D1432433

DEATH IN QOHELETH AND EGYPTIAN BIOGRAPHIES OF THE LATE PERIOD

SOCIETY OF BIBLICAL LITERATURE

DISSERTATION SERIES

Michael V. Fox, Old Testament Editor
Mark Allan Powell, New Testament Editor

Number 170
DEATH IN QOHELETH AND
EGYPTIAN BIOGRAPHIES
OF THE LATE PERIOD
by
Shannon Burkes

Shannon Burkes

DEATH IN QOHELETH AND EGYPTIAN BIOGRAPHIES OF THE LATE PERIOD

Society of Biblical Literature
Atlanta, Georgia

BS
1475.2
.B86
1999

Death in Qoheleth and Egyptian Biographies of the Late Period

by
Shannon Burkes
Ph.D., University of Chicago, 1997
John J. Collins, Advisor

Copyright © 1999 by the Society of Biblical Literature

All rights reserved. No part of this work may be reproduced or transmitted in any form or by any means, electronic or mechanical, including photocopying and recording, or by means of any information storage or retrieval system, except as may be expressly permitted by the 1976 Copyright Act or in writing from the publisher. Requests for permission should be addressed in writing to the Rights and Permissions Office, Scholars Press, P.O. Box 15399, Atlanta, GA 30333-0399, USA.

Library of Congress Cataloging-in-Publication Data
Burkes, Shannon.
    Death in Qoheleth and Egyptian biographies of the late period / Shannon Burkes.
        p. cm. — (Dissertation series / Society of Biblical Literature ; no. 170)
        Revision of author's dissertation (doctoral)—University of Chicago, 1997.
        Includes bibliographical references and indexes.
        ISBN 0-88414-005-9 (cloth : alk. paper)
        1. Bible. O.T. Ecclesiastes—Criticism, interpretation, etc. 2. Death—Religious aspects. 3. Egypt—Biography—History and criticism. I. Title. II. Series: Dissertation series (Society of Biblical Literature) ; no. 170.
    BS1475.2.B86   1999
    291.2'3—dc21   99-38480
                                                 CIP

        08 07 06 05 04 03 02 01 00 99   5 4 3 2 1

Printed in the United States of America
on acid-free paper

JESUIT - KRAUSS - McCORMICK - LIBRARY
1100 EAST 55th STREET
CHICAGO, ILLINOIS 60615

To
John J. Collins

CONTENTS

Acknowledgments

This project is a slightly revised version of my dissertation, completed at the University of Chicago in 1997. It would never have been possible without the assistance and support of many people. I want to thank Adela Collins for her interest and help, even though she was not serving on my dissertation committee. My readers, Michael Fishbane and Janet Johnson, cheerfully read multiple drafts and provided indispensable advice, correction, and encouragement, not only in their capacity as members of the committee but in the classes I took with them as a student. The former showed me the worlds that a careful reading of texts can open up, the latter revealed the richness and beauty of late Egyptian history and literature.

As I was finishing the original dissertation, C. L. Seow graciously allowed me to see a copy of his new Anchor Bible commentary on Ecclesiastes before it had come out, and Christoph Uehlinger sent me the proofs of his article on Qoheleth in the context of Persian and Hellenistic period wisdom literature. I want to thank both of them for their generosity.

I also appreciate deeply the opportunity given to me by Michael V. Fox, editor of the Society of Biblical Literature Dissertation Series, for accepting the book and then helping me through the intricacies of the publication process.

My advisor, John J. Collins, several years ago took me under his wing and saw me through the trials of graduate school with patience, discipline, and good humor. His efforts with the dissertation were tireless, and so I dedicate this project to him.

Last but not least, I need to point out that nothing I have done would have been possible without the support and understanding of my parents, whose encouragement over the years, both as a graduate student and now as a teacher, has been unfailing. (Look, I finally did it!).

INTRODUCTION

The book of Qoheleth is a work that has long been considered bizarre and something of a misfit within the biblical canon, and it has generated ongoing discussion throughout the centuries by commentators of all stripes.[1] The first known recorded reaction to Qoheleth appears within the book itself, in the final verses (12:9–14), which sum up for the reader what this particular editor would like one to take away from the work, in case one might be led to the wrong conclusions. Not surprisingly, a number of different readings of the text have been proffered, but the following project understands the driving theme and main concern of Qoheleth to be the problem of death. It is death that really dominates the stage and forms the core of the author's melancholy. Part of what makes the book so distinctive is the novelty of its central theme within the canon. One could no doubt identify many obsessions in the biblical corpus, but with the exception of Qoheleth, death would not be one of them. When it comes to this particular issue in the Hebrew Bible, Qoheleth has cornered the market.

This is not to say that Qoheleth's ancestors did not have to deal with the fact of death or have any feelings about it. The Hebrew Bible does provide something of a window into how death was incorporated into the cosmic framework. Essentially, it seems to have been considered the end of one's personal existence, but the culture had forms of continuity that were a response to the potential rupture mortality represents. One achieved endurance through one's descendants, through the survival of the nation as a whole, through the memory of a good name, and could even delay death by choosing to follow the paths of

---

[1] The word "Qoheleth" is the Hebrew title of the book, as well as the designation of the speaker in the text. "Ecclesiastes" is the Greek translation rendered in the Latin alphabet.

wisdom and God's law. A natural end that came in the fullness of time was not a cause for crisis. The tradition had little to say about death as a principle of the universe and instead concerned itself with the responsibilities, struggles, and events of this world. This is why Qoheleth stands out so sharply from the preceding tradition, because he is utterly fixed on mortality and its implications. Qoheleth is certainly not the only surviving example of a sceptical or pessimistic view in biblical thought. Scepticism in itself was not new to the ancient Near Eastern civilizations, and is a facet of human reflection long attested. What makes Qoheleth distinctive within his culture is his particular focus on death, which for him represents the chief flaw that embraces and subsumes all other problems in the world.

Modern scholars have tried to understand how such an unusual Jewish book could be possible. Early on in the scholarship it was suggested that Qoheleth reflects foreign influence, almost always Greek, and although some have demurred from time to time, this notion became an ingrained thread in scholarly investigation. Recently, people have seemed less enthusiastic about itemizing specific points of contact, but the notion remains that Qoheleth was probably influenced at least in a general way by Greek thought. However, the Greek influence theory is neither persuasive nor necessary to explain the text's existence. At this point the comparison with selected Egyptian tomb biographies becomes relevant.

In a very different culture, but in the same time period, the last few centuries BCE, attitudes toward death that are similar to Qoheleth's begin appearing in Egyptian biographies. The biographical genre in ancient Egypt was an old one, always associated with the mortuary context. Either in the tomb or on a funerary stela the deceased presents his life to the public, with a view to eliciting the proper offerings or invocations that will maintain his comfort in the netherworld. Unlike Israel, Egyptian culture had a very deep interest in death and a complex mortuary tradition for dealing with it. The individual hoped to attain a quite corporeal and personal immortality in a blessed afterlife. Scepticism appears from time to time, but never in the biographies, which were a standard part of the mortuary complex and had never strayed from the positive view of mainstream belief.

Nevertheless, in the late period of ancient Egyptian history, a few of the biographies begin to express astonishing views of death, that there is no pleasant life on the other side, that the netherworld is a land of deprivation, that the dead do not remember their loved ones, that death is in fact a terrible thing. What is interesting about the comparison with Qoheleth is not merely to see that a similar distress in the face of death appears in both sets of material, but to set the texts within their preceding traditions and see what exactly it is that they are saying. In both cases, the gloom over death is expressed in ways that specifically annul the methods each culture had formulated for ameliorating mortality. Qoheleth systematically knocks down every means of continuity his culture had to offer, through children, community, or memory, and he denies that one's moral status and actions have any bearing on the manner or timing of death. The selected Egyptian biographies negate their tradition's teaching that death is just a stage before reunion with one's family, ongoing enjoyment of life's pleasures, and a serene existence in a pleasant afterlife. In other words, these are not random expressions of melancholy, but are precise denials of what each society had to offer by way of comfort in the confrontation with death. And in both cases, a common refrain is that a person should enjoy life to the fullest while alive, because that is all there is.

Although the Egyptian biographies are part of a well-defined genre of their own, it is of interest to note that in Egypt, biography and wisdom literature are related. Miriam Lichtheim puts it most succinctly when she states "Egyptian autobiographies reflect the teachings of Egyptian wisdom literature."[2] Biographies could explicitly provide wisdom instructions of their own, and even when they did not, the moral defense of the speaker is based directly on the ethic promulgated in Egyptian wisdom texts.[3] A good example of the convergence of biography and

---

[2] Miriam Lichtheim, *Maat in Egyptian Autobiographies and Related Studies* (Göttingen: Vandenhoeck & Ruprecht, 1992) 99. Note: this project refers to the genre as "biography," while Lichtheim calls it "autobiography."

[3] Lichtheim, *Maat in Egyptian Autobiographies*, 117. She elsewhere describes the biographies as being "the principle sources for the affirmations of having fulfilled the ethical demands which the Instructions taught" (143). See also Baudouin van der Walle, "Biographie," in Wolfgang Helck et al, eds., *Lexikon der Ägyptologie*, Vol. I (Wiesbaden: Otto Harrassowitz, 1975) 819, who says of the biographies that they "se présentent parfois comme des 'enseignements' ce qui montre combien les rédacteurs de ces inscriptions étaient conscients de la connexion entre les deux genres." Similar comments are found in Christoph

instruction can be seen in an article by Goedicke which he entitled "A Neglected Wisdom Text." In fact, the article's subject is a biographical stela that does consist, in part, of an instruction. The speaker runs through the typical offering formula, personal description of the offices held in life, and account of deeds performed, then says "My instruction to my children is as follows...." What ensues could be found in any standard Egyptian wisdom work.[4] Biography and wisdom, then, had an affinity for one another in the content of their ethic and manner of reflecting on what it is that people ought to do in life. They are not the same, but they are related. Lichtheim describes the *difference* between the two genres thus: both assert a model of human nature, but where the teachings "stressed types of character," the biographies "articulate selfhood and self-understanding in the frame of rank and profession."[5]

This genre overlap is relevant because Qoheleth is an example of Israelite wisdom. While the project at hand is based on an idea, changing attitudes towards death, and so does not set limitations on the type of genre that will clarify these attitudes, it happens that the focus of the comparison rests on two sets of material, a Jewish wisdom text and Egyptian biographies, which from the point of view of genre are not entirely different. Furthermore, the line can be blurred a bit more in view of the fact that Qoheleth takes on autobiographical overtones in the insistent first-person form of presentation. The author is emphatically sharing *his* experiences and views of the world. C. L. Seow discusses Qoheleth as a fictional autobiography of King Solomon.[6] The book is

---

Uehlinger, "Qohelet im Horizont mesopotamischer, levantinischer und ägyptischer Weisheitsliteratur der persischen und hellenistischen Zeit," in Ludger Schwienhorst-Schoenberger, ed., *Das Buch Kohelet. Studien zur Struktur, Geschichte, Rezeption und Theologie* (Berlin: de Gruyter, 1997) 41.

[4] Hans Goedicke, "A Neglected Wisdom Text," *Journal of Egyptian Archeology* 48(1962) 25.

[5] Miriam Lichtheim, "Autobiography as Self-Exploration," in G. Zaccone, ed., *Sesto Congresso Internazionale di Egittologia*, Vol. I (Torino, Italy: International Association of Egyptologists, 1992) 414.

[6] C. L. Seow, "Qohelet's Autobiography," in Astrid B. Beck et al, eds., *Fortunate the Eyes that See: Essays in Honor of David Noel Freedman in Celebration of His Seventieth Birthday* (Grand Rapids, MI: Eerdmans, 1995) 278. He considers it comparable to Akkadian royal autobiographies. See also Tremper Longman III, *The Book of Ecclesiastes* (Grand Rapids: Eerdmans, 1998) 17–20, who describes Qoheleth as a "framed wisdom autobiography," a subgenre of

actually not a biographical text, nor are the Egyptian biographies properly regarded as wisdom literature, but the fact that the two sets of material brush against one another in terms of genre helps explain why they lend themselves to dealing with similar issues, and why the scholar might be inclined to think of them comparatively.

Not many people work with the late Egyptian material, but insofar as it has been studied, some have suggested that it, like Qoheleth, is the result of Greek influence. The following project however makes a different move, since in neither case does the theory persuade. First of all, and the argument has been made more emphatically with respect to Qoheleth, there are no expressions or ideas which must be explained by Greek sources; certainly the Hebrew and Egyptian works are noticeably different from preceding tradition, but while such situations *may* reflect cases of outside influence, this is not the only possible answer. The arguments also tend to be scattered, in that often no particular Greek composition, school, or philosophy is credited as being the fountainhead, but rather an entire range of material through time and across genres, which seems to imply an unlikely breadth and level of familiarity with the Greek world.

Secondly, it helps to see not only how the writings under discussion relate to their own foregoing traditions, but also what is happening in the contemporary cultural contexts. Although Qoheleth and some of the Egyptian biographies are definitely saying things that run counter to their respective cultural traditions, neither is a complete anomaly in the religious trends of the time. Changes are taking place in both societies which suggest that others are starting to raise questions about the old worldviews, and to offer a variety of new ones. New religious movements and texts emerge at this time in Judah and Egypt alike. In other words, deep-seated shifts are occurring in both places of which the texts under discussion here are only one example. That something as basic as death should come to the fore of concern is not particularly surprising at a time when people are starting to rethink all kinds of religious and philosophical matters.

It appears, then, that by contextualizing the materials and seeing what is going on around them that the content of their message is not as

---

Akkadian fictional autobiographies to which Qoheleth is analogous in form, if not in content.

inexplicable as it might first seem. Neither set of material has influenced the other, nor do they reflect influence from yet a third source; trends internal to the cultures offer the most powerful explanation for how these works came into existence. The next question is what exactly *was* taking place in the ancient Near East in the second half of the final millennium BCE. Simply put, the power structures of the ancient world were undergoing permutations that were felt far and wide. A succession of kingdoms, from the Assyrians down to the Greeks, passed control of the region back and forth. In the meantime, the Jews had lost their native kings, while the Egyptian kingship experienced a variety of changes as it alternately disintegrated, was reestablished, overrun by foreign empires, and finally was adopted by the Ptolemaic line. Both cultures become subject to political and economic forces beyond their control. For the Jews, their shorter royal tradition ceased abruptly in 587, while the Egyptians saw their longer tradition of pharaonic rule die by fits and starts. More broadly, a number of political, social, economic, as well as religious and psychological repercussions were bound together in the subsequent centuries. Whatever the specifics of circumstances in both places, one thing is certain; the old ways of doing business were changing, and with the changes came concomitant pressure on previously established worldviews which no longer fit the new realities. People had to reorient themselves in the cosmos, and reorient themselves they did. The era known variously as the "Second Temple" or "Post-exilic" period in Judah and as the "Late Period" in Egypt was a time of dynamism and creativity as people attempted anew to understand their place, purpose, and destiny within the surrounding world.

The ensuing investigation looks at Qoheleth with an eye to understanding what he feels about death and what conclusions he draws from it, and then compares this text with a selection of Egyptian biographies which also express similar feelings. The final conclusion will be that the changing views of death in each of the two traditions is not due to the result of one literature's influence on the other, but to a paradigm shift which is taking place across the ancient Near East in this period, and is manifested analogously in both cultures. The first chapter surveys what had been the Jewish attitudes towards death before Qoheleth for the purpose of highlighting how distinct his own views are. The second chapter looks at the book in detail in order to see what it is about death that bothers him and how this contradicts the tradition. The third chapter considers what might underlie his thoughts by looking at some of the Jewish writings that soon followed, surveying the common arguments for Greek influence and, after deciding that these are not compelling, turning to the circumstances of the day. In chapter four the argument shifts to the Egyptian side, and reviews the traditional views of death in Egypt so as to provide the preceding context, once again, for the study of the texts themselves in chapter five. Chapter six then examines the political and social factors of the time with a focus on other writings and trends that provide a context for the biographies.

The final chapter is the conclusion. It draws out the point of the comparison, and suggests that perhaps scholarship has not asked enough questions of these texts in the search for influences. A short section surveys changes that were occurring in Greek life and finds shifts similar to those in Judah and Egypt. One would suggest then that perhaps students of the Hellenistic era in the Near East should think about the period somewhat differently than has been the norm. First, instead of regarding Greece as the home source for ideas in other cultures which are questioning, sceptical, or critical of tradition, it would be useful to take a history of religions approach in order to see if any patterns emerge across the cultural spectrum. In fact, it seems that all three places were undergoing contemporaneous shifts in worldview. Secondly, these shifts appear to have been getting underway before Alexander appeared on the scene, so that while the Hellenistic period is certainly an important one, it may not be as distinct an historical watershed for the region as is usually assumed; it may be instead one part of broader cultural metamorphoses that began earlier. Rather than a matter of the influence of any given culture on another, a more promising approach is to try to understand the nature and consequences of the changes in traditional systems across the ancient Near Eastern and Mediterranean world, "systems" including the political/economic as well as religious/intellectual, since all of these facets comprised individual parts of the larger cultural wholes.

This chapter argues that what one finds in Qoheleth and the Egyptian biographies is intelligible within the framework of pressures and shifts within each culture, that Greece itself was part of, not simply the source for, this pattern of change, and that broader religious and intellectual shifts can be seen across the entire region. J. Z. Smith's theory of the move from locative to utopian forms of religiosity is helpful for understanding the period and, with some modification, provides a lens for viewing the texts under discussion. Qoheleth was not a renegade blip on the screen of Jewish tradition, nor are the biographies inexplicable in Egyptian tradition. Once one pulls back far enough to take in the fuller context, both within the tradition and across traditions, the fact that something as fundamental as death should come to the fore, and that there were at least some people for whom their own traditions could not provide the answers they needed on the matter, no longer appears to be so strange. In a time of spiritual distress, one of the first things likely to come up is the disjunction caused by death.

Chapter 1
DEATH IN THE HEBREW BIBLE

Earlier in this century, Dylan Thomas penned a poetic verse which has entered the popular consciousness as a cry against death:

> Do not go gentle into that good night.
> Rage, rage against the dying of the light.[1]

It has been remarked that in this verse death is "a symbol of that absurdity or futility which many poets and philosophers have considered the most salient characteristic of life in our century. It is a force against which the will of man must continually struggle."[2] The comment is on the mark, but one should notice the specification "in our century." Although the struggle against the very idea of death is a universally human instinct, the same scholar goes on to observe that the instinct has not asserted itself to the same degree at all times and in all places. As it happens, most of the writings in the Hebrew Bible do not seem to be especially exercised by the fact of death and have little to say about it, turning their attention instead to other problems and questions.[3] This is not to suggest that death was considered a negligible event, or ignored, but that it did not confront the writers and compilers of what became the Hebrew Bible as a serious snag in the fabric of the cosmos or human society within that cosmos.[4]

---

[1] Dylan Thomas, *The Collected Poems of Dylan Thomas* (New York: New Directions, 1957) 128.

[2] Milton McC. Gatch, *Death: Meaning and Mortality in Christian Thought and Contemporary Culture* (New York: Seabury Press, 1969) 3.

[3] Gatch, *Death*, 35.

[4] "Every society is confronted with the reality of death. It is an important confrontation, philosophically because it challenges the assumption of continuity

The societies represented in the biblical texts appear to have integrated death into the religious system in an unobtrusive, if sometimes melancholy, way. The one exception to this observation is the book of Qoheleth.[5] Death seems to be a clarion call of the unjustness of the world for Qoheleth in a manner that it had not been in the previous traditions. While he does not exactly *rage* against the dying of the light, he does lament it in an unnervingly relentless fashion. The oddity of the book in its biblical surroundings can best be brought forth, first, by an examination of how death figures in the earlier biblical traditions, followed by an inquiry into what it means to Qoheleth in particular. This chapter will do the former, and the next chapter the latter task.

HEBREW CONCEPTIONS OF DEATH

A methodological point needs to be stated at the outset, and that is that it is not possible today to speak of "the Israelite view of death" in complete confidence, inasmuch as only a few texts and debated archeological evidence have survived from the culture in which one might investigate the question. Different types of literature from different periods, some of which no doubt reflect minority opinions and interests, are what the scholar has to work with on the literary level. And of that material, little looks at death in its own right. Moreover, even this limited body of material does not offer one, monolithic view of death, but reveals different nuances and emphases. If the Israelites had shared a single and culturally homogeneous view of death, they would probably be the only people in human history to

---

and permanence that societies make about themselves; organizationally because it requires the replacement of personnel in all the various statuses that make up the social order; interpersonally because it dislocates role networks and has immense emotional tone; psychologically because it requires each and every actor on the human scene to acknowledge the transitory nature of his own existence," notes Ernest Q. Campbell, "Death as a Social Practice," in L. O. Mills, ed., *Perspectives on Death* (Nashville: Abingdon, 1969) 211. The argument of this chapter will not be that the Hebrew Bible exempted itself from this confrontation with death, but that it did not consider the confrontation to be at the top of its list of important religious questions.

[5] Daniel 12 is also an exception to the mainstream, as will be discussed further below, but in a very different way from Qoheleth.

have done so. Before discussing the general trends which emerge, however, it makes sense to begin with the actual texts. For convenience, these texts are here loosely grouped into categories, even though the categories may tend to overlap and blur somewhat.[6]

The first consists of those passages which express the idea of human ephemerality.[7]

Ps 39:4–6
Lord, let me know my end,
    and what is the measure of my days;
    let me know how fleeting my life is.
You have made my days a few handbreadths,
    and my lifetime is as nothing in your sight.
Surely everyone stands as a mere breath.
    Surely everyone goes about like a shadow.

Ps 90:3–6
You turn us[8] back to dust,
    and say, 'Turn back, you mortals.'
For a thousand years in your sight
    are like yesterday when it is past,
    or like a watch in the night.
You sweep them away; they are like a dream,
    like grass that is renewed in the morning;
in the morning it flourishes and is renewed;
    in the evening it fades and withers.

Job 7:9–10
As the cloud fades and vanishes,
    so those who go down to Sheol do not come up;
they return no more to their houses,
    nor do their places know them anymore.

---

[6] The quotations in this chapter are from the NRSV: Bruce M. Metzger and Roland E. Murphy, eds., *The New Oxford Annotated Bible: New Revised Standard Version* (New York: Oxford University Press, 1991).

[7] For similar ideas see II Samuel 14:14, Isaiah 40:6–8, Psalms 39:11, 49:10–15, 89:47–48, 90:9–10, 103:13–16, 104:29, 144:3–4, 146:3–4, Job 14:1–5 [note the interesting comment in vv. 7–12 that the trees have better hope than a mortal, because even if cut down a tree will sprout again, unlike a human being], and Job 34:14–15.

[8] Heb *humankind*.

Consistent imagery and themes emerge from these passages. Human beings are by nature transitory creatures, and this impermanence is often expressed in the same terms: like a shadow, a dream, a passing cloud, an empty breath, the dust, withering grass, fading flowers, a sigh. Not too surprisingly, the majority of the passages come from the psalms and wisdom literature, where one would expect to find occasion for reflection on human nature and its weaknesses. The observations do not seem to function as a cri de coeur, but as simple comments on an obvious fact, which sometimes serve to contrast the transience of mortals with the eternity of God's power and existence. They are not the focus of attention in the larger context in which they appear. In other words, the speaker is not interested in human mortality in itself, but brings it into the discussion as a piece of a larger argument, such as God's omnipotence.[9]

The second category of texts more specifically describes what Sheol is like, what a person there can or cannot do.[10]

> Ps 30:9
> What profit is there in my death,
>   if I go down to the Pit?
> Will the dust praise you?
>   Will it tell of your faithfulness?

> Ps 88:10–12
> Do you work wonders for the dead?
>   Do the shades rise up to praise you?
> Is your steadfast love declared in the grave,
>   or your faithfulness in Abaddon?
> Are your wonders known in the darkness,
>   or your saving help in the land of forgetfulness?

---

[9] James P. Carse, *Death and Existence: A Conceptual History of Human Mortality* (New York: John Wiley & Sons, 1980) 177, remarks "Never in these passages "is death *as such* isolated and discussed as a subject or issue."

[10] See also Isaiah 38:18–19, Psalm 6:4–5, Psalm 115:17, and Job 3:17–19 (note that Isaiah 14:10ff. is similar to this last passage in its portrayal of Sheol as the great equalizer).

Job 10:20–22
Are not the days of my life few?[11]
    Let me alone, that I may find a little comfort[12]
before I go, never to return,
    to the land of gloom and deep darkness,
the land of gloom[13] and chaos,
    where light is like darkness.

Although the passages speak of being in Sheol, as if one might exist and have consciousness there, this is obviously existence only in the most technical sense of the word. Sheol is a place of gloom, silence, forgetfulness, and darkness. One has no memory there, nor does one express hope in or praise of the Lord.[14] Though the Hebrew words נֶפֶשׁ and רוּחַ are often translated "soul" or "spirit," they do not convey the notion of anything like the Platonic soul,[15] and it is not the case that Sheol represents a place for the enduring reality of a "soul" in the sense of a vital existence. What survives in Sheol is not the "soul," but "a weakened and fragmented shadow of oneself."[16] This notion of death is common to the Semitic cultures of the era, and finds parallels in Babylonian and Sumerian writings.[17] Again, the belief that one will

---

[11] Compare Gk Syr: Heb *Are not my days few? Let him cease!*

[12] Heb *that I may brighten up a little.*

[13] Heb *gloom as darkness, deep darkness.*

[14] Robert Martin-Achard, *From Death to Life* (Edinburgh and London: Oliver and Boyd, 1960) 17, says that a person's state in Sheol "is such a pale and pitiful reflection of human existence that it has no longer any reality, and is only a metaphorical expression of non-being."

[15] John Bowker, *The Meanings of Death* (Cambridge: Cambridge University Press, 1991) 52. Leonard J. Greenspoon, "The Origin of the Idea of Resurrection," in Baruch Halpern and Jon D. Levenson, eds., *Traditions in Transformation: Turning Points in Biblical Faith* (Winona Lake, IN: Eisenbrauns, 1981) 250, writes that the nephesh is not treated as "a higher, more divine substance than any or all of the body," nor is the body "a corruptive agent for man."

[16] Antonio R. Gualtieri, *The Vulture and the Bull: Religious Responses to Death* (Lanham, MD: University Press of America, 1984) 82.

[17] S.H. Hooke, "Israel and the Afterlife," *Expository Times* 76(1965) 236. Klaas Spronk, *Beatific Afterlife in Ancient Israel and in the Ancient Near East* (Kevelaer: Butzon und Bercker; Neukirchen-Vluyn: Neukirchner Verlag, 1986) 111–12, describes the ways that the ancient Mesopotamians sought to address their mortality. The Gilgamesh Epic teaches that one should not fret about death but enjoy what can be had in the present; another route of consolation was to be found in the immortality of one's name due to famous deeds. The underworld was not

essentially cease to maintain the actions and characteristics of human identity is not the main interest of the speaker, but an observation usually brought into the discussion in order to point out to God that the living are better able to offer him admiration and praise than the dead, so it would be in the deity's own interest to spare his afflicted worshipper.

In the third category of passages, the shared theme is the notion that God can save his devotee from death/Sheol.[18]

> Ps 16:9–11a
> Therefore my heart is glad, and my soul rejoices;
>   my body also rests secure.
> For you do not give me up to Sheol,
>   or let your faithful ones see the Pit.
> You show me the path of life....

> Ps 30:3
> O Lord, you brought up my soul from Sheol,
>   restored me to life from among those gone down to the Pit.[19]

Although on the face of it these passages suggest that God can and will save a person from death, a contradiction of the earlier quotations which pointed out that it is human nature to die, the contexts suggest that this is a way of expressing salvation from present troubles.[20]

---

generally a place to which one looked forward, even though one's shade has some sort of minimal existence there.

[18] See also Psalm 33:18–19, Psalm 36:9, and Psalm 68:19–20.

[19] Or *that I should not go down to the Pit.*

[20] There are also passages in which God's power is described in terms of his authority over life and death which come to mind here. "See now that I, even I, am he; there is no god beside me. I kill and I make alive; I wound and I heal; and no one can deliver from my hand" (Deut 32:39). "The Lord kills and brings to life; he brings down to Sheol and raises up. The Lord makes poor and makes rich; he brings low, he also exalts" (I Sam 2:6–7). For similar ideas see Is 45:7, Lam 3:38, and Ben Sira 11:14. The impression is less one of God raising people from the dead as it is a declaration of God's power over every facet of the world, the good as well as the bad. The only other thing that is ever said to be equal to or greater than death in power is love. See Song of Songs 8:6–7, "Set me as a seal upon your heart, as a seal upon your arm; for love is strong as death, passion fierce as the grave...." Roland Murphy, "Dance and Death in the Song of Songs," in John H. Marks and Robert M. Good, eds., *Love & Death in the Ancient Near East: Essays in Honor of Marvin H. Pope* (Guilford, CT: Four Quarters Publishing Company, 1987) 118,

Escape from death means escape from premature, unnatural death. The psalmist had already slipped down to Sheol under the burden of his troubles, to be subsequently rescued by God.[21]

The final set of texts continues a variation on this theme. All are found in Proverbs, and speak of wisdom sparing its practitioner from death.[22]

> Prov 8:35–36
> For whoever finds me [Lady Wisdom] finds life
> > and obtains favor from the Lord;
> but those who miss me injure themselves;
> > all who hate me love death.

> Prov 14:27
> The fear of the Lord is a fountain of life,
> > so that one may avoid the snares of death.

---

says that in the last instance the strength of love is being compared to "one of the most powerful figures that confronted ancient Israel, Death." This comment also provides some understanding of the other quotations in this footnote. God's power is naturally described in terms of that other powerful aspect of creation; omnipotence requires authority over death.

[21] Nicholas J. Tromp, *Primitive Conceptions of Death and the Nether World in the Old Testament* (Rome: Pontifical Biblical Institute, 1969) 213, says that things such as "persecution, oppression, need, and illness are felt as forms of partial but real death." Greenspoon, "The Origin of the Idea of Resurrection," 251, quotes J. Pedersen, *Israel: Its Life and Culture* (London: Oxford University, 1926 [vol. 1], 1940 [vol. 2]) 153, as follows: "Life and death are not two sharply distinguished spheres, because they do not mean existence or non-existence. Life is something which one possesses in a higher or lower degree. If afflicted by misfortune, illness, or something else which checks the soul, then one has only little life, but all the more death. He who is ill or otherwise in distress may say that he is dead, and when he recovers, he is pulled out of death." (It should be noted that James Barr, *The Semantics of Biblical Language* [Oxford: Oxford University Press, 1961] 41 and passim, expresses considerable reservations about Pedersen's yen for extrapolating "Semitic thought" from "Semitic language," but this particular comment by Pedersen does seem apt). See also Nico van Uchelen, "Death and the After-Life in the Hebrew Bible of Ancient Israel," in J. M. Bremer et al, eds., *Hidden Futures: Death and Immortality in Ancient Egypt, Anatolia, the Classical, Biblical and Arabic-Islamic World* (Amsterdam: Amsterdam University Press, 1994) 83, who notes that death grows in power when the quality of life goes down, and adds "dangerous cases and ominous domains may be full of death in human life."

[22] See also Proverbs 1:32–33, 3:18, 10:16–17, 11:4, 11:30, 12:28, and 16:22.

Prov 15:24
For the wise the path of life leads upward,
  in order to avoid Sheol below.

Prov 21:16
Whoever wanders from the way of understanding
  will rest in the assembly of the dead.

Proverbs also refers four times (3:18; 11:30; 13:12; 15:4) to the "tree of life" in contexts of comparison.[23] Like the passages in the psalms where God will save the afflicted from Sheol, the point here is not that the wise person will never die, but that wisdom leads one into the kind of life which preserves one from a bad, early death, and into a long, full, and prosperous length of days. The kind of treatment that the issue of mortality receives in Proverbs has been described as a "qualitative understanding of life and death."[24] In a similar fashion, Moses can insist, "I call heaven and earth to witness against you today that I have set before you life and death, blessings and curses. Choose life so that you and your descendents may live...." (Deut 30:19). The question is not simply one of a person's biological state, but of manner of life. Mere physical viability is not "life" in the fullest sense, and someone who dies in old age, with a large family, having lived righteously, and under the favor of the Lord, can be said to have been spared from the paths of death. This is a "derivative" idea of death, not death in biological terms alone.[25] Though Proverbs will proclaim "an absolute life which is offered by wisdom, that life does not undermine the reality of either physical life or physical death. Rather, the transcendent life of wisdom embraces both physical life and death as a

---

[23] Tikva Frymer-Kensky, "The Planting of Man: A Study in Biblical Imagery," in John H. Marks and Robert M. Good, eds., *Love & Death in the Ancient Near East: Essays in Honor of Marvin H. Pope* (Guilford, CT: Four Quarters Publishing Company, 1987) 131–32, points out that in the Hebrew Bible the tree is an image for long life, while grass connotes impermanence and thus lends itself to expressions of human mortality.

[24] John J. Collins, "The Root of Immortality: Death in the Context of Jewish Wisdom," *Harvard Theological Review* 71(1978) 180.

[25] N. Lohfink, *The Christian Meaning of the Old Testament*, trans. R. A. Wilson (Milwaukee: Bruce, 1968) 147.

complementary pair. Death is the necessary limit of life."[26] This description can largely be applied to the Hebrew Bible in general.[27]

The argument of this chapter so far brings forth several points. The Israelite view of human mortality, as represented in the surviving texts, was consistent in that life was felt to be ephemeral. There is an idea of a place where the dead go, Sheol, but this place is almost a metaphorical way of speaking of non-existence. Nothing of notice happens there. A small but fairly robust stream of thought appears in the psalms and in wisdom writings that speaks of the follower of the Lord/wisdom as escaping death and walking on the path of life, but this is not a literal message of life after death. Instead the idea is that one can choose what *kind* of a life to pursue, and this, too, fits with the general ideas that have emerged from the study. In a nutshell, earthly existence is the only shot one gets, and so the most should be made of it.[28] This conception is nowhere a cause for a crisis, but a matter of accepted fact. Death is not an occasion for discussion in its own right, but is tied to other issues, such as obtaining the Lord's aid, the manner in which one should live, how adhering to God's precepts brings divine protection, and so on.

It should be pointed out that there are a few passages which have raised questions among scholars about a possible life after death in the Hebrew Bible. They include Psalm 49:15, Psalm 73:26, Job 19:26, Hosea 6:1–2, Hosea 13:14, Isaiah 25:7, Isaiah 26:19, Isaiah 53:10, Ezekiel 37:12–14, and Daniel 12:2–3.[29] However, most of the passages

[26] Collins, "The Root of Immortality," 181.

[27] Bruce Vawter, "Intimations of Immortality and the Old Testament," *Journal of Biblical Literature* 91(1972) 170, says "not mere existence but meaningful existence is what the OT understands as synonymous with life."

[28] Martin-Achard, *From Death to Life*, 18, notes that "man is born mortal and his death is regarded as entirely natural. In this no problem is raised, the fact of death is simply noted." Cf. Alan Segal, "Some Observations about Mysticism and the Spread of Notions of Life after Death in Hebrew Thought," *Society of Biblical Literature: 1996 Seminar Papers* (Atlanta: Scholars Press, 1996) 385, who writes "rather than discuss the notion [of death], as was quite common in the literature of Israel's neighbors, the advice of the Bible is curt and practical, 'Teach us to number our days that we may gain a wise heart' (Psalm 90:12). This life with its inevitable death is what the Bible wants to emphasize."

[29] Other items which might bring into question the statement that the Israelites speculated little on death or an afterlife are the revivals of the dead by Elijah and Elisha, and the translations of Elijah and Enoch. However, these events

do not make it clear that a literal and individual, rather than a figurative or national, restoration to life is meant. Daniel 12:2–3 is the only indisputable affirmation of an afterlife in the Hebrew Bible. The rest of the evidence "is ambiguous at best."[30] Isaiah 26:19 is debatable, but is probably, like Ezekiel 37, a description of Israel's renewal after the exile.[31] Some scholars have found such passages to be fairly explicit glimpses of an idea of immortality,[32] but others are more reticent,[33] and even a lenient view would lead one to conclude that the notion was, at most, a very small element within the Hebrew Bible as a whole.[34]

Occasional references have also led scholars to wonder if Israel had a cult of the dead. Some texts suggest that consultation of the dead,

---

are the exceptions to the rule. See Martin-Achard, *From Death to Life*, 152–65; John J. Collins, *Daniel* (Minneapolis: Fortress Press, 1993) 394.

[30] Collins, *Daniel*, 394. Kaiser and Lohse believe this conclusion is too restrictive, and point to redactional additions in Isaiah 24–27, Psalm 49:15, and Psalm 73:24ff. Cf. Otto Kaiser and Eduard Lohse, eds., *Death and Life* (Nashville: Abingdon, 1981) 79. Moore, "Resurrection and Immortality," 33, specifically questions Collins's argument that most of the debated passages are not literally speaking of resurrection or life after death. While there is room for disagreement over interpretation, the view espoused by Collins is the more persuasive.

[31] Collins, *Daniel*, 395. For an opposite view, see Émile Puech, *La croyance des Esséniens en la vie future: Immortalité, résurrection, vie éternelle? Histoire d'une croyance dans le judaïsme ancien, Vol I: La résurrection des morts et le contexte scripturaire* (Paris: Librairie Lecoffre/J. Gabalda, 1993) 66–73, who believes that Isaiah 26 definitely refers to punishment of the unrighteous and resurrection of the just.

[32] R. H. Charles, *A Critical History of the Doctrine of a Future Life* (London: Black, 1913) 51–81; Mitchell Dahood, *Psalms*, 3 Vols. (Garden City, NY: Doubleday, 1966–1970) 3.xli–lii. Dahood reaches his conclusions by comparisons between Hebrew and Ugaritic and finds that the interpretation of Hebrew words based on their Ugaritic counterparts reveals many references to immortality or resurrection in the Bible, particularly in Psalms and Proverbs. Greenspoon, "The Origin of the Idea of Resurrection," 319, believes that the idea of bodily resurrection appears in biblical material dating from the ninth to second centuries, and that it arises out of the network of images tied to God as the Divine Warrior.

[33] Martin-Achard, *From Death to Life*, 164–65; Vawter, "Intimations of Immortality and the Old Testament," 158–71. Vawter points out that Dahood is mistaken to read passages "according to the philologically possible rather than according to the theologically probable" (161–62).

[34] Collins, *Daniel*, 395.

or necromancy, was a familiar phenomenon among the Israelites. Deuteronomy 18:11 proscribes a number of practices that the people might be inclined to adopt when they enter the promised land, among which is the consultation of ghosts or spirits. Twice Leviticus 20 (vv. 6 and 27) forbids mediums and wizards.[35] In Isaiah 65:4 God castigates the people because they take part in improper rituals, including spending the night in tombs for divinatory purposes. Isaiah 8:19 portrays the people requesting that the prophet: "Consult the ghosts and the familiar spirits that chirp and mutter; should not a people consult their gods, the dead on behalf of the living, for teaching and instruction?" This kind of thing is then strictly forbidden by Isaiah.[36] Yet something very similar actually happens in I Samuel 28 when the king has the woman from Endor summon up the spirit of Samuel to give him advice.[37]

Other texts provide glimpses of rituals and practices connected with the dead which imply mortuary procedures that may have been fairly common. Deuteronomy 26:14 commands a recitation when making offerings to God that includes a promise from the speaker that he has not offered any of the material to the dead. Deuteronomy 14:1 forbids self-laceration or shaving of the head for the dead. But in Jeremiah 16:5–9, it seems that the mutilation and hair-cutting are forbidden not because they are improper, but as a punishment for disobedience. The passage describes a scene of horror in which the people will die in droves and lie unburied. Further, God forbids that anyone should mourn them; "there shall be no gashing, no shaving of

---

[35] II Kings 21:6, in a description of Manasseh's depraved reign, lists his dealings with mediums and wizards as one of his failings. In 23:24, Josiah as part of his clean-up operation gets rid of the mediums and wizards, among a number of other things.

[36] Isaiah 19:3 speaks of the Egyptians consulting idols, the spirits of the dead, ghosts, and familiar spirits.

[37] Spronk, *Beatific Afterlife*, 257, says that Deut 18, Isaiah 8, and I Samuel 28 suggest "an under-current in the ancient religion of Israel next to the mainstream of Yahwism," usually associated with the common people but also linked with kings such as Saul, Manasseh, and Amon. Theodore J. Lewis, *Cults of the Dead in Ancient Israel and Ugarit* (Atlanta: Scholars Press, 1989) 117, remarks that it is strange that the Deuteronomist not only preserves this story but shows necromancy to be effective. He suggests that the story was too well-known to excise, and so it is used instead as part of the narrative "to articulate Saul's demise."

the head for them." Isaiah 22:12 demands shaving of the head along with mourning and wearing of sackcloth. The significance of this group of passages has been variously described. Some have inferred that the Israelites practiced ancestor-worship, a cult of the dead,[38] or some form of veneration of the ancestors.[39]

Deuteronomy 26 does make it clear that an idea was present among the Israelites that the dead needed sustenance, and the remains of grave goods suggests that people were believed to exist in some sense after death.[40] Mourning customs as described in the biblical texts have also been considered by some to be part of a cult of the dead. Typical customs include lamentation with cries (I Kings 13:30, Jer 22:18, Amos 5:6), or in some cases with a qinah or lament song (II Sam 1:17–27, 3:33–34), tearing of the clothes (Gen 37:34, II Sam 1:11), removal of sandals (II Sam 15:20, Micah 1:8), donning of sackcloth (Gen 37:34 and II Sam 3:31), cessation of bathing (II Sam 14:2), rolling in ashes and dust (Jer 6:26, Ezek 27:30, Micah 1:10), and throwing dust on the head (Josh 7:6, I Sam 4:12). The mourner might

---

[38] Spronk, *Beatific Afterlife*, 247, defines a cult of the dead as "a veneration of the dead which can be compared to the veneration of deities."

[39] See Herbert C. Brichto, "Kin, Cult, Land and Afterlife—A Biblical Complex," *Hebrew Union College Annual* 44(1973) 1–54. Brichto offers a multi-layered argument for this view. Isaiah 14 and I Sam 28 show that the afterlife was a matter of accepted fact. Gen 23, about Abraham's acquiring the field of Machpelah, reveals a crucial link between burial site and ownership of land. The purpose of levirate law is to guarantee that the dead would have descendants to care for them. Deut 26 shows that rites for the dead were permitted even within the Bible, since it prohibits them only in one specific case. The fifth commandment is about honoring one's parents after their death, and in general, the desire for burial and the close ties to the land are both aspects of a cult of the dead. Brichto concludes that the evidence "testifies overwhelmingly to a belief on the part of Biblical Israel in an afterlife," where the dead retain their personality, are involved with their descendants, and depend on them for care in their existence after death (48). However, his analysis relies on the work of Foustel de Coulanges on worship of the dead, which is now outdated, and while the Israelites, or at least some of them, clearly knew practices involving care of the dead and took part in mourning rituals, Brichto jumps from that to a concept of reward and punishment after death which is not obvious. See Spronk, *Beatific Afterlife*, 50, for his rebuttal.

[40] Spronk, *Beatific Afterlife*, 241. See also George E. Mendenhall, "From Witchcraft to Justice: Death and Afterlife in the Old Testament," in Hiroshi Obayashi, ed., *Death and Afterlife: Perspectives of World Religions* (New York: Greenwood Press, 1992) 72.

tear out or cut off the hair (Ezra 9:3, Is 22:12, Jer 41:5, Job 1:20), or cover the beard and head (II Sam 19:5, Ezek 24:17, 23). One might beat (Is 32:12) or cut oneself (Jer 16:6, 41:5) and fast (I Sam 31:13, II Sam 1:12), or take part in a funeral meal (Jer 16:7, Ezek 24:17, 22).[41]

Spronk notes that this is all standard among ancient Near Eastern mourning procedures, and the likeliest explanation for such actions is that these are ways for the living to make themselves like the dead as an act of communion, to imitate decay and return to the dust, rather than expressions of fear or veneration of the dead.[42] He feels that the eating and drinking in Jeremiah and Ezekiel were probably felt to have been shared by the dead, especially since Deut 26 shows that some people made food offerings to them, but such offerings in themselves do not indicate a cult of the dead, since little is known about the status of the departed.[43] All in all, while the Israelites had mourning rituals like everyone else, and clearly thought that the dead had some kind of existence in the beyond, the evidence for a cult of the dead in Israel is slight, and the kind of life after death, if the biblical references to Sheol are to be believed, seems to have been considered quite pale in contrast to life on earth. Spronk notes, "compared to Canaanite religion Yahwism is remarkably silent with regard to the afterlife."[44] The reason for this, he believes, is that ideas of the afterlife in Israel are so closely tied to the fight against Baalism and its associated notions of life and death. The Israelites believed their god to have just as much power over death as anyone's, but the surviving

---

[41] See Sponk, *Beatific Afterlife*, 244, for this list.

[42] Sponk, *Beatific Afterlife*, 244–47; Gashing and shaving are forbidden in Leviticus and Deuteronomy probably because they were associated with the Baal cult.

[43] Sponk, *Beatific Afterlife*, 245–48; In Jeremiah 16 the "bread of mourning" and "cup of consolation" are tied to the "house of the Marzeah," which in Ugarit was part of the cult of the dead, though as Sponk remarks, the living also took part in the marzeah meals. Other hints of a cult of the dead in Israel are the cult of Baal Peor, Psalm 16, which could be about the deified dead, and the royal cult of the dead (249–50). Brian B. Schmidt, *Israel's Beneficent Dead: Ancestor Cult and Necromancy in Ancient Israelite Religion and Tradition* (Tübingen: J. C. B. Mohr [Siebeck], 1994) 262–63, says that the Marzeah in Jeremiah 16 was probably mostly concerned with the economic interests of its members and not primarily tied to mortuary events, though members might arrange a colleague's funeral.

[44] Sponk, *Beatific Afterlife*, 281.

texts usually restrict themselves to the present life and God's saving power from premature death or death-like conditions. The traces that do survive in the Hebrew Bible of such things as a cult of the dead or necromancy are signs of the syncretistic beliefs among some of the people in distinction to official Yahwistic religion.[45]

Spronk's analysis has been criticized by other scholars for treating the textual evidence in a synchronic, rather than a diachronic, fashion. When viewed diachronically, one learns that condemnations of practices associated with the dead do not start to appear until the middle of the eighth century, which, it has been suggested, may be a response to the competition necromancy was giving prophecy.[46] If this is the case, the assertion that an official "Yahwism" was opposed to a popular or folk religion is doubtful. The religion developed over a long period of time and to make a distinction between different degrees of orthodoxy is anachronistic.[47] Spronk's critics conclude that the sparseness of the evidence makes it impossible to draw definitive conclusions about the existence of resurrection or beatific afterlife in ancient Israel.[48]

However, Elizabeth Bloch-Smith does believe that a cult of the dead[49] was a central part of society in Judah and probably also Israel.[50]

---

[45] Spronk, *Beatific Afterlife*, 344–45. In later parts of the Hebrew Bible the hope in God after death, he says, is set apart from Canaanite notions on the matter.

[46] Mark S. Smith and Elizabeth Bloch-Smith, "Death and Afterlife in Ugarit and Israel," *Journal of the American Oriental Society* 108(1988) 281. Other practices such as feeding the dead did not come under criticism until the seventh century (Deut 26:14).

[47] Smith and Bloch-Smith, "Death and Afterlife in Ugarit and Israel," 281–82.

[48] Smith and Bloch-Smith, "Death and Afterlife in Ugarit and Israel," 284. The best evidence, they say, for at least a "modified form" of a beatific afterlife is in royal prayers such as Psalm 21:3–5, where God gives the king "length of days forever and ever" (283).

[49] Elizabeth Bloch-Smith, *Judahite Burial Practices and Beliefs about the Dead* (Sheffield: Journal for the Study of the Old Testament Press, 1992) 109, notes the following names for the dead in the Hebrew Bible: "those who pass over" (Ezek 39:11, 14, 15), "divine ones" (I Sam 28:13, Is 8:19), "mutterers" (Is 19:3), "dead ones" (Is 26:14, Ps 106:28), "being" (Lev 19:28, Num 5:2, Hag 2:13), "ghosts" (Is 29:4), "knowing ones" (Is 8:19), "corpse" (Is 14:19), "holy ones" (Ps 16:3), and "healers [?]" (Is 14:9, 26:14, Ps 88:11).

[50] Elizabeth Bloch-Smith, "The Cult of the Dead in Judah: Interpreting the Material Remains," *Journal of Biblical Literature* 111(1992) 222.

The consultation of Samuel by Saul in I Sam 28 shows that the dead were thought to have special knowledge. II Kings 13:20–21, where Elisha's bones revivify a dead man, indicates a belief in the power of at least some dead to bring others back to life. II Sam 4:12 and Isaiah 57:11 may reveal a fear that the dead could harm the living. Therefore they were appeased with tithed food (Gen 28:17–18, Deut 26:14), oil (Gen 28:17), and sacrifices (Gen 31:53, 46:1, Is 57:6–7).[51] Ancestral tombs functioned as physical claims to the patrimony, and the family had to stay nearby in order to take care of and venerate their ancestors.

The first prohibitions of feeding the dead and of necromancy appear in the Deuteronomic and Holiness Codes, as well as Isaiah.[52] These prohibitions are the result, she feels, of the fall of the northern kingdom and subsequent immigration of cultic functionaries to the south. The priests and prophets in Judah wanted to centralize their cult and ensure their own authority, which was achieved in part by forbidding consultation of the dead by official functionaries to gain knowledge from sources other than Yahweh. Priests, prophets, and nazirites could no longer consult the dead, but the common people were still allowed to feed them (except tithed food) or consult them on their own, without cultic assistance. An additional consideration of the reforms was to weaken the family-based cult of the dead.[53] The masses, however, did not modify their beliefs in spite of the changes that were taking place in Jerusalem, and until the reforms of Hezekiah and Josiah, the cult of the dead, in her view, was universal. The archeological data from the material remains of the culture also reveals that there was no shift in practices, even in Jerusalem. The authorities could curb, but not really suppress the cult.[54]

Schmidt reads the data differently. He points out, as did Spronk, that caring for, feeding, and commemorating the dead "neither presupposed nor necessitated the belief in the supernatural beneficent power of the dead as expressed in ancestor veneration or worship or in

---

[51] Bloch-Smith, *Judahite Burial Practices and Beliefs about the Dead*, 146.
[52] From the late 8th to the 7th centuries BCE.
[53] Bloch-Smith, *Judahite Burial Practices and Beliefs about the Dead*, 146–47.
[54] Bloch-Smith, *Judahite Burial Practices and Beliefs about the Dead*, 151. See also Bloch-Smith, "The Cult of the Dead in Judah: Interpreting the Material Remains," 222–24.

the deification of the dead."[55] The belief in an afterlife or grave goods in tombs do not indicate anything one way or the other about the conceptions of the dead and their powers. In Israel, he says, the dead had a "weak and marginal role."[56] The evidence of necromancy might contradict this view, except that necromancy, he says, was not native to the Israelite traditions. It was a late introduction brought in by the Assyrians. The evidence for this includes the following: divination achieved popularity under late Assyrian rulers, references to Mesopotamian necromancy in particular are many from this period forward, the Mesopotamian nations of Assyria and Babylon controlled Judah in the mid first millennium, the religious life in Judah in this time was influenced by Mesopotamian practices, either because the locals wished it or were compelled to it, the biblical texts which speak of necromancy are all late, and apart from these late references, the practice is unattested in Israel.[57]

He suggests that the post-Deuteronomic redactor slipped references to necromancy into "early" texts about the beginning of the nation, treated it as a Canaanite practice, and proscribed it in the speech of Moses in Deut 18:10–11. This served as a "precedent" for excoriating Manasseh in II Kings 21:6 and 23:24. Further redaction included Saul's encounter with Samuel's spirit in I Sam 28, which foreshadowed the downfall of the later monarchy under Manasseh, just as Saul's was overthrown.[58] More anti-necromancy rhetoric appears in Isaiah 8:19, 19:3, and 29:4, where it was set in the near past under Ahaz and ascribed to the whole people.[59] Schmidt also disputes the argument that ancestor cults always existed in Israel but were later suppressed by Yahwist writers, which is supposedly why the evidence

---

[55] Schmidt, *Israel's Beneficent Dead*, 275.

[56] Schmidt, *Israel's Beneficent Dead*, 282.

[57] Schmidt, *Israel's Beneficent Dead*, 241. He says also that long-term social crises and the failure of the traditional religion in the face of foreign invasion contributed to the adoption of this foreign custom, which was an effort to regain a way of interacting with the transcendent and preserving group cohesion (see 275 and 292).

[58] Lewis, *Cults of the Dead in Ancient Israel and Ugarit*, 174, believes that in I Sam 28 the Deuteronomist is preserving an older story, which he adds is surprising considering Deuteronomy's polemic against necromantic practices. Schmidt's analysis may explain better what the tale is doing here.

[59] Schmidt, *Israel's Beneficent Dead*, 247.

for them is so sparse. His argument is as follows. Necromancy was shown by the biblical editors to have been popular in late pre-exilic Judah; those editors handled the problem of necromancy's existence by prohibiting it in the biblical material (retroactively), instead of simply editing it out of the texts altogether; one would therefore expect that ancestor cults, if they had truly existed, would get the same treatment as necromancy had at the hands of the same editors. Yet earlier biblical traditions make no mention of either necromancy or ancestor cults, and later traditions mention only necromancy. This suggests not that the fact of ancestor-related practices were suppressed by those who later compiled the biblical texts, since these same people acknowledged the existence of necromancy when it came on the scene, but that the practices did not exist.[60]

If the prohibitions of necromancy and some of the mourning practices were not a struggle against Baalism, as suggested by Spronk, or part of the centralization of the cult in Jerusalem and assertion of authority against previously accepted ways of attaining supernatural knowledge, as argued by Bloch-Smith, what motivated them? Schmidt reconstructs the origin of the prohibitions as part of an effort to reestablish social cohesion in the exilic and post-exilic periods. After the disruption of the Babylonian invasions, a new national identity was needed, and this was achieved by sharply redefining boundaries of all kinds in order to strengthen social solidarity. One of these boundaries was that between the living and the dead. Mourning rites such as self-mutilation, which were an imitation of the dead, and necromancy, which involved an actual meeting of the worlds of the dead and the living, blurred this boundary in the extreme. So all competing religious systems, indigenous (self-mutilation, child sacrifice, the Asherah cult) as well as foreign (Mesopotamian necromancy), were labelled by the deuteronomists as Canaanite and condemned through the voices of Moses, Isaiah, and Josiah.[61]

---

[60] Schmidt, *Israel's Beneficent Dead*, 276.

[61] Schmidt, *Israel's Beneficent Dead*, 292–93. Schmidt also states that the idea of worship of the ancestors as underlying Israel's mortuary customs is "a cherished relic of nineteenth century anthropology."

Conclusions

The fact that the same textual and archeological data can lead to so many different theories about the views the Israelites had of the dead shows how problematic the matter is. The references to death and the dead which have survived are few and far between in the texts, and the reader who looks to the Hebrew Bible for reflections on death has to look hard. Of course, the biblical texts are a select group of materials that may not represent the interests of all facets of the culture; the archeological evidence provides a somewhat fuller insight into ancient practices. Yet it also does not reveal a very extensive cultural focus on the dead. This is not to say that the Israelites did not have funerary rituals, mourning practices, and even leave offerings to the dead, but none of these things necessarily signifies full-blown ancestor worship, for example. When taken together, the most persuasive interpretation of the various data is that as a people the Israelites did not appear to spend a large amount of time, from the side of belief or of practice, on the dead in particular or death in general.

Contrary to this chapter's argument, however, some scholars have argued that mortality was in fact a fearsome idea to the Israelites. The poetic sections of the Hebrew Bible alone show that the matter "was not a peripheral phenomenon in Hebrew thought."[62] Death was a misfortune, and hideous.[63] Others have pointed out that this is only a fair description on certain occasions, and one needs to be aware of the exact circumstances under which death is treated as a calamity. There certainly are times when death is viewed as a bad thing, but not because death in itself is necessarily an evil. The reason is instead that something about the cause, manner, or timing of the death is unfortunate.[64] In II Sam 18, David bitterly mourns the death of his

---

[62] Tromp, *Primitive Conceptions of Death and the Nether World in the Old Testament*, 211.

[63] Bruce Vawter, "Post-exilic Prayer and Hope," *Catholic Biblical Quarterly* 37(1975) 470; H.W. Wolff, *Anthropology of the Old Testament* (Philadelphia: Fortress Press, 1973) 102: cited in Bailey, *Biblical Perspectives on Death*, 122. Cf. also Wolfram Herrmann, "Human Mortality as a Problem in Ancient Israel," in Frank E. Reynolds and Earle H. Waugh, eds., *Religious Encounters with Death: Insights from the History and Anthropology of Religions* (University Park, PA: The Pennsylvania State University Press, 1977) 162, who writes that "death was greeted by the Israelite not with joy but with fear."

[64] Bailey, *Biblical Perspectives on Death*, 47.

young son Absalom. Hezekiah also laments his own upcoming death at age 39, saying "in the noontide of my days I must depart" (Is 38:10). Violent death is also to be feared. Examples of this include Joab's efforts to avoid execution (I Kings 2:28–33), Saul's terror at the prediction that he will fall in battle (I Sam 28:15–20), and threats to the wicked of dying by the sword (various prophetic texts). Death without children is grim. The concern for acquiring offspring is apparent in Abraham's worries about his childlessness in Gen 15, and Boaz's marriage of his childless kinsman's widow, Ruth, "to maintain the dead man's name on his inheritance, in order that the name of the dead may not be cut off from his kindred and from the gate of his native place" (Ruth 4:10).[65]

Others, taking a somewhat different tack, have suggested that the theory that the Israelites were not much concerned with death is an imprecise way of stating the issue, and argue that an original perception by the Israelites of death as a problem, a perception common to all humanity, is being confused with the religious *responses* to this problem, which transforms the threat of human mortality into an acceptable part of the cosmos. Thus survival of one's offspring, name, and nation are the answers given by the Israelite tradition to the universal problem of death.[66] The distinction is a good one. The Israelites were well aware of death, and did not treat it with a cavalier attitude. Survival of the person through community conduits is indeed a response to the danger of individual annihilation. Death was not an inconsequential event, and could moreover be the source of great grief. Part of the debate here has to do with differences between cultural and individual responses to death. A culture can have an effective way of dealing with it, while an individual will still feel the common emotions of sorrow and distress.

The point of the argument is not to claim that the Israelites did not care about death, have rituals associated with it, experience normal human emotions because of it, or offer answers to it, but to suggest that the existence of death as an unavoidable phenomenon of human life had been confronted by the religious tradition in a way that

---

[65] Bailey, *Biblical Perspectives on Death*, 47–51. Cf. also Deut 25:5–10 on levirate marriage, as well as Gen 38.

[66] Gualtieri, *The Vulture and the Bull: Religious Responses to Death*, 74–75.

successfully offered solace, so that death did not continue to stand as a live religious or philosophical problem. How did the Israelites arrive at their particular approach? Societies can take any of a number of views of death, and the situation among the Israelite culture itself eventually changed after a number of centuries. The following section will attempt to address the question in more detail.

SOCIAL BACKGROUND

Scholars approach the matter by investigating the social factors that shaped Israelite society.[67] The core idea which is cited as the anchor of Israelite views of death often appears under the rubric "corporate personality," a term which was coined by H. Wheeler Robinson earlier in the century. The phrase describes Robinson's view of how "personality" functioned in ancient Israel in terms of legal responsibility. "The larger or smaller group was accepted without question as a unity.... The whole group, including its past, present, and future members, might function as a single individual through anyone of those members conceived as representative of it."[68] The practical outcome of this notion was that for purposes of guilt and punishment, one individual's actions could initiate consequences which would

---

[67] L. H. Silberman, "Death in the Hebrew Bible and Apocalyptic Literature," in L. O. Mills, ed., *Perspectives on Death* (Nashville: Abingdon, 1969) 14, writes that "ideas of death did not exist by themselves but rather within a constellation of other ideas and attitudes with which they cohered. Whatever ideas and attitudes toward death the Israelites held, such ideas and attitudes stood in some crucial relationship to what they believed about life." Cf. also Thomas J. Hopkins, "Hindu Views of Death and Afterlife," in Hiroshi Obayashi, ed., *Death and Afterlife: Perspectives of World Religions* (New York: Greenwood Press, 1992) 144, who points out that one's views of life and afterlife are interrelated, sharing metaphysical assumptions and beliefs in the same realities.

[68] H. Wheeler Robinson, *Corporate Personality in Ancient Israel* (Philadelphia: Fortress Press, 1964) 1. Typical cases cited by proponents of Robinson's theory include the annihilation of Achan and his family in Joshua 7, David's handing over of seven of Saul's sons to the Gibeonites to remove the bloodguilt of Saul's line in II Sam 21, the procedure for a town's collective absolution of guilt when a murder victim is found nearby in Deut 21:1–9, and the attribution of the nation's misfortunes to the sins of Manasseh in II Kings 21:10–16 and 24:3–4.

equally effect other members of the group with which he was identified, family, clan, tribe, nation, or whatever the case might be.[69]

Although this analysis of Israelite society initially received widespread support, it gradually came under criticism on a variety of points, such as the question of whether Israelite law was based on the group or the individual, and the specific kinds of situations in which punishment was meted out on a community level.[70] Further suspicion of the usefulness of Robinson's theory arose as scholars considered the fact that he was influenced by the anthropological studies of Lévy-Bruhl, which have since come under fire for poor methodology and lack of sophistication in lumping cultures from around the globe under the over-simplified label "primitive."[71]

---

[69] Cf. Ex 20:5, 34:7, Num 14:18, Deut 5:9, and Jer 32:18 for one formulation of the principle in the epithet of God who visits "the iniquity of the parents upon the children and the children's children, to the third and the fourth generation."

[70] J. R. Porter, "The Legal Aspects of the Concept of 'Corporate Personality' in the Old Testament," *Vetus Testamentum* 15(1965) 361–80, took issue with the argument that the place where one mainly finds examples of corporate personality is in the legal setting. According to him, Israelite law was primarily based on an assumption of *individual* responsibility, going all the way back to what many take to be the earliest Hebrew law-code, the "Book of the Covenant" (Exodus 20–23). Most of the laws begin with the phrase "if a man does X," et cetera. That is, if an individual acts in a certain way, such and such shall be done to that particular person. As far as the legal sections of the Hebrew Bible go, "it may be questioned whether the principle of communal responsibility really appears in them at all" (365). In those cases where the notion of group responsibility does apply, matters of personal property or religious beliefs about the contagiousness of holiness and sin are the guiding considerations of what scholars have incorrectly been treating under the rubric of "corporate personality."

[71] J. W. Rogerson, "The Hebrew Concept of Corporate Personality: A Re-Examination," *Journal of Theological Studies* 21(1970) 1–16, notes that Lévy-Bruhl's contribution to the academy was his work on primitive cultures, which he concluded were characterized by pre-logical thought, a mystical approach to the world where distinctions could not be made between objective and subjective experiences, and that Robinson used this idea to explain that in a similar manner, the Israelite could not conceive of individual personality as something separate from the larger structures of community organization (7). Rogerson concludes that though Robinson did not classify the ancient Israelites as primitives, his treatment of them suffers from the same flaws inherent to the assumptions borrowed from Lévy-Bruhl.

While recent scholarship might suggest that the whole idea ought to be consigned to the trash heap, however, a deeper look at the arguments about corporate thought cautions against a wholesale rejection of it. The original theory of corporate personality has been well and properly criticized, but the fact remains that there are situations in the Bible where the people, or God, deal with matters on a corporate level.[72] Scholars now give the biblical corpus a more nuanced treatment in this matter. Even within the same biblical books one can find examples of both individual and corporate-oriented cases of retribution, such as in Numbers[73] and Deuteronomy.[74] One must question the romanticism inherent in the earlier treatment of Israelite religion exemplified by Robinson and those like him, but this does not mean that the entire substance of the idea was wrong. Corporate "personality" is not a useful classification, since it assumes a theory of Israelite mentality and an inability to think in terms of the individual which is erroneous, but to deny the corporate aspect of some of the

---

[72] Cf. Joel S. Kaminsky, *Punishment Displacement in the Hebrew Bible*, Dissertation, 2 Vols. (University of Chicago, 1993) 16; published as *Corporate Responsibility in the Hebrew Bible* (Sheffield: Sheffield Academic Press, 1995) 22, who makes this point and provides a level-headed treatment of the question of the corporate nature of action and decisions in the Hebrew Bible.

[73] Cf. Gordon H. Matties, *Ezekiel 18 and the Rhetoric of Moral Discourse* (Atlanta: Scholars Press, 1990) 127, who shows that in Numbers 14, 15, and 16, three different answers are offered to the question of whether the consequences of part of the community's actions will effect everyone in the community together and/or subsequent generations. In Numbers 14, when the people balk at entering the land, God swears that the entire generation will die in the wilderness, including the children (v. 33). In Numbers 16, the account of Korah's rebellion, Moses and Aaron successfully turn away God's wrath from the congregation as a whole. "O God...shall one person sin and you become angry with the whole congregation?" (v. 22). In the intervening 15th chapter, a series of cultic regulations, the extent of punishment depends on whether or not the offense was intentional.

[74] While on the one hand Deuteronomy repeats the statement that God visits the sins of the fathers to the third and the fourth generation (5:9–10), one law declares (24:16) "Parents shall not be put to death for their children, nor shall children be put to death for their parents; only for their own crimes may persons be put to death." See Matties, *Ezekiel 18 and the Rhetoric of Moral Discourse*, 128. He concludes that Israel acknowledged "two foci, both of which were valid," depending on the circumstances (130). See also Ezekiel 18:20 and Jeremiah 31:29–30.

episodes in Israel's history is to go too far.[75] Keeping in mind, then, that the notion of corporate personality as initially applied by Robinson is far too simplistic, and that biblical traditions reveal a more complex and nuanced approach to individual and community identity than the original theory allows, the basic idea that the ancient Israelites shared a worldview which tended to have a group-oriented outlook on life is not without value.

The ability to conceive of the individual as in some sense part of a larger community body who affects and is affected by that body provides some understanding of Israelite attitudes towards death. Because of the corporate view, "death, though no less the dissolution of the individual, lost its ultimacy, for the corporate person, family or clan or all Israel, endured."[76] Each person is one small part of a larger entity comprising ancestors and descendents alike. Although the individual Israelite would probably not fully and exclusively identify himself with his compatriots, he would nonetheless be aware of his relation to the people as a whole.[77] The Israelites had practically no notion of an afterlife for the individual because of their finely honed sense of the people's survival in general under God's guidance; community continuity provided comfort in the face of death.[78] The individual focus that appears in the psalms and the wisdom literature proves that the Israelites were quite capable of showing an interest in personal concerns, but does not negate the fact that for the most part, the biblical writings emphasize the history and experiences of Israel as a nation.

---

[75] Kaminsky, *Punishment Displacement in the Hebrew Bible*, 21.

[76] Silberman, "Death in the Hebrew Bible and Apocalyptic Literature," 26; similarly Gatch, *Death*, 35.

[77] Martin-Achard, *From Death to Life*, 210, speaks of one's "solidarity with a whole people, whose merits and faults he shares; his lot is dependent on the attitude of his family or nation towards God." See also Hooke, "Israel and the Afterlife," 238; Roland E. Murphy, "The Sage in Ecclesiastes and Qoheleth the Sage," in J. G. Gammie and Leo G. Perdue, eds., *The Sage in Israel and the Ancient Near East* (Winona Lake: Eisenbrauns, 1990) 268.

[78] Hiroshi Obayashi, "Introduction," in Hiroshi Obayashi, ed., *Death and Afterlife: Perspectives of World Religions* (New York: Greenwood Press, 1992) xiv. Whether the lack of a notion of an individual afterlife is the cause, or result of, the community-oriented worldview, or exactly how these two facts are related, may be impossible to unravel.

Within this framework of thought, an individual death is not the kind of shattering event which would bring the culture's entire idea of God, society, and nature into question, although of course the individual's surviving loved ones still had to deal with their loss on a personal level. But as a whole the tradition could handle the potential disruption death might offer through its own version of immortality, which consisted of several related points: survival through one's offspring, a kind of corporate memory of the just,[79] and the continuation of the people as a nation. Family and name are double insurance against annihilation.[80] In all respects personal continuity depends on the community at large. Moreover, if one lives properly and under God's law, then a ripe old age and a peaceful death are to be expected, and appreciated. The book of Proverbs shows how death can be comfortably incorporated into an ordered system. "Because the qualitative 'life' of wisdom prevails unambiguously over the qualitative 'death' of the fool, the fact that every human life ends in death seems less important."[81]

The definitions of life and death, then, from a more modern and literalistic point of view, are finessed into multiple shades of meaning, so that children and memory, national survival and quality of experience, all serve as ways of protecting the individual's life in the face of death. All of these are "symbolic immortalities" which establish human continuity not by preservation of the individual's consciousness after death, but by maintaining the feeling that something both part of and larger than the individual survives.[82]

"So the exploration of death in the Biblical period is not one of seeking for each individual an immortal compensation with God. It is an exploration of

---

[79] Murphy, "The Sage in Ecclesiastes and Qoheleth the Sage," 268. For examples of the importance of memory, see Prov 10:7 (The memory of the righteous is a blessing, but the name of the wicked will rot); also Isaiah 56:5 and Ben Sira 41:11.

[80] Howard N. Bream, "Life Without Resurrection: Two Perspectives From Qoheleth," in H.N. Bream et al, eds., *A Light Unto My Path (Jacob M. Myers Festschrift)* (Philadelphia: Temple University Press, 1974) 54.

[81] Collins, *The Root of Immortality*, 185.

[82] Carol Zaleski, "Death, and Near-Death Today," in John J. Collins and Michael Fishbane, eds., *Death, Ecstasy, and Other Worldly Journeys* (Albany: State University Press of New York, 1995) 387.

how...the order and stability of the process of life and of succeeding generations can be maintained in conjunction with God."[83]

In summary, it is not so much the case that death was a non-issue for people living in Canaan many centuries ago, but that their traditions met the problem of death in a way that prevented it from remaining an urgent theological question for society as a whole. Eventually, however, the traditional solutions began to lose their powers of persuasion, and one of the first places where one can see this is in the book of Qoheleth.

---

[83] John Bowker, *The Meanings of Death*, 54.

Chapter 2
DEATH IN QOHELETH

None of what was said in the preceding chapter applies to the book of Qoheleth. One of the interesting things that the reader becomes aware of when going through the secondary literature about the book is that the same adjectives keep cropping up. One commentator dubs it "the strangest book in the Bible,"[1] while another calls it "the Bible's strangest book."[2] Yet a third goes one better by declaring it "one of the most remarkable works in world literature."[3] The astonished reaction is fairly consistent across the spectrum of interpretation. The reason for this is perhaps that Qoheleth's denial of any perceivable order in the workings of the world, or even of the human capacity to arrive at an understanding of why things are the way they are, whether by divine instruction or human reason, is the rock against which the systems of cosmic and moral coherence offered by priest, prophet, and sage threaten to shatter. The linch-pin in his despair is the inevitability of death, death which recognizes no distinctions of age or virtue, and is the ultimate negation of knowledge. Or put another way, he consistently expresses his dissatisfaction with the world and human existence within that world through the idea, imagery, and fact of death.

---

[1] R. B. Y. Scott, *Proverbs-Ecclesiastes* (New York: Doubleday, 1965) 191.
[2] James Crenshaw, *Ecclesiastes: A Commentary* (Philadelphia: The Westminster Press, 1987) 23.
[3] Robert Gordis, *Koheleth-The Man and His World* (New York: Bloch Publishing Company, 1955) vii.

THE TEXT: DATE AND LANGUAGE

Qoheleth's style of Hebrew, in both vocabulary and grammatical forms, is noticeably different from that in most of the rest of the Hebrew Bible. On the basis of this fact scholars have offered a number of theories with respect to both the text's time of composition and original language.

Date

The majority view is that the book is linguistically late compared to those in the rest of the canon, and this is the position taken here as well. Among its features are Persian words, Aramaisms, late developments in forms and syntax in Biblical Hebrew, and forms also found in the Mishna.[4] These suggest to many scholars that the language

---

[4] Cf. Barton, *The Book of Ecclesiastes* (New York: Charles Scribner's Sons, 1908) 52–53 for a reliable summary:

Persian words: פרדס, פתגם. (Crenshaw, *Ecclesiastes*, 49, considers מדינה to be a Persian word as well, while Barton categorizes it as an Aramaism).

Aramaisms: נכסים, על, על-עמת ש-, שבח, מדינה, תקן, ענין, כבר, עבד, משלחת, שלטון, פשר, חשבון, על-דברת ש-, תקיף, אלו, מענה, דרבנות, בטל, ילדות, מדע, בן חורים, סכן, גומץ, קרב.

Late developments in Hebrew forms: An article and preposition when attached to the beginning of a noun are each written out, as in כהכבם (8:1); repeated use of abstracts ending in ון and ות; confusion of III-א and III-ה stems; always אני instead of אנכי; אספה (12:11) found only I Chron 26:15, 17 and Neh 12:25 where the plural is formed differently.

Late developments in Hebrew syntax: Waw-consecutive with the imperfect appears only three times (1:17, 4:1,7); frequent use of participial constructions, often accompanied by the personal pronoun as the subject; negation of participial constructions with אין; use of pronoun plus verbal adjectives, as in אני עמל; pleonastic use of אני with first person verb; בש- and באשר as "because"; עד אשר לא as "while not."

Similarities to Mishna: אי as "woe," cf. Mish. *Yebamoth* 13:7; אביונה as "caperberry," cf. Ma'aseroth 4:6 etc.; זה for זאת, cf. זו *Erub.* 4:6 and *Yom.* 3:3; זה הוא, where הוא is a copula, cf. Mishnaic זה הוא *Kel.* 5:10 etc.; the use of זה with nouns without the article, as in כל זה, like Mishnaic זה איש and זה...זה as "this...that," also without article; אי זה as "what" or "what then," cf. *Peah* 7:8; יצא as "be guiltless" or "quit from," cf. *Berakoth* 2:1; מראה as "the power of seeing," cf. *Yoma* 74b; מי and מי אשר as "whoever," cf. *Sheb.* 9:8, 9; ש- instead of אשר 89 times (by the Mishna it replaces אשר completely, while in Qoheleth both appear).

is very late Biblical Hebrew and closer in time to the Mishna.[5] Whitley lists a number of words and phrases in Qoheleth which otherwise appear only in the Mishna and the Talmud. Examples include חוּץ, מִן עַנִין, בֵּית־עוֹלָם, אֲבִיוֹנָה, and חֵפֶץ (in the specific sense of "matter/thing").[6] Schoors offers a sane analysis of the different arguments and concludes that though Qoheleth's language is not identical to Mishnaic Hebrew this does not mean there is no similarity whatsoever. The constellation of linguistic features in the book suggests a late date.[7] Wise believes that Qoheleth wrote a type of Hebrew that was closer to the spoken language than any of the other postexilic biblical books. His language "approaches that of the spoken Hebrew of Jerusalem in the third century BCE."[8] Isaksson agrees that Qoheleth's language was closer to spoken Hebrew than classical narrative Hebrew, possibly a local dialect.[9] Michael Fox accepts "the nearly universal placement of Qoheleth in the fourth to third centuries BCE, primarily on linguistic grounds."[10] However, in a recent study which examines the book's vocabulary in comparison with Aramaic words, especially Aramaic economic terms that are attested in the

---

[5] Cf. also Gordis, *Koheleth*, 59–50; Crenshaw, *Ecclesiastes*, 50; H. W. Hertzberg, *Der Prediger* (Leipzig: A. Deichertsche Verlagsbuchhandlung D. Werner Scholl, 1932; Gütersloh: G. Mohn, 1963) 6–7; Kurt Galling, "Der Prediger," in Ernst Würthwein, ed., *Die Fünf Megilloth* (Tübingen: J. C. B. Mohr [Siebeck], 1969) 74–75; and Aarre Lauha, *Kohelet* (Neukirchen-Vluyn: Neukirchener Verlag, 1978) 7–8, for a similar discussion.

[6] Charles F. Whitley, *Koheleth: His Language and Thought* (Berlin, New York: Walter de Gruyter, 1979) 137–39. He in fact believes that Qoheleth is so close in syntax and vocabulary to the Mishna that he dates the book later than most, to around 150 BCE.

[7] Antoon Schoors, *The Preacher Sought to Find Pleasing Words: A Study of the Language of Qoheleth* (Leuven: Departement Oriëntalistiek, 1992) 15.

[8] Michael Wise, "A Calque from Aramaic in Qoheleth 6:12; 7:12; and 8:13," *Journal of Biblical Literature* 109(1990) 250. He notes that the only other works that are close to the spoken Hebrew of the time are 4QMMT, the Copper Scroll, and maybe the laws of the Damascus Covenant.

[9] Bo Isaksson, *Studies in the Language of Qoheleth: With Special Emphasis on the Verbal System* (Stockholm: Almqvist & Wiksell International, 1987) 196–97. He rejects the belief, however, that it is all that close to Mishnaic Hebrew and finally questions whether the book can be dated on linguistic grounds alone. See also Daniel C. Fredericks, *Qoheleth's Language: Re-Evaluating Its Nature and Date* (Lewiston, NY: The Edwin Mellen Press, 1988) 5–6.

[10] Michael Fox, *Qohelet and His Contradictions* (Sheffield: The Almond Press, 1989) 151.

documents of the fifth and fourth centuries BCE, C. L. Seow suggests that Qoheleth most likely is datable to this period, instead of the somewhat later dating most scholars accept, as indicated by Fox.[11] James Kugel also considers the book to be a little older than most, no later than mid-fourth century BCE at the latest.[12]

Any one of the characteristics of Qoheleth's style would not necessarily be enough to assume a late stage of the language, but the argument is cumulative, so that overall the evidence suggests a time when Hebrew grammar was showing new developments and Aramaic was starting to influence Hebrew significantly.[13] The presence of Persian words makes it almost certain that the Persian era is the period *non ante quem* for the text.[14] Because fragments of the book found at Qumran have been placed in the mid-second century BCE,[15] the window for Qoheleth's composition is typically set between the fifth and second centuries. Modern commentators rarely fail to quote the apt comment of Delitzsch: "Wenn das B. Koheleth altsalomisch wäre, so gäbe es keine Geschichte der hebräischen Sprache."[16]

---

[11] C. L. Seow, "Linguistic Evidence and the Dating of Qohelet," *Journal of Biblical Literature* 115(1996) 654, 666. Thus he puts Qoheleth in the Persian era, "specifically between the second half of the fifth century and the first half of the fourth" (666). See also Seow, *Ecclesiastes* (New York: Doubleday, 1997) 13–15. An example of an Aramaic economic term which he uses for dating the text is the verb שׁלט, and the nominal forms of the root, which in fifth century documents pertains to property control. It has this semantic sense in Qoheleth as well (likewise in Neh 5:15, Ezra 4:20 and 7:24, he notes). By the time of Daniel, however, the root has come to mean "rule." After the Persian period it no longer denoted property rights (14).

[12] James L. Kugel, "Qohelet and Money," *Catholic Biblical Quarterly* 51(1989) 47. He points to the presence of Persian words but complete lack of Greek vocabulary, the apparent commercial vitality of the author's world, and absence of national consciousness (47–48).

[13] Gordis, *Koheleth*, 59–60. Robert Polzin, *Late Biblical Hebrew: Toward an Historical Typology of Biblical Hebrew Prose* (Missoula, MT: Scholars Press, 1976) 11, cautions "one cannot prove a chronologically questionable text to be late simply on the evidence of Aramaisms alone. There must be a heavy concentration of late linguistic elements (non-Aramaic as well as Aramaic) in the text under investigation." Qoheleth fulfills this requirement, though see pp. 5–6 for a different view.

[14] Gordis, *Koheleth*, 59.

[15] Crenshaw, *Ecclesiastes*, 49.

[16] Franz Delitzsch, *Biblischer Commentar IV, Hoheslied und Koheleth*

Since the book's comments on the state appear to reflect none of the upsets that arose in the second half of the third century BCE, when Israel bounced between the warring Seleucids and Ptolemies three times (249, 217, and 198), nor of the Maccabean period, a likely date is sometime before the mid-third century BCE.[17] Seow's arguments for a date in the Persian period are persuasive, although one is always aware that the specifics of any dating on the basis of language alone must be accepted cautiously, since the data that has survived from the time is limited. Nevertheless, based on what linguistic evidence there is, Qoheleth may well have originated in the Persian period. In any event, a pre-mid-third century date is plausible.[18]

(Leipzig: 1875) 197; reprinted as *Commentary on the Song of Songs and Ecclesiastes* (Grand Rapids: Eerdmans, 1982).

[17] Gordis, *Koheleth*, 63–68. Gordis also believes that Ben Sira knows the book. Since this wisdom text dates to ca. 180 BCE, and the text of Qoheleth would no doubt need to have existed at least a little while to gain circulation, a date of composition by the mid-third century is again suggested. Cf. also Crenshaw, *Ecclesiastes*, 50.

[18] A few have gone against the current and argued that a proper interpretation of the data does not support a late dating of the text. Fredericks believes that the common linguistic analyses of the book have ignored the relevance of Qoheleth's genre and dialectical uniqueness, as well as similarities to early Biblical Hebrew, which in fact make Qoheleth a pre-exilic work (*Qoheleth's Language: Re-Evaluating Its Nature and Date*). See also Isaakson, footnote #9, for doubts about dating on linguistic grounds period. However, in response Fox, *Qohelet and His Contradictions*, 154, asks among other things why vernacular, northern elements would predominate in an early work and then lie dormant until much later times. "Fredericks' approach is to take each feature individually and try to show that it could have existed in pre-exilic times—assuming that Qohelet wrote an unparalleled form of Hebrew.... Qohelet's Hebrew is certainly not the language known from definitely pre-exilic sources, and it is gratuitous to explain its peculiarities from unknowns." Schoors, *The Preacher Sought to Find Pleasing Words*, 222, has a similar reaction. He adds that while scholars like Fredericks are right to criticize the casual use of linguistic features, such as Aramaisms, for positing a late date, nevertheless some of the Aramaisms in Qoheleth's language are late traits. He cites nouns ending in "וֹת," repeated use of אֲשֶׁר/שֶׁ as a conjunction, and numerous composite conjunctions as examples (223). The argument that the book of Qoheleth cannot reasonably be given a post-exilic date is unpersuasive. William H. U. Anderson, *Qoheleth and Its Pessimistic Theology: Hermeneutical Struggles in Wisdom Literature* (Lewiston: Edwin Mellen Press, 1997) 87–94, also argues for a pre-exilic setting of the book, partly based on its view of death, since he suggests that such a view comes from an early period and shows no acceptance of the later notions of an afterlife. The present chapter will

Language

An issue related to the question of dating on the basis of Aramaisms is the hypothesis that Qoheleth was originally written entirely in Aramaic and subsequently translated into Hebrew.[19] This theory has been refuted by others and appears to have passed its heyday.[20] Gordis, a key critic of the idea, made his argument based on two fundamental points. First of all, while the text of Qoheleth is undeniably difficult in places, the expectation that a difficult text must be the result of a translation process does not necessarily conform to the logic of translation. Original texts may be misread, emended, and misunderstood, but generally the translator will convey his own, possibly incorrect understanding, into a clear translation; problems tend to be written out of, not written into, a translation.[21] Secondly, the fact that Hebrew fragments were found at Qumran means that a very short time would have existed for Qoheleth to be written in Aramaic, disseminated, translated into Hebrew, further disseminated in Hebrew, and then achieve a high enough

---

argue, however, that Qoheleth does show a new attitude towards death, while refusal of an afterlife belief is not evidence that a text is not from the late period. By the turn of the millennium, a wide range of opinions on that issue existed in Jewish circles.

[19] F. C. Burkitt, "Is Ecclesiastes a Translation?" *Journal of Theological Studies* 23(1921–22) 22–26; F. Zimmermann, "The Aramaic Provenance of Koheleth," *Jewish Quarterly Review* 36(1945–46) 17–45, and "The Question of Hebrew in Qohelet," *Jewish Quarterly Review* 40(1949–50) 79–102; C. C. Torrey, "The Question of the Original Language of Qohelet," *Jewish Quarterly Review* 39(1948–49) 151–60; H. L. Ginsberg, *Studies in Koheleth* (New York: Jewish Theological Seminary of America, 1950) 1–40.

[20] Robert Gordis, "The Original Language of Qohelet," *Jewish Quarterly Review* 37(1946–47) 67–84; Gordis, "The Translation Theory of Qohelet Re-examined," *Jewish Quarterly Review* 40(1949–50) 103–16; Gordis, "Koheleth—Hebrew or Aramaic," *Journal of Biblical Literature* 71(1952) 93–109; Gordis, *Koheleth*, 60–62. See also the later edition of *Koheleth: The Man and His World* (New York: Schocken, 1968), Supplementary Note A: The Theory of an Aramaic Origin of Koheleth, pp. 413 ff., and Whitley, *Koheleth: His Language and Thought*, 106–110.

[21] Gordis, *Koheleth*, 60–61. Schoors, *The Preacher Sought to Find Pleasing Words*, 8, concurs. He says of the Aramaic translation theory in general, "why should somebody want to translate an Aramaic text into Hebrew when he neither properly understands the Aramaic original nor sufficiently masters the Hebrew language to offer a flawless translation?" He adds that the theory requires too many mistranslations, and fundamental ones, to persuade.

status to crop up at Qumran.[22] The numerous Aramaic features simply set Qoheleth among the other late Biblical writings, including Daniel, Esther, Ezra, Nehemiah, and Song of Songs.[23]

Whybray points out that although Qoheleth has more Aramaic words than any book except Esther, Aramaic was becoming the lingua franca of Palestine and so this should not be cause for much surprise.[24] Fox on the other hand is attracted to the theory of Qoheleth's translation from Aramaic, more to the formulation of Ginsberg than Zimmermann, because he feels that it is plausible and sometimes facilitates interpretation. However, although he does not believe that Gordis and other scholars have fully disproven the theory, he says they have often been partially effective and thus shown that the case for an Aramaic original has not been made.[25] Sheldon Blank briefly sums up the core of each side of the argument. On the one hand, some of the odd expressions in the Hebrew are nicely explained as a misreading of an Aramaic original. An example is 12:13, which in Hebrew is "כִּי זֶה כָּל הָאָדָם," "for this is the whole man," and makes sense as a misunderstanding of an Aramaic "דִּי יְדִן כָּל אֱנָשׁ," "who will judge every man." Perhaps "יְדִן" was read as "דֵּן," which in Hebrew would be "זֶה." On the other hand, he notes, there are cases of paranomasia in the Hebrew which do not work well in Aramaic. An example of this is 7:1, where "טוֹב שֵׁם" balances "שֶׁמֶן טוֹב." In the end, he considers Gordis's view to be the "less hazardous."[26]

In sum, the accumulated evidence implies that the book of Qoheleth was originally written in Hebrew, probably in the fifth to third centuries BCE. A further piece in the argument that Qoheleth originated in this period is the very fact that the book is so fixed on the subject of death, something which is new among the interests of Jewish writers, but does emerge as a concern in a number of later apocryphal and pseudepigraphal works. The purpose of this chapter and the next is to fill this argument out. The bulk of the present chapter will attempt to

---

[22] Crenshaw, *Ecclesiastes*, 49; Cf. also Gordis, *Koheleth*, 62.

[23] Gordis, *Koheleth*, 49.

[24] R. N. Whybray, *Ecclesiastes* (Grand Rapids: Eerdmans, 1989) 15.

[25] Fox, *Qohelet and His Contradictions*, 155.

[26] Sheldon Blank, "Prolegomenon" to Christian D. Ginsburg, *The Song of Songs and Coheleth (Commonly Called the Book of Ecclesiastes)* (reprinted New York: Ktav Publishing House, Inc., 1970) xviii–xix.

demonstrate the text's focus on death, while the next one will look at some of the other writings of the period and how they deal with the issue. The aim of these two chapters is to show that a new interest in death appeared in Jewish thought in the last centuries BCE and turn of the millennium. The linguistic arguments for placing Qoheleth in this era, then, are reinforced by the concerns of the book itself, though the full scope of the latter will not be apparent until the end of chapter 3.

THE TEXT: STRUCTURE

While a general consensus exists with regard to Qoheleth's language and date, the same cannot be said for the question of its structure, or even the question of whether it has a structure. Opinions range from the view that the book is highly organized to the theory that it consists of a random compilation of sayings. Both camps can claim a number of respected scholars.

One approach analyzes the book numerologically, where the numerical value of the phrase הבל הבלים הכל הבל is 216, which is also the number of verses in 1:1–12:8. Since הבל appears three times in 1:2, and its value is 111 (37 x 3), 111 verses comprise the first half of the book, up to 6:9. This half divides into six sections, each ending with the *hebel* refrain. The second half falls into ten sections, the first four of which end "not find out" and the following six in "do not know."[27] Another view argues that Qoheleth used a Greek structure called a palindrome, where a work is balanced to the extent that the same reading emerges forwards or backwards. The book is divided accordingly, though the proponent of this theory admits that the palindrome structure is imperfect.[28] A different analysis explores the "polar structures" of Qoheleth, along with thirty-eight chiastic structures. The polarities comprise a positive point followed by a negative point which together unveil a *hebel*.[29]

---

[27] Addison D. G. Wright, "The Riddle of the Sphinx: The Structure of the Book of Qoheleth," *Catholic Biblical Quarterly* 30(1968) 313–334, "The Riddle of the Sphinx Revisited: Numerical Patterns in the Book of Qoheleth," *Catholic Biblical Quarterly* 42(1980) 35–51, "Additional Numerical Patterns in Qoheleth," *Catholic Biblical Quarterly* 45(1983) 32–43.

[28] Norbert Lohfink, *Kohelet* (Wurzburg: Echter Verlag, 1980) 10.

[29] J. A. Loader, *Polar Structures in the Book of Qoheleth* (Berlin and New

Another scholar does not argue for an internal structure of the work but tries to see how the epilogue (12:9–14) relates to the body of the text. In this view, the book from beginning to end is the coherent product of one author, who speaks through the character or persona of Qoheleth. The frame-narrator in the epilogue is doing a number of things with respect to the rest of his book. By speaking of Qoheleth as someone who really lived, he testifies to the reality of this strange person with his mysterious name and claims of royalty. The narrator also protects Qoheleth by treating him with respect, which is important because the character has very unconventional ideas that would not appeal to many. Though respectful, he is also non-committal to this person. He writes that Qoheleth "sought to find" words of truth, without stating whether he succeeded. He then ends with a completely conventional summary: fear God and keep his commandments. This allows one to choose which person to accept as the key speaker, Qoheleth or the narrator.[30] In the most recent commentary on Qoheleth, the book's structure is divided into four segments which comprise two halves. The segments are 1:2–4:16, 5:1–6:9 (Heb 4:17–6:9), 6:10–8:17, and 9:1–12:8. Segments one and three describe an aspect of the human situation, while two and four explain how one can best deal with the situation.[31]

Others fail to find any structure in the book. One person treats it as

---

York: Walter de Gruyter, 1979) 13–14.

[30] Michael V. Fox, "Frame-Narrative and Composition in the Book of Qohelet," *Hebrew Union College Annual* 48(1977) 83–106. In his *Qohelet and His Contradictions*, 157, he notes that the book in detail does not reveal a complex structure because it is "a journey of consciousness," although it is not without coherence, either: it has a central thesis (all is absurd) which is defended with uniform tone, style, and ideas. He sees the text neither as a treatise nor as a random collection. For a defense of 12:9–14 as a coherent and consistent part of the author's overall message rather than the introduction of "an orthodox safety net" (90), see Andrew Shead, "Reading Ecclesiastes 'Epilogically,'" *Tyndale Bulletin* 48(1997) 67–91. See also C. L. Seow, "'Beyond Them, My Son, Be Warned': The Epilogue of Qoheleth Revisited," in Michael L. Barre, ed., *Wisdom, You Are My Sister* (Washington, D. C.: The Catholic Biblical Association of America, 1997) 125–41, who argues that 12:9–13a was probably original, while vv. 13b–14 may be secondary.

[31] Seow, *Ecclesiastes*, 46. Seow cites F. J. Backhaus, *"Denn Zeit und Zufall trifft sie alle": Studien zur Komposition und zum Gottesbild in Buch Qohelet* (Frankfurt am Main: Anton Hain, 1993), who suggests a very similar structure.

a collection of unrelated sayings.[32] A similar approach divides the text into twelve sections, but does not regard these units as united into a single argument.[33] Yet another reading sees the text as a kind of notebook full of reflections without a logical progression of thought, though the book is not completely random. Its unity consists of "mood and worldview."[34] In an analogous opinion, a different scholar agrees that Qoheleth is unified in style and thought, but says there is no logical plan overall.[35] It has been argued as well that the book is not a systematic treatise, but has a more cyclical tendency. The shifts between poles reflect Qoheleth's own tensions of thought.[36] Finally, one of the main Qoheleth scholars regards the superscription, epilogues, and occasional internal verses as secondary, but feels that the other tensions of the text reflect the understandable ups and downs of human existence over a lifetime.[37] Both the book's form and content, as well as consistently used vocabulary, imply a sustained argument.[38] The conclusion is that in the face of death nothing is permanent.[39]

The arguments which aim to show a detailed and complex structure in the book of Qoheleth are often interesting, but not ultimately persuasive. The tendered plan always has irregularities and is usually so subtle that even multiple readings do not allow such structures to emerge naturally. However, the text does not seem to be a random collection of largely unrelated sayings, either, as a number of the above scholars acknowledge. Although there is no apparent structural framework that one can trace from one chapter to another, the book is broadly unified through a select body of motifs and topics that cohere through repetition of subject and consistent vocabulary. Moreover, the book has an introduction and a conclusion that complement one another and powerfully bracket the main theme, which is progressively developed

---

[32] Galling, "Der Prediger," 76–77.

[33] Hertzberg, *Der Prediger*, 13–19.

[34] Gordis, *Koheleth*, 110–11.

[35] Lauha, *Kohelet*, 4–7.

[36] Whybray, *Ecclesiastes*, 17–19.

[37] Crenshaw, *Ecclesiastes*, 48–49.

[38] Crenshaw, *Ecclesiastes*, 35–36.

[39] The one area in which Crenshaw finds an unchanging attitude in the text is in its allusions to death; see James L. Crenshaw, "Qoheleth in Current Research," in Reuben Ahroni, ed., *Hebrew Annual Review, vol. 7: Biblical and Other Studies in Honor of Robert Gordis* (Ohio: Ohio State University, 1983) 51.

through the course of the work. In other words, Qoheleth does appear to have an argument that he wants to make, and he never wanders very far from his prevailing theme, which is the transitory nature of everything in human experience and of life itself; in short, death. The following pages study the text in detail to see how exactly the author draws out his theme. First is a short investigation of hebel, one of the most important keywords for Qoheleth and basic to his understanding of the world. An analysis of the text's introduction and conclusion and how they function together follows. Finally the chapter turns to the main body of the text and how the notion of death is developed in it.

THE SHADOW OF DEATH IN QOHELETH

Hebel

After the superscription in 1:1, the book opens with its main motif, הבל הבלים אמר קהלת הבל הבלים הכל הבל. Probably the best known translation into English of this line is "vanity of vanities, says Qoheleth, vanity of vanities, all is vanity."[40] Other translations are "breath of breaths,"[41] "utter futility,"[42] and "emptiness, emptiness."[43] The word הבל appears in the text 38 times,[44] which comprises over half of its occurrences in the Hebrew Bible.[45] Elsewhere in the Bible one of its common uses is to describe idols and false gods or the transience of life; the word is also the name "Abel" in Genesis 4. Nuances of translation vary from scholar to scholar. One says that *hebel* is breath, or vapor, which is "a) unsubstantial and b) transitory."[46] Elsewhere in the Hebrew Bible the word denotes what is useless and "fleeting, ephemeral, or

---

[40] Cf. Gordis, *Koheleth*, 195; Whybray, *Ecclesiastes*, 36. "Vanity" is the translation in the KJV, NAB, and NRSV among others.

[41] Leo Perdue, *Wisdom and Creation*, 204; Scott, *Proverbs-Ecclesiastes* (New York: Doubleday, 1965) 209.

[42] Crenshaw, *Ecclesiastes*, 57.

[43] NEB.

[44] Perdue, *Wisdom and Creation*, 206. Graham Ogden, *Qoheleth* (Sheffield: Journal for the Study of the Old Testament Press, 1987) 28, notes that 9:2 actually reads הכל, but the Septuagint emends to הבל. So do many commentators, though Ogden is not one of them.

[45] The Septuagint translates הבל "ματαιότης," "emptiness, futility, purposelessness, transitoriness."

[46] Gordis, *Koheleth*, 195.

insubstantial."[47] Another scholar states that the word denotes what is "empty of substance, and also transient."[48] A recent commentary says that the word in Qoheleth has two meanings, "temporal ("ephemerality") and existential ("futility" or "absurdity")."[49] A slightly different tack argues that the word signifies not "vanity" but the fact that life is enigmatic, "that there are many unanswered and unanswerable questions."[50] Yet another makes use of existentialism's terminology by rendering *hebel* as "absurdity." The absurd is "a disparity between two phenomena that are supposed to be joined by a link of harmony or causality but are actually disjunct...." It exists not in a thing, act, or event in its own right, but "in the tension between a certain reality and a framework of expectations."[51] Typically the main connotation of *hebel* in Qoheleth is expressed in terms of evanescence and ephemerality.[52]

---

[47] Whybray, *Ecclesiastes*, 36.

[48] Scott, *Proverbs-Ecclesiastes* (New York: Doubleday, 1965) 209.

[49] Crenshaw, *Ecclesiastes*, 57.

[50] Ogden, *Ecclesiastes*, 17–22.

[51] Fox, *Qohelet*, 31. See Jean-Jacques Lavoie, *La penseé du Qohélet: Étude exégétique et intertextuelle* (Quebec: Fides, 1992) 207–25, who also opts for the translation "absurde."

[52] Perdue, *Wisdom and Creation*, 206–07. In relation to his argument he makes an interesting suggestion with regard to the repeated statement הכל הבל ורעות רוח (see 1:14; 2:11, 17, 26; 4:4, 16; 6:9). Different interpretations exist for the phrase, the most common being "all is vanity and pursuit of/chasing after the wind." However, Perdue suggests "all is ephemeral and a desire for (life's) vital spirit." Here רוח would be the divine force that animates the body and thus sustains life. He cites Job 27:3; Is 42:5; Zech 12:1; Ps 104:29–30 for רוח in this sense. See also Gen 6:17; Gen 7:15; Ezek 37:5. רעות may come either from the Hebrew root "to pasture" (רעה) or the Aramaic root "to take pleasure in/desire" (רעא). BDB, 946, cites the latter root as the source for the word in Qoheleth, as well as רעיון. The translation "pasturing the wind" is possible and would connote the futile act of trying to shepherd/control the wind, but Whitley, *Koheleth: His Language and Thought*, 13, says that Hosea 12:2 suggests the root "to desire" is also possible. He adds that the Aramaic in Ezra 5:17 and 7:18 has the same root (רעות as the construct of רעו) where it means "pleasure," and the verbal form of the root appears again in Prov 15:14 and Ps 37:3. If "a desire for the life-breath" is the meaning, then the entire phrase, all is הבל and רעות רוח, would be an expression of the basic paradox of human existence, that life is fleeting yet characterized by the desire to hold on to life, by craving for the רוח. A mortal being hopelessly yearns for immortality. See Perdue, *Wisdom and Creation*, 207. An additional argument that comes to mind is that Qoheleth does use רוח as "life-breath" in his text; see 3:19, 11:5, and 12:7. An especially interesting verse is

The main theme that emerges from most of the commentators is that *hebel* signifies what is insubstantial and ephemeral, and while it certainly carries different nuances throughout the text of Qoheleth, these do seem to come closest to its core meaning. "Insubstantial" and "ephemeral" do not of course mean exactly the same thing; something can be one without being the other. But for Qoheleth the ideas are closely linked. Human life and experience are both insubstantial, or frail, and fleeting. On occasion, though, the sense of the word *hebel* is clearly more that act and result are mismatched. This is one advantage of Fox's suggested translation "absurdity," because it points at the underlying quality of all of the nuances, that in some way a thing is other than what Qoheleth would want and expect it to be in a reasonable universe.[53] But the frailty and transience of life is certainly an absurdity in Qoheleth's eyes, and the presence of death throughout the book (to be discussed

---

8:8 where he says that no one has power over the רוח "to restrain/withhold" (לכלוא) the רוח, or power over the day of death. One wonders if the two ideas, the inability to withhold the רוח and death, might be associated here in his mind as analogous in some way. Ginsburg, *The Song of Songs and Cohelet*, 396–97, translates the verse: "No man is ruler over his spirit to retain the spirit." Gordis, *Koheleth*, 280, translates רוח "the spirit of life." Fox, *Qohelet and His Contradictions*, 248, argues for "life-spirit." Crenshaw, *Ecclesiastes*, 152 believes "life-breath" to be the best. Elsewhere, of course, the רוח is just the wind, as in chapter one. Perdue's translation of the phrase הכל הבל ורעות רוח remains tentative, then, but suggestive nonetheless.

[53] It should be pointed out that contrary to this chapter's argument, Fox, *Qohelet and His Contradictions*, 47, says that the book as a whole is not mainly bewailing life's brevity. "Qoheleth is not at root saying that everything is insubstantial, or transitory, or useless, or trivial. He does indeed observe these qualities in many beings and actions, but he mentions them mainly to reinforce and exemplify his main complaint, the irrationality of life as a whole." As Fox himself points out, though, even if a person does experience what is appropriate to his actions in life, "death sets the seal on life's absurdity" (45). Roland Murphy, "On Translating Ecclesiastes," *Catholic Biblical Quarterly* 53(1991) 573, expresses reservations about Fox's translation "absurdity." He feels that the categories of rational/irrational are not Qoheleth's; better is know/not know, which means that "incomprehensible" rather than "irrational" is the most precise translation. This distinction is fair enough, though one could argue that what is incomprehensible for Qoheleth is also that which does not match his expectations. In both categories the problem is one of outcome not fitting action, or effect fitting cause. God is just, or so people have been led to expect, yet the world is not just. We cannot understand how this can be, as it is unintelligible according to human standards of reason. The idea seems amenable to expression as both "incomprehensible" and "irrational."

below) suggests that this transience is the overriding theme, the chief absurdity, which rivets the author's attention.[54] Death is that event which is most unlike what Qoheleth would desire and expect it to be. The repeated message of *hebel* in the sense of the disjunction created in human expectation by ephemerality, the ephemerality of everything in human experience and human life itself, is one of the ways that Qoheleth keeps the reader fixed on his theme. It is this ultimate *hebel* which embraces all the other manifestations of *hebel* and expresses life's overarching irrationality. The organization of the book suggests that death as the core of Qoheleth's message is borne out in other ways.

The Opening and Conclusion of Qoheleth

The reader cannot help but feel that the opening (1:2–11) and close (12:1–8)[55] of the book are not accidental. This observation returns to the discussion of Qoheleth's structure. While the book is not a tightly knit argument that moves with rigorous steps from one verse to the next, it does have a loose organization in that it has a beginning which serves as a good introduction to the body of the book, and an end that neatly brings it all to a close and serves as a fulfillment of the beginning. Most obviously, the phrase in 1:2 (הבל הבלים אמר קהלת הבל הבלים הכל הבל) is almost repeated in 12:8 (הבל הבלים אמר הקוהלת הכל הבל), so that the first and last lines form a literary frame for the material in between. The book opens with the statement of universal ephemerality, and ends with the description of death in the final chapter.

In the opening, after the thematic note about הבל in 1:2, Qoheleth asks what יתרון there is in human toil. The word יתרון, which appears only in Qoheleth (1:3; 2:11,13; 3:9; 5:8,15; 7:12; 10:10–11) and shows up for the first time here in verse 3, is usually translated by "what

---

[54] C. D. Ginsburg, *The Song of Songs and Coheleth*, 259, interprets the opening phrase in 1:2 as the expression of the impact on the author of "the brevity of man's life" and "the conviction that no human effort can protract man's existence here."

[55] Taking 1:1 as a superscription, 12:9–14 as a later addition. Regarding 12:9–14, Michael Fishbane, *Biblical Interpretation in Ancient Israel* (New York: Oxford University Press, 1985) 30–31, points out that the addendum follows a well-known colophonic pattern throughout the ancient Near East, as "texts were not simply summed up, but were often annotated with references to the scribal activities performed on it." Vv. 9–12 give the reader a version of standard scribal tasks along with praise of the scribes.

profit/advantage is there to a man in all his labor...." But the basic meaning of the root is "to remain," or "to be left over".[56] This is not to quibble with the standard translation, but it is illuminating to keep in mind that the word literally means "what is left over" or "what endures," and Qoheleth is asking, "what endures from the labor at which one toils?"[57] Qoheleth asks this question in 1:3, 3:9, and 5:15. In 2:11 he considers all his toil and answers that "there is no יתרון under the sun,"[58] that is, there is nothing that is enduring or permanent in human efforts.[59]

---

[56] Perdue, *Wisdom and Creation*, 207, cites as an example of the root's basic meaning I Sam 25:34, where the verb means to survive or remain after a battle. The Septuagint has "περισσεία" "surplus, abundance." See also Anson F. Rainey, "A Study of Ecclesiastes," *Concordia Theological Monthly* 35(1964) 150–51.

[57] Perdue, *Wisdom and Creation*, 207–08. This especially makes sense considering that Qoheleth "is obsessed with discovering something that endures, that would enable one to live beyond the grave, at least in human memory" (208).

[58] Says James G. Williams, "Proverbs and Ecclesiastes," in Robert Alter and Frank Kermode, eds., *The Literary Guide to the Bible* (Cambridge: Harvard University Press, 1987) 280, Qoheleth is frank about the fact that because of death, "there is no profit of any sort, material, intellectual, or spiritual." Some of the later interpretations of 1:3 have interesting ways of avoiding this conclusion. The translation of the Targum, which tends toward midrash, reads "What profit does a man have after he dies from all his labor which he labors under the sun in this world unless he occupies himself with Torah in order to receive a complete reward in the world to come before the Master of the world" (cf. Knobel, *The Targum of Qohelet*, 20, for the translation). The Targum rereads the verse to be an affirmation of יתרון in light of Torah study, and adds the promise of nothing less than an eternal reward. It further translates 2:11 that there is no יתרון under the sun "in this world, except that I have a complete reward for my good deeds in the world to come." The Midrash remarks at 1:3 that the sages sought to suppress the book because it contains "words which savour of heresy." It continues, "WHAT PROFIT HATH MAN OF ALL HIS LABOUR? Is it possible that the words may also be applied to man's labour in the Torah! On reconsidering the matter they declared: He did not say 'Of all labour' but OF ALL *HIS* LABOUR—In HIS LABOUR one should not labour, but one should toil in the labour of the Torah!" Another interpretation is "A man's labour is UNDER THE SUN, but his treasury of reward is above the sun." Cf. Cohen, *Midrash Rabbah: Ecclesiastes*, 6–7. The Midrash, by careful reading of the language, counters the literal implications of the verse.

[59] Ogden, *Qoheleth*, 14, believes that the purpose of the book in fact is to find an answer to the question of whether there is any יתרון in the world. Clearly it cannot be found in the present life, which means that the semantic field of the word "must be defined broadly enough to include the possibility of 'advantage' beyond death for the faithful." The deuteronomic view of God's reward and punishment of

He follows this with the observation that human generations constantly come and go, while the earth remains as it was. Interestingly, the only things which Qoheleth ever says are eternal are the earth, here in 1:4 (וְהָאָרֶץ לְעוֹלָם עֹמָדֶת: but the earth stands forever),[60] and the grave, in 12:5 (כִּי־הֹלֵךְ הָאָדָם אֶל־בֵּית עוֹלָמוֹ: and man is going to his eternal home);[61] creation in the beginning and death in the end are the only eternal constants.[62] The poem continues that the sun, wind, and rivers all persevere on their unceasing and unchanging circuits.[63]

---

the righteous and wicked was often not confirmed by reality. Qoheleth cannot prove that distinctions between these categories were made after death, "yet it is inherent in his belief in divine justice that something of that order must be considered" (25). Ogden reads יתרון then, as Qoheleth's word for "wisdom's reward both here and after death" (29). Death is Qoheleth's most pressing problem, because it is impartial, and because יתרון cannot be had before or at death; this "leads the reader to question along with him" whether it will be had after death (44–45). While Ogden's argument that Qoheleth does not see any יתרון in life is correct, his belief that the author is forced to contemplate options after death is not supported by the text. Certainly the *reader* might wonder this, and other subsequent Jewish authors did come to this conclusion, but not Qoheleth.

[60] Qoheleth later echoes this statement in 3:14 where he says that he knows that everything which God has made will last לְעוֹלָם.

[61] Gordis, *Koheleth*, 337, states that the "eternal home" is the grave, and cites the following parallels: Tobit 3:6, the Talmud (B. Sanh. 19a), and the Quran (41:28), also the phrase in Latin, Palmyrene, and Punic. Crenshaw, *Ecclesiastes*, 188, notes that although the phrase בֵּית עוֹלָמוֹ appears only here in the Bible, it was common in the ancient world. He cites Gordis's examples as well as the Targum on Isaiah 14:18.

[62] One notices with interest where the train of thought on 1:4 leads in the Midrash. In the course of discussion is the following: "the distinction which I [God] made between the celestial creatures and the terrestrial, viz. that the former endure while the latter die, holds good only in this world, but in the Messianic future there will be no death at all; as it is stated, *He will swallow up death for ever* (Isa. xxv,8)." Cf. Cohen, *Midrash Rabbah: Ecclesiastes*, 12. The passing of the generations in contrast to the earth elicits an assurance in the Midrash that death is not a permanent aspect of human existence.

[63] Ginsburg, *The Song of Songs and Coheleth*, 260–61, comments on the fact that the ongoing endurance of the earth and of nature contrasts with the rapid passing of human generations; "the ruthless hand of death violently shakes him [man] off the tree of life... while the earth, upon which he displays his ingenuity, abides forever." He adds later in the paragraph that this "is the burden of the argument, that man, who was made a little lower than the angels, who is capable of developing such intellectual life, should especially be so ephemeral, while inferior nature abides permanently." Ibn Ezra draws a similar conclusion from the opening

Everything is "weary" or "wearisome" (יְגֵעִים) beyond words. The eye is not satisfied with seeing[64] nor the ear filled with hearing. Everything that will be done has already been done, but there is no memory of any of it now, nor will there be in the future.[65]

The passage in a calm but haunting fashion thereby introduces the discussion to come. All is *hebel*, human toil yields nothing, life itself does not endure in contrast to the earth, God's creation rolls through its cycles oblivious to the comings and goings of the creatures within it,[66] and

---

verses of chapter 1. In his interpretation, the question in v. 3, "what advantage has man," is explicated in the following lines. The wind blows continually, in contrast to a man who must go to his grave; his works cease and he is no longer remembered. Similarly, the rivers keep flowing into the sea, and the system maintains its equilibrium, "but man leaves his course and habit, he vanishes away from the world." Cf. Ginsburg, *The Song of Songs and Coheleth*, 44, for the translation.

[64] This phrase has an interesting parallel in Proverbs 27:20: "Sheol and Abaddon are never satisfied; and human eyes are never satisfied." Here as in Qoheleth, the sense appears to be that there are some things which never appear to hit their limit, whether the cycles of nature, human senses, or Sheol (death).

[65] Rashbam makes the argument that the animals are better off than people with respect to memory, because each person is different from all others, and when that individual dies there is no one like him to preserve his likeness. Animals, however, all look alike within their species, so when one dies another that looks just the same takes its place. See Ginsburg, *The Song of Songs and Coheleth*, 45.

[66] Fox does not believe that 1:4 is about human transience in contrast to the permanence of the earth. He says that הָאָרֶץ means not the physical earth, but humanity. The word עֹמֵד signifies "remains as is." His translation, then, is "A generation goes and a generation comes, but the world remains forever the same." The succeeding verses are about the unchanging nature of things, not the disappearance of them. In addition, he notes that if the verse were about human mortality, one would expect the order to be "a generation *comes* and a generation *goes*." The point is that humanity as a whole remains unchanged by the movement of the generations. See Michael V. Fox, "Qohelet 1.4," *Journal for the Study of the Old Testament* 40(1988) 109; Graham S. Ogden, "The Interpretation of דּוֹר in Ecclesiastes 1.4," *Journal for the Study of the Old Testament* 34(1986) 91–92 [to which Fox is responding in the afore-cited Fox article]; and Fox, *Qohelet and His Contradictions*, 168–171. The suggested translations of הָאָרֶץ and of עֹמֵד are certainly possible, but not demanded by the context. While it is true that the verses following 1:4 are about the unchanging nature of things, this does not contradict the idea that verse 4 is a statement that humans are transient, in contrast to the permanently enduring earth; the nature of this permanent earth is then simply described in the following verses in terms of those aspects of it which also never change or disappear (day and night, the wind, the rivers). The contrast with the

human memory is too short and fleeting even to acquire any sense of time's passage and what has happened over the course of it.[67] From verse 12 on through the rest of the chapter Qoheleth ṣteps forward and describes his efforts to understand "everything that is done under heaven." The experiment he runs and his observations on its results follow. In the next chapter he specifically describes the test that he had made of pleasure, and being a king ("son of David," 1:1), he was in a position to make the test a fair one. None of the works, gardens, possessions, money, or pleasures undermine his belief that everything is vanity and nothing can be gained under the sun (2:11). The opening verses are not a random beginning, then. They present the essence of creation, of humanity, and the problem which motivates Qoheleth's inquiry.

The conclusion of the book corresponds to the introduction in that it expands in a personal way the significance of the *hebel* raised in 1:2

---

transience of humanity is not therefore contradicted; rather, it is expanded. Moreover, הארץ in its physical sense seems a likelier translation since what follows is in fact a description of the planet's component cycles. The fact that the generations go before they come is a chicken-and-egg problem. Previous generations have to make room for the succeeding ones. Jeffrey H. Tigay, "What is Man that You Have Been Mindful of Him? (On Psalm 8:4–5)," in John H. Marks and Robert M. Good, eds., *Love & Death in the Ancient Near East: Essays in Honor of Marvin H. Pope* (Guilford, CT: Four Quarters Publishing Company, 1987) 170, notes that the heavens, sun, moon, and so on are typically used in ancient literatures as symbols of permanence. In Psalm 8:4–5, the psalmist sets up a contrast between the (permanent) heavenly bodies and (ephemeral) humanity. Something similar seems to be happening here in Qoheleth, this time using the earth as the point of contrast. Jean-Jacques Lavoie, *La penseé du Qohélet*, 194–95, who studies Qoheleth by examining its parallels and differences with Gen 1–11, notes that unlike Genesis, where a stable universe is a sign of God's grace, the stable universe in Qoheleth simply sets human finitude in sharper relief. "Dans *Gn* 1 la théologie de la création est d'une certaine façon anthropocentrique: Dieu crée l'univers très bon pour que l'être humain puisse y vivre comme le maître et le roi. Dans le Qohélet la théologie de la création est plutôt géocentrique car seule la terre subsiste: les humains sont éphémères, fragiles, et impuissants."

[67] This failure of memory is also filled out in the repeated insistence that people are incapable of knowing what will come after them, and there is no one who can tell them. These statements really make every individual an isolated being: one is cut off from the past and from the future by the inability of human knowledge to extend in either direction. Knowledge is curtailed like everything else. Cf. 2:16, 2:19, 3:22, 6:12, 7:14, 8:7, 8:17, 9:5, 9:12, 10:14, 11:2, 11:6.

and following. It consists of a beautiful but grim reflection on human death.

> Now remember your creator[68] in the days of your youth, before the troublesome days come, and the years draw near, about which you will say, "I take no pleasure in them"; before the sun and the light and the moon and the stars grow dark, and the clouds return after the rain, on the day when the keepers of the house tremble, and the mighty men are bowed down, and the grinding-women cease because they are few, and the women who look through the windows become dark, and the doors on the street are shut; when the sound of the grinding is low, and one rises at the call of the bird, and all the daughters of song are prostrated; also one is afraid[69] of a height, and terrors are on the road, and the almond-tree blossoms,[70] and the grasshopper drags itself along,[71] and the caperberry[72] fails,[73] because man is going to his eternal home, and the mourners go about on the street; before the silver chain is snapped,[74] and the

---

[68] The word is בּוֹרְאֶיךָ, which contains an unexpected yod. See below for discussion.

[69] Reading יראו as יִירָא. Cf. Gordis, *Koheleth*, 334, who suggests taking the word as a singular, despite the versions which mostly read יִירְאוּ. Since the rest of the context is singular, he regards the final ו as dittography. Crenshaw, *Ecclesiastes*, 187, translates it as a plural, as does Fox, *Qohelet and His Contradictions*, 305, and Whybray, *Ecclesiastes*, 165.

[70] Reading וְיָנֵץ for וְיָנֵאץ, from the root נצץ, as implied by the versions. Cf. Crenshaw, *Ecclesiastes*, 187.

[71] From סבל, "to bear a load." BDB has it in the Hithpael form *as "drag oneself along*, as a burden." Some manuscripts read the root as סכל, "to be foolish."

[72] The word הָאֲבִיּוֹנָה is entered in BDB under the root אבה, to be willing or to wish. It's a hapax in the Bible but appears in the Mishna, and the versions take it as "caperberry." Since it may be tied to sexual desire, some give it the translation "desire" here in verse five (as in the Targum). Cf. Crenshaw, *Ecclesiastes*, 188. Whybray, *Ecclesiastes*, 166–67, says that the aphrodisiac sense of the word does not appear until the medieval Jewish commentaries, so he interprets it as related to the appetite, since the fruit of the bush is used as a flavoring for food.

[73] תָּפֵר as a Hiphil of the root פרר, "break, frustrate," though everywhere else it is transitive. In BDB the tentative translation for this verse is "fails," though it suggests the word may be a Hophal, as do others.

[74] The ketib is יִרְחַק, "to be distant," which has no clear meaning in this context. The Qere, יֵרָתֵק, is listed in BDB as a Niphal from רתק, "to bind," here meaning "to be snapped." Gordis, *Koheleth*, 336, says this could be a privative Niphal. Both BDB and BHS believe יִנָּתֵק to be the likeliest reading, meaning "to be torn apart, snapped." The Peshitta, Symmachus, and Vulgate translate "cut" or "break," which supports יִנָּתֵק. Cf. Crenshaw, *Ecclesiastes*, 188; Whybray, *Ecclesiastes*, 167. Fox, *Qohelet and His Contradictions*, 307, is leary of Gordis's

golden bowl is crushed,[75] and the pitcher is broken at the spring, and the wheel is broken at the cistern, and the dust returns[76] to the earth as it was, and the ruah returns to God, who gave it. Vanity of vanities, says the Qoheleth, all is vanity.

Scholars have debated what exactly is taking place in the passage, actually, because the imagery is so allusive, and not entirely clear at every step. Gordis separates the common approaches into four groups. In the first, the chapter is treated as a description of the waning of strength in the bodily organs. The second method understands the subject to be the end of a life described as a coming storm which terrifies the residents of a household. The third angle also thinks the chapter is about the end of a life, but portrayed through the metaphor of nightfall. Some regard the imagery as the ruin of an estate which describes the increasing weakness of a person approaching death.[77] Another approach takes the context as a funerary one, though this reading has gaps like the others.[78]

The first verse of chapter 12 opens with the command that one should "remember your בּוֹרְאֶיךָ in the days of your youth." Many translate the word as "creator," but the presence of the yod in the Massoretic text makes the word a plural. Some have suggested that this is "the plural of majesty," or that the yod is the result of mixing III-א and III-ה verbs.[79] The earliest known interpretation of the text, by Rabbi

---

"privative niphal" and believes a nun/resh interchange, for either phonetic or graphic reasons, is possible. Antoon Schoors, "Ketibh-Qere in Ecclesiastes," in J. Quaegebeur, ed., *Studia Paulo Naster Oblata II: Orientalia Antiqua* (Louven: Department Oriëntalistiek, 1982) 220–22, is also doubtful of the "privative niphal" solution and goes with ינתק.

[75] BDB lists תֵּרֹץ in this verse as possibly an intransitive Qal from the root רצץ, "to crush." It also proffers the possible Niphal reading תֵּרוֹץ, as does BHS, Fox, *Qohelet and His Contradictions*, 307 and Whybray, *Ecclesiastes*, 167–68.

[76] וְיָשֹׁב is a jussive, for no obvious reason. The indicative יָשׁוּב would be expected.

[77] Gordis, *Koheleth*, 328–29. Gordis's own opinion is that old age is depicted through shifting points of reference, some literal and others metaphorical.

[78] Fox, *Qohelet and His Contradictions*, 286–289.

[79] Gordis, *Koheleth*, 330; Crenshaw, *Ecclesiastes*, 184–85; Fox, *Qohelet and His Contradictions*, 299–300; Whybray, *Ecclesiastes*, 163. Crenshaw feels that a reference to God the Creator here does not fit the context very well. He points to other alternative readings, "your vigor, well-being," "your well" (symbolic of one's wife), or "your pit" (the grave) (see Gordis, 330). Gordis, Fox, and Whybray think "creator" works fine. As Fox says, "in this context to think on one's creator is to

Akabia ben Mahalalel in Abot 3:1, says "reflect upon three things and thou wilt not come within the power of transgression: know whence thou art come, and whither thou art going, and before Whom thou wilt in the future render account and reckoning. 'Whence thou art come'—from a fetid drop; ' and whither thou art going'—to a place of dust, worms, and maggots; 'and before Whom thou wilt in the future render account and reckoning'—before the Supreme King of kings, the Holy One, Blessed be He." Y. Sota [II, 18a] says that Rabbi Akabia is using Qoheleth 12:1 for this teaching, and reading בוראיך in three ways: your well (womb), your pit (grave), and your creator.[80] It is not impossible that all of these ideas lie in the background, though "creator" itself actually incorporates all three, in a sense. God is the source of everything that exists, and the end of everything as well. Since God stands at both ends of human existence, to remember either one's creation at birth or one's dissolution at death *is* to remember God, who is the reason for both.[81]

The somber opening warning continues with the fact that one should be keeping the creator (the source and the end of all) in mind before the troublesome days come, and the years which are empty of pleasure, before the sun, light, moon, and stars are darkened, and the clouds return after the rain. The meaning of the clouds and rain is uncertain. Sometimes clouds signify misery (Joel 2:2, Zeph 1:15), while clouds covering the sun is an eschatological image in Ezek 32:7. But they may just suggest gloom,[82] or simply be another way of expressing the disappearance of light. In verse three the imagery begins to become even more difficult. Who are the keepers of the house, the mighty men, the grinding women, and the ones looking through the windows? They probably refer to male servants, free men, female servants, and free women.[83] But why does the grinding cease, and why are the women of status "darkened"? The uncertainties here lead some to take the images symbolically, as the body described in terms of a house. The keepers could be the hands, the mighty men the back, the grinders the teeth, and

---

think of death," since 12:7 claims that the ruah goes back to its source, God, at death.

[80] Perdue, *Wisdom and Creation*, 233.

[81] Isaiah 44:6 may be brought to mind: "אני ראשון ואני אחרון."

[82] Fox, *Qohelet and His Contradictions*, 300–01.

[83] Crenshaw, *Ecclesiastes*, 186.

the window-peerers the eyes.[84] Thus, the hands tremble, the back is bent, the teeth are few, and the eyes dim. This would be a description of old age. Or perhaps an estate is declining and its workers are idle.[85] Another interpretation is that the people in the verse are in mourning and going through the manifestations of grief, writhing and getting blurred vision because of the tears.[86]

Verse four continues with further allusions: shut doors, grinding noises at a minimum, one rising at a bird's sound, the daughters of song brought low. Some stay with the interpretation of the bodily limbs becoming decrepit, or imagine an approaching storm which drives everyone inside, or the declining estate falling into disuse.[87] Perhaps the elderly are sleeping fitfully and waking at the mere sound of a bird? The daughters of song could be an allusion to the weakness of the voice, though they might also refer to songbirds.[88] Fox notes that the allegorical interpretations get quite difficult from this point, and reads the verse as a funeral scene, when the doors are closed and the mill stops because people are joining the funeral procession. The bird image is not obvious, though it might refer to a bird of ill-omen, while the daughters of song he takes as mourning women, possibly professionals, who bow low in the posture of lament.[89]

The going does not get any easier for the interpreter in the first half of verse five. Fear of heights, terrors on the road, a blossoming almond tree, a dragging grasshopper, and the caperberry have elicited a number of theories. Most seem to agree that the first two items describe the timidity an old person feels when out and about. As for the rest, at least two interpretations are possible. The images describe the effects of spring which contrast with human deterioration, when the almonds blossom, the locusts stuff themselves to immobility, and caperberries burst open; or, the body ages with hair turning white like almond blossoms, joints becoming so stiff that they make it hard to move, and fading sexual

---

84 Crenshaw, *Ecclesiastes*, 186.

85 Gordis, *Koheleth*, 332–33. Whybray, *Ecclesiastes*, 164, says that these are undoubtedly metaphors for a house or palace and those who live in it, though whether it is simply falling into decay or has been hit by a storm is not a clear.

86 Fox, *Qohelet and His Contradictions*, 301–03.

87 Gordis, *Koheleth*, 333. Whybray, *Ecclesiastes*, 165, follows the estate analysis until the verse reaches the part about the sound of the grinding being low.

88 Crenshaw, *Ecclesiastes*, 187. For the songbirds he cites Job 30:29.

89 Fox, *Qohelet and His Contradictions*, 303–04.

desire.[90] In line with the funereal reading, it is the songstresses who are afraid of the height, and this along with the terrors on the way express the fearful emotions of the mourners in the funeral cortege.[91] The rest of this part of the verse would be to contrast how nature, unlike humanity, is reborn every spring.[92] The second half of verse five is more straightforward. Everything described above comes about because all must go to their eternal home, that is, their grave, when the mourners will go out into the streets. The fact that the Hebrew uses a participle to express the idea of dying is interesting: humanity "is going" to the grave, at all moments of a human life the direction is constantly towards death. The action is continuous.

In verse six, the silver cord, golden bowl, pitcher, and wheel are all broken or snapped so that they no longer function. These are metaphors for death. The first two images may be trying to evoke a lamp whose cord breaks and is shattered in the ensuing fall, while the second set might describe the breaking of the wheel which raises the pitcher out of the well and the subsequent loss of the pitcher.[93] In any case it seems clear that the ideas express sudden destruction and loss of utility. Any doubt about the implication of this is removed by verse seven which continues the thought, that [when someone dies] the dust returns to the earth and the רוח to God.[94] Just as the cord, pitcher et al are broken up, the individual

---

[90] Crenshaw, *Ecclesiastes*, 187; Gordis, *Koheleth*, 334–37; Whybray, *Ecclesiastes*, 165–67.

[91] Fox, *Qohelet and His Contradictions*, 305. He admits that the cause and context of the fear are vague.

[92] Fox, *Qohelet and His Contradictions*, 305–06. He cites a similar idea in Job 14:7–10, "A tree has hope: if it is cut off, it may be renewed...But man dies and is helpless. A human expires and disappears."

[93] Cf. Whybray, *Ecclesiastes*, 167–68. Gordis, *Koheleth*, 337–38, thinks the change in metaphor would be too harsh, and suggests that all four images are part of the same idea: a well used by means of cord manipulated by a wheel, in which one end of the cord has the pitcher, and the other a ball as a counterweight. Once the cord is broken, all the other elements crash to the bottom of the well. Crenshaw, *Ecclesiastes*, 188, notes that in Prov 13:9 an extinguished lamp is a metaphor for death. Fox, *Qohelet and His Contradictions*, 306–8, adds that a broken vessel represents loss of life in Jer 18:6, Is 30:14, and Ps 2:9.

[94] Cf. Gordis, *Koheleth*, 339; Crenshaw, *Ecclesiastes*, 188–89; Whybray, *Ecclesiastes*, 168, who all say that this is not a suggestion that there is any kind of afterlife, or a contradiction with 3:21. The life-breath is a component that returns to its source, not an aspect of personality. Gen 2:7 and 3:19 have a similar conception of the human make-up. Fox, *Qohelet and His Contradictions*, 308, remarks that the

breaks down into the component parts of existence. Verse eight is the grand conclusion, הבל הבלים הכל הבל.[95]

It has been pointed out that along with the more basic readings of 12:1–8, which try to interpret what the figures literally signify, some of the imagery also evokes a cosmic disaster. The totality of the darkness and breadth of the silence, from the servants to the powerful men to the heavenly bodies, goes beyond the normal, everyday events of a person's death.[96] The portrait suggests something more on the order of the prophetic descriptions of the end of the age, characterized by universal destruction.[97] A commonplace, if unhappy, human experience is thus considerably heightened. For the person who is dying, it really is the end of the world. Civilization, nature itself, fails along with the dying individual.

Throughout his book Qoheleth always comes around to death,[98] which makes it fitting that he should end his argument with this passage, full of images of decrepitude, enervation, dissolution, and destruction.[99]

---

verse is a contradiction with Qoh 3:21, but neither verse affirms an afterlife, and the contradiction is not significant for the book's meaning. Probably Qoheleth in 3:21 is countering a newly spreading idea of the soul's ascent, which he discounts. 12:7 is a traditional way of speaking of the loss of the life-breath at death. The Targum of 12:7, however, takes the meaning to be that the individual faces judgment. "Then will your flesh which was created from dust return to the earth as it was previously and the spirit of your soul will return to stand in judgment before the Lord who gave it to you." Cf. Knobel, *The Targum of Qohelet*, 54.

[95] Fox, *Qohelet and His Contradictions*, 309, calls this "the most prominent and powerful inclusio in the Bible."

[96] The disappearance of the light is found in cosmological reversals, prophetic eschatology, and apocalypticism (Job 9:7; Jer 4:23–26; Amos 5:8; Hab 3:11), cf. Perdue, *Wisdom and Creation*, 235.

[97] Fox, *Qohelet and His Contradictions*, 290–91, quotes Jer 25:10–11a; Ezek 32:7–8; Joel 2:2a, 6, 10b; Is 13:9b–10. "Both Qoheleth and the prophets draw upon images of mourning and universal cataclysm. For the prophets, these images depict the disaster to a nation or the world at large. For Qoheleth they represent the demise of the individual" (293).

[98] "Qoheleth reveals an obsession with death unparalleled in biblical literature" (Fox, *Qohelet and His Contradictions*, 294). Note also Mathias Delcor, "Jewish Literature in Hebrew and Aramaic in the Greek era," in W. D. Davies and Louis Finkelstein, eds., *The Cambridge History of Judaism*, Vol. I (Cambridge: Cambridge University Press, 1984) 361, who similarly writes that the thought of death "obsesses" Qoheleth.

[99] Lavoie, *La penseé du Qohélet*, 99, observes that in chapter 12 God functions almost as a "dé-Créateur." In contrast to Genesis 1–11, which can be

In the beginning of the book, the generations are coming and passing out of existence again, just as they are when Qoheleth concludes. The eternal earth is checked by humanity's eternal grave. All things are wearisome at the first, and sink into complete stasis at the last. Everything at the start is hebel, and so it is at the end. The final movement of the argument is the description of human mortality, the last image the reader is given is the return of the body to dust and the breath to God. The beginning and conclusion of the book neatly fit together, and bring the reader to the understanding that death is the ubiquitous, inescapable, and even apocalyptic aspect of the universe that counters all others. The death in chapter twelve is the full expression of the *hebel* that begins chapter one.

The Body of the Text

It seems plain that the author framed his book with an awareness of shaping his argument to carry as much impact as possible. Can a deliberate structure can be found in the body of the text as well? If the question means to ask whether there is a verse by verse structure on the order of the proposals of Wright, et al, the answer is no. The book does not appear to be a rigidly systematic argument. Nevertheless, this does not mean that it is a scattered collection of thoughts or that it cannot carry a sustained proposition. Within the opening and closing chapters, Qoheleth has a loose but constant set of interrelated points from which he never strays very far, all of which gird the main theme. These reflections can be divided for convenience of discussion into three categories. The first consists of the observations he makes about death itself, the second of the comments which imply death's presence by observing how short life is, and the third of the places where Qoheleth counsels enjoyment, but almost always in view of death.

Explicit References to Death. In the first category, references to death appear in every chapter between one and twelve with only one exception.[100] The first time is just after 2:13–14a, where Qoheleth says

---

schematized in terms of creator/creation/revelation of divine kindness, Qoheleth's framework is built around an opposite move, creator/de-creation/hiddenness of God (100). Elsewhere he remarks that Qoheleth can be read as a reflection on "l'être-humain-au-sortir-de-l'Eden" (15, 257).

[100] These are 2:14–16; 3:2, 19–21; 4:2–3; 5:15–16; 6:3–6; 7:1–2, 4, 17, 26; 8:8; 9:2–12; and 11:8. Only chapter ten, a collection of aphorisms, is without even

that wisdom excels folly and then throws in a proverbial expression on the wise and fools for emphasis: "The wise has eyes in his head, but the fool walks in darkness."

> But I know that the same happening befalls all of them. Then I said to myself, "according to the outcome of the fool, so also will it happen to me; why then have I been so wise?" And I said to myself that this also is *hebel*, because there is no lasting remembrance of the wise or of the fool, since in the days to come everything will have been forgotten. And how can the wise die just like the fool? (2:14–16)

This makes Qoheleth bitter about his toil in particular and life in general. Everything is pain and vexation (2:23). His statement in 2:14–16 that all die alike,[101] and the melancholy this stimulates in the following

---

one verse on death. Lavoie, *La penseé du Qohélet*, 53, remarks that death is "la véritable *nemesis* du Qohélet" (emphasis his).

[101] The Targum of 2:14 is: "The sage sees at the beginning what will be in the end, and he prays and annuls the evil decrees from the world, but the fool walks in darkness. And I also know that if the sage does not pray and annul the evil decrees from the world when punishment comes upon the world, one fate will befall all of them." Cf. Knobel, *The Targum of Qohelet*, 26. According to the Targum, the wise man who prays can expect to come to a different end than the fool. The Midrash interprets this section as an affirmation that the wise and the fool do not experience the same end by offering a series of examples where the opposite is the case. Abraham thinks himself no better off than Nimrod, since all are forgotten; but, in adversity Israel calls on the memory of Abraham, while the heathens do not call on the memory of Nimrod. Thus, the wise and the fool are not the same. Similar contrasts are offered between Moses and Balaam, David and Nebuchadnezzar, one who prepares for a famine and one who does not, and a diligent student of the Torah versus a lax one. Cf. Cohen, *Midrash Rabbah: Ecclesiastes*, 64–66. Rashi says of the passage "to think in this fashion is also vapor; for the memory of the righteous and of the wicked are not equal after death. One leaves behind him a good remembrance and the other leaves behind an evil remembrance. In the days to come, the evil ones now existing will be forgotten. I know this, because the wicked ones who lived in former times, no matter how strong and how successful they were, have been forgotten. Does the wise man die as does the fool? He most assuredly does not. Even after they are dead, the wise are triumphant and bring blessing to their descendants." See David Eichhorn, *Musings of the Old Professor: The Meaning of Koheles* (New York: Jonathan David, 1963) 32. Ibn Ezra concludes from the passage that *worldly* things and *earthly* knowledge are valueless (33–34). An interesting text that comes from the Cairo Geniza (dubbed WKG for "Die Weisheitsschrift aus der Kairoer Geniza") and dates to the late first millenium CE is a running critique of Qoheleth. It reverses the meaning of

verses, significantly modifies the view of v. 14a that wisdom so greatly excels folly. The reader learns that in one instance, at least, that of death, wisdom makes no difference.

Soon after, chapter 3 opens with a poem on the times in which all things and their opposites have a proper time and season. The very first pair declares that there is a time to be born[102] and a time to die (v. 2).[103] This seems to be a lifeboat of order in a sea of mayhem, if everything has its appointed time within a larger cosmic schedule, yet verses 10 and 11 undo whatever comfort one might have derived from this. Qoheleth says that he has seen the business that God has given people to be busy with,[104] and God "has made everything beautiful in its time; also he has

Qoheleth 2:16 and says that wisdom and fear of the lord will exalt one's memory forever, which is the opposite of the verse's original sense. Cf. A. P. Hayman, "Qohelet, the Rabbis, and the Wisdom Text from the Cairo Geniza," in A. Graeme Auld, ed., *Understanding Poets and Prophets: Essays in Honour of George Wishart Anderson* (Sheffield: Journal for the Study of the Old Testament Press, 1993) 156–58. It should be noted that there is some disagreement about the date of this text. K. Berger, *Die Weisheitsschrift aus der Kairoer Geniza: Erstedition, Kommentar, und Übersetzung* (Tübingen: Franke, 1989), suggests a date in the late first century CE while H. P. Rüger, *Die Weisheitsschrift aus der Kairoer Geniza* (Tübingen: J. C. B. Mohr [Siebeck], 1991) 1–19, considers it to be medieval. See John J. Collins, "Wisdom, Apocalypticism, and Generic Compatibility," in Leo G. Perdue et al, eds., *In Search of Wisdom: Essays in Memory of John G. Gammie* (Louisville, KY: Westminster/John Knox Press, 1993) 180–81.

[102] Literally, a time to give birth and a time to die. Most translators take the Qal infinitive of לֶדֶת as an intransitive so as to better fit the second half of the pair. Cf. Fox, *Qohelet and His Contradictions*, 192.

[103] The Midrash on 3:2 provides an interesting story, in the course of which R. Simeon is walking home at night and meets the angel of death. R. Simeon asks to have his fate revealed, and the angel of death answers "'I have no jurisdiction over you and your colleagues.' 'Why?' he asked. 'Because every day you labour in the Torah and the commandments, and perform righteous acts, and the Holy One, blessed be He, adds to your days.'" Cf. Cohen, *Midrash Rabbah: Ecclesiastes*, 78. According to the Midrash, those who are virtuous escape death's power.

[104] This harks back to 1:13 where he says that "it is an unhappy business" God has given people to busy them, so the reader is cued to recognize the nature of this "business" as nothing cheerful. Norbert Lohfink, "Qoheleth 5:17–19— Revelation by Joy," *Catholic Biblical Quarterly* 52 (1990) 628–29, has a different analysis. His rendition of 1:13 is: "I set my mind to study and to seek out (traditional) wisdom. My question was whether (as certain teachers say) everything which is done (by human beings) under the sun is (or is not) an unfortunate business transaction which God gave men to be busy with." The fact that in 3:10 Qoheleth drops the adjective (רָע) suggests to Lohfink that this section is not all

put הָעֹלָם into their hearts, so that humanity cannot find out the work that God has done from beginning to end" (3:11). The Hebrew word עֹלָם has received a variety of translations, including "a sense of past and future,"[105] "the world,"[106] the "timeless,"[107] "a sense of duration,"[108] "the unknown,"[109] and "an enigma."[110] It seems to be the case that whatever the thing may be which God has put into the human heart,[111] it makes it inherently impossible for people really to comprehend God or God's creation.[112] God gives us our intellect, but no means of satisfying it.[113] "This is a fantastic statement of divine sabotage."[114] The fact that there is a time to die in God's plan is cold comfort if it is not within the human

---

that negative. However, his translation of 1:13 so changes the meaning of the verse that it borders on midrash. Qoheleth is in no doubt about the fact that "this is an unhappy business" that God has given people (עַל is taken by Lohfink to mean "whether"). This being the case, the fact that Qoheleth refers to עִנְיָן in 3:10 without the accompanying רָע only suggests that he considers he has already made his estimation of עִנְיָן clear.

[105] New Revised Standard Version.

[106] King James Version. Cf. also Gordis, *Koheleth*, 221–22 who has "love of the world."

[107] New American Bible.

[108] Roland E. Murphy, *Ecclesiastes* (Dallas: Word Books, 1992) lxvi.

[109] Crenshaw, *Ecclesiastes*, 91.

[110] Scott, *Proverbs-Ecclesiastes*, 220.

[111] Murphy, "On Translating Ecclesiastes," 573, divides the translations into four categories: eternity, duration, the world, and ignorance. "One can be sure only that Qoheleth thinks that there is something in the human heart (divinely implanted!) which prevents humans from comprehending the divine work." Murphy himself prefers "temporal duration." Fox, *Qohelet and His Contradictions*, 194, emends עֹלָם to עָמָל.

[112] The Midrash offers a number of readings, one of which is: "R. Nathan said: A dread of the Angel of Death He set in their heart." Cf. Cohen, *Midrash Rabbah: Ecclesiastes*, 91. Others are "a love of the world He set in their heart" (91), "a love of the world and a love of children He set in their heart" (92), and "the Ineffable Name was hidden from them" (reading ha'olam as hu'alam, "concealed") (92).

[113] Morris Jastrow, *A Gentle Cynic* (Philadelphia: J.B. Lippincott Company, 1919) 135, points out that we have no "power to carry our search to any satisfactory conclusion"; Perdue, *Wisdom and Creation*, 239, says that God gives humankind the "olam" but not the power to understand it.

[114] Murphy, *Ecclesiastes*, 39. The idea is echoed in 7:14, where Qoheleth advises the reader that God has made the day of prosperity and the day of adversity alike, "so a person may not find out anything that will come after him."

ken to understand it.[115] In 7:17, interestingly, Qohelet advises that a person be neither especially bad nor foolish, for "why die before your time?" Since one cannot learn what the times are, of course, it would be difficult to know if one is dying before one's time. What Qoheleth seems to be saying is that a person should be careful not to hasten inadvertently an already mysterious event.

Chapter three develops Qoheleth's ideas about death further. The author soon observes after 3:11 that wickedness is in the place of justice and righteousness (3:16; also see 7:15 and 8:14). Though he next counters his own complaint with the statement that God will judge both righteous and wicked, since there is a time for everything (a time, however, which cannot be understood by mortals) (3:17), he also adds that God is trying to show people that they are just animals (3:18). And here appears his next explicit comment on death (3:19–21).

> Because the outcome of humans and the outcome of beasts is the same; as one dies, so dies the other, for they all have the same breath, and the superiority[116] of humans over beasts is nought; for all is *hebel*. All are going to one place; all are from the dust, and all return to the dust. Who knows whether the life-breath of mortals goes upward and the life-breath of animals goes downward to the earth?[117]

In 2:15–16 we learn that death eradicates the differences between wise and fool. In 3:2 death, as well as birth, have their appropriate times, but these times cannot be known by humans as God has made such

---

[115] 8:5–7 states that there is a time and a way (עת ומשפט) for every purpose and the wise person will know what they are—but, the author goes right on to say "indeed there is no one who knows what will be, because who can tell him what will be?"

[116] The Hebrew is מותר, from the same root as יתרון. Literally, "the enduring aspect," or "thing that remains" of human over beasts.

[117] In the MT this verse is not vocalized according to the usual pattern of the interrogative *He*. Gordis, *Koheleth*, 228, says that this does not represent an attempt by the MT to make the line more "orthodox," and remarks on a tendency to vocalize the interrogative with a full vowel and dagesh in some cases. He refers the reader to Gen 19:9, Lev 10:19, Num 16:22, as well as Job 23:6. The Peshitta, the Aramaic Targum, and the Vulgate all treat the verse as a question, as the context requires. So does the Septuagint.

knowledge impossible. In 3:19–21 death brings humans and beasts to the same level.[118]

The next remark about death comes at the beginning of chapter four, where Qoheleth observes that the oppressed are comfortless. This drives him to say,

> And I praise the dead, who have already died, more than the living, who are still alive, but better than both of them is the one who has not yet been, because he has not seen the evil business which is done under the sun (4:2–3).

Here he takes a somewhat different approach from his earlier reflections. Previously he has treated death as the great annihilator of distinctions whose time is unknowable, a theme to which he will return. But the present comment does not serve to undermine assertions of wisdom's value or of the protection of righteousness. Its context is instead an observation on the unrelieved suffering of the oppressed, in which case death, as oblivion, is a better state than consciousness. The reader notices that Qoheleth does not argue in favor of non-existence because it prevents oppression, but says that awareness of the unhappy elements of life by the

---

[118] The Targum for this section, 3:19ff., has "For the fate of *guilty* people and the fate of the unclean beast is the same for all of them. And as an unclean beast dies, so dies the one who does not turn in repentance before his death. And the life breath of both of them is judged alike in all respects... Who is so wise that he knows if the life breath of man goes up on high to the sky and the life breath of the beast goes down below to the earth? And I saw that there was nothing better in this world than that a man rejoice in his good deeds and eat and drink and be of good cheer. For it is his good portion in this world to acquire by it the world to come...." Cf. Knobel, *The Targum of Qohelet*, 30. The Midrash for the passage states that the wicked are like beasts. "In the same way that a beast is condemned to death and does not enter the life of the World to Come, so are the wicked condemned to death like a beast and do not enter the World to Come." Cf. Cohen, *Midrash Rabbah: Ecclesiastes*, 105. Lavoie, *La penseé du Qohélet*, 77–78, draws a set of contrasts between this passage in Qoheleth and the story of creation in Genesis 1–11. Both address the same issues of the nature of humanity, but come up with different conclusions. In Genesis humans are in the image of God, and have dominion over the rest of the earth's creatures. In Qoheleth, people share the same essence as the animals and have no higher telos than to end, like them, as dust. A few pages later (88) Lavoie offers an interesting conclusion on this passage, which is that for Qoheleth "la réflexion sur la mort est au service d'une description de l'être humain." In the book's conclusion (249) he adds that death is profoundly dehumanizing; it undoes all that seems to make one special and different from the beasts. In fact, there is no difference.

one who *observes* the oppression ceases. Better still is the one who has not passed through life at all. This person never sees the evil business of the earth. Also, though this is not stated by Qoheleth, such a one avoids the need to die by virtue of not living.[119]

A number of exhortations and observations follow, but soon Qoheleth comes back to death. In chapter 5:14–15 he reflects on the unhappy person who loses his fortune, and adds,

> As he came out from his mother's womb, naked shall he return again, just as he came, and he can take nothing from his toil, which he may carry in his hand. This also is a grievous ill—just as he came, so shall he go, and what gain[120] has he in his toil for the wind?

Here Qoheleth goes back to his earlier theme of the levelling effect of death, which is extended to yet another sphere, from the wise and the foolish, humans and animals, to the rich and the poor.[121] Distinctions of intelligence, virtue, species, and wealth make no difference in the face of death. Birth and death, moreover, appear to be equal states of being. One comes and one goes in the same condition, naked, helpless, and empty-handed. The equation between the two brings out the complete futility of all that happens in between. A lifetime of experience, knowledge, struggle, and acquisition counts as nothing. The entire span

---

[119] Note that earlier in 2:17 Qoheleth says "I hated life" after his comments about the equality of wise and fool alike in death. Hatred of life and praise of the dead do not testify, however, to a sense of peace about or gratitude for death. His feelings are the result of his deep sense of injustice regarding the state of the world and frustration that death in the end treats all creatures exactly the same.

[120] Literally, "what endures to him" (יִתְרוֹן).

[121] The Targum on this passage has "Just as he came out of his mother's womb naked without merit and without anything good so shall he return going to his tomb lacking merit just as he came into the world. He shall receive no good reward whatsoever for his labor to carry with him in the world where he is going to be a merit in his hand. And also this is a grave illness and there is no cure for it. As he came into this world lacking merit so will he go into the world to come and what advantage did he have that he labored for his spirit?" Cf. Knobel, *The Targum of Qohelet*, 35. Knobel notes that the word "naked" in the MT is interpreted to mean "without commandments." The Midrash says at the end of its discussion of these verses "It has been taught in the name of R. Meir: When a person enters the world his hands are clenched as though to say, 'The whole world is mine, I shall inherit it'; but when he takes leave of it his hands are spread open as though to say, 'I have inherited nothing from the world.'" Cf. Cohen, *Midrash Rabbah: Ecclesiastes*, 155.

of a person's existence is voided at death and so the individual ends up right back at square one; nothing has been gained.

As for the person who has the material means to enjoy life, but does not do so, a stillborn is better off than he is. There are those who have material possessions and honor, but do not enjoy them and end up handing them over to a stranger (6:1–5).

> Even if he should live a thousand years twice over, but see no good—are not all going to one place? (6:6).[122]

The interesting feature of this passage is that an unusually lengthy life is not the solution to Qoheleth's problem. For one thing quality of life is as important as quantity. Better never to live at all than to live without enjoyment. The stillborn who does not see the sun or have any knowledge avoids the dark side of existence. But what if the person in this passage not only had the advantages necessary to enjoy life but also made use of them? Would this not answer Qoheleth's complaint? Since the realities of the world make a long and happy life an extremely uncertain proposition, one example of a person who was able to do so would not establish a rule by which Qoheleth could be satisfied. In any event the wicked are just as likely to enjoy the good life while the innocent are oppressed, and in the end there still looms the inevitable fact of annihilation, no matter what kind of life a person has led. Length of life just puts off the inevitable. Whether happy or sad, all "are going to one place."

In 7:1–2 Qoheleth adds that the day of death is better than the day of birth, and the house of mourning than the house of feasting, "because

---

[122] The Targum says that even if a person lives two thousand years "but he does not occupy himself with the Torah and did not do justice and charity," his soul goes to Gehenna where all sinners go. Cf. Knobel, *The Targum of Qohelet*, 36. Murphy, "On Translating Ecclesiastes," 577–78, discusses an interesting translation of the verse following 6:6, which is usually rendered "All human toil is for the (literally, his/its) mouth, but the appetite is never satisfied." He suggests that since 6:6 is an explicit reference to Sheol (the place to which all go), one might take "its mouth" in 6:7 as referring back to Sheol. Thus, all human labor is for *Sheol's* mouth, the appetite of which is never satisfied. Murphy notes that the idea of a devouring Sheol appears in Is 5:14 and Hab 2:5. The verse is ambiguous, however, and he points out that Sheol is not mythologized elsewhere in the book.

this is the end of everyone, and the living will lay it to heart."[123] In chapter five he has already equated the day of birth and the day of death with one another since at both times a person is naked and empty-handed. Beginning and end are the same. In chapters four and six he said that the dead and/or the unborn are better off than the living when the latter are unable to enjoy life. Now the day of death is better than the day of birth as a general principle. The reason he gives seems to be not that death is the cessation of suffering, as before, but that it serves as a reminder of the reality of existence, namely, that it is fleeting. One might prefer not to be reminded of the fact that death is inescapable, but Qoheleth seems to feel that knowledge of a thing, even if melancholy, is better than ignorance. This is suggested by 7:4 where he adds that the heart of the wise is in the house of mourning, of fools in the house of mirth.[124] The wise person's heart may be in the house of mourning because he fully understands his own ephemerality; perhaps he mourns his own upcoming death.

In chapter 8, "no one has power over the wind (or the life-breath?) to withhold the wind, or power over the day of death" (8:8).[125] A few

---

[123] The Midrash says that this is so because "When a person is born he is designated for death; when he dies he is designated for life [in the Hereafter]." Moreover, one does not know what manner of person a newborn will be, but if someone dies with a good name and in peace, there is reason to rejoice. Cf. Cohen, *Midrash Rabbah: Ecclesiastes*, 170. The Targum remarks "The good name the righteous acquire in this world is better than the anointing oil which was poured on the head of kings and priests and the day that a man dies and departs for the tomb with a good name and merits (is better) than the day when a wicked man is born into the world." Cf. Knobel, *The Targum of Qohelet*, 38.

[124] A few verses further into the chapter (11–12) appears a little commentary on wisdom which, in view of what Qoheleth has already said about life and death, is quite ironic. He claims that wisdom is an advantage (יֹתֵר) to "those who see the sun," but since no one can ever see the sun for more than a few decades at the most, the advantage is a relative one. He then says that wisdom's protection is like that of money, which chapter 5 has already shown to be no protection at all against the final oblivion. Finally he remarks that the יִתְרוֹן of wisdom is that it gives life to its possessor. This, of course, is not true in the grand scheme of things. Wisdom's life-giving properties may exist temporarily but it cannot prevent the final arrival of death, which abolishes wisdom along with everything else. So its יִתְרוֹן is short-lived.

[125] See footnote #52 for רוּחַ as "life-breath." The Targum for 8:8 says "There is no man who rules over the breath of the spirit to restrain the breath of life so that it will not depart from the human body." Cf. Knobel, *The Targum of Qohelet*, 42. The Midrash reports "The Rabbis say: A man has no power over the

verses later Qoheleth insists that all will be well with those who fear God, while the wicked will not prolong their days (vv. 12–13), which is a proper rendition of the traditional view of divine reward and retribution to be found in both wisdom and deuteronomic traditions. Thus death is a means of God's judgment. He then immediately goes on to say that there is a *hebel* that happens in the world, that there are righteous who are treated like the wicked and vice versa. The reader takes this to mean, in light of the preceding, that there are righteous who die early, as the wicked should, and wicked who prolong their days, instead of being cut off as they deserve. In other words, when he says in verse 8 that no one has power over the day of death, he means it on every level. Not only can no one avoid death in the end, one cannot even exercise the limited power over it that living a righteous life was traditionally supposed to provide.[126]

In chapter nine the reader arrives at a particularly intense exposition on the implications of death. In fact, the chapter has a climactic feel to it and would have served as a decent conclusion to the book in its own right if it had ended at verse 10 or 12.[127] Everything that people face is vanity,[128]

---

wind of the Angel of Death to make him withhold it from him." Cf. A. Cohen, *Midrash Rabbah: Ecclesiastes*, 219. Rashbam explains 8:8 by saying "no man has control over his soul on the day of death, to withhold his soul from being handed over to the angel of death." See Sara Japhet and Robert B. Salters, *The Commentary of R. Samuel Ben Meir Rashbam on Qoheleth* (Leiden: E. J. Brill, 1985) 170. Ginsburg, *The Song of Songs and Coheleth*, 396–97, translates the verse: "No man is ruler over his spirit to retain the spirit." Gordis, *Koheleth*, 280, translates "the spirit of life." Fox, *Qohelet and His Contradictions*, 248, argues for "life-spirit." Crenshaw, *Ecclesiastes*, 152 believes "life-breath" to be the best.

[126] At the end of verse 8 he adds that wickedness does not rescue its practitioner. Crenshaw, *Ecclesiastes*, 152, points out that some have emended רשע to עשר, a reading also proposed by BHS. But the original is not a problem for the thrust of the argument. Even those who throw morality to the winds and do whatever they can to further their own ends are still not going to avoid the inevitable.

[127] Gordis, *Koheleth*, 292, notes that Qoheleth's basic themes, death and joy, reach heights in this passage "which is virtually the culmination of the preceding."

[128] This is an emendation. The Hebrew has הכל, instead of הבל, but the latter is supported by the Septuagint, and an orthographic error from ב to כ is easily understandable, especially since הכל appears twice in the vicinity, almost immediately before and after the word.

since one event comes to all, to the righteous and to the wicked, to the good [and the evil] and to the clean and to the unclean, to the one who sacrifices and to the one who does not sacrifice; as is the good, so is the sinner, the one who swears like him who shuns an oath. This is an evil in all that is done under the sun, because one end comes to everyone, and also the heart of mortals is full of evil, and madness is in their hearts during their lives and after that—to the dead. But whoever is joined[129] to all the living has hope, because a live dog is better than a dead lion, since the living know that they will die, but the dead do not know anything,[130] and they have no more reward, because memory of them is forgotten. Their love and their hate and their jealousy have already perished. They have no more portion forever[131] in all that is done under the sun.

Go, eat your bread with joy, and drink your wine with a happy heart, for God has already accepted what you do. At all times let your clothes be white, and let there be no lack of oil for your head. Enjoy life with a woman whom you love, all the days of your brief life which he has given you under the sun, all your passing days, for it is your portion in life and in your labor in which you are laboring under the sun. All that your hand finds to do, do in your strength, because there is no act or thought or knowledge or wisdom in Sheol, to which you are going.[132]

---

[129] "Joined" is the Qere (יחבר). The ketib is from the root "to choose" (יבחר).

[130] The Midrash says that "the living" refers to the righteous, who even in death are called living. "The dead" refers to the wicked, who are called dead even when alive. Cf. Cohen, *Midrash Rabbah: Ecclesiastes*, 229.

[131] The Midrash takes לעולם as "for the world" instead of "forever," and renders: "Neither have they (that is, the wicked) a portion for the World [to Come], whereas Israel has a portion and a good reward...." Cf. Cohen, *Midrash Rabbah: Ecclesiastes*, 230.

[132] This section of chapter 9 (vv. 7–10) is thought by some to be based on a passage in the Epic of Gilgamesh where the barmaid Siduri advises the hero to stop his quest for immortality and enjoy his present life while he can. Bruce William Jones, "From Gilgamesh to Qoheleth," in William W. Hallo et al, eds., *The Bible in the Light of Cuneiform Literature: Scripture in Context III* (Lewiston, NY: The Edwin Mellen Press, 1990) 369–73, notes the following: both texts refer to food in the context of joy twice, both refer to clean clothes and to washing/anointing the head, both speak of enjoying one's spouse or a woman, and each has a summary statement, all of which are in similar order. See also Crenshaw, *Ecclesiastes*, 162–63. Gordis, *Koheleth*, 293–94, however, feels that the parallels are too general to be a question of borrowing. Jean-Jacques Lavoie, "Bonheur et Finitude Humaine: Étude de Qo 9,7–10," *Science et Esprit* 45(1993) 323, notes that there are a number of differences between the passages, too. The vocabulary is not the same, the Jewish text offers reasons for its advice which are lacking in Gilgamesh, and the contexts are different. He concludes that in light of similar themes in other cultures, the case for influence in neither necessary nor compelling.

> I saw again under the sun that the race is not to the swift, nor the battle to the strong, nor bread to the wise, nor wealth to the discerning, nor favor to those who know, because time and chance befall all of them (vv.10–11).[133]

All distinctions disappear in the end. Everyone, despite their moral or cultic standing, is off to the dead. This is a continuing theme in the text and it reaches its fullness here. In addition, Qoheleth now insists that life of any sort is better than death, even if that life is like a dog's. The dead know nothing at all, whereas the living have one piece of knowledge ("hope"): that they will die. It has been suggested that this statement is ironic,[134] and in light of what Qoheleth has already said about the advantage of missing out on life altogether in chapters four and six this may be true. However, the word בטחון may not signify "hope" as much as something that one can rely on,[135] in which case his claim could be taken literally. The one and only thing that can be relied on, in fact, is death.[136] Although he has said that non-existence is better than a bad life, when Qoheleth actually confronts the utter void of death he is willing to laud any form of consciousness no matter how meager or gloomy. The reader also notices that he never wishes for death, and only once actually considers the dead fortunate (4:2). Elsewhere he says that the one unborn (4:3), or the stillborn (6:3–5), are better off than the living because they have never had to bear the weight of human awareness. This is different

---

[133] The Targum, not too surprisingly by this point, reinterprets this passage in light of reward and punishment after death. 9:5 runs as follows: "For the righteous know that if they sin, they will be considered as dead in the world to come. Therefore, they guard their ways and do not sin, and if they sin, they return in repentance." 9:10 says, after the part describing the lack of thought, wisdom, and so on in Sheol (here, the grave), "and nothing will help you but good deeds and charity alone." Cf. Knobel, *The Targum of Qohelet*, 44–45.

[134] Cf. Crenshaw, *Ecclesiastes*, 161: "Although many commentators view this theoretical knowledge as positive, Qoheleth's words appear ironic. No comfort derives from knowing that the dead have already received their rewards and are completely forgotten, for the living will experience the same oblivion. Awareness of such grim prospects can hardly form a basis for hope. In this instance, ignorance is preferable."

[135] Fox, *Qohelet and His Contradictions*, 258.

[136] Even though this is not a happy thing of which to be assured, earlier the author has not quailed before knowledge even when that knowledge is not comforting. In 1:18 he asserts that wisdom includes grief, and knowledge brings sorrow, while in 7:4 he has said that a wise person's heart is in the house of mourning.

than wanting to die. Once one has life in hand, one does not want to let it go.

Chapter ten is the one chapter free of any reference to death.[137] Chapter eleven reminds the reader again that the days of darkness will be many (11:8).[138] The crescendo of the repeating drumbeat of death is reached in chapter twelve, the conclusion, which as discussed earlier draws the entire argument to a close with a powerful description of an individual death. These reflections on mortality assert themselves in the book at regular intervals, in one chapter right after another, and they lead in an unswerving line to the climax at the end. No matter what he is discussing, Qoheleth continually finds himself butting against the same insurmountable wall. By the end of the book, the reader has been given a full account of what death is and what it means for life. It eradicates all distinctions of good and evil, wise and foolish, rich and poor, young and old, human and animal, and all others that can be imagined. The inequities of life are many, and they find their consummation in the final inequity of death. Death along with all other events has a "time," but whatever the nature and schedule of these times may be are known only to God. Humans are by nature incapable of ever understanding them. Death is the complete absence of all those things which characterize human existence, thought, knowledge, work, wisdom, and emotion. Even meager life is better than the void, which is why Qoheleth can say that someone who has never tasted existence is better off than those who have only to know that they will lose it again, but also never suggests suicide. The process of death on a personal level is one of dissolution. From the point of view of the one who is dying, it is the end of the world. Death is, in sum, ultimately dehumanizing in every sense of the word: literally, because it undoes the components of existence, and metaphorically, because it makes humans no different from any other form of life.

---

[137] Perhaps after the intensity of chapter nine Qoheleth needed a breather.

[138] The Targum reads "And let him remember the dark days of death and not sin. For many are the days which the deceased lies in the grave and it is proper for him to receive judgment from Heaven for his life which he loved, all the time that punishment comes upon him for the vanity which he has done." Cf. Knobel, *The Targum of Qohelet*, 52.

The Brevity of Life. Even when Qoheleth is not specifically speaking of death, one cannot help but notice that almost every time he mentions life, he can hardly refrain from attaching "hebel (ephemeral)" or "few days of"[139] to the word.

> 2:3 what is good for people to do "during the few days of their life?"
> 5:17 find enjoyment "the few days of life" God allows.
> 6:12 what is good for humanity "the days of their *hebel* life?"
> 7:15 Qoheleth has seen all in the "days of my *hebel*...."
> 9:9 Enjoy what you can "all the days of your *hebel* life."
> 11:10 youth is *hebel*.

In these cases, life is colored by the reminder that it is marked by brevity.[140]

The Counsel to Make Merry. Qoheleth's repeated advice amongst all these comments on death is to enjoy life to the fullest while one can. "There is nothing better for mortals than to eat and drink, and find enjoyment in their toil" (2:24).[141] Yet in the vast majority of cases, these counsels lead Qoheleth back to the brevity of life, death itself, or *hebel*. The test of pleasure he makes in 2:1ff. turns out in verse 11 to be vanity.[142] In 2:24 the advice also leads to the conclusion that all is vanity as well.[143] In 5:17–19 one should rejoice during the brief span of a life,

---

[139] The Hebrew for "few days of" is מספר, indicating a small number of days; cf. Gordis, *Koheleth*, 206.

[140] See Graham S. Ogden, "Qoheleth IX 1–16," *Vetus Testamentum* 32(1982) 164, who rightly notes that life is always lived under "the shadow of our common fate in death"; also cf. Roland E. Murphy, "The Sage in Ecclesiastes and Qoheleth the Sage," in J. G. Gammie and Leo G. Perdue, eds., *The Sage in Israel and the Ancient Near East* (Winona Lake: Eisenbrauns, 1990) 271, who says the emphasis on the enjoyment of life is limited, since it is in "the perspective of Sheol and the nothingness to come," and depends on God's arbitrariness; J.A. Loader, *Ecclesiastes*, trans. by John Vriend (Grand Rapids: Eerdmans, 1986) 14, says "the joy of life is subordinate to the vanity of life."

[141] See also 2:10; 3:1–13, 22; 3:22; 5:18–20; 6:3, 6; 7:14; 8:15; 9:7–9; 11:9.

[142] The Midrash has its own interpretation of the idea of pleasure as vanity. In 2:1 it comments on the phrase "and enjoy pleasure": "i.e. the pleasure of the World to Come. R. Jonah said in the name of R. Simon b. Zabdi: All the prosperity which a man experiences in this world is 'vanity' in comparison with the World to Come; because in this world a man dies and bequeaths his prosperity to another, but in connection with the World to Come it is written, *They shall not build, and another inhabit* (Isa. LXV, 22)." Cf. Cohen, *Midrash Rabbah: Ecclesiastes*, 51.

[143] The Midrash of 2:24, which advises eating, drinking, and finding

because embracing what life has to offer has the advantage of inhibiting any inclination to dwell on one's fate: "for he will not much remember the days of his life, since God keeps him busy with the joy of his heart."[144] The busier one is, the less time one has for melancholy.[145] Even a thousand-year life span twice over would end in Sheol (6:6). In chapter 9 a person's enjoyment again ends in Sheol (9:10), while in 11:9 God will bring one into judgment for it. Some have taken the counsel to make merry as the main theme of the book, and therefore read the text largely

---

enjoyment in one's toil, reads: "All the references to eating and drinking in this Book signify Torah and good deeds. R. Jonah said: The most clear proof of them all is, *A man hath no better thing under the sun than to eat and drink, and to be merry, and that this should accompany him in his labour*—'amalo (Eccl. VIII, 15). The last word should be read as *'olamo* (his world)—in this world; All *the days of his life* (ib.) alludes to the grave. Are there, then, food and drink in the grave which accompany a man to the grave? It must then mean Torah and good deeds." The Midrash states the same principle also in 3:12, 5:17, and 8:15. Cf. Cohen, *Midrash Rabbah: Ecclesiastes*, 71–72, 94, 156–57, 224. The Targum says in 3:12 that there is nothing good for humanity "except to rejoice in the joy of the Torah and to do good during the days his life." Cf. Knobel, *The Targum of Qohelet*, 28. Jerome states that 2:24 is a reference "to the Sacrament of the Lord's Supper." See R. B. Salters, "Qoheleth and the Canon," *Expository Times* 86(1975) 342. He further explains that to have joy in life means giving alms, which prepares treasure for the giver in heaven (Svend Holm-Nielsen, "On the Interpretation of Qoheleth in Early Christianity," *Vetus Testamentum* 24[1974] 176). Augustine also interprets the counsel to eat and drink as a reference to the eucharist. See Ginsburg, *The Song of Songs and Coheleth*, 105.

[144] The Targum of 5:17–18 adds to the counsel in the MT that one should also avoid violence, keep the Torah, and have compassion on the poor; the reward will be in the world to come. Cf. Knobel, *The Targum of Qohelet*, 36.

[145] Lohfink, "Qoheleth 5:17–19," 626, takes the sense in a different way. He thinks the root meaning for מענה here is not from "to be occupied, to be busy with," but from "to answer, reveal." So the verse should read "He will not brood much over the days of his life; on the contrary, God reveals himself (to him) by the joy of his heart" (634). This joy is a kind of divine revelation, then. The Midrash also uses the root "to answer." Grammatically Lohfink's translation is possible, but as God is completely enigmatic everywhere else in the book and purposefully arranges things so that people may not understand the ways of the world (cf. 3:11, 7:14), it seems unlikely, whereas the idea of being busy with pleasure to avoid dwelling on the inevitable makes perfect sense in the book. Murphy, "On Translating Ecclesiastes," 578–79, concludes after praising the case Lohfink makes that in the end it probably is not correct, as the pleasures that God gives are themselves too erratic to comprise an answer or revelation from the deity. The usual translation, he feels, is more in keeping with Qoheleth's mood.

as a "divine imperative of joy."[146] However, the context as a whole suggests that these notes of joy are a meager tune in a work that plays in a somber key.

Of course Qoheleth discusses other things, such as nature, human society, the lack of justice, the dangers of politics, as well as more mundane, proverbial topics. Yet at no point can the reader get very far from the theme of death. The book begins that all is hebel, and ends with a long reflection on death. Injustice, human limitation, and God's inscrutability are all sore trials to bear, but the disquiet they arouse finds its highest expression in the ultimate injustice, the consummate limitation, the token of God's inscrutability par excellence: death.[147]

Death in Qoheleth Versus the Rest of the Tradition

This message stands in stark contrast to everything else in the canon. Nowhere else is death the theological problem that it is for Qoheleth. Other voices in the Hebrew Bible certainly hold forth on theological problems of great importance, and probe the nature of humanity, God, history, and justice, among other topics. The argument is not that the rest of the biblical texts have no grievances and make no protests, only that death had not figured among these. With Qoheleth,

---

[146] Robert Gordis, *Koheleth*, 58. Also R. N. Whybray, "Qoheleth, Preacher of Joy," *Journal for the Study of the Old Testament* 23(1982) 94, who says that joy "is what Qoheleth above all wished to commend to his readers." Whybray in his later commentary, *Ecclesiastes*, 28, seems to be a little more reticent about stating that Qoheleth is a preacher of joy. He sums up his discussion of the question by saying simply that whether Qoheleth was "a pessimist or an optimist, therefore, will remain a matter of opinion; what is certain is that he was a realist." See Anderson, *Qoheleth and Its Pessimistic Theology*, 71–74, for a discussion which counters the view that joy is a basic message of Qoheleth; similarly Tremper Longman III, *The Book of Ecclesiastes* (Grand Rapids: Eerdmans, 1998) 34–35.

[147] Chapter 9 is a perfect example of this, where Qoheleth reduces everything to the same problem. Ogden, "Qoheleth IX," 168–69, says "the question of justice, of evil in high places, of oppression, of one's inability to enjoy the fruits of one's labours, and of all the other frustrations of human experience, all its inequities, become so problematic theologically because of our common death"; cf. also R. N. Whybray, *Ecclesiastes* (Grand Rapids: Eerdmans, 1989) 139, "from v. 4 onwards Qoheleth turns from a general discussion of the inequities inherent in human life to one of his favorite themes; the levelling effect of death." Lavoie, "Bonheur et Finitude Humaine: Étude de Qo 9,7–10," 317, writes "c'est la finitude humaine qui est la véritable obsession du Qohélet.... Autrement dit, la vie, même avec son lot de jouissances, n'est rien d'autre qu'une marche vers la mort."

however, death makes its entrance into the Hebrew traditions as a phenomenon to be reckoned with. The difference does not lie in his view of what death is; he agrees with his predecessors that physical death is the end of individual consciousness. But he goes beyond the tradition in his belief that physical death is the end of every other conceivable means of continuation as well. The symbolic immortalities offered elsewhere in the Bible, the memory and endurance of a good name, survival through one's children and people, even the qualitative good life that negates the "death" of folly and unrighteousness, fail utterly in Qoheleth's opinion. First, he emphasizes that memory is discontinuous from one generation to the next.

> 1:11 There is no memory of the people of long ago, nor will there be any memory of the people to come by those who will come after them.

> 2:16 There is no lasting remembrance of the wise or of the fool, since in the days to come everything will have been forgotten.

> 9:5 The dead do not know anything, and they have no more reward, because their memory is forgotten.

Second, one cannot know who will inherit after him, or whether that person will even be deserving.

> 2:18–19 And I hated all my toil for which I was toiling under the sun, since I must give it to the man who comes after me, and who knows whether he will be wise or foolish? Cf. 2:21

> 6:1–2 There is an evil that I have seen under the sun, and it lies heavy on humanity: a man to whom God gives wealth, and possessions, and honor, so that he lacks nothing of all that he desires, but God does not give him power to make use of them, because a stranger devours them.

And finally, the ability to make choices regarding the kind of life to lead based on the expected result of the choice is circumscribed in the extreme by God's mysterious whim, because happenstance and chance befall everyone.

> 9:12 For a man doesn't know his time—like fish that are seized in a cruel net, and like birds caught in a trap, like these mortals are snared at a bad time, when it falls upon them suddenly.

One is unable to predict, then, just how events will play out.[148] Death is the event that neutralizes memory, offspring, and choice.

"Thus death, as the mind becomes aware of it, deprives the wisdom of the wise of its meaning in an increasingly radical way. Death has become the frontier situation which forces man to reflect upon it."[149] This comment is right on target in describing death as a *frontier* situation, that heretofore undeveloped boundary area which becomes a place of exploration.[150] Death is now "the great adversary" which collapses the previous, traditional understandings in which it properly fits into creation and can be more or less chosen, with occasional exceptions, depending on one's path of life. In Proverbs, for example, the sages treat death as something that can be calculated, and pass over the disruptive aspects, addressing the proper timing of it while ignoring the ramifications of its existence.[151] Humanity has still a relative power against death.[152]

Not so, says Qoheleth: "In my vain life I have seen everything; there is a righteous man who perishes in his righteousness, and there is a

---

[148] Ogden, "Qoheleth IX," 165. Jean-Jacques Lavoie, "Temps et Finitude Humaine: Étude de Qohélet IX:11–12," *Vetus Testamentum* 46(1996) 439–47, provides an interesting discussion of this passage. He comments that humanity is "au contrôle arbitraire du créateur qui détermine le sort funeste de chacun" (447).

[149] N. Lohfink, *The Christian Meaning of the Old Testament*, trans. R. A. Wilson (Milwaukee: Bruce, 1968) 152.

[150] In Qoheleth we find a "completely distinctive radical consideration of death," writes Walther Zimmerli, "Concerning the Structure of Old Testament Wisdom," trans. Brian W. Kovacs, in James L. Crenshaw, ed., *Studies in Ancient Israelite Wisdom* (New York: Ktav Publishing House, 1976) 192; also cf. Murphy, "The Sage in Ecclesiastes," 268, who says that Qoheleth "radicalizes Death/Sheol." Antoon Schoors, "Koheleth: A Perspective of Life After Death?" *Ephemerides Theologicae Lovanienses* 61(1985) 303, says "in Koheleth's view, death renders the aporia of human life complete."

[151] Zimmerli, "Concerning the Structure of Old Testament Wisdom," 193.

[152] Cf. Prov 13:6, "Righteousness guards one whose way is upright, but sin overthrows the wicked." See also texts such as Psalm 37, which declare that in no case does God permanently allow the wicked to prosper and the righteous to suffer. "I have been young, and am now old, yet I have not seen the righteous forsaken or their children begging bread" (v. 25). Job 4:7–9 contains part of a discourse by Eliphaz the Temanite wherein he says "Think now, who that was innocent ever perished? Or where were the upright cut off? As I have seen, those who plow iniquity and sow trouble reap the same. By the breath of God they perish, and by the blast of his anger they are consumed." Similarly Bildad the Shuhite states in 8:20 "See, God will not reject a blameless person, nor take the hand of evildoers."

wicked man who prolongs his life in his wrongdoing" (7:15).[153] Earlier participants in the biblical traditions on this matter were not much shaken by exceptions to their rule, while Qoheleth zeros in on the exceptions.[154] He does not insist that the righteous always die early, or that the wicked will never get their comeuppance in a timely manner, but that sometimes events do not unfold the way they should from the point of view of moral justice.[155] It has been suggested that in this regard the book of Qoheleth

---

[153] The Targum of 7:15 says: "For there is an innocent man who perishes in his righteousness in this world, but his merits are preserved for him in the world to come and there is a guilty man who prolongs his days in his sin, but his evils are preserved for him in the world to come to exact punishment from him on the great judgment day." Knobel, *The Targum of Qohelet*, 40. This interpretation neatly removes the problem of death since afterwards the inequities of the present world will be sorted out. (Interestingly, a little later in the Targum, in 7:29, the serpent and Eve are blamed for causing the "day of death" to happen to Adam and all people in the world.) A somewhat different interpretation appears in 8:14, where the Targum states that the righteous experience evil to repay their minor sins so their reward in the world to come will be complete, and the sinners experience good to recompense their minor merit so that they may have no portion in the world to come. Cf. Knobel, *The Targum of Qohelet*, 43.

[154] Job, of course, has similar comments on the experiences of the righteous and the wicked. Chapter 21 is a particularly detailed example. "How often is the lamp of the wicked put out? How often does calamity come upon them? How often does God distribute pains in his anger.... Let their own eyes see their destruction, and let them drink of the wrath of the Almighty" (vv. 17, 20). Habakkuk writes, "Your eyes [God] are too pure to behold evil, and you cannot look on wrongdoing; why do you look on the treacherous, and are silent when the wicked swallow those more righteous than they?" (1:13–14). One notes with interest in Malachi an impatience with this kind of thinking. "You have wearied the Lord with your words. Yet you say, 'How have we wearied him?' By saying, 'All who do evil are good in the sight of the Lord, and he delights in them.' Or by asking, 'Where is the God of justice?'" (2:17). See also Malachi 3:17–18, "They shall be mine, says the Lord of hosts, my special possession on the day when I act, and I will spare them as parents spare their children who serve them. Then once more you shall see the difference between the righteous and the wicked, between one who serves God and one who does not serve him." Of interest is the implication that in the present, the differences between the righteous and the wicked are not obvious. The distinctions will be restored in the future.

[155] For this reason "death casts its shadow over every meaningful interpretation of life," says Gerhard Von Rad, *Wisdom in Israel* (Nashville: Abingdon Press, 1972) 228. W. Lee Humphreys, *The Tragic Vision and the Hebrew Tradition* (Philadelphia: Fortress Press, 1985) 129, describes death as a "cancer."

represents a "mutation in structure" compared with earlier wisdom traditions.[156] He is not simply altering the subject matter of his teaching. The change in content reflects an entire shift in the basic framework of thought with which he begins. A person's actions have no bearing whatsoever on whether one will experience good or evil in life. Or, if by chance act and outcome do appear to be related, this will only be so in the short term, since death awaits no matter what. Death is especially that event which transpires regardless of conduct, because in the end it happens to everyone alike.[157] The correlation of the timing and manner of death with personal righteousness fails, and so death voids human efforts.[158] It becomes a kind of "final solution" to human understanding.[159]

Not everyone agrees with this assessment. Although death comes closer to being a real problem theologically than it does anywhere else in the canon, "the question of the appropriateness of that universal fate is not raised," and death is accepted within the larger sphere of divine wisdom.[160] That Qoheleth does not explicitly question the appropriateness of death is technically true, inasmuch as he does not explicitly question the appropriateness of anything, oppression, injustice, misfortune, ignorance, God's elusiveness, or any of the other things that trouble him. His approach is not Job's. It does not even occur to him to rail against God or demand explanations, because his God would not answer. His style is instead one of resigned observation, and he "accepts" the problems he sees because he has no other choice. This does not mean, however, that he likes the situation or takes any comfort in it, and the

---

[156] Hartmut Gese, "The Crisis of Wisdom in Koheleth," in James L. Crenshaw, ed., *Theodicy in the Old Testament* (Philadelphia: Fortress Press, 1983) 143.

[157] Gese, "The Crisis of Wisdom in Koheleth," 144.

[158] Crenshaw, *Ecclesiastes*, 25.

[159] Murphy, "The Sage in Ecclesiastes," 268.

[160] Lloyd R. Bailey, *Biblical Perspectives on Death* (Philadelphia: Fortress Press, 1979) 55–57. See also Roy B. Zuck, "God and Man in Ecclesiastes," *Bibliotheca Sacra* 148(1991) 46–56; and Barry C. Davis, "Ecclesiastes 12:1–8— Death, and Impetus for Life," *Bibliotheca Sacra* 148(1991) 298–318, for other opinions contrary to that of this chapter. Davis writes (298) that death is the most devastating barrier Qoheleth faces in his search for the meaning of life, but believes that he overcomes the problem in chapter 12 by portraying death as the "beginning of an everlasting existence" (304). This chapter of course argues that Qoheleth does not overcome the problem.

statements he makes, his entire attitude and tone, all suggest that he is making a serious break with the tradition. The break is not one of rejecting his Jewish heritage; no doubt Qoheleth would not have conceived of being anything other than a Jew. But his thought does undermine the teaching of the tradition in an acute fashion.

Another scholar acknowledges the importance of the theme of transience in the book, but feels that the darker side of this theme is often over-emphasized. Since everything is ephemeral, so is the evil that one encounters in life.[161] Qoheleth actually offers consolation for life's brevity, such as the fact that God is in complete control of all events, and the hope that one might prolong one's life through wisdom.[162] While Qoheleth stresses the more somber facets of life, this does not signify a full-fledged crisis or break with tradition, and the notes of death are countered by the call to pleasure in life.[163]

A different scholarly approach to death in Qoheleth acknowledges the profound problem it creates for the author, but tries to find an otherworldy solution to it.[164] Qoheleth bluntly states that present-life injustices do not work themselves out, and that in the end death annuls any apparent distinctions between types of people and even between people and animals. "It is apparent that Qoheleth believes some distinction is required, even though it presently lies beyond proof."[165] This is certainly true. Qoheleth most emphatically believes some distinction is required, but death makes this impossible. Yet the interpretation goes on to find, in spite of the admitted fact that Qoheleth sees no evidence for any restitution after death, "a clear note of hope" that

---

[161] Daniel C. Fredericks, *Coping with Transience: Ecclesiastes on Brevity in Life* (Sheffield: Journal for the Study of the Old Testament Press, 1993) 31.

[162] Fredericks, *Coping with Transience: Ecclesiastes on Brevity in Life*, 37–38.

[163] Fredericks, *Coping with Transience: Ecclesiastes on Brevity in Life*, 95–97.

[164] This approach is taken by Graham Ogden in his commentary on the book. See footnote #59 for his discussion of יתרון. Cf. also Davis in footnote #160.

[165] Ogden, *Qoheleth*, 62.

there is something beyond this life.[166] That Qoheleth feels a distinction to be required, however, does not mean that he in fact finds it. The interpretation has insight in recognizing that according to the way Qoheleth frames his argument, the only solution which would be possible would have to come after death. But that Qoheleth himself accepts this solution is not persuasive. For Qoheleth, there is no solution. The injustices of life are sealed by the final and absolute injustice of death.

---

[166] Ogden, *Qoheleth*, 63. This discussion is specifically related to the commentary on 3:21–22. For a different view, see Isak J.J. Spangenberg, "Irony in the Book of Qohelet," *Journal for the Study of the Old Testament* 72 (1996) 69, who says that Qoheleth's "hunger for immortality in the face of the inevitability of death," among other things, a hunger which is not satisfied, is one example which contributes to the irony of the book as a whole.

Chapter 3
QOHELETH'S HISTORICAL CONTEXT

Qoheleth is not the only Jewish thinker in this period who is troubled by death, as it turns out, though one must go outside the canon to realize that he is the forerunner of an emerging trend. No other extant Jewish works says exactly what he does, but not long after Qoheleth's composition death suddenly becomes a main topic of reflection. Although there is not enough room here to analyze the other texts in any kind of detail, it is important to understand that Qoheleth is not an isolated phenomenon in his concern about death among Jews in the last centuries before the turn of the millennium. This fact is relevant to the question of foreign influences on the book, which is the second section of this chapter. The final section explores the political and social realities of the time as a possible way of understanding the text and its interest in death.

OTHER LATE JEWISH RESPONSES TO DEATH

In the second century BCE, the issue of death emerges in a variety of ways for Jewish writers.[1] The book of Ben Sira is the closest in time to Qoheleth. The translator, Ben Sira's grandson, begins with a statement about his own arrival in Egypt and subsequent translation of the book into Greek that suggests a date of composition around 180 BCE. Ben Sira cannot be described as a work that spends a special amount of time contemplating death. In fact, it stands closer to Proverbs in its view of the world. Practical advice and standard hortatory material make up the bulk

---

[1] Possibly death received attention in texts that were produced even earlier, in the fourth and third centuries BCE, which is to say practically coeval with Qoheleth (if Seow is correct in his dating, the second half of the fifth century could even be relevant), but if so they did not survive to posterity.

of the book. Nevertheless, Ben Sira is not unoriginal. For one thing, his work goes beyond the usual interests of didactic wisdom in its explicit incorporation of the torah (24:8–12, 23) and Israel's history (44–50). He also feels compelled to take several shots at explaining the source of evil in the world. His first attempt (15:11–20) is traditional deuteronomic theology, where everyone has the ability to choose between good and evil, "life and death" (15:17). But later (33:10–15) he explains that God blesses some and curses others, as is the deity's prerogative, because all things come in pairs; "good is the opposite of evil, and life the opposite of death" (33:14). Then he suggests (39:25–27) that the basic ingredients of the world are good or bad relative to whether they are used by the good or by sinners. These three explanations are not, strictly speaking, compatible, though Ben Sira would probably insist on theodicy number one if pressed. The interesting thing is that he apparently feels pressure to keep trying to address the question of evil in the world.

A further item of interest is that death itself, while not the central issue that it is for Qoheleth, does take on more somber tones than it had in the rest of the Hebrew Bible. "Like his near-contemporary Qoheleth, and unlike the older Hebrew tradition, Sirach is haunted by the shadow of death: 'a heavy yoke is laid on the children of Adam... perplexities and fear of heart are theirs and anxious thought of the day of their death' (40:1–2; cf. 41:1–4)."[2] Moreover,

> From the one who sits on a splendid throne to the one who grovels in dust and ashes, from the one who wears purple and a crown to the one who is clothed in burlap, there is anger and envy and trouble and unrest, and *fear of death*, and fury and strife (40:3–5).

Death and divine judgment "are significant motivating factors in Sirach's ethical system."[3] Ben Sira's attitude is not as adamant as Qoheleth's, since he can follow the thought of death's bitterness with an admonition not to fear death's decree because it is the Lord's will (41:3–4; cf. 14:16–19; 17:1–2, 27–28, 30–32), but death is still on his mind. Unlike Qoheleth, he also still insists that the memory of a good name is eternal

---

[2] John J. Collins, *Jewish Wisdom in the Hellenistic Age* (Louisville: Westminster John Knox Press, 1997) 78.

[3] Collins, *Jewish Wisdom in the Hellenistic Age*, 79.

(41:13, 44:8,14), and that a righteous person's children endure forever (44:13).

> "When a father dies, he will not seem to be dead, for he has left behind one like himself, whom in his life he looked upon with joy and at death, without grief. He has left behind him an avenger against his enemies, and one to repay the kindness of his friends" (30:4–6).

The perpetuity of one's name and offspring is straight out of the tradition, but Ben Sira still shows a gloom over death which is not. Death is not the radical aporia for him that is for Qoheleth, but it does appear to weigh on his mind in a way that one does not find in Proverbs, for example. The children of Adam bear a heavy yoke, because they fret over death (40:1–2, above). This is a new idea for a Jewish text. Unlike Qoheleth, however, Ben Sira struggles to reconcile this view with the tradition.

Many other writers of the time were confronting death from an entirely different angle, particularly those who had an apocalyptic worldview. Within the canon, the only example of such a work is Daniel. Its most relevant passage occurs in chapter 12, where the angel states that at the end of the age "many of those who sleep in the dust of the earth shall awake, some to everlasting life, and some to shame and everlasting contempt. Those who are wise shall shine like the brightness of the sky, and those who lead many to righteousness, like the stars forever and ever" (12:2–3). The date of the visions of Daniel, chapters 7–12, is 167–163 BCE, during the time of uprising and persecution under Antiochus Epiphanes.[4] The assurance that the righteous dead will receive their reward makes sense in a period of war and calamity, when many Jews had paid the ultimate price in the revolution. The idea of the righteous receiving vindication after death appears also in I Enoch 22. Here Enoch is shown the place where the spirits of the dead are kept until the time of judgment.[5] I Enoch 104, which may be older than Daniel,[6] says that Enoch will "shine like the lights of heaven" and join the heavenly host (104:2). This last is quite similar in conception to Daniel 12:3. As in Daniel, the individual does not appear to be resurrected in the body, but

---

[4] John J. Collins, *Daniel* (Minneapolis: Fortress Press, 1993) 61.

[5] See also chapter 27, in which Enoch sees where the wicked await their judgment in the last days. In chapter 91, "the righteous one shall arise from his sleep, and the wise one shall arise" (91:10), as in chapter 93.

[6] Collins, *Daniel*, 396.

to be raised in a spirit state among the angels. Yet another example of non-physical resurrection appears in the mid-second century book of Jubilees.[7] In 23:31 it is said of the righteous that "their bones will rest in the earth and their spirits will increase in joy."

In other texts, survival after death is emphatically in embodied form. 2 Maccabees 7 is the star example. Here all seven sons and their mother gladly accept martyrdom, confident that God will raise them "to an everlasting renewal of life" (7:9). That their bodies will be restored to them is made clear. One brother says of his hands "I got these from Heaven, and because of his laws I disdain them, and from him I hope to get them back again" (7:11).[8]

The approaches of the second century BCE continued to be developed and modified in the subsequent centuries. The Wisdom of Solomon shows the range of responses to death that can be found within the genre of wisdom literature. This is a late work, and the likeliest date for the book is the first century CE, though it has been placed as far back

---

[7] On the date of Jubilees see O. S. Wintermute in James H. Charlesworth., ed. *The Old Testament Pseudepigrapha*, Vol. II (New York: Doubleday & Company, 1983) 44. The collection of the later Qumran writings is a debated case when it comes to the question of the physicality of the post-mortem existence. Physical resurrection is scantily attested at best, although retribution after death and eternal life for the righteous in general is without doubt. The Community Rule, column 4, promises everlasting life for the children of light and eternal torment for the children of darkness. The Qumran sect appears to express its hopes for continuing life in terms of participating in an angelic life in the present, which would continue after death. In the War Rule and the rule books, there is at least partial co-mingling with the angels before death. The Hodayot in particular support such a view.

[8] See also the Testaments of the Twelve Patriarchs, which comprises a combination of Jewish and Christian material with the Jewish perhaps dating to the second century BCE; on the dating cf. John J. Collins, *Between Athens and Jerusalem: Jewish Identity in the Hellenistic Diaspora* (New York: Crossroad, 1983) 155–56; and John J. Collins, *The Apocalyptic Imagination: An Introduction to the Jewish Matrix of Christianity* (New York: Crossroad, 1989) 107. The work contains a repeated pattern of future predictions which tend to include resurrection of the dead, along with appearances of the cosmic foe Beliar and a messiah; see Collins, *The Apocalyptic Imagination*, 110. Cf. especially T. Judah 25, T. Benjamin 10:6–10, T. Zebulun 10:1–4, T. Simeon 6:7, and by implication, T. Levi 18:10–14, in ibid., 236 note 96.

as the third century BCE.[9] The two most striking statements Pseudo-Solomon utters about death are quite straightforward. He says,

> "...God did not make death, and he does not delight in the death of the living. For he created all things so that they might exist; the generative forces[10] of the world are wholesome, and there is no destructive poison in them, and the dominion[11] of Hades is not on earth. For righteousness is immortal" (1:13–15).

Later one learns that

> "God created us for incorruption, and made us in the image of his own eternity,[12] but through the devil's envy death entered the universe, and those who belong to his company experience it" (2:23–24).

These sorts of assertions paint a dualistic picture of the world by claiming that death was never meant to be part of the human experience and never would have been if not for the devil's envy. Furthermore, only those who follow the devil actually experience death even now. The ungodly wrongly believe (like Qoheleth) that once a person dies that is the end of existence, so one should just enjoy the good things in life while possible (2:1–9). Unlike Qoheleth, they also figure they might as well oppress the righteous in the meantime (2:10–20). But they err in their reasoning, because God will reward the just with eternal life and they will be punished (3:5–10).

The author has no reservations about acknowledging that everyone undergoes the same physical process.[13] His point seems rather to be that this process, for the righteous, is ultimately irrelevant. "The complexity of the notion of death in Wisdom does not lend itself to a fine line of

---

[9] David Winston, *The Wisdom of Solomon* (New York: Doubleday, 1979) 20–23.

[10] Or *the creatures*.

[11] Or *palace*.

[12] Other ancient authorities read nature.

[13] In his speech on wisdom, Pseudo-Solomon says "there is for all one entrance into life, and one way out" (7:6), and he describes man by nature as "weak and short-lived" (9:5). See also where he says of the race that "after a little while [they] go to the earth from which all mortals were taken" when their borrowed souls return whence they came (15:8). Fools do not grasp the fact "that mortals are destined to die or that their life is brief" (15:9).

demarcation between physical and spiritual death."[14] The key to attaining immortality is virtue. Better than raising wicked offspring is "childlessness with virtue, for in the memory of virtue is immortality" (4:1).[15] Life and death, then, are determined by virtue, virtue which in its own right is eternal and confers eternal life by varying means on its practitioners, both through preservation of the soul and of the individual's memory on earth (cf. 8:13).[16]

In this wisdom text, death has definitely become an issue that needs to be addressed, more so than for Ben Sira, an example of the genre that appears between this book and Qoheleth. The Wisdom of Solomon also takes a dualistic view of the cosmos, where death was not even meant to be a part of the world, which is unlike Ben Sira as well. The latter is traditional in that it offers no extension of life beyond death, as the Wisdom of Solomon does. Part of the difference may lie in the circumstances of the time; Wisdom of Solomon appears to be addressing a particular problem in which the righteous are being martyred by an unnamed foe. Ben Sira finds the thought of death oppressive, but still tries to work within a traditional scheme. In this regard he backs off from the new boundaries Qoheleth establishes. Wisdom of Solomon, on the other hand, takes a sharp step beyond the tradition, but his step is different from Qoheleth's. He turns to a post-mortem existence for a solution to the problem of death. But for all these differences the three books still share something in common. Each takes a general wisdom approach in its mode of discourse, in that none appeal to law, prophetic inspiration, or apocalyptic revelation. They all are trying to deal with death in their own, non-revelatory, fashion.

By Wisdom of Solomon's time, presumably the first century CE, other types of texts are addressing the question of the very existence of death, even treat it as a kind of personal adversary. For these books, the

---

[14] Michael Kolarcik, *The Ambiguity of Death in the Book of Wisdom 1–6* (Rome: Pontifical Biblical Institute, 1991) 151.

[15] Righteousness is immortal (1:15). Solomon declares wisdom to be the ground of righteousness and the virtues (8:7), going on to say that because of wisdom "I shall have immortality" (8:13, cf. also 8:17).

[16] Gerhard Von Rad, *Wisdom in Israel* (Nashville: Abingdon Press, 1972) 305, remarks that death in the Jewish tradition only becomes a real problem which demands attention when confidence in the world's regulation begins to fail, and that the Wisdom of Solomon is the first wisdom book to handle the difficulty by removing death from God's plan.

problem is heightened yet one more degree as death itself takes center stage. A good example is the Testament of Abraham, which despite redactional activity and copying by Christian scribes is a Jewish work that perhaps dates to around 100 CE.[17] The story is that Abraham's time to die has come. "But even to him came the common and inexorable bitter cup of death and the unforeseen end of life" (1:3). God sends the archangel Michael to fetch him, but Abraham does not want to go, that is, to die, and he requests a revelation, which he gets in the form of a chariot ride all over the world. Sixteen chapters later the ride is over, but Abraham still refuses to come with Michael, so God sends Death. At Abraham's urging Death reveals his true form, "and he put on (his) robe of tyranny, and he made his appearance gloomy and more ferocious than any kind of wild beast and more unclean than any uncleanness....(17:13). Finally Death tricks Abraham into dying, and the angels come and take his soul to paradise where there is "endless life" (20:15). The text itself is actually somewhat humorous, but the subject matter is serious. Death is a horrible monster who ravages the world and whom someone as righteous and obedient as Abraham wants to avoid at all costs. This tale contrasts sharply with the biblical account of Abraham's death in Genesis 25:8–10, where he simply breathes his last and dies in a good old age. That death should be the focus of interest in this fashion for a Jewish writing is a far cry from the older Israelite traditions.

4 Ezra may be the biggest standout on the matter of death. The book is a Jewish apocalypse probably written about the same time as the Testament of Abraham in the late first century CE.[18] Ezra reflects on Adam, whose transgression in the garden was the beginning of the world's troubles, since "immediately you [God] appointed death for him and for his descendants" (3:7). The evil heart in Adam remained in all his offspring, who fill the world with woe (3:20–22). And yet, "you endure those who sin, and have spared those who act wickedly... and have not shown to anyone how your way may be comprehended" (3:30–31). This is essentially what Qoheleth says too. It would have been better if the dust from which the first human was made had itself not been born, because with existence comes sentience (7:63). "But now the mind grows with us,

---

[17] E. P. Sanders, "Testament of Abraham," in James H. Charlesworth., ed. *The Old Testament Pseudepigrapha*, Vol. I (New York: Doubleday & Company, 1983) 875.

[18] Collins, *The Apocalyptic Imagination*, 156.

and therefore we are tormented, *because we perish and we know it*" (7:64). For this reason the animals are better off than humanity because they have no such knowledge (7:65–66). The angel does not really answer these points, and instead turns Ezra's attention to the future age and away from the present world, which is winding down. He does say, however, that for Ezra himself and the few other righteous ones in the world, evil, illness, death, and Hades are fled and immortality awaits (8:51–54).[19] The gist of the advice to the audience is to turn away from mortal life and look to the judgment in the hereafter (14:14–15, 35).[20] The depth of Ezra's despair over suffering and human mortality is striking.

Conclusion

Even this brief survey shows that Qoheleth was in the vanguard of a phenomenon in which the older biblical approach to death was no longer felt to be sufficient. Qoheleth himself regards it as a breach in the framework of coherence supplied by his traditions, but he has no real solution to the problem. All he can do is advise the reader to make the most of a bad situation, and with luck, maybe pleasure can be wrested from the present. By the second century the concern with death is blossoming. Ben Sira is uneasy about death at times, at other times resigned, and does his best to defend the standard, deuteronomic view of the world. A number of the apocalypses which began appearing on the scene soon after Ben Sira simply claim that God will judge everyone after death or at the end of the age and that all the injustices of mortal experience will be righted. Sometimes a bodily resurrection will be the means of preserving the life of the just, sometimes the spirit will live forever. Interestingly, the apocalypses reject the empirical epistemology of Qoheleth. Their solution, they readily admit, is not something to be

---

[19] Part of this scenario includes a resurrection after the destruction of humanity, though here persecution is no longer the problem as it was in the case of Daniel 12 and 2 Maccabees 7. George W. E. Nickelsburg, *Resurrection, Immortality, and Eternal Life in Intertestamental Judaism* (Cambridge: Harvard University Press, 1972) 172, observes that "resurrection of the body has become a formalized *topos*, cut off from the *ad hoc* interpretation of scripture that motivated it in Daniel 12 and the specific theological problem to which it is addressed in 2 Maccabees 7." He adds that late texts overall "generalize the scope of resurrection" from specific cases of persecution to reward or retribution on a broad level "unrelated to one's former lot in life" (173).

[20] Collins, *The Apocalyptic Imagination*, 168.

attained without a heavenly revelation. These texts thereby neatly neutralize the problem which faces Qoheleth, that his eyes are giving him bleak data and bleaker conclusions.

After the turn of the millennium, the Wisdom of Solomon comes right out and assures its readers that the righteous live in an exalted state after their deaths, but it does not appeal to revelation in the manner of an apocalypse or anticipate an imminent and radical new order or re-creation. The book is concerned to defend the goodness of God's creation, so does not look for the cosmic cataclysms that the apocalypses await. It just declares that death is the devil's fault and is not even truly real for the righteous. In a sense, it denies death altogether, or at least denies it with respect to one portion of the population. In this same time, the Testament of Abraham and 4 Ezra in particular agonize over death. The former conveys the consoling message that God is merciful and death for the just leads to paradise. The latter also proclaims that the righteous will be given immortality, but their numbers are so few that the comfort is rather limited. Ezra's cry that "we are tormented, because we perish and we know it" (7:64) is particularly poignant, and epitomizes Qoheleth's state of mind.

It seems apparent that in the final centuries BCE older models for approaching religious questions in Israel such as death were breaking down, and that religious thinkers were confronting the new situation in a variety of ways. Qoheleth is one of the first, among those writings that have survived, to face the question. His response is not a comforting one, but he remained true to what he saw in the world, and expressed himself with great power and beauty. The question that naturally arises in the mind of Qoheleth's reader is what has lead to his grim analysis of life and fixation on death? The book stands out from earlier Jewish tradition so markedly in this respect that one wants to know why. One possible answer of course is simply that the author was an anomaly, that he had an unhappy life or a gloomy temperament, and that there is no other explanation beyond individual peculiarity. The "anomaly" explanation, however, is blunted by the fact that the book was accepted into the canon, which suggests that it struck a chord with a number of people who must have shared similar feelings, and also by the ensuing developments in subsequent Jewish writings, as discussed above. The most common approach to the question is that Qoheleth was influenced by the writings or thought of another culture. Although the star candidate for this influence is Greece, scholars have looked to Babylon and Egypt as well. None of the attempts to find foreign causes for Qoheleth's thought are ultimately persuasive, but because they are an important part of the scholarship they should be investigated.

FOREIGN INFLUENCE

Egyptian and Babylonian

Humbert is the person best known to have defended the theory of Egyptian influence on the book. He argues that Greek influence is not convincing but states that Qoheleth definitely had stayed in Egypt.[21] Similarities he points to between Qoheleth and various Egyptian works include royal authorship, a dialogue with one's heart, pessimism, carpe diem advice, references to female singers, ideas of the time and season, social injustice, counsel to keep one's words few when in worship, reversal of social positions, and the description of old age.[22] This Egyptian influence is what explains the fact that Qoheleth's themes are un-Jewish.[23]

Others have turned to Babylonian traditions. Barton feels that Qoheleth 9:7–9 was possibly a translation in part of Siduri's advice to Gilgamesh in the "Epic of Gilgamesh."[24] Oswald Loretz, the key defender of Mesopotamian influences on Qoheleth, specifically rejects the Egyptian hypothesis,[25] and argues that Qoheleth also did not use Greek expressions or even more generally draw from Greek philosophy, either.[26] He favors Babylonian influence,[27] essentially agreeing with Barton on passages like 9:7–8, and adding further suggestions, such as the comparison of Qoheleth's idea of "hebel" to Gilgamesh's remark that everything one does is "wind."[28] Lauha also remarks on some of the

---

[21] Paul Humbert, *Recherches sur les Sources Égyptiennes de la Littérature Sapientale d'Israel* (Neuchatel: Delachaux & Niestlé, 1929) 124.

[22] Humbert, *Recherches sur les Sources Égyptiennes*, 107–24.

[23] Humbert, *Recherches sur les Sources Égyptiennes*, 124.

[24] George Barton, *The Book of Ecclesiastes* (New York: Charles Scribner's Sons, 1908) 39.

[25] Oswald Loretz, *Qohelet und der alte Orient: Untersuchungen zu Stil und theologischer Thematik des Buches Qohelet* (Freiburg: Herder, 1964) 57–89.

[26] Loretz, *Qohelet und der alte Orient*, 45–57.

[27] Loretz, *Qohelet und der alte Orient*, 90–134.

[28] Loretz, *Qohelet und der alte Orient*, 126–28.

similarities in thought and tone between Gilgamesh and Qoheleth, though he stops short of positing a direct connection between the two.[29] The reigning explanation for the book's worldview, however, has been that Qoheleth was influenced, more or less directly, by the Greeks. The details of this theory have varied from one scholar to another. Sometimes Qoheleth is thought to have read specific texts, or to have been influenced by philosophical schools, or to have acquired his Greek ideas through more indirect methods. The hypothesis is so pervasive in the scholarship,[30] and the question so central, that it is worth looking at its progress to see how the theory is formulated and the ups and downs of its existence throughout the decades.

Greek Influence

The first to tender the proposition that Qoheleth reflects Greek thought were van der Palm in 1784 and Zirkel in 1792.[31] The idea became a commonplace of Qoheleth scholarship, which took a two-pronged approach to the issue, a search for Greek influence on the language and on the thought of the text.[32] Zirkel was followed by Hitzig (1847), Kleinert (1864), Tyler (1874), Plumptre (1881), Pfleiderer (1886), Siegfried (1898), and Haupt (1905).[33] Renan (1882) and McNeile (1904) stood on the opposite side of the fence and insisted that the content of Qoheleth was strictly Semitic.[34] They were supported by Barton (1908)

---

[29] Aarre Lauha, *Kohelet* (Neukirchener Verlag: Neukirchen Vluyn, 1978) 12–14.

[30] James L. Crenshaw, *Ecclesiastes: A Commentary* (Philadelphia: The Westminster Press, 1987) 51, writes "the question of the extent of exposure to Greek thought affects every interpretation of the book."

[31] J. van der Palm, *Ecclesiastes philologice et critice illustratus* (Leyden, 1784), and G. Zirkel, *Untersuchungen über den Prediger mit philosophischen und kritischen Bermerkungen* (Würzburg, 1792). Cf. Sheldon Blank, "Prolegomenon" to Christian D. Ginsburg, *The Song of Songs and Coheleth (Commonly Called the Book of Ecclesiastes)* (reprinted New York: Ktav Publishing House, 1970) xix, and George A. Barton, *The Book of Ecclesiastes* (New York: Charles Scribner's Sons, 1908) 23, for discussion.

[32] Charles G. Forman, "The Pessimism of Ecclesiastes," *Journal of Semitic Studies* 3(1958) 336–37.

[33] Cf. Barton, *The Book of Ecclesiastes*, 23–24.

[34] Barton, *The Book of Ecclesiastes*, 34. A.H. McNeile, *An Introduction to Ecclesiastes* (Cambridge: Cambridge University Press, 1904) 44, remarks that with respect to the question of Stoic influence, Zeno was of Phoenician origin and his

who agreed that Qoheleth was independent of Greek influences.[35] Hertzberg (1932) noticed a number of parallels with various Greek, Babylonian, and Egyptian works, but concluded that these parallels demonstrated simply that some ideas are common to many cultures.[36] Yet the search for examples of and sources for a Greek background to the book seemed to have caught the scholarly imagination, because in spite of occasional voices of disagreement, this is the trend that remained dominant.[37]

Ranston especially made determined efforts in the 1920's to establish the theory once and for all. His conclusion about the author of Qoheleth was that "at heart he is more Greek than Jew."[38] More specifically, he argued that Hesiod and Theognis were Qoheleth's particular sources, as opposed to the abstract philosophers.[39] In a number of places he felt Qoheleth must be taking individual aphorisms from one of the two Greek authors. For example, in 6:9 Qoheleth says "better is the sight of the eyes than the roaming of desire." Hesiod's *Works and Days*

---

followers came from Syria and Carthage, among other places. Stoicism is Semitic in root, then, which in itself explains similarities to other Semitic works like Ecclesiastes.

[35] Cf. Barton, *The Book of Ecclesiastes*, 43. He writes that the book is "an original development of Hebrew thought, thoroughly Semitic in its point of view, and quite independent of Greek influence."

[36] H. W. Hertzberg, *Der Prediger* (Leipzig: A. Deichertsche Verlagsbuchhandlung D. Werner Scholl, 1932; Gütersloh: G. Mohn, 1963) 54, sums up: "Qoh. ist die natürliche Reaktion des scharf beobachtenden und denkenden Menschen gegen die übliche Weisheit. Der Blick in die Umwelt lehrt uns, daß das etwas Typisches ist, daß Skepsis und Aufbegehren, Problematik und Pessimismus urewige Dinge sind, die unter gewissen Gegebenheiten und bei gewissen Persönlichkeiten zu allen Zeiten und unter allen Völkern möglich sind."

[37] Diethelm Michel, *Qohelet* (Darmstadt: Wissenschaftliche Buchgesellschaft, 1988) 59, remarks that since the late nineteenth century "gehört es zur Pflicht eines jeden Auslegers, sich mit dem Problem des hellenistischen Einflusses auf Qohelet auseinanderzusetzen...."

[38] Harry Ranston "Koheleth and the Early Greeks," *The Journal of Theological Studies* 24 (1923) 163.

[39] Cf. Ranston "Koheleth and the Early Greeks," 169: "in view of the many general parallels in idea, and the similarities in language found here and there, the best explanation of the facts seems to be found in some connexion between Koheleth and Hesiod and Theognis, especially the latter." See also his book on the question, *Ecclesiastes and the Early Greek Wisdom Literature* (London: Epworth Press, 1925), where he comes to same conclusion.

366 has "Foolish is he who leaves what he has and pursues what he has not." Further, in both Qoheleth and Hesiod (*Works and Days* 83; *Theogony* 589f.) women are a snare.[40] In 6:10 Qoheleth says [Ranston's translation] "He (man) is not able to contend with Him who is mightier than he." Theognis 687–88 has "'Tis not for mortals to fight with Immortals, or to argue with them." Both authors make remarks on human ignorance, both believe that God treats everyone the same, whether good or evil, neither expects redress after death, success or lack thereof is due to chance for both of them, and each has the same advice, carpe diem. Moreover, Qoheleth repeatedly uses the phrase "under the sun," which probably comes from the Greek ὑφ᾽ἡλίω.[41]

The last point, the belief that the Hebrew expression "under the sun" came from a Greek phrase, was a common feature of the argument for Greek influence in the lingusitic sphere, probably the strongest one, but the same phrase was later found in two Phoenician inscriptions, and then in Elamite, which fairly soundly proved that the expression existed in semitic circles on its own.[42] The other points of contact that Ranston offers are all quite general, on the order of broad observations about the world which could quite plausibly arise independently of one another, and with nothing in the specific phrasing or arrangement of the statements to suggest the influence of the Greek material on Qoheleth. However, Ranston's arguments reinforced the power of the Greek hypothesis in Qoheleth scholarship. By 1934 Pfeiffer wrote "It is hardly conceivable that Ecclesiastes would have lost his assurance in the validity of the Jewish faith, worship and rule of conduct, unless he had come into

---

[40] Ranston "Koheleth and the Early Greeks," 160.

[41] See Ranston "Koheleth and the Early Greeks," 161–68, for further details of the argument.

[42] Forman, "The Pessimism of Ecclesiastes," 337, sets the Phoenician inscriptions in the third century BCE. Charles F. Whitley, *Koheleth: His Language and Thought* (Berlin, New York: Walter de Gruyter, 1979) 8, sets them in the sixth century (Tabnit) and fifth century (Eshmunazar). He says that the Elamite documents date to the twelfth century. He adds further that Qoheleth also uses the similar phrase תחת השמים which appears elsewhere in the Hebrew Bible. Most recently, C.L. Seow, "Linguistic Evidence and the Dating of Qohelet," *Journal of Biblical Literature* 115(1996) 657–58, dates both Phoenician inscriptions to the fifth century.

contact, more or less indirectly, with Greek thought."[43] This forthright statement is very revealing. It leads one to wonder whether the real driving force of at least some of the effort to find Greek influence in Qoheleth has not been the assumption that surely a Jew, left to his own devices, would never come up with such "unorthodox" observations about the world.

Even those who have been cautious about finding specific sources of influence tend to be drawn in that general direction by the force of gravity the idea exerts, and one observes with interest how this happens. Gordis writes in his fine commentary (1955) that the fact that Qoheleth shows similarities to some ideas in Greek writings merely demonstrates that "similar material conditions in different societies will produce similar spiritual and intellectual tendencies, *mutatis mutandis*."[44] This is certainly a circumspect enough position to take. Later, he states that there is no evidence Qoheleth knew Greek or that he was a student of any Greek philosophical school, but that "Greek culture was an aggressive worldview," that the region of Israel was susceptible to Greek influences through both Syria and Egypt, and that it would be strange if Qoheleth were entirely isolated from Greek ideas. What interests him is not so much that the author would be familiar with popular ideas from Greek philosophy, "but his *completely original and independent use of these ideas to express his own unique world-view* [author's italics]...."[45] By the

---

[43] Robert H. Pfeiffer, "The Peculiar Skepticism of Ecclesiastes," *Journal of Biblical Literature* 53(1934) 109. Another scholar states it thus: "The way he conducts the debate shows Qoheleth to be a thinker of great individuality, whose spiritual attitude one might want to make intelligible by reference to Greek spirituality." He then continues, "But, repeated attempts to prove conclusively a Greek source for Ecclesiastes have not yet succeeded." Cf. Ernst Würthwein, "Egyptian Wisdom and the Old Testament," trans. Brian W. Kovacs, in James L. Crenshaw, ed., *Studies in Ancient Israelite Wisdom* (New York: Ktav Publishing House, 1976) 128.

[44] Robert Gordis, *Koheleth—The Man and His World* (New York: Bloch Publishing Company, 1955) 29.

[45] Gordis, *Koheleth—The Man and His World*, 56. The more one thinks about this statement the more intriguing it becomes. On the one hand Gordis is making the claim that Qoheleth is using ideas formulated by an outside culture, yet notice the emphatic repetition of the adjectives, "completely original," "independent," and "unique," not to mention the italics. What exactly does it mean to say someone uses another person's/school's/culture's concept or worldview in a *completely original, unique and independent* way? If the idea comes from another

time he gets to the discussion of date, he offers a variety of plausible reasons why the text's latest date would be the mid-third century BCE. Then he adds "nor can its date be much earlier, since time must be allowed for the penetration of Greek ideas into Jewish Palestine."[46] This is an interesting progression to observe in the commentary. First there seems to be no claim for Greek and Semitic interaction, then an acceptance of influence on a very broad level, and finally a belief that the influence of Greek thought on Qoheleth is certain enough to require judgments of date on that basis.

Similar ambiguity appears in Hengel's discussion of Qoheleth (1974).[47] He starts out by expressing caution about the typical treatment of the text. Although scholars may claim the book is essentially unoriental, he says "we should not lay excessive emphasis on the contrast between 'Greek' and 'oriental' which is made here and suppose any dependence on the part of Koheleth." He immediately adds, "The intellectual revolution with which the third century began made more room for new, independent beginnings of thought, though movement in this direction had already begun in the Persian period."[48] Yet he later has come around to saying that Qoheleth became acquainted with Greek criticism of religion through Ptolemaic officials, merchants, and soldiers.[49] Under the impact of the spiritual crisis taking place in the

---

source, then by definition, even if one puts a personal spin on it, it cannot be entirely original, unique, or independent. This is a contradiction in terms, and probably reflects Gordis's ambivalence about the claim. He really seems to think that Qoheleth is a work that does not need explanation from other sources, yet accepts that there is Greek coloring of some degree as a kind of unavoidable universal truth.

[46] Gordis, *Koheleth—The Man and His World*, 67.

[47] Martin Hengel, *Judaism and Hellenism: Studies in their Encounter in Palestine during the Early Hellenistic Period*, 2 Vols. (Philadelphia: Fortress, 1974).

[48] Hengel, *Judaism and Hellenism*, 117–118. Somewhat earlier he writes that Qoheleth could hardly have shut himself off from the spirit of the times, but that the attempts to enumerate parallels are not successful, since they are too disparate, and since wisdom literature is so universal by nature that the existence of shared themes between cultures says nothing of the origins of those themes (116).

[49] Hengel, *Judaism and Hellenism*, 125. He further adds "In a completely individualistic way he fused stimuli from this direction with traditional 'wisdom' and his own observations" (125). One notes with interest that he uses the same language as Gordis, in that Qoheleth is taking Greek ideas yet is "completely individualistic." See footnote #45.

Hellenic world, Qoheleth could "no longer make sense of traditional wisdom and, consequently, of traditional piety and the cult," yet he was too conservative to break from his ancestral religion.[50]

Hengel briefly summarizes in a later work (1984) his view of the book, which seems to have evolved somewhat.[51] "The spirit of the new era, and even direct influence of Greek thought" is to be found in the Jewish text. "מקרה" and "חלק" "remind us of the Greek *moira* and *tyche*." Other items he cites are "הבל" ("typhos"), "עשה טוב" ("eu prattein" or "eu dran"), and "טוב אשר יפה" ("kalos kagathos" or "to kalon philon"). The stress on time as destiny is paralleled in Greek literature, as is the impersonal notion of God, reserve toward cultic activities, absence of Jewish history and law, the concept of fate, carpe diem advice, and the belief that after death the breath goes upwards. "A comparison with the Greek gnomic traditions shows that Ecclesiastes must have been conversant with it," either in oral or written form. "For nearly every verse parallels can be cited from Greek poetry and popular philosophy."[52]

---

[50] Hengel, *Judaism and Hellenism*, 127. He also says in a later essay ("The Political and Social History of Palestine from Alexander to Antiochus III (333–187 B.C.E.)," in W. D. Davies and Louis Finkelstein, eds., *The Cambridge History of Judaism*, Vol. I [Cambridge: Cambridge University Press, 1984] 62–63) that the book alludes to a number of specific conditions of the Ptolemaic era. 5:8, which speaks of one official being watched by a higher one, refers to the Ptolemaic bureaucracy. 10:20 is about the number of informers in a Hellenistic kingdom. 5:10f. describes how the lover of money will never be satisfied with money, which is about Hellenistic-oriental managers. A postscript to 5:8 (a text he admits is uncertain of translation) "clearly refers to the interest of the Ptolemies in increasing the return in agriculture." However, as these verses do not seem to contain anything specifically pointing to Ptolemaic adminstrators, such as technical terms or references to offices that existed only at this time, such specificity is not persuasive. The book may be from the period of Ptolemaic rule in Judea, but official bureaucracies, informers, and greed are features common to many eras and societies. The final citation in 5:8 is too garbled to draw any conclusions.

[51] Martin Hengel, "The Interpenetration of Judaism and Hellenism in the Pre-Maccabean Period," in W. D. Davies and Louis Finkelstein, eds., *The Cambridge History of Judaism*, Vol. I (Cambridge: Cambridge University Press, 1984) 222–23.

[52] Hengel, "The Interpenetration of Judaism and Hellenism in the Pre-Maccabean Period," 223, adds here "But it must be emphasized that Ecclesiastes combined in a highly original and artistically accomplished way" the Greek ideas with traditional Jewish teaching.

The reader sees here the same kind of evolution of thought as before, from a rejection of the theory that Qoheleth depends on Greek conceptions to a tacit conclusion that such is the case, and finally an outright acceptance of it. Inherent in the idea is that Qoheleth's traditional piety was nullified by exposure to Greek beliefs. Yet such an assumption does not carry a compelling internal logic. Pace Hengel, why should exposure to a *Greek* spiritual crisis necessarily have any bearing whatsoever on Qoheleth's attitudes toward his own *Jewish* religiosity? While it is no doubt the case that the Jews were not living their lives in isolation from the Greek power structures, this does not therefore mean that Jewish thinkers necessarily echoed Greek intellectual movements, or that Jews were even always particularly interested in Hellenic thought. Specific points of contact between the text of Qoheleth and Greek writings, philosophy, or worldview would at least provide some evidence that Qoheleth's beliefs had been undermined by a Greek crisis, but Hengel at first openly acknowledges that such parallels are general and prove nothing about origins. His later listing of parallels are, as such lists tend to be, general in scope and do not demonstrate that Greek material must be the source.[53] Some of the features in fact, such as the reticence Qoheleth shows toward the cult, and the absence of Jewish history and law in the text, are typical of the wisdom genre. Nevertheless, the assumption of Greek influence has a powerful hold on the scholarly imagination, and has been hard to resist.[54]

---

[53] See footnote #48 where Hengel himself had earlier opined that parallel lists prove nothing in particular.

[54] Another example of the power of the idea appears in Peter Machinist, "Fate, *miqreh*, and Reason: Some Reflections on Qohelet and Biblical Thought," in Ziony Zevit, Seymour Gitin, Michael Sokoloff, eds., *Solving Riddles and Untying Knots: Biblical, Epigraphic, and Semitic Studies in Honor of Jonas C. Greenfield* (Winona Lake, IN: Eisenbrauns, 1995). In this article the author convincingly demonstrates that the Hebrew Bible provides passages which form a semantic tradition from which Qoheleth could extract his usage of "miqreh," in the sense of an event which happens to people while being beyond their ability to predict, comprehend, or control. The new feature Qoheleth provides is the equation of miqreh specifically with death, which creates a more abstract notion of the word (170). Near the end of the article, the author points out that native Hebrew tradition was discussing the issue long before the Hellenistic period, and that Qoheleth is heir to that discussion. Moreover, the term is not equivalent to any of the Greek words for fate (heimarmene, tyche, or moira). Nevertheless, although we must be circumspect, "the [Greek/Hellenistic] influence may reside not so much in the use

Braun's study (1973), more or less contemporaneous with Hengel's *Judaism and Hellenism*, is entirely devoted to trying to demonstrate the effect of Greek material on Qoheleth.[55] He argues that Greek pessimistic themes appear in the text and definitely must be the book's source. Most parallels come from Homer, Theognis, Euripides, and Menander, which shows that Qoheleth reflects the sentiments of his surrounding environment in that he was confident in the thought found in these Greek writings.[56] He makes a number of observations about the book which are valid, such as the fact that Qoheleth ponders the situation of a person as an individual instead of as a member of a people, and that his idea of God is a distant, impersonal one, which is not typical of the rest of the Hebrew Bible. He then concludes that Qoheleth took over Greek thought and teaching and gave it Hebraic formulation.[57] This statement is stronger than scholars such as Gordis and Hengel make, though differs only in degree, not in kind. Braun's analysis implies that the book would not exist without the Greek material that underlies it. Qoheleth's contribution is one of style, not content.[58]

Occasionally recent commentators have demurred from the general push to explain Qoheleth in terms of Greek influences. Lauha (1978) points out that while Qoheleth has some general similarities with Stoic, Epicurean, and gnomic writings or philosophical schools, in each case there are a number of differences that separate the Jewish work from the

---

of *miqreh* for fate per se, as in the ability to write about *miqreh* in a way that indicates both a rational process at work and, even more, a reflection on what rationality consists of" (174). If Qoheleth is already building on Hebrew tradition, cannot a Jew also reflect independently on rationality? The preceding argument suggests that outside influence is not necessary to explain Qoheleth's observations on miqreh, yet here it is.

[55] Rainer Braun, *Kohelet und die frühhellenistische Popularphilosophie* (Berlin: Walter de Gruyter, 1973).

[56] Braun, *Kohelet und die frühhellenistische Popularphilosophie*, 149–150.

[57] Braun, *Kohelet und die frühhellenistische Popularphilosophie*, 170. As he puts it, "ihr Denken und ihre Lehren übernahm und in seiner Lehrschrift hebraisch formulierte."

[58] James L. Crenshaw, ed., *Studies in Ancient Israelite Wisdom* (New York: Ktav Publishing House, 1976) 8, says that the urge to demonstrate Greek influence on Qoheleth has finally lost its momentum, though he adds in a footnote that Braun may reopen the whole question. Considering the fact that the recent commentaries still discuss the question and give some measure of credence to the theory, Crenshaw's footnote would seem to be correct.

thought-worlds of the Greek writings.[59] Stoic pantheism, optimism, and apathy towards the interplay of life and death are quite different from Qoheleth. The book's only real similarity with Epicureanism is the shared attitudes toward pleasure. Qoheleth holds some ideas in common with Theognis, but lacks other central points which appear in the Greek composition. Although Qoheleth might have known a number of Greek authors or texts, "eine direkte Abhängigkeit von griechischen Einflüssen bleibt unbewiesen. Die Problematik Kohelets ist nicht griechisch, sondern orientalisch."[60]

Loader (1979) takes a somewhat unusual approach. He is one of the few people who sets Qoheleth in its religio-historical situation, and he concludes that, like other Jews after the Exile, Qoheleth regarded God as a distant deity; the tensions in the book are to be explained by this fact, rather than "the acceptance of influence of Greek philosophy."[61] Thus, he regards Braun's thesis as unpersuasive in this matter. However, he also says that this does not mean that there is no Greek influence on Qoheleth. There certainly is, but it does not explain the polarity of the book, which "is to be found in the religio-historical development of Judaism."[62] He thinks such influence is probably there, "but this is not a fundamental argument."[63] He concludes that efforts to explain Qoheleth's uniqueness through Greek influence should cease; similarities do not prove that Qoheleth has borrowed.[64]

That same year, however, Whitley (1979) testifies to the continuing power of the majority trend with his discussion of Greek influences on the book.[65] Epicurus treats the deity as a being remote from the world, which is similar to Qoheleth's own view. The former also

---

[59] Lauha, *Kohelet*, 11.

[60] Lauha, *Kohelet*, 11–12.

[61] J. A. Loader, *Polar Structures in the Book of Qoheleth* (Berlin and New York: Walter de Gruyter, 1979) 129.

[62] Loader, *Polar Structures in the Book of Qoheleth*, 130.

[63] Loader, *Polar Structures in the Book of Qoheleth*, 131.

[64] Loader, *Polar Structures in the Book of Qoheleth*, 132.

[65] Charles F. Whitley, *Koheleth: His Language and Thought* (Berlin, New York: Walter de Gruyter, 1979) 146, makes a remark in a chapter which appears before his discussion of Greek parallels that nonetheless provides an interesting insight to his approach. He says that Qoheleth reveals a "negative attitude to Judaism" and "susceptibilities to Hellenic culture." This view seems to be fairly common to a number of scholars, if not explicitly expressed in this way.

believed that death is total extinction, and described it in terms of the body's dissolution and the subsequent release of the soul which then also disperses. These ideas probably influenced Qoheleth as well. Another parallel is the Epicurean notion of achieving pleasure during life.[66] With respect to Stoicism, the Jewish author probably is thinking of the Stoic idea of the cyclical creation and destruction of nature when he observes in 3:15 that all that is has been already. On the other hand, Qoheleth questions the Stoic doctrine of the world's moral governance.[67] Hesiod's view that life is a struggle and full of toil is likely the basis for the concept of "hebel" in the book. Homer, Theognis, Sophocles, Pindar, Menander, and Euripides all offer grim observations about the suffering of life and often suggest that the shorter life is the better.[68] Whitley concludes that there is no evidence for literary dependence on the literature to which Qoheleth shows similarity, whether Greek, Egyptian, or Babylonian, but "it may be that he consulted certain sources and presented their substance in his own words, or again such material may have been current in oral form in the intellectual world of his day."[69]

The following year (1980) Lohfink in his commentary adds additional arguments to the Greek hypothesis.[70] In form the book of Qoheleth is a palindrome, in content a diatribe. Among various Greek sources for Qoheleth are the Cynics, Epicureans, Satirics, Menander, Euripides, Homer, Hegesias, Pindar, Archilochos, Diogenes Laertius, Simonides, and Theognis.

Subsequent to these publications (1986), J. G. Gammie writes that it "may be established that Qoheleth did not remain unaffected by the

---

[66] Whitley, *Koheleth: His Language and Thought*, 166–69.

[67] Whitley, *Koheleth: His Language and Thought*, 170–71.

[68] Whitley, *Koheleth: His Language and Thought*, 173–74.

[69] Whitley, *Koheleth: His Language and Thought*, 183. The author earlier sums up his response to others who have argued for Egyptian influence on Qoheleth and although he feels the parallels are relevant, he adds that the assumption of "exclusive" influence of the Egyptian material on Qoheleth is weakened by the fact that similar parallels can be found in Babylonian and Greek literature (156). This is fair enough, yet he goes on to speak as if the Greek parallels are examples of actual influence, which according to his own argument is a conclusion weakened by the existence of parallels in other literatures.

[70] Norbert Lohfink, *Kohelet* (Wurzburg: Echter Verlag, 1980). See James Crenshaw, "Qoheleth in Current Research," in Reuben Ahroni, ed., *Hebrew Annual Review, Vol. 7: Biblical and Other Studies in Honor of Robert Gordis* (Ohio: Ohio State University, 1983) 49–50, for his analysis of Lohfink's argument.

gnomic utterances of the Greeks (especially those of Hesiod and
Theognis), by Greek philosophical discussion (especially that of the
Skeptics and Cynics) and by Greek attitudes toward nature (especially
those of the Stoics)."[71] Gammie is not incorrect in his assessment of the
scholarship, and he moves on to add his own observations on the relation
between Qoheleth and the Greeks. He notes that Qoheleth gives attention
to the pain and vexation of life, which is important to the thought of
Epicurus. Both also advise enjoying what one can. Qoheleth shares Greek
philosophical ideas about the world's composition, as he refers in chapter
one to the four primal elements (earth, fire/sun, air/ruah, and water).[72] The
idea that the generations come and go while the earth remains is close to
a statement Cicero ascribes to the Stoics: "all things both fall back to the
earth and arise from the earth." Events for both Qoheleth and the Stoics
are cyclical. Both make clear distinctions between the wise and foolish,
good and bad. Both consider knowledge of the proper action in a given
situation to be important.[73] Gammie says that Qoheleth may also have
been actively trying to *counter* some Stoic ideas. The closest Greek
parallel to the statement that all is "hebel" comes from the Cynic
philosopher Monimus who said "everything grasped [by humans] is a
delusion ("typhos," or mist)."[74] Another aspect of Qoheleth's deliberate
anti-Stoicism is in his rejection of the Stoic view of death and its
significance.[75]

---

[71] John G. Gammie, "Stoicism and Anti-Stoicism in Qoheleth," in Reuben
Ahroni, ed., *Hebrew Annual Review, Vol. 9: Biblical and Other Studies in Memory
of S. D. Goitein* (Columbus: Ohio State University, 1986) 171.

[72] Gammie, "Stoicism and Anti-Stoicism in Qoheleth," 174.

[73] Gammie, "Stoicism and Anti-Stoicism in Qoheleth," 175–76.

[74] Gammie, "Stoicism and Anti-Stoicism in Qoheleth," 180.

[75] Gammie, "Stoicism and Anti-Stoicism in Qoheleth," 181–85. Differences
between Qoheleth and the Stoics on this topic include the following: for the Stoics,
the code of virtue was so high that in reality no one could fulfill it, while Qoheleth
feels that there are those who can claim to be righteous, and when death cancels out
the real distinctions between righteous and wicked, he has a problem. For the
Stoics, the virtuous man would be praised and remembered after death, which
Qoheleth thought was not true. While the Stoics saw virtue as its own reward and
believed the virtuous man could not, by definition, be unhappy, Qoheleth observed
the righteous suffering, which was not alleviated either in the present or at death.
Finally, unlike the Stoics, Qoheleth could not view events from the point of view of
"the big picture," because human knowledge is curtailed regarding the past and
the future.

Schwienhorst-Schönberger (1994) takes a somewhat more nuanced approach to the question of Greek influence on Qoheleth. Instead of regarding the matter as an either/or situation, he suggests that Qoheleth is in part responding to internal developments in Israelite wisdom, as well as Hellenistic influences.[76] The book's central theme, he feels, is "die Frage nach dem Inhalt und den Bedingungen der Möglichkeit menschlichen Glücks," which is also the concern of Hellenistic philosophy; thus arises the possibility that Qoheleth takes up this theme not only as a question of Israelite wisdom but also in the context of Hellenistic philosophy.[77] Like Lohfink, he believes that the form of the book is best understood as a diatribe, although he also discusses differences between Qoheleth's view of the world and that of Greek philosophical schools, so that Qoheleth retains one foot in his Israelite traditions.[78] He also remarks that he is less interested in simple individual parallels with Greek thought, though these are important, and more intent on seeing how Qoheleth as a whole can be compared with Hellenistic philosophy "in ihrem Grundansatz."[79]

Blenkinsopp (1995), continuing in the direction of Gammie, adds his voice to the argument for the existence of specifically Stoic ideas in the book.[80] His particular focus of investigation is 3:1–15, which he believes comprises a long quotation of another source (vv. 2–8) followed by Qoheleth's commentary on this source (vv. 9–22). The first part of the section does not conform to Qoheleth's own ideas, which is made apparent by his own following comments. Further, Blenkinsopp says that if one follows the literal translation of "laledet" in verse two, which is not "to be born" as most people render it but "to give birth," then the following "lamut" would be left as the only action in the entire set of 28 items in this poem which is not under human control. So to preserve

---

[76] Ludger Schwienhorst-Schönberger, *"Nicht im Menschen Gründet das Glück" (Koh 2,24): Kohelet im Spannungsfeld jüdischer Weisheit und hellenistischer Philosophie* (Freiburg: Herder, 1994) 3.

[77] Schwienhorst-Schönberger, *"Nicht im Menschen Gründet das Glück" (Koh 2,24)*, 246.

[78] Schwienhorst-Schönberger, *"Nicht im Menschen Gründet das Glück" (Koh 2,24)*, 274–332.

[79] Schwienhorst-Schönberger, *"Nicht im Menschen Gründet das Glück" (Koh 2,24)*, 250.

[80] Joseph Blenkinsopp, "Ecclesiastes 3.1–15: Another Interpretation," *Journal for the Study of the Old Testament* 66(1995) 55–64.

consistency, he suggests that the word be translated "to put an end to one's life."[81] This translation further suggests to him the poem may reflect influence from the Stoics, for whom suicide was not an immoral act. The passage could be the work either of a "stoicizing Jewish sage" or a "Stoic composition translated into Hebrew."[82]

These latest arguments offered for Greek influence on Qoheleth are, like those of their predecessors, quite broad and diffuse in nature. An idea from a philosophy here, a phrase from a saying there, are culled together to provide a patchwork of parallels to items in the Jewish text, which items are in many cases well-attested in Hebrew tradition.[83] The separation of the body and ruah at death is a common conception in Hebrew anthropology. The mention of the earth, sun, wind, and the rivers together is nothing out of the ordinary since there was an established tradition of creation theology and reflection on God's world. They certainly do not require the Greek primal elements.[84] More general items, such as recognition that life is bound with suffering and that humans cannot know the ways of God are also attested in earlier wisdom literature, the Psalms, and elsewhere in the Hebrew Bible. Nor has the problem yet been overcome that in these lists of parallels simple similarity proves nothing in itself about origins. The assumption is that

---

[81] Blenkinsopp, "Ecclesiastes 3.1–15: Another Interpretation," 56–57.

[82] Blenkinsopp, "Ecclesiastes 3.1–15: Another Interpretation," 59. Although Qoheleth does indeed undermine the sense of the world's harmony in the opening of chapter three by his subsequent comments, the rest of this argument is not persuasive. Even if one translates "to give birth," such a translation does not pose the kind of difficulty Blenkinsopp suggests. Giving birth is not exactly something over which one has much control; the birth process happens on its own, and is not in the power of the mother to stop. In any event, the translation of "to die" in the sense of killing oneself is a very long stretch. Both birth and death are beyond human control.

[83] Schwienhorst-Schönberger, *"Nicht im Menschen Gründet das Glück"* *(Koh 2,24)*, wants to treat the book of Qoheleth as a whole and get away from lists of isolated parallels, so his argument does not suffer from this criticism as much. He still concludes that there is Greek philosophical influence on the book and regards it as a diatribe in structure, a point which is not compelling since Qoheleth's structure does not appear to be so formally organized.

[84] Ernest Horton, Jr., "Koheleth's Concept of Opposites," *Numen* 19(1972) 21–22, points out that although 1:2–11 "brings to mind the familiar Greek tetrad of the earth, air, fire, and water, there is little resemblance beyond this point. When Koheleth looks at nature, he describes it simply and its processes as being external, real, and independent of each other."

Qoheleth was not simply taken with one philosophy or school or author, but that he was aware of a whole library of Greek materials and drew from them eclectically, whether through written or oral contacts. Although such a conclusion is not impossible, it is much harder to demonstrate because of the the lack of specificity.[85]

In the most recent commentaries scholars have tended to accept some sort of idea that Qoheleth has been influenced by Greece, while backing off from suggesting specific parallels. Crenshaw (1987) notes that people have gone overboard with claims of literary dependence, though he feels that Hellenistic influence is likely.[86] Whybray (1989) reverses the general trend by starting out in favor of Greek influence and then backing off a bit later. First he says that the "personal tone" of the book almost certainly is due to the Greek cult of the individual.[87] Qoheleth reflects a time when the old values had been undermined by the intellectual power of Hellenism and the new commercial world that existed under the Ptolemies. He is not persuaded that Qoheleth knew Greek, but says that his knowledge of Greek culture is typical of any educated Jew of the time living in the Ptolemaic empire.[88] A little later, though, he takes a somewhat more distant view of the idea of Greek influence when he says that Qoheleth's thought is parallel in that similar situations will produce similar observations on life.[89] He goes on to say that the book's ideas are fundamentally Hebraic, and could have been written only by a Jew.[90]

---

[85] Also, C. L. Seow, *Ecclesiastes* (New York: Doubleday, 1997) 16, makes a good point when he remarks that it is odd, if Qoheleth is familiar with and using Greek thought, that there are no grecisms in the book. By the Hellenistic period Greek loanwords are common in Palestine, while they are unattested in the Persian period. Seow takes this as evidence that not only does Qoheleth not use Greek material, the book also dates to the Persian era.

[86] Crenshaw, *Ecclesiastes*, 51.

[87] R. N. Whybray, *Ecclesiastes* (Grand Rapids: Eerdmans, 1989) 6.

[88] Whybray, *Ecclesiastes*, 11–13.

[89] Whybray, *Ecclesiastes*, 23.

[90] Whybray, *Ecclesiastes*, 28. "The list of characteristically Old Testament beliefs which he fully accepted, explicitly or implicitly, is a long one: it includes belief in a sole God who is transcendent and omnipotent, who created the world and created it a good world, and in mankind as weak and dependent on God, made from the dust and animated by him with breath, but destined after a short span of life to return to dust and to descend to the comfortless and shadowy realm of Sheol. Qoheleth was also in full agreement with biblical teaching in recognizing, within

Fox (1989) also takes a restrained position. He says that he does not claim that Qoheleth's ideas have a specific Greek source, only that he shared "the concerns and attitudes of various philosophies known in the Hellenistic period."[91] He observes Greek parallels but draws no conclusions. In reference to Braun he notes that he has reopened the question of Greek influence on the Jewish text; even if many of his parallels are not compelling, he does show that Qoheleth was not isolated from the intellectual climate.[92] Murphy (1992) reviews the pros and cons of the debate, ending with a summary of Braun's study, and concludes "The nature of such evidence boils down to this: while there is no proof that Ecclesiastes is directly dependent upon Greek sources, the parallels between many facets of Qoheleth's thought and the common stock of Greek philosophical literature are sufficiently frequent and striking to suggest some relationship."[93] However, he says that while a "Greek connection" is easy to accept, the way the influence would be mediated is not clear.[94]

Conclusion

Thus runs the range of scholarly opinions on the question of whether Qoheleth was influenced by the texts, philosophy, or popular thought of Greece. The majority answer is that he was, with differences

---

these limits, man's freedom: that it is not God but men themselves who are responsible for the present corrupt state of the world. 'God made man upright, but they have sought out many devices' (7:29). Some of these beliefs can be paralleled from non-Israelite sources (see Loretz); but taken together they have an unmistakable Jewish flavour" (28–29).

[91] Michael Fox, *Qohelet and His Contradictions* (Sheffield: The Almond Press, 1989) 16.

[92] Fox, *Qohelet and His Contradictions*, 16. He adds "The most significant parallels will, I believe, be the least provable—similarities of attitude, epistemology, fields of inquiry, underlying questions addressed, and the types of answers offered (though not necessarily the specific answers)."

[93] Roland E. Murphy, *Ecclesiastes* (Dallas: Word Books, 1992) xliv. He does add that he is reticent about Braun's contention that Qoheleth actually translates Greek thought into Hebrew idiom.

[94] Murphy, *Ecclesiastes*, xlv.

of opinion as to the details.[95] What is interesting to observe is how even those scholars who in recent decades have expressed reticence about drawing lists of parallels between the Jewish and various Greek writings usually come around to some idea that Qoheleth has been influenced nonetheless, even if only in broad terms. In fairness, it is true that one might recognize an expression or idea from one culture in a composition from another without being able to cite exact source and means of contact. However, in the case of Qoheleth the cited parallels are such a grab-bag that the argument must be made on strictly generic terms and is consequently considerably weakened. The fact that the Greek parallels come from a broad swath of different genres and time periods further dilutes the power of the theory.

One can reasonably argue, on the other hand, that a large body of potential influences, even if they cannot be specifically traced, would also carry some weight, but many of the parallels cited find their source in the Jewish traditions or are so general as to appear in a variety of cultures, which again weakens the argument. This is a type of smorgasbord approach to the question. On this basis, similar parallels can also be culled from the Egyptian and Babylonian bodies of literature, as has in fact been noted above. In short, *a parallel and an influence are two different creatures*. The tendency, however, is to make a leap from one to the other as if they were interchangeable.

Finally, one wants to ask why exactly it is that with nothing definite to point to, the Greek hypothesis nevertheless endures. This leads back to the question that initiated the investigation into Greek (or other foreign) influence in the first place: why does Qoheleth stand so far outside his own tradition regarding his view of death and the significance this has for life? Everyone is trying to respond to this question. Something new and different is happening in Qoheleth. How to explain it? Looking for foreign contacts is a reasonable move, because it is certainly a possible explanation. Yet two centuries of the investigation have turned up little, while in the meantime the question "is Qoheleth's oddity explained by Greek influence?" has almost become, perhaps by dint of repetition, an embedded declarative statement in the framework of Qoheleth scholarship.

---

[95] Michel, *Qohelet*, 52, remarks that currently "neigt sich das Pendel der Meinungen wieder einmal der Annahme eines griechisch-hellenistischen Einflusses zu."

Pfeiffer's opinion that it is "hardly conceivable" that the book would ever have been written without the influence of Greek thought is telling.[96] So is the belief that Qoheleth is essentially "un-Jewish,"[97] "more Greek than Jew,"[98] or that he feels negatively toward his own tradition.[99] The Jewish author has indeed forged new frontiers in his tradition in a number of ways, but that this can be explained *only* by Greek influence, or outside influence from any source, is not a self-evident principle of the universe. The inconceivability of the book being penned by a full-fledged Jew is a mental block only for moderns, and may originally have been related to a desire in some cases, possibly unconscious, to protect the "orthodoxy" of Jewish thought in the face of an unusual, but canonical, book. If the work is essentially Greek, then it becomes something of an interloper and orthodoxy is saved. But it must be remembered that a myriad of writings originate in this period, all quite Jewish, which offer the fullest imaginable array of ideas, some of which seem bizarre today only because a subsequent canonical process weeded many of them out. Qoheleth's era was not defined by today's standards of orthodoxy.

Instead of the search for outside influences, there may well be explanations for Qoheleth's worldview from within the history of the Jewish tradition, which, as some have suggested, also reflects changes similar to those taking place in Greek religious and philosophical beliefs. This does not mean that parallels cannot be made between Qoheleth and Greek movements, but that the influence of one on the other is not necessarily the correct way to approach the matter. Greece may not be the hub of the cultural wheel radiating out to influence the other traditions of the ancient Near East; although Greek ideas certainly did have an influence on the cultures surrounding them, the question of "influences" is probably a fair deal more complicated. Greece may be exhibiting changes in religious thought alongside its neighbors, all of whom are reacting to transitions in the political, economic, and social horizons of the region.[100] A more useful move in the attempt to determine what might

---

[96] Pfeiffer, "The Peculiar Skepticism of Ecclesiastes," 109.

[97] Humbert, *Recherches sur les Sources Égyptiennes*, 124.

[98] Ranston "Koheleth and the Early Greeks," 163.

[99] Whitley, *Koheleth: His Language and Thought*, 146.

[100] See chapter 7 for the full exposition of this idea, which is only adumbrated here.

be driving Qoheleth's reflections is to look at what was happening in Jewish life at the time.

SOCIAL CONDITIONS

Although scholars on occasion turn to the history of the times to determine why Qoheleth may have been motivated to say the things that he does, not all scholars find such a move to be useful, since trying to match individual historical events with new religious or philosophical ideas is a hazardous project.[101] However, this chapter does not intend to discover *specific* events and causes for Qoheleth's thought. Its purpose is to see instead if there are broader trends of the time that would explain how a book like Qoheleth's might be possible. Many people have placed Qoheleth within the "spirit of the time," but as can be seen in the preceding discussion, usually define that spirit as one where Greek culture stamps itself and its ideas on a receptive Orient. This discussion will be taking a somewhat different approach. The spirit of the time is important for understanding Qoheleth, but the question is what is the nature, or the driving force, of this Zeitgeist? The discussion in chapter one about the corporate attitudes of the Israelites vs. individualistic views again becomes relevant. There it was decided that, contrary to the scholarly theories of the early twentieth century, ancient Israel well knew of individual identity and consciousness, and from early days, too. Nonetheless, it seems safe to say that the people did tend to conceive of their obligations, purpose, and destiny from a corporate point of view, and that this approach largely undergirded their conceptions and feelings toward death. Has this state of affairs changed by Qoheleth's time? The

---

[101] Fox in particular expresses scepticism at trying to find "external 'causes'" for a person's thought. Historical and material factors might provide the context for an individual's ideas and responses, but they cannot explain them. He says this in answer to the idea that economic realities had so extensively changed in Hellenistic Palestine that the well-established norms had finally broken down, thereby eliciting Qoheleth's observations on the world. The problems that Qoheleth mentions, however, such as oppression, corrupt officials, power abuses, and incompetent leaders are all attested by the prophets, while economic success was quite possible in Hellenistic times. So it does not, he feels, seem to be especially plausible that Qoheleth is reacting to such specific historical-social conditions. See Fox, *Qohelet and His Contradictions*, 143.

answer seems to be yes, and is tied to a number of historical changes that had taken place over the last half millennium BCE.

Probably the most serious event that affected the history of the Israelites was the fall of Judah to the Babylonians in 587 BCE. The defeat by Babylon, loss of the temple and king, and exile of the upper classes removed any last vestige of Israelite nationhood and resulted in a number of shifts in self-perception. Although the exiles received permission from Cyrus only a few decades later to return to the homeland and rebuild their temple, the rebuilding process, of temple and peoplehood alike, was fitful, and the results were different from what they had previously been. The temple cult would endure in its resurrected form until the Romans swept through Jerusalem in 70 CE, which was another watershed in Jewish history, but one that had been foreshadowed and in some sense set in motion over six centuries earlier. The foundation for the shift from a cultic religion to a book religion was laid in 587. Some have characterized the period following the Babylonian defeat as a time when the Jewish tradition became persistently concerned with the question of God's justice, since obedience and long life, or disobedience and early death, seemed to be entirely unconnected with one another. Job, Qoheleth, Ben Sira, and the Wisdom of Solomon all offer different answers.[102] Rainer Albertz begins vol. II of his history of the Old Testament with the remark that the exile represents a breaking point in Israelite religion.[103]

Even after the decree of Cyrus, the political upheavals were really just getting underway. Subjugation by the Babylonian empire ceased only

---

[102] Otto Kaiser and Eduard Lohse, eds., *Death and Life* (Nashville: Abingdon, 1981) 14. Claudia Camp, *Wisdom and the Feminine in the Book of Proverbs* (Sheffield: Journal for the Study of the Old Testament Press, 1985) 239, describes the political and economic situation as a time when not only was Jerusalem destroyed, but also the other towns and probably the farms of the southern part of the country. The villages that did survive existed without the political and economic stucture of the past. The Edomites were pushing in from the south, as they themselves were being edged out by the Nabateans, and the Samaritans had control of the north.

[103] Rainer Albertz, *A History of Israelite Religion in the Old Testament Period*, Vol. II (Louisville, KY: Westminster/John Knox Press, 1994) 369. He goes on to add (370) that the destruction of the political and cultic institutions led to religious realignments, and centralized authority was replaced with decentralized organization based on the family (375).

because it was replaced by Persian domination, followed by Greek, then Egyptian, then Syrian, and a last brief gasp of independence quickly quashed by the Romans. In short, the era of Israelite independence, such as it was, had come to an end and stayed ended. Robert Gordis gives an analysis of the new situation which is worth quoting in full.

> A fundamental revolution in men's thinking now took place. The ancient Semitic outlook, which was shared by the Hebrews, had placed the well-being or decline of the group, the family, tribe or nation in the center of men's thoughts. This collective viewpoint now gave way to a heightened interest in the individual. Prosperity and freedom for a tiny weak people were not likely to be achieved in a world of mighty empires. All that remained was for each human being to strive to attain his personal happiness. What qualities were needed, what pitfalls had to be avoided by a man seeking to achieve success and a respectable place in society? These perennially modern and recurrent questions, which indeed had never been suppressed even during the pre-Exilic days of national independence, now became the pivot on which men's convictions and doubts revolved. To help the individual attain to well-being had always been the function of Wisdom. It now became a central element in the religio-cultural pattern.[104]

One has to be careful not to overstate the case. What happened is not that the Jews suddenly acquired a brand new interest, but that an older, less central interest now came to the fore. Albertz describes the situation in terms of a shift from national to family concerns. God, it seemed, had rejected the people as a national entity, but was still accessible in the "everyday realm" to the individual.[105]

The process was a gradual one, which some think may even have begun before the exile but was certainly accelerated after it.[106] Any number of factors, political and economic as well as religious, fed into the phenomenon, but the series of wars initiated by Assyria and lasting under other auspices for more or less the rest of the 1st millenium BCE added a special impetus to it, particularly by destroying the central authority and thus throwing responsibility back onto local entitities.[107] Added to this

---

[104] Gordis, *Koheleth—The Man and His World*, 25.

[105] Albertz, *A History of Israelite Religion in the Old Testament Period*, 401.

[106] Robert Martin-Achard, *From Death to Life* (Edinburgh and London: Oliver and Boyd, 1960) 210.

[107] Martin-Achard, *From Death to Life*, 210; see also R. N. Whybray, *Ecclesiastes* (Grand Rapids: Eerdmans, 1989) 11, who notes the breakdown of the

was the prophetic demand that the listeners make their own choices between right and wrong, which added moral and religious backing to the strengthening sense of individual responsibility.[108] Ezekiel 18 is a prime example of such a prophetic text, which declares that each person is personally responsible for his own actions, rejects the idea that the innocent will be punished along with the guilty, and in so doing implies a new concept of identity, a concept which no longer relies on ethnicity but on one's choice of action within a particular ethnic group. The group as the unit of decision begins to give way to the individual.[109]

The argument in the first chapter was that the existence of death was met by a mindset related to a group-oriented or community-based outlook on life. Even though personal consciousness dissipates at death, continuity remains through the survival of one's family and name in the community at large. If this corporate approach should fail in the face of new historical and social realities, presumably the related aspects of a people's worldview are also going to need to be readdressed, and this in fact is what seems to happen. "Concomitant with this emergence of individualism, the problem of death assumes an increasing importance

---

closely-knit community life of earlier days. Camp, *Wisdom and the Feminine in the Book of Proverbs,* 241, cites Sara Japhet, "Sheshbazzar and Zerubbabel: Against the Background of the Historical and Religious Tendencies of Ezra-Nehemiah," *Zeitschrift für die alttestamentliche Wissenschaft* 94(1982) 66–98, for the observation that the power vaccum left by the fall of the state was gradually filled by local and family leaders. See also Camp, 243–250, where she further elaborates on the argument. "Although the political entity of Judah was decimated, the family remained an ongoing social and economic unity. Consequently, the sense of community built on royal symbolism now encountered a void, while family symbolism remained viable. The relationship of the individual and God nutured by the family was able to withstand the historical break. As long as the individual draws breath, he or she can still turn in trust to the God who is known as Creator and Parent" (247) The book of Proverbs is a testimony to the shift in weight from the national, royal locus of authority to the local. This is not unlike Gordis's argument on the preceding page, that wisdom and its individual concerns now come to the fore, and that of Albertz.

[108] Martin-Achard, *From Death to Life,* 210.

[109] Hiroshi Obayashi, "Introduction," in Hiroshi Obayashi, ed., *Death and Afterlife: Perspectives of World Religions* (New York: Greenwood Press, 1992) xvi, says that the shift in "the locus of religious faith" began under the prophets and was heightened by events in the reign of Antiochus Epiphanes. "The logic of salvation that focused only on corporate or collective survival was no longer sufficient."

and tends to become the great anxiety of the living."[110] Once political events or social changes overly stress those structures which had preserved the sense of continuity in the past, continuity itself is also taxed. This is exactly what one finds in Qoheleth. Even Michael Fox, who rightly says "not every literary phenomenon has social or historical causes,"[111] notes that Qoheleth's obsession with death is tied to another oddity of his book, that he has no sense of the nation or community. "All his values are solitary, measured by benefit or harm to the individual. This individualism imposes itself on his attitude toward death. Every death is an unmitigated loss, for its shock cannot be buffered by communal continuity."[112]

The shift in perspective from older tradition in Qoheleth manifests itself in other, related ways. Several scholars have noticed that for the first time, the author of a biblical writing emerges forcefully as an individual, as is pointedly expressed in the prevalence of first person singular verbs and even more, by the repeated but grammatically unnecessary first person singular pronoun "אֲנִי."[113] This kind of a "confession style" is symptomatic of Qoheleth's disconnection from the community.[114] Although the word "Qoheleth" is a pseudonym, his personality is fully present; in a book of only 222 verses, 82 of the verbs are in the first person singular.[115] Fox points out that, beyond the simple grammatical features, the book has gone much farther than any other in the canon in its focus on the "organizing consciousness of the sage,"

---

[110] Robert Martin-Achard, *From Death to Life*, 211. Cf. also Antonio R. Gualtieri, *The Vulture and the Bull: Religious Responses to Death* (Lanham, MD: University Press of America, 1984) 83, where he says that "the emergence of the individual" is a key factor in the changing Hebrew approach to death and the afterlife.

[111] Fox, *Qohelet and His Contradictions*, 294.

[112] Fox, *Qohelet and His Contradictions*, 294.

[113] Elias Bickerman, *Four Strange Books of the Bible* (New York: Schocken Books, 1967) 154.

[114] R. J. Williams, "What Does it Profit a Man?: The Wisdom of Koheleth," in James L. Crenshaw, ed., *Studies in Ancient Israelite Wisdom* (New York: Ktav Publishing House, 1976) 376.

[115] Whybray, *Ecclesiastes*, 6.

meaning that rather than disappearing into the text his personality is a primary factor.[116]

Related to the importance of Qoheleth as an individual is the fact that his epistemology is empirical. Some of the book's material is traditional enough, but his procedure in principle is to base his conclusions on personal experience. He pursues, investigates, and reports on his own experience as the basis of his argument.[117] "Qoheleth is unusual in his emphasis on validation, especially validation by empirical evidence," and unique in claiming to have learned something new apart from what he was taught.[118] If one were to ask a typical sage how he knew his teaching, he would answer that he *learned* it; the same question to Qoheleth would elicit the answer that he *saw* it.[119] This suggests once again that Qoheleth does not conceive of himself as a small part of a larger community body in the way he might have done earlier in Israelite history. He is not a cog in a greater unit passing on the tradition, but feels compelled, apparently, to do the legwork himself in his efforts to comprehend the world. "I... applied my mind to seek and to search out" (1:12–13); "I saw all the deeds" (1:14); "I perceived that" (1:17; 2:14); "I considered all that my hands had done" (2:11); "This also, I saw, is from the hand of God" (2:24), etc.[120]

---

[116] Fox, *Qohelet and His Contradictions*, 159. The reader also sees the "I" in Ezra and Nehemiah, but the overall effect is not the same, and the individual speaker in the psalms is not as personal, but conventional, for which see Whybray, *Ecclesiastes*, 6. The teacher in Proverbs 1–9 speaks in the first person, but is a generic father type, as Fox, *Qohelet and His Contradictions*, 159–60 points out. Martin Hengel, *Judaism and Hellenism*, 116, refers to the "marked 'individuality' of authorship" in the book.

[117] Michael Fox, "Wisdom in Qoheleth," in Leo G. Perdue, B. B. Scott, and W. J. Wiseman, eds., *In Search of Wisdom* (Louisville, KY: Westminster/John Knox Press, 1993) 121.

[118] Fox, *Qohelet and His Contradictions*, 85–86; also "Wisdom in Qoheleth," 121. Fox, *Qohelet and His Contradictions*, 87, 98, considers this to be revolutionary, that a sage should base his understanding on his own experience, since the wisdom tradition across the ancient Near East attempted not so much to find new truths as to drive home well-learned tradition.

[119] Fox, "Wisdom in Israel," 122.

[120] One wonders if Qoheleth's empirical approach is related to the fact that he insists memory fails from one generation to the next. Taken most literally, such a failure would require each generation to start from scratch in building up its store of knowledge, and this obviously does not happen. Qoheleth himself assumes much from the tradition. Nevertheless, he assumes less than would normally be expected.

Associated with the individualism and empiricism is also a level of detachment which is new to the books of the Bible. Qoheleth still has mundane advice to give, but seems to experience a certain distance from the world.[121] Earlier wisdom had been concerned with the smooth operation of the community organism. Advice was directed at the individual, but with the understanding that the individual was operating within a particular social context. "This detachment from the common life is an aspect of Qoheleth's independent stance. Every commonly accepted notion must be put to the test of his personal experience of the world; nothing is to be taken for granted."[122] Qoheleth's distance from his surroundings is matched by God's. Not once does he refer to the deity as YHWH, using rather the more generic "Elohim."[123] He never questions that God exists, but his God is unlike the God to be found in the rest of the Hebrew Bible.[124] This is no personal being involved with his people,

James Crenshaw, "Qoheleth's Understanding of Intellectual Inquiry," in Antoon Schoors, ed., *Qohelet in the Context of Wisdom* (Leuven: Leuven University Press, 1998) 212–13, has raised the question whether Qoheleth was actually as empirical as Fox argues. He lists a number of items of knowledge which Qoheleth simply asserts, and makes a good point when he says that Qoheleth accepted many teachings from his tradition "without submitting them to the test of experience" (213). The argument may be one of degree, since in an article in the same volume, Fox agrees that, like all people, Qoheleth has an "inherited world construction" based on a number of presuppositions about reality. Cf. Michael Fox, "The Inner-Structure of Qohelet's Thought," in Antoon Schoors, ed., *Qohelet in the Context of Wisdom* (Leuven: Leuven University Press, 1998) 234–35.

[121] Whybray, *Ecclesiastes*, 7. Hengel, *Judaism and Hellenism*, 117, remarks "as far as the person of Koheleth is concerned, the most significant thing here is his cool detachment, in which any sense of responsibility for the community of his people is lacking...."

[122] Whybray, *Ecclesiastes*, 7.

[123] Morris Jastrow, *A Gentle Cynic* (Philadelphia: J.B. Lippincott Company, 1919) 134.

[124] Hengel, *Judaism and Hellenism*, 117, writes that Qoheleth "denationalizes" God. Of the 38 times he uses "Elohim," only 8 cases appear without the article. Stephan de Jong, "God in the Book of Qohelet" A Reappraisal of Qohelet's Place in Old Testament Theology," *Vetus Testamentum* 47(1997) 164, offers a different view from the one presented here by suggesting that Qoheleth's portrayal of God is not intended to be a systematic theology, but is a selection of ideas intended specifically to highlight human limitation. This is an instructive point, but unless Qoheleth has pressed his effort to actual distortion, he presents a God which it is difficult to imagine he might in another context portray as tender or responsive towards human beings.

no deity carefully marking every good and evil action, not even the somewhat distant yet benevolent God of Proverbs, nor even yet the almost frightening power in the book of Job. God is so utterly unknowable, so distant, that the deity becomes "a sort of *Fatum*, or impersonal power."[125] God seems to be as disassociated from the world as Qoheleth is from the community.[126] "God is in heaven, and you upon earth" (5:1).

The fact that death should suddenly take on an importance and an overtone of menace at this stage of Israel's history is not accidental, since the new conditions of the post-exilic period lent themselves to all kinds of theological, intellectual, questioning. Along with the realignments of social structure from royal/centralized to local and an increasing interest in the individual, other features of life came to the fore in Jewish experience. Crüsemann discusses the economic implications of these specifically with regard to Qoheleth's fixation on death. He notes, as do many, that the old order was destroyed by the Babylonian conquest. By the Hellenistic era conditions had altered considerably. The economy became increasingly based on money and coinage, which with the heavy tax burdens imposed from the outside by foreign overlords undermined the abilities of farms and villages to carry on as before. Farmlands began to be converted to orchards and vineyards, which reduced the number of productive families. Economic prosperity was experienced by the aristocratic classes who became part of the tax-raising system, and thus the agents of the foreign rulers. The traditional family-based structures

---

[125] Oliver S. Rankin, *Israel's Wisdom Literature* (Edinburgh: T&T Clark, 1936) 94. Jastrow, *A Gentle Cynic*, 135, observes that God "represents the Power that is behind all phenomena, but a power who, so far as man is concerned, is beyond knowledge...." Perdue, *Wisdom and Creation*, 239, calls God a deus absconditus, removed from humanity and hidden in the heavens. Hengel, *Judaism and Hellenism*, 126, also uses the phrase deus absconditus, saying that if Qoheleth's conception were pushed any farther he would end up with "impersonal fate."

[126] In a discussion of late period psalms, Gunther Wanke, "Prophecy and Psalms in the Persian Period," in W. D. Davies and Louis Finkelstein, eds., *The Cambridge History of Judaism*, Vol. I (Cambridge: Cambridge University Press, 1984) 187, makes the observation that along with the growing idea that God is sovereign over all the nations is a sense of the great distance between God and humanity. Also the notion of human ephemerality becomes more pronounced (Pss 90, 103). Of interest here is the association of transience and a distant God in other late biblical texts besides Qoheleth.

and solidarity were not well able to withstand the new economic realities, however. "Tradition and experience were diverging".[127]

According to Crüsemann, people responded to the new situation in a variety of ways, one of which is represented by Qoheleth, who in his view comes from the aristocracy. Qoheleth's problem is not one of material want, but the result of what happens when everything in one's world is related to wealth. He wants to know what "gain" there is in life, but if one attributes a "commercial category to life as a whole, then, given the fact of death, the answer can only be: no gain (2:11)."[128] Death is now the ultimate expression of the meaninglessness of life. Crüsemann notes that others were offering opposite conclusions about death in this time period,[129] but everyone is essentially working from the same basis, specifically, the new social and economic structures of Hellenistic Israel which created among some of the social strata a sense of injustice, pointlessness of effort and absence of divine interest in the world.[130] The

---

[127] Frank Crüsemann, "The Unchangeable World: The 'Crisis of Wisdom' in Koheleth," in Willy Schottroff and Wolfgang Stegemann, eds., *God of the Lowly: Socio-Historical Interpretations of the Bible* (Maryknoll, NY: Orbis Books, 1984) 63.

[128] Crüsemann, "The Unchangeable World: The 'Crisis of Wisdom' in Koheleth," 66.

[129] See the first part of the present chapter for a survey.

[130] Albertz, *A History of Israelite Religion in the Old Testament Period*, 495–96, places the beginnings of the increasing social divergence between the classes in Judea in the second half of the fifth century when Nehemiah laid a tax burden on the people in the form of forced labor. The same text tells of an outcry by the poor against the nobles. A tax reform by Darius then required tax payment in silver coin in an amount set without regard for yearly harvest variations. This could only be fulfilled by converting crop surpluses to money, and something like bad weather or labor conscriptions would ruin an already borderline situation. Although Nehemiah sided with the complainants in this incident, the structural problem remained. Albertz further discusses a split among the upper classes between those who took advantage of the situation for themselves and those who felt a moral duty towards the impoverished. He feels that the book of Job came from the latter group who were trying to deal with the fact that unlike their more ruthless colleagues, they were susceptible to material losses in spite of their concern for the poor. This raised a problem of theodicy. Job is a wealthy aristocrat who loses everything although he showed piety towards the poorer classes. "The whole book of Job can be seen as one long pastoral scheme seeking to cope with this difficult problem" (502–03; see also 513–517). Setting the texts from this period in their economic and social setting is interesting and informative, though in the case of Job the Sitz im Leben seems a little too specific. Albertz points to a number of late texts where

collapse of group identity and focus on the individual and his "gain" is what "gives death a fascination that eclipses everything else."[131] The interesting thing about this analysis is that the author of the book of Qoheleth would be the one benefitting, not suffering from, the economic conditions. Yet the melancholy, according to the argument, is the result of the all-encompassing focus on the economic profit to be gotten from life.[132] This is an interesting argument, and provides good background to the conditions of Qoheleth's times, but is probably an overly economic reading of the book. While the economic and social conditions of the period probably do underlie the author's melancholy, one questions whether Qoheleth himself is so fixated on material goods. His problem does not seem to be merely that of a frustrated aristocrat, or even of a successful one who has put all his efforts into money-making. Qoheleth has a keen understanding that material goods, along with everything else in the human realm, are worth little in the big picture.

One should state here that it is no part of this chapter's argument that historical conditions require certain, necessary theological responses.

---

the concern for the poor and their problems figures prominently, so it seems that his general historical reconstruction has merit. But nothing in Job itself suggests that it can be pinpointed to a particular branch of the aristocracy. The problems it raises would actually be relevant to the lower classes as well.

[131] Crüsemann, "The Unchangeable World: The 'Crisis of Wisdom' in Koheleth," 68.

[132] Albertz, *A History of Israelite Religion in the Old Testament Period*, 536–37, agrees that the economic hardships and social divisions of the Persian period continued and even deepened in the hellenistic era; he sees Qoheleth as a testament to the oppression of the poor by the wealthy. See also C. L. Seow, "The Socioeconomic Context of 'The Preacher's' Hermeneutic," *Princeton Seminary Bulletin* 17(1996) 168–195, for a careful discussion of the economic situation in Qoheleth's time, which he dates to the Persian period, and the effect this had on society's view of the world. He explains how the new monetary economy differed from the mostly subsistence-level agrarian economy of pre-exilic Judah (174), and examines a number of individual sayings in Qoheleth in light of particular economic changes. In some cases the sayings may be read in an overly specific economic fashion, but generally he is persuasive that this was a "new world of rapid political, social, and economic innovations" which were overwhelming (189). This thesis would apply in the later Hellenistic era as well. Seow, *Ecclesiastes*, 21–36, specifically discusses the impact of the Persian tax system, which required payment in precious metal, and the standardization of the monetary system. Money was not an unknown before this, but under the Persians it became the basis of the economy. Money "had become a commodity" (21).

Any number of responses are possible, and the surviving writings of Qoheleth's era and later, which are no doubt a small fraction of the total number that once existed, reveal a wide range of these possibilities. However, the argument does assume that if one cannot reliably predict exactly how an individual, community, nation, or region will respond to changing historical circumstances, one can at least reasonably expect that there will be a response, or responses, of *some* kind. It may be one of adamant resistance to evolving historical horizons, or it may consist of different degrees of adaptation, or of acceptance, or despair, or confusion, or any of a number of other things. Considering the degree of change that had occurred not just for the Jews, but throughout the ancient Mediterranean in the last centuries of the millennium, and considering that the Jewish canon in particular consists of a body of writings that is highly sensitive to the successive events of history, it is only fitting that there should be a response to these changing social and religious realities, of which Qoheleth is one possible variant.

It appears then that Qoheleth is a book that was made possible by a convergence of historical, political, and social factors, initiated by the loss of the kingdom and the destruction of the nation in 587 and continued by a succession of foreign overlords. These same factors are responsible for the prolific composition of all kinds of texts in the last centuries BCE, both within and without the canon, and probably for the canonical process itself. The atmosphere of distress, confusion, and chaos induced people to react in a variety of ways, some by attempting to solidify and preserve traditions of the past, some by seeking explanations for the present, some by looking for hope in the future. Understandably, in a world where the symbolic system of the past no longer matches the realities of the present, fundamental human questions such as the meaning and nature of death are susceptible to reappraisal. This is exactly what happens in Qoheleth, as well as in subsequent Jewish texts.

Qoheleth's sense of problem does not emerge in a vacuum, then. It seems to be tied to a feeling of isolation from the broader community, expressed through a finely developed sense of individualism; to a personal, empirical approach to discovering the nature of the world; and to a much more impersonal, detached conception of God than one hitherto finds in the tradition. Because of the fact that the Jews were only one people among many in the ancient Near East at this time who were experiencing the same invasions and shifts in power across the

Mediterranean, the question at this point is whether anything comparable in the realm of religious thought was taking place in other cultures in the region. Egypt, as it happens, shows that similar concerns about death were cropping up in the same way, at the same time. The following chapters will explain.

Chapter 4
DEATH IN ANCIENT EGYPT

Probably no other ancient Near Eastern culture stands out in modern minds more than Egypt when it comes to the topic of death, and for obvious reasons.[1] The bulk of what remains from the society is related in one way or another to death and the dead. Because of this fact, scholars from time to time point out that present-day conceptions tend to be skewed by the evidence. The physical reasons for the survival of so much of the funerary materials of the culture are straightforward. Egypt consisted of a long narrow strip of fertile black soil, which lay on each side of the Nile, and which quickly gave way to the desert, where the tombs and burials were located. "The result is that our evidence on the ancient Egyptians is disproportionately strong in material on their mortuary beliefs and formal temple worship but weak on such lay matters as business, government, economics, and social organization. The view that the ancient Egyptians were excessively concerned with death and the next world is conditioned by the accident that materials dealing with death and the next world lay out in the desert sands and survived down to our day, whereas materials dealing with life in this world lay chiefly on the fertile alluvial soil; were subject to moisture, chemical destruction, and human wear and tear; and so did not survive."[2]

---

[1] Miriam Lichtheim, *Ancient Egyptian Literature: A Book of Readings*, 3 Vols. (Berkeley: University of California Press, 1973, 1976, 1980) II:119 remarks, "No other nation of the ancient world made so determined an effort to vanquish death and win eternal life."

[2] John A. Wilson, *The Burden of Egypt: An Interpretation of Ancient Egyptian Culture* (Chicago: University of Chicago Press, 1951) 15–16. See also Leonard H. Lesko, "Death and the Afterlife in Ancient Egyptian Thought," in Jack M. Sasson, ed., *Civilizations of the Ancient Near East*, Vol. III (New York: Charles Scribner's Sons, 1995) 1763, who writes "the Egyptians' attitude toward death and

This is a good point and the caution should be kept in mind when dealing with death in ancient Egypt. Nevertheless, while a disproportionate amount of funerary material has survived in comparison to other aspects of society, the fact remains that Egypt is still a standout among its neighbors when it comes to its responses to death. This would be apparent even if the full remains of the culture could be retrieved for context. Egypt's cult and mythology with respect to death is approached by no one else for detail and importance in society as a whole.[3] However, a second caution is in order. As in the case of ancient Israel, and probably all societies, even Egypt with its highly formalized mortuary apparatus cannot be said to have had "a" view of death. Attitudes would have been affected by any of a number of possible factors, among which are time period, region, social class, and individual personalities. Naturally many such nuances are lost to the modern observer, but some still come through and must be acknowledged if one hopes to have any reliable conception of what death meant to the ancient Egyptians.

One of the most common pitfalls when studying any aspect of Egyptian culture is the view that it was conservative and consistent.

---

burial preparations through several millennia was such and the quantity of burial equipment so great that at times these subjects might seem to have preoccupied them totally. Yet although death and the world of the dead are predominant features in much of the surviving record, the documentation points not to excessive morbidity, but rather to a preoccupation with life and a desire to continue living after death." Similarly A. J. Spencer, *Death in Ancient Egypt* (New York: Penguin Books, 1982) 73: "The Egyptians were not obsessed with death; the study of their funerary beliefs shows that it was the love of life which drove them to make such elaborate preparations for burial, since death accompanied by the correct rituals was only the beginning of eternal life. Their fear of losing this second existence is very apparent."

[3] Cf. Herman te Velde, "Funerary Mythology," in Sue D'Auria et al, eds., *Mummies and Magic: The Funerary Arts of Ancient Egypt* (Boston: Museum of Fine Arts, 1988) 27: "Although our knowledge of ancient Egyptian culture is doubtless one-sided, since most of its non-funerary aspects are lost forever, it must be said that the ancient Egyptians focused on questions of life and death to a degree unsurpassed, before or since. In the millennia of their history they developed an imposing, extensive, and intricate funerary mythology to answer the riddle of death and to make its prospect more acceptable." Alan H. Gardiner, *The Attitude of the Ancient Egyptians to Death and the Dead* (Cambridge: Cambridge University Press, 1935) 6, uses stronger language when he writes "the Egyptians conceived a fanatical abhorrence of death, and devoted no small part of their wealth to devising means of defeating it."

Ancient Egypt's history is so long, yet remained so recognizably "Egyptian" in the culture's socio-political structure, artistic achievements, and literary output, that clearly there was a kind of conservatism of attitude which allowed for such a high degree of continuity.[4] Sometimes, however, this leads to a misconception that the culture was in fact unchanging, which is emphatically not the case. Continuity is not the same as stasis.[5] In a number of ways Egypt changed over time, and one of these is in the varying approaches to death. As noted on the preceding page, different factors would have played a role in the matter, but the following will be an attempt to understand the overall shape of Egyptian mortuary religion through time, since this is necessary in order to understand the context for what will appear in the late period tomb biographies.

---

[4] William J. Murnane, "Taking It With You: The Problem of Death and Afterlife in Ancient Egypt," in Hiroshi Obayashi, ed., *Death and Afterlife: Perspectives of World Religions* (New York: Greenwood Press, 1992) 35, writes "Fascination with death is credited to no nation more widely than it is to Egypt of the pharaohs. Alone among the peoples of the ancient Near East, the Egyptians have left us a considerable body of monuments, artifacts, and written records that attest to essentially the same view of death and the afterlife for more than 3000 years."

[5] "Ancient Egypt has long been described as a land where consistency reigned supreme. Once a system was developed, little change occurred over the thousands of years of civilization. This uniformity of structure and its continuity are often considered the hallmarks of Egyptian culture.... [But] looking at the broad picture, what may first appear as a totally homogeneous system is in reality an evolving structure. Egyptian religion is also prone to similar misconceptions about its conservatism, given the longevity and seeming immutability of its concepts, deities, and texts. But here too, evolution was taking place...." See David P. Silverman, "Textual Criticism in the Coffin Texts," in William Kelly Simpson, ed., *Religion and Philosophy in Ancient Egypt* (New Haven: Yale University Press, 1989) 30. Also see Barry J. Kemp, *Ancient Egypt: Anatomy of a Civilization* (New York: Routledge, 1989) 184, who writes "Ancient Egypt has a modern reputation for extreme cultural conservatism. But the New Kingdom demonstrates that this is itself something of a myth, brought about by a confusion between form and substance."

EGYPTIAN MORTUARY TEXTS AND PRACTICES

Although it can probably never be known for certain just how the people of the Nile valley were first led to what would become the standard practice of mummification, probably the best known feature of their funerary practices, one hypothesis is that people observed the phenomenon occurring naturally when bodies left in the desiccating desert sands were rediscovered. Perhaps this, as Breasted opined early in the century, is what led to the belief in an afterlife.[6] Of course other cultures and religions have come to a belief in life after death without having a particular interest in the preservation of the body in this way, so the question will have to remain open. But whatever the cause, the Egyptians did develop both an early notion of a hereafter as well as a concern for bodily preservation. In the early dynastic period, however, it has been suggested that the realm of the afterlife was open only to royalty, and possibly only to the king alone by virtue of his participation in divinity even on earth.[7] Since the Egyptians left an extensive body of

---

[6] James Henry Breasted, *Development of Religion and Thought in Ancient Egypt* (New York: Charles Scribner's Sons, 1912; reprinted New York: Harper & Row, 1959) 49: "Among no people ancient or modern has the idea of a life beyond the grave held so prominent a place as among the ancient Egyptians. This insistent belief in a hereafter may perhaps have been, and experience in the land of Egypt has led me to believe it was, greatly favored and influenced by the fact that the conditions of soil and climate resulted in such a remarkable preservation of the human body as may be found under natural conditions nowhere else in the world." See also Edward F. Wente, "Egyptian Religion," in David Noel Freedman, ed., *The Anchor Bible Dictionary*, Vol. II (New York: Doubleday, 1992) 411. He writes "Already in archaic times natural dehydration of the body in a shallow grave suggested the permanent existence of the deceased...." Gardiner, *The Attitude of the Ancient Egyptians to Death and the Dead*, 5, summarizing Petrie about the climate, says it is so dry that "the problem is rather to discover why anything should perish than why it should survive. Where permanence is thus the rule, could man be the exception?" He adds that in reality one can never really know all the reasons for the existence of Egyptian mortuary traditions.

[7] See Wilson, *The Burden of Egypt*, 64–65: "Here we claim that, in the earliest dynasties, only those were sure of eternal life after death who carried within them the germ of divinity—king and queen, prince and princess—and that the noble class apparently depended upon royal need of their services in order to gain such eternal life. This was the doctrine of divine kingship carried out in grim earnest." Also see Philippe Derchain, "Death in Egyptian Religion," in Yves Bonnefoy, ed., *Mythologies*, Vol. 1 (Chicago: The University of Chicago Press,

literary texts which relates their various responses to death and the dead, this chapter will begin by looking at the main collections in order to lay a foundation for the discussion.[8] The writings which provide the window into this matter in the Old Kingdom are the oldest known corpus of Egyptian religious material, called the Pyramid Texts.

The Pyramid Texts

These texts include all those inscriptions to be found within the inner chambers of the pyramids.[9] They first appear in the pyramid of the final ruler of the Fifth Dynasty, Unas, and continue to be used throughout the remainder of the Old Kingdom,[10] more specifically in the pyramids of

1991) 111. On the other hand, the fact that there were cemeteries for the nobles, paid for by the king, may suggest that some were able to gain access to the afterlife with royal assistance. The evidence is sparse.

[8] The Egyptians did not collect their writings into an official canon, and the subject matter considered worthy of explication included a variety of topics. Important texts were copied and created in the "House of Life," which was the name for the part of a temple complex where scribal activity took place. "The sacred books studied by the theologians of the House of Life contained the myths or 'annals' of the gods and goddesses, catalogues of divinities, hymns and specific ritual texts, rituals for embalming, and source texts for the *Book of the Dead* and other funerary literature as well as magical, medical, veterinary, astronomical, and mathematical books, books on the sacred geography and topography of Egypt, on history, the interpretation of dreams, and many other subjects. In the House of Life, the sacred and secret traditions of Egyptian knowledge were brought together. In form and content, they constituted holy scripture. They were written in the sacred scripts of hieroglyphs and hieratic, not in demotic. This holy scripture contained ancient theology or philosophy, including ancient science." Cf. Herman te Velde, "Theology, Priests, and Worship in Ancient Egypt," in Jack M. Sasson, ed., *Civilizations of the Ancient Near East*, Vol.III (New York: Charles Scribner's Sons, 1995) 1747. (N. B.: in the late period some of these texts do appear in demotic). See also Gertie Englund, "Gods as a Frame of Reference: On Thinking and Concepts of Thought in Ancient Egypt," in Gertie Englund, ed., *The Religion of the Ancient Egyptians: Cognitive Structures and Popular Expressions* (Stockholm: Almqvist & Wiksell International, 1989) 8, who notes that Egyptian "religion" (and equally, Egyptian "scripture") includes philosophy, psychology, science, and so on.

[9] Breasted, *Development of Religion and Thought in Ancient Egypt*, 142, points out that the pyramid is a solar tomb which is associated with the sun god, Re.

[10] Siegfried Morenz, *Egyptian Religion* (New York: Cornell University Press, 1973) 227. Jan Assmann, "Death and Initiation in the Funerary Religion of Ancient Egypt," in William Kelly Simpson, ed., *Religion and Philosophy in Ancient Egypt* (New Haven: Yale University Press, 1989) 136, remarks that the

Teti, Pepi I, Mernere, and Pepi II, all of the Sixth Dynasty.[11] Those which appear in the pyramid of Unas, the oldest collection, comprise 228 separate spells in all, and most of them reappear in later pyramids, although some were dropped and new ones added.[12] They contain a variety of utterances, all of which focus on the king and his experiences or needs after the end of his mortal life.[13] The main theme is the king's journey heavenward, often to join the sun god Re as he travelled across the daytime sky.[14] He might do this in a number of ways, such as using a reed boat, flying there in the form of bird, climbing a ladder, or going up on offerings of incense. Sometimes the king actually becomes Re, or even greater than the god.[15] On other occasions his fate is related to the "imperishable stars," which are the circumpolar stars that never set. The king might take his position as their leader, or again, be identified with them.[16] A sample of spells related to the king's heavenly destination provides a flavor of this theme.

> ....Behold, I have reached the height of heaven.... the hailstorms of the sky have taken me, and they raise me up to Re' (utterance 262).[17]

> ....Here comes the ascender, here comes the ascender!
> Here comes the climber, here comes the climber!
> Here comes he who flew up, here comes he who flew up!
> I ascend upon the thighs of Isis,
> I climb up upon the thighs of Nephthys,
> My father Atum seizes my hand for me,

Pyramid Texts "represent the oldest substantial corpus of religious texts known to mankind."

11 Lichtheim, *Ancient Egyptian Literature*, I:29. She adds that other texts appear in the pyramids of Pepi II's three queens, as well as in an Eighth Dynasty king's pyramid, that of Ibi.

12 Lichtheim, *Ancient Egyptian Literature*, I:29. The total is 759.

13 Some of the spells may also have had a cultic or magical function before the king's death.

14 Lesko, "Death and the Afterlife in Ancient Egyptian Thought," 1767.

15 Beatrice L. Goff, *Symbols of Ancient Egypt in the Late Period: The Twenty-first Dynasty* (The Hague: Mouton Publishers, 1979) 20.

16 Goff, *Symbols of Ancient Egypt*, 20. Carol Andrews, "Introduction," in R. O. Faulkner, *The Ancient Egyptian Book of the Dead* (Austin: The University of Texas Press, 1993) 11, states that the belief in the astral afterlife predates the solar ideas of those who built the pyramids.

17 R. O. Faulkner, *The Ancient Egyptian Pyramid Texts* (Oxford: Oxford University Press, 1969) 71.

And he assigns me to those excellent and wise gods,
The Imperishable Stars (utterance 269).[18]

Another common category of spells in the Pyramid Texts is related to food and drink. They are concerned that the king be provided with sustenance in his new, post-mortem existence. Among many examples are the following:

O Hunger, do not come for me; go to the Abyss, depart to the Flood! I am satisfied, I am not hungry by means of this ḳmḥw-bread of Horus which I have eaten, which my chief woman has prepared for me, and I am satisfied thereby, I assume my (normal) condition thereby. I will not be thirsty by reason of Shu, I will not be hungry by reason of Tefenut; Hapy, Duamutef, Kebhsenuf, and Imsety will expel this hunger which is on my lips (utterance 338).[19]

O my father the King, raise yourself upon your left side, place yourself upon your right side for this fresh water which I have given to you. O my father the King, raise yourself upon your left side, place yourself upon your right side for this warm bread which I have made for you (utterance 482).[20]

Interestingly, the Pyramid Texts are not consistent in mood. Sometimes the spells are confident declarations that the king will ascend to the sky and take his rightful place in the heavens. In one particularly striking example, the king actually goes on a rampage among the gods, devouring them in gory detail and thereby acquiring their magic.[21] Yet in a different spell, the very same king is nothing more than Re's obedient

---

18 Faulkner, *The Ancient Egyptian Pyramid Texts*, 78. In utterance 481 the Imperishable Stars, and thus the king's destination, are in the east: "I ferry across in order that I may stand on the east side of the sky in its northern region among the Imperishable Stars...." (169). Later the west became the direction in which the dead headed.

19 Faulkner, *The Ancient Egyptian Pyramid Texts*, 109. See also utterances 339–349 for similar material.

20 Faulkner, *The Ancient Egyptian Pyramid Texts*, 169.

21 This occurs in utterances 273–74, in the pyramid of Unas. Although Teti's pyramid also uses the spell it was subsequently dropped, "a clear indication that this very primitive text was not suited to the thinking of later generations" says Lichtheim, *Ancient Egyptian Literature*, I:30. An analogous if somewhat less graphic example is spell 217, in which the king's arrival is repeatedly announced with the statement that king will let live or kill whomever he wishes among the gods and spirits.

secretary.[22] Self-assertion alternates with requests and pleas. From time to time a spell will declare that the king is alive and whole with an insistence that borders on desperation: "you have gone, but you will return, you have slept, [but you will awake], you have died, but you will live...."[23] In addition, some spells make it apparent that the dead pharaoh's passage into the beyond was not exactly a safe and unhindered trip. One counsels that the subject seek protection "from all wrath of the dead."[24] Another assures him that "the earth-gods shall not lay hold of you."[25] Others specifically identify Osiris as a potential threat. Re "will never give me to Osiris, for I have not died the death...."[26] "May Osiris not come with this his evil coming; do not open your arms to him...."[27] "....look down upon Osiris when he governs the spirits, for you stand far off from him, you are not among them and you shall not be among them"[28]

Regarding the role of Osiris in the Pyramid Texts, it seems evident that this god is something of an interloper in what is mainly and originally a solar theology, and moreover that he is an ambivalent figure. Breasted noted that the Pyramid Texts are testimony to an earlier time when Osiris was a hostile force to the celestial dead,[29] but that they also show a process of "Osirianization," in which the god is integrated into the

---

[22] See utterance 309 in Faulkner, *The Ancient Egyptian Pyramid Texts*, 96, or in Lichtheim, *Ancient Egyptian Literature*, I:39. The latter translates in part "Unas squats before him, Unas opens his boxes, Unas unseals his decrees, Unas seals his dispatches, Unas sends his messengers who tire not, Unas does what Unas is told." Lichtheim comments on how unlike the "cannibalistic bluster" of utterance 273–74 this is.

[23] Faulkner, *The Ancient Egyptian Pyramid Texts*, 285, utterance 670.

[24] Faulkner, *The Ancient Egyptian Pyramid Texts*, 21, utterance 93.

[25] Faulkner, *The Ancient Egyptian Pyramid Texts*, 206, utterance 703.

[26] Faulkner, *The Ancient Egyptian Pyramid Texts*, 74, utterance 264.

[27] Faulkner, *The Ancient Egyptian Pyramid Texts*, 201, utterance 534. This spell goes on to hope that Horus will not come, nor Seth, nor Thoth, Isis, and Nephthys, among others. Faulkner remarks that all the deities of the Osirian circle are regarded as hostile.

[28] Faulkner, *The Ancient Egyptian Pyramid Texts*, 58, utterance 245.

[29] Breasted, *Development of Religion and Thought in Ancient Egypt*, 142; see also J. Zandee, *Death as an Enemy According to Ancient Egyptian Conceptions* (Leiden: E. J. Brill, 1960) 210.

heavenly framework.[30] Part of the time Osiris is a benefactor to the king and seems to function to some extent in the heavenly regions with Re. Wilson describes the situation as one in which there were two kinds of mortuary religion, one solar, one Osirian.[31] As time wore on, changes in religious perspective came about which led to the dominance of Osiris in the realm of the dead. This will be discussed further in the next section.

The Pyramid Texts, then, are not full of sunshine and roses. Some parts express assertion and confidence, but others reveal concern and anxiety about the king's possible experiences after death. There are dangers which must be avoided, journeys which must be successfully completed, and physical requirements for sustenance that must continue to be met. The spells collectively engage in an attempt to ensure that the deceased king can continue to function as if still alive and attain a kind of beatification in the sky. Death is to be thoroughly overcome.

The Coffin Texts

The perspective on death and the afterlife changes considerably by the time the Coffin Texts come into existence. Before examining this material a few comments on the historical background of the time will help put them into context. Five centuries of a strong central government, with Pharaoh at the head, came to an end in the early twenty-second century BCE and were followed by about 150 years in which the locus of authority shifted to provincial centers of power. This is called the First Intermediate Period.[32] One theory is that the massive efforts poured into the construction of the royal pyramids and mortuary complexes, along

---

30 Breasted, *Development of Religion and Thought in Ancient Egypt*, 150. In his view the combination of Re and Osiris in the texts, followed in later times by the eventual triumph of Osiris as the god of the afterlife, reflects a struggle between state and popular religion, with the popular winning out. This interpretation has been questioned by more recent scholars (see Wilson in the following footnote).

31 Wilson, *The Burden of Egypt*, 65–66. Wilson explicitly rejects the notion that Osiris was inherently a popular deity. Although Osiris eventually achieved dominance in the mortuary realm this was not because he was originally more "democratic." For most of the Old Kingdom both systems were royal religions to which the masses had no access.

32 B. G. Trigger et al, *Ancient Egypt: A Social History* (Cambridge: Cambridge University Press, 1983) 71. "The First Intermediate Period seems essentially to represent a loss of equilibrium between a powerful court and provincial aspirations" (115).

with the ongoing commitment of wealth in the form of goods to accompany the dead, finally depleted the strength of the pharaonic power structure.[33] An entirely unrelated phenomenon that may have contributed to the collapse of the Old Kingdom court was that the Nile ran at extreme lows in this period, which led to famine.[34] In any event, the socio-political status quo had changed in significant ways since the time period of the Pyramid Texts, and therefore it is no great surprise to see that the contemporary mortuary literature also acquires a new character.[35]

The Coffin Texts comprise a set of writings inscribed in private coffins mostly during the First Intermediate Period,[36] with a few in the late Old Kingdom and early Middle Kingdom. Although they are related to the older Pyramid Texts and even contain some of the same spells, many of them are new.[37] One of the most important aspects of this material is that its view of the hereafter is no longer restricted to the king. These writings represent the aspirations of private, if elite, citizens to achieve a life after death.[38] Most likely this appropriation of privilege is

---

[33] B. G. Trigger et al, *Ancient Egypt*, 176. They remark that possibly this was true in the sense that the official class was starting to exercise demands of a mortuary nature on their own, which might have overburdened a limited agricultural economy.

[34] B. G. Trigger et al, *Ancient Egypt*, 181. It is further stated that although it would be simplistic to view governmental decline as the result of an ecological disaster, the Nile lows might have added one more burden on a system already under strain.

[35] Jørgen Podemann Sørensen, "Divine Access: The So-called Democratization of Egyptian Funerary Literature as a Socio-cultural Process," in Gertie Englund, ed., *The Religion of the Ancient Egyptians: Cognitive Structures and Popular Expressions* (Stockholm: Almqvist & Wiksell International, 1989) 117, takes it as a given that the change in the political structure of the Old Kingdom lies behind the increasing access to the divine for private persons, although he comments that the causes for the political changes are not well understood.

[36] Morenz, *Egyptian Religion*, 227. Unlike the Pyramid Texts, which were carved in hieroglyphs, the Coffin Texts are written in hieratic; cf. Andrews, "Introduction," 12.

[37] Lichtheim, *Ancient Egyptian Literature*, I:131.

[38] Sørensen, "Divine Access: The So-called Democratization of Egyptian Funerary Literature as a Socio-cultural Process," 114–17, says that in terms of the literature there is no distinction between royal and non-royal, although he goes on to say that there were still limits in some areas to what a private person could appropriate. One of these was in iconography; a non-royal could not be portrayed worshipping a god face to face in the Middle Kingdom. Nevertheless, some ritual scenes do start appearing for the first time in private tombs, which in the Old

related to the devolution of authority from a single royal family to more numerous provincial centers, though whether it reflects changes in attitude that were part of the cause or of the effect of the devolution is uncertain. Certainly the rising influence of the nobility is a factor. In any event, one scholar gives a vivid description of the process in a single sentence: "The nobles seized the Pyramid Texts and had them inscribed upon their coffins."[39] The opening up of the hereafter in this way to non-royal persons is often described as a "democratization."[40]

In the Coffin Texts one could become a star in the sky with the moon god Thoth, or dwell in the Fields of Offerings with Osiris, or travel with Re on the sun-bark. Individuals may have had personal preferences, but all must have been options.[41] Unlike the Pyramid Texts, a solar or celestial destiny is no longer the main theme, but one of many choices.[42] Osiris has become a much more prominent figure, and consequently non-solar realms come into the spotlight; now there is an underworld in

---

Kingdom is not found. By the new Kingdom, non-royals can be shown adoring a god, though at first still not face to face; this was not possible until the Ramesside period (119–21).

[39] Wilson, *The Burden of Egypt*, 116. He adds that although it is difficult to know, this wider access to the hereafter may have extended beyond the well-to-do to the lowest classes. In six coffins a spell appears in which the creator-god implies that all are equal. The god states, "I did four good deeds within the portal of the horizon. I made the four winds that every man might breathe thereof like his fellow in his time. That is (the first) deed thereof. I made the great inundation that the poor man might have rights therein like the great man. That is (the second) deed thereof. I made every man like his fellow. I did not command that they do evil, (but) it was their hearts that violated what I had said. That is (the third) deed thereof. I made their hearts to cease from forgetting the West, in order that divine offerings might be given to the gods of the nomes. That is the (fourth) deed thereof" (117–118).

[40] Breasted, *Development of Religion and Thought in Ancient Egypt*, 252; Lesko, "Death and the Afterlife in Ancient Egyptian Thought," 1768; Andrews, "Introduction," 12; James P. Allen, "Funerary Texts and Their Meaning," in Sue D'Auria et al, eds., *Mummies and Magic: The Funerary Arts of Ancient Egypt* (Boston: Museum of Fine Arts, 1988) 48; Derchain, "Death in Egyptian Religion," 1:111.

[41] Lesko, "Death and the Afterlife in Ancient Egyptian Thought," 1767.

[42] For examples of celestial utterances see R. O. Faulkner, *The Ancient Egyptian Coffin Texts*, 3 Vols. (Warminster: Aris & Phillips, Ltd., 1973, 1977, 1978) spells 12, 44 and 53 (I:8, 36, 52).

addition to the heavenly sphere.[43] Osiris functions as the judge of the dead.[44] As in the Pyramid Texts, spells related to staving off hunger and thirst are frequent.[45] A new category of interest is a motif that dwells on the deceased's reunification with family in the netherworld. One poignant example is the following:

> ASSEMBLING A MAN'S FAMILY FOR HIM IN THE REALM OF THE DEAD. O Re'! O Atum! O Geb! O Nut! See, N goes down (sic) in to the sky, he goes down into the earth, he goes down into the waters seeking his family, seeking his father and mother, seeking his children and brethren, seeking his loved ones, seeking his friends, seeking his associates and his servants who worked for N on earth and seeking his concubines whom he has known, because N is you (sic) whom the Great One created. There are assembled for N his children and his concubines whom N's heart has accepted, and there are assembled for N his servants who worked for N on earth. If there delay, be prevented or impeded the giving of his father to N and the releasing of his mother to him and the assembling for N of his family [etc....] there shall be taken away the choice joints from upon the altars of the gods, p3ḳ-cakes shall not be kneaded [etc.... and if the family be given to N, then the offerings will be continued] ....N has gone down rejoicing and happy-hearted, for his family has been given to him. The great ones of N's family have gone down joyfully and their hearts are happy at meeting N.... ASSEMBLING THE FAMILY, FATHER, MOTHER, FRIENDS, ASSOCIATES, CHILDREN, WOMEN, CONCUBINES, SERVANTS, WORKERS AND EVERYTHING BELONGING TO A MAN FOR HIM IN THE REALM OF THE DEAD. A SPELL A MILLION TIMES RIGHT.[46]

As in the Pyramid Texts, a number of dangers await the deceased and must be conquered or avoided.

---

[43] Jan Assmann, "Death and Initiation in the Funerary Religion of Ancient Egypt," 143.

[44] Andrews, "Introduction," 12, points out that the term "the Osiris so-and-so," an expression of the dead person's identification with this god, is so frequent that it comes to mean little more that "the deceased."

[45] Examples include Faulkner, *The Ancient Egyptian Coffin Texts*, spells 70, 164–67, 173–221 (I:66, 142–44, 147–75). The latter set is largely concerned with not being forced to consume one's own feces or urine in the realm of the dead. See also spells 581, 661, 772 (II:184–85, 234, 302). Similarly cf. spells 1011 and 1012–14 (III:110–12, 112–15).

[46] Faulkner, *The Ancient Egyptian Coffin Texts*, spell 146 (I:123–24). See also spells 131–145 (I:113–124).

SPELL FOR THE VINDICATION OF A MAN AGAINST HIS FOE IN THE REALM OF THE DEAD.... may you have power over your enemies, may you have power over those who would harm you in the realm of the dead, may you have power over those who would command you to be harmed in the realm of the dead....[47]

....may you save me from the fishers of Osiris who cut off heads and sever necks and who take souls and spirits to the slaughter-house of those who eat fresh (meat). My head will not be cut off, my neck will not be severed, my name will not be unknown among the spirits, I will not be caught in a net, the food which is at my mouth will not be taken away, my heart (ib and ḥ3ty) will not be cut out, my soul will spend the night watching over my corpse, my face will not be sad, my heart will not be forgetful, I will not be ignorant of my path to the realm of the dead, for I am a spirit whose mouth is hale, and magic is what equips me according to my desire.[48]

BECOMING A FALCON. I am a falcon on that night of enriching the years. He has set dread of me in those who are over destruction, and respect for me in the lords of butchery; I will not be taken to the slaughter-house of the god, the destroyers will not use the whip-lashes on me, for I am the guide to the horizon of the sky.[49]

---

[47] Faulkner, *The Ancient Egyptian Coffin Texts*, spell 225 (I:177).

[48] Faulkner, *The Ancient Egyptian Coffin Texts*, spell 229 (I:182–83). In a similar vein spell 236 fends off the messengers of Osiris: "....O you terrible ones, you messengers of Osiris who close the mouths of the spirits because of what is in them, you are powerless to close my mouth, you cannot take away the movement of my legs.... Be far from me, you executioners of Osiris; you have no power over these feet of mine, for I possess the funerary meal in On; I know what I should know" (I:185). On not losing one's heart, see spells 387–388, 459 and 715 (II:17, 88, 271).

[49] Faulkner, *The Ancient Egyptian Coffin Texts*, spell 273 (I:206). Other spells express this fear of being killed and devoured in the netherworld. Cf. spell 265: "....I will never be given over to the killer, the hostile serpents have not eaten me...." (I:202); also cf. spell 335, part II: "....[to Re'] save me from that God whose shape is hidden and whose eyebrows are the arms of the balance on that day of reckoning with the robbers in the presence of the Lord of all, who puts bonds on the evil-doers at his slaughter-house, who kills souls; save me from those who deal wounds, the slayers whose fingers are painful. Their knives shall not have power over me, I will not go down into their cauldrons, I will not enter into their shambles, because I know their names, because I am one who proceeds on earth with Re' and who moors happily with Osiris...." (I:261); and spell 336 "....O Atum who are in the Great Mansion, excelling the gods, save me from that god who lives by slaughter, whose face is that of a hound, whose skin is that of a man, who is in charge of the windings of the Lake of Fire, who swallows shades, who snatches

SPELL FOR AVOIDING THE NET AND OF ESCAPING THE PURSE-NET
BY A SPIRIT IN THE REALM OF THE DEAD....[50]

A consistent concern is that the deceased regain all his faculties just as when alive on earth. The eyes blinded by death and the body's bent limbs will be restored to normal; the heart, soul, and body will reunite; bread, water, and air continue to be available for consumption.[51] A related motif is the worry that the subject retain a functioning memory. This is often expressed in terms of remembering one's name.[52] In other words, both the physical and mental status of the individual must remain at their best pre-mortem levels. Interestingly, the Coffin Texts do not necessarily deny that the individual has died, but the first death is followed by a new life. What is important is that one avoid the second death, which is irreversible. Statements such as "I died yesterday, I raised myself today," or "I have died the death, I have returned alive,"[53] show that in the worldview of the Coffin Texts, death is not the end, but a transition. The danger is dying the second death. "NOT DYING A SECOND DEATH.... May I live like Re every day, who lives after death...."[54] On other occasions, though, one can find denials that death has occurred at all: "O N! You depart living, you do not depart dead.... Raise yourself, N; live, for you are not dead."[55]

In some ways then, the Coffin Texts continue themes from the Pyramid Texts. The deceased might still join the sun-god or the

hearts, who casts the lasso, but who is not seen...." (I:270).

[50] Faulkner, *The Ancient Egyptian Coffin Texts*, spell 343 (I:277). Other net spells include 473–481 (II:112–27).

[51] Faulkner, *The Ancient Egyptian Coffin Texts*, spell 20, I:11.

[52] Faulkner, *The Ancient Egyptian Coffin Texts*, spells 410–412, 453–454 (I:63–64, 84–85).

[53] Faulkner, *The Ancient Egyptian Coffin Texts*, spells 513 and 515, II:145–46. Jan Assmann, *Egyptian Solar Religion in the New Kingdom: Re, Amun and the Crisis of Polytheism*, trans. Anthony Alcock (London and New York: Kegan Paul International, 1995) 202, writes "Death in this case does not mean physical death, which the Egyptians regarded merely as an opportunity for the just to make the transition to life on a different plane of existence, but rather the absolute end, non-existence (tm-wnn)."

[54] Faulkner, *The Ancient Egyptian Coffin Texts*, spell 424, II:69. See also spells 458, 787, and 896 (II:87–88, 308; III:55).

[55] Faulkner, *The Ancient Egyptian Coffin Texts*, III:22. Cf. Morenz, *Egyptian Religion*, 205, who points to another example of this denial, "Rise alive, you did not die; rise to life, you did not die."

circumpolar stars, want to acquire food and drink, and need to be careful of the threatening forces which could inflict harm. Nevertheless, the newer material does have its own character. Osiris and his realm come to the fore, and this pulls the main interest away from a solar teleology. The potential dangers which one might encounter seem to be greater in number and detail, and are quite horrific. The deceased has a persistent interest in rejoining family and associates. This is tied to perhaps the most important innovation the Coffin Texts have to offer, which is a widening of access to the afterlife from the king to the upper levels of society in general, if not to society in its entirety. The concern is that one be able to maintain one's family and social circle intact. The theological significance of bodily death is subordinated to the danger of a second and final death. The first death is simply a means to the transformation to eternal life. However, while happiness and security are the goal, the reader of the Coffin Texts comes away with a powerful sense of how dangerous the post-mortem journey can be. The deceased must be prepared to fend off all kinds of unpleasant creatures and experiences.

The Book of the Dead

The Book of the Dead is the next collection of mortuary literature and continues in the tradition of the Pyramid Texts and Coffin Texts. The name is modern; to the ancient Egyptians it was known as "The Spell(s) for Coming Forth by Day (prt m hrw)."[56] The material consists of almost two hundred chapters written on papyrus sheets. No individual copy contains all two hundred; this was the total from which some number would be chosen. The wealthy could have their own versions compiled based on personal selections of spells, while others would be able to buy pre-fabricated copies with spaces left empty for their name and titles.[57] The earliest version dates to the mid-fifteenth century BCE.[58] The Book of the Dead was the mortuary corpus for the New Kingdom and the rest of ancient Egyptian history.

---

56 Allen, "Funerary Texts and Their Meaning," 42. Spencer, *Death in Ancient Egypt*, 144, adds "this title alludes to the power of the inscriptions to enable an individual to emerge from the tomb after death."

57 Andrews, "Introduction," 11; Spencer, *Death in Ancient Egypt*, 149, adds "mass-produced coffins could be purchased in the same way."

58 Andrews, "Introduction," 11. Allen, "Funerary Texts and Their Meaning," 42, says that there are versions from the late Middle Kingdom, as well.

Although the number[59] and order of chapters varied, every known copy of the collection contains Chapter 1, Coming Forth by Day after Burial, Chapter 17, Coming Forth by Day Triumphant, and chapter 64, Coming Forth by Day in Various Transformations.[60] As in the case of the Coffin Texts, some of the spells go all the way back to the Pyramid Texts, others descend from the Coffin Text corpus, while yet others are new.[61] Because of this, the Book of the Dead reflects all of the antecedent mortuary traditions—the hope for an astral afterlife, the solar destiny, and union with Osiris in the Field of Reeds.[62] Beginning in the Eighteenth Dynasty, the Book of the Dead "became the standardized form for funerary literature until the end of Egyptian civilization."[63]

The best known chapter is 125, which is usually called "the negative confession."[64] Here the judgment scene before Osiris, the most important event the deceased faces,[65] is laid out in detail as he proceeds to defend himself and insist on his moral worthiness.[66] The chapter

---

[59] Andrews, "Introduction," 12. In the earliest copies the chapters as well as the vignettes are few in number. Throughout the New Kingdom both increased.

[60] Andrews, "Introduction," 14. She adds that starting in the Twenty-Sixth Dynasty the order of chapters was made more consistent and the total set at 192. This text is called the Saite Recension, as opposed to the earlier and more varied papyri, known as the Theban Recension.

[61] Allen, "Funerary Texts and Their Meaning," 42, states that sixty percent of the Book of the Dead goes back to the Pyramid and/or Coffin Texts.

[62] Andrews, "Introduction," 12.

[63] Allen, "Funerary Texts and Their Meaning," 42.

[64] Although many scholars are quick to point out that nothing in this chapter is like a confession, since the speaker emphatically denies any type of wrongdoing. See A. J. Spencer, *Death in Ancient Egypt*, 145: "the deceased does not confess to anything; instead, he simply enumerates his virtues."

[65] Alexandre Piankoff and N. Rambova, *The Mythological Papyri* (New York: Pantheon Books, 1957) 5.

[66] Book of the Dead papyri contain illustrations which represent a number of the places and events described in the chapters, and naturally the all-important judgment scene comes in for attention. Typically the dead man or woman stands to one side of a large set of scales, on which the heart is weighed against the feather of truth (Maat). Osiris watches over the proceeding, often attended by Isis and Nephthys. Anubis or Horus operates the balance, while Thoth records the results. Others can appear too, such as the Forty-Two Assessors. Cf. J. Gwyn Griffiths, *The Divine Verdict: A Study of Divine Judgement in the Ancient Religions* (Leiden: E. J. Brill, 1991) 226–227. In the Papyrus of Ani, which provides a particularly good example of the judgment scene, Ani enters the judgment hall with his wife and makes a speech in which he pleads with his own heart not to betray him. Cf.

contains a hodgepodge of methods. Some of the time the speaker insists that he has done no wrong, and lists all of the crimes he has avoided. These include such standard moral items as murder, slander, or oppression of another person, as well as cultic offenses such as skimping on the divine offerings. The deceased also gains ground in his movement into the hall of judgment by virtue of his knowledge about various esoteric matters. An example is his ability to give the obscure names of the architectural components of the hall itself, as well as being able to identify the names of the gods. Other common themes in the Book of the Dead in general are the concern to secure the dead individual's ability to move freely between the realms of the living and the dead;[67] to prevent attacks by snakes and other hostile creatures, slaughter, decapitation and similar maladies;[68] to have air and water;[69] to achieve a variety of transformations;[70] to have knowledge of various spirits;[71] to be a worthy spirit;[72] and to get food.[73] The Fields of the Blessed are where the deceased dwells, for which a good example is chapter 149.[74]

Spencer, *Death in Ancient Egypt*, 144. John Baines, "Society, Morality, and Religious Practice," in Byron E. Shafer, ed. *Religion in Ancient Egypt: Gods, Myths, and Personal Practice* (Ithaca, NY: Cornell University Press, 1991) 151, says that the actual judgment scene is not found before the Eighteenth Dynasty, but the idea of an ethical judgment was probably quite old.

[67] Cf. R. O. Faulkner, *The Ancient Egyptian Book of the Dead* (Austin: The University of Texas Press, 1993) for examples including spells 2, 9, 12, 13, 66–68, 71–72, 122, 180, 188 (36–37, 69–70, 71–72, 113–114, 177–180, 185).

[68] Faulkner, *The Ancient Egyptian Book of the Dead*, examples include spells 31–37, 39–50, 153A–154, 163–164 (56–58, 60–65, 149–153, 158–160).

[69] Faulkner, *The Ancient Egyptian Book of the Dead*, examples include spells 54–59, 62 (65–68).

[70] Faulkner, *The Ancient Egyptian Book of the Dead*, examples include spells 77–88 (73–84). Beatrice L. Goff, *Symbols of Ancient Egypt*, 31–32, lists the following forms the deceased could take: "the falcon, lotus, goose, phoenix, heron, swallow, scorpion, snake, crocodile, and in addition the form of different gods, as Ptah, Re, Atum, and Hathor."

[71] Faulkner, *The Ancient Egyptian Book of the Dead*, examples include spells 108–109, 112–115 (101–102, 108–113).

[72] Faulkner, *The Ancient Egyptian Book of the Dead*, examples include spells 130, 133–136A (117–120, 121–126).

[73] Faulkner, *The Ancient Egyptian Book of the Dead*, examples include spells 148–149, 178, 189 (137–145, 176, 185–188).

[74] Jan Assmann, "Death and Initiation in the Funerary Religion of Ancient Egypt," 143, comments on the fact that this mortuary knowledge becomes a science

While Re still holds a place of authority in this literature, Osiris has without question become the dominating figure. His myth, however, is in none of the writings discussed so far related in full from beginning to end. Instead it is assumed as common knowledge, which means that although a full account is lacking, much of it can be pieced together from the many references and allusions. Nowhere is the actual murder of Osiris described, a fact due to a reluctance by the ancient Egyptians to enunciate in any way such an ominous event.[75] The full narrative appears for the first time in the account of Plutarch, who relates the tale in his "De Iside et Osiride," which was written around 120 CE.[76] Briefly, in days of yore when Osiris was king and his wife Isis queen, his evil brother Seth devised a plan with his followers in which he killed Osiris and seized the kingship. After much effort on the part of Isis, she finally found her husband's body, used her magic to resuscitate him, and became pregnant with their son Horus, who had to fight and overcome his uncle in order to claim his rightful place as the new king. Osiris became ruler of the netherworld.[77] Eventually a tradition formed in the Middle Kingdom that Osiris had been buried in Abydos, and people began to make pilgrimages, some of them having cenotaphs set up near by. Every year the story of Osiris and his resurrection was performed there by actors and attracted

---

in its own right and reflects "the typical bureaucratic and systematic style of Egyptian daily life, transposed to the next world."

[75] Cf. Erik Hornung, *Conceptions of God in Ancient Egypt: The One and the Many*, trans. John Baines (Ithaca, NY: Cornell University Press, 1982) 152. "Texts speak of the tomb and the resurrection of Osiris, and both are even depicted pictorially; there are allusion to what his enemies 'did' to him, his 'deathly tiredness,' and the laments of his sisters, Isis and Nephthys, are mentioned—but Egyptian texts of the pharaonic period never say that Osiris died. In the cult celebrations of the Osiris myth at the festival of Abydos this detail—the god's violent death—remains unmentioned."

[76] See J. Gwyn Griffiths, *Plutarch's De Iside et Osiride* (Cambridge: University of Wales Press, 1970) sections 12–19. Plutarch is not infallible by any means, but his version seems to tally in general with what is known from the Egyptian sources.

[77] This myth was also important with respect to the status of the pharaoh, who functioned in the role of Horus Triumphant and who had successfully overcome the forces of chaos. Upon his death he was identified with Osiris while his own heir became Horus.

large audiences.[78] In the Book of the Dead, even though there is still room for Re and others, this myth provides the main structural frame.[79]

Innovations in the mortuary textual traditions did not stop with the Book of the Dead, even though it remained the primary source throughout the rest of ancient Egyptian history.[80] In royal tombs of the New Kingdom a series of materials that mostly consisted of illustrations appeared.[81] These are sometimes referred to by scholars as "guides to the beyond," and they portray maps of the underworld, the different gatekeepers and demons there, and the spells needed to get by them.[82] Examples include "The Book of Gates," "The Book of Caves," and the "Amduat."[83] Later in the Twenty-First Dynasty a collection of texts called the Mythological Papyri became current. The examples that have survived were largely made for priests and priestesses, and were also mostly pictorial in nature, although a number of the scenes illustrate chapters found in the Book of the Dead.[84] Copies of the Book of the Dead might contain illustrations of their own, but there appears to have been a trend among some circles within the royal and priestly spheres that favored iconography over text, with a focus on the geography of the underworld and the various stages and creatures that awaited each step of the way.

---

78 Beatrice L. Goff, *Symbols of Ancient Egypt*, 28.

79 Osiris and Re are completely identified with one another when Re travels through the underworld each night. There he meets Osiris and they become the "United Soul." Cf. Piankoff and N. Rambova, *The Mythological Papyri*, 6. Re's myth, where he continually fights off the cosmic enemy in the form of Apophis, joins the Osiris cycle of death and resurrection (7).

80 The Book of the Dead itself underwent a process of systematization, an evolution that has led to the treatment of papyri in terms of different recensions, as mentioned in footnote #60, Andrews, "Introduction," 14.

81 In the late New Kingdom in general a big change came about in which the usual scenes of daily life in the tombs disappeared and were replaced by scenes of the netherworld. Cf. Baines, "Society, Morality, and Religious Practice," 196; Wilson, *The Burden of Egypt*, 296–97.

82 Leonard H. Lesko, *The Composition of the Book of Two Ways*, Dissertation (The University of Chicago, 1969) 2. The earliest example of this kind of highly pictorial material is "The Book of Two Ways," which actually appears in the Coffin Texts (3). It was usually placed on the inside bottom of the coffin, and portrayed a pair of paths, an upper waterway and a lower land path, on which the deceased could travel to the mansion of Osiris or the "Field of Offerings" (4).

83 Lesko, "Death and the Afterlife in Ancient Egyptian Thought," 1768.

84 Piankoff and N. Rambova, *The Mythological Papyri*, 3.

Mortuary Practices

Such is the main content of the different collections of mortuary texts that have survived to the present day. Clearly beliefs about and responses to death evolved throughout Egyptian history. Not only did the content of the traditions shift emphases and scope, but so did the manner of recording, from carvings in stone, to inscriptions in coffins, to papyri. So far, however, the picture is one-sided. Although the ancient Egyptians by anyone's reckoning had a huge body of literary materials relating to death, they also had an extensive funerary cult which accompanied the texts (or vice versa). At this point it would be useful to look at the main features of their burial procedures and tomb apparati.

The Pyramid Texts, of course, were part of the mortuary ritual of the pharaoh and inscribed in the pyramid chambers. This discussion, however, will focus on the typical practices of later periods when a broader range of people had access to the afterlife. After the age of the pyramids drew to a close, the rock-cut or stone-built tomb became the locus of burial for king and commoner alike.[85] The exact layout of the tomb varied, but it always had a chamber for burial and a chapel, which usually comprised a single complex, but not always. The burial chamber was not open to the public and was below ground or deep within a cliff wall, while the chapel was accessible to priests and passersby for offerings.[86] Some people left inscribed invitations outside for visitors to come into the chapel and make an offering, describing how beautiful the chapel was and the exalted rank of the owner.[87] Offerings could consist of everything from actual food and drink to a recitation of an offering

---

[85] Ann Macy Roth, "The Social Aspects of Death," in Sue D'Auria et al, eds., *Mummies and Magic: The Funerary Arts of Ancient Egypt* (Boston: Museum of Fine Arts, 1988) 53, writes: "Building and equipping a tomb was one of the main occupations of adult Egyptians of the upper classes."

[86] Roth, "The Social Aspects of Death," 54. The chapel could consist of many rooms, or a single niche; it could be covered with inscriptions and paintings, or be left bare.

[87] Roth, "The Social Aspects of Death," 55. She also notes, "Aware of these potential visitors, tomb owners often included amusing scenes and jokes in their tomb decoration."

formula by a visitor.[88] Since even uttering the deceased's name could keep him alive, many people also had memorials and offering requests placed in temples and pilgrimage spots where there was a heavy flow of traffic.[89]

Every effort was made to preserve the body through the process of mummification before it was sealed up in the tomb along with the grave goods.[90] This involved the removal of various internal organs, desiccation by a drying agent like natron, padding, and bandaging with strips of linen. The goal was to keep the body in one piece so that it continue to function as it had in life; in short, it became a "living corpse."[91] The importance that bodily preservation played in the cultural psyche is apparent in chapter 154 of the Book of the Dead, "Spell for preventing a corpse decomposing." It reads in part: "My members shall endure forever. I have not decayed, I have [not become bloated], I have not decomposed, I have not become rotten.... I exist, I exist, alive, alive, enduring, enduring."[92] The mummified individual was identified with Osiris.[93]

In the funeral itself, the mummy was carried in a procession of family, mourners, and priests to the tomb. The event always included an

---

88 Eberhard Otto, *Die biographischen Inschriften der ägyptischen Spätzeit* (Leiden: E. J. Brill, 1954) 57, cites examples of the common plea to the visitor for an offering recitation with the assurance that uttering the formula does not cause the speaker to become weary, that is, it is effortless, and does not require giving up something out of one's own possessions.

89 Roth, "The Social Aspects of Death," 55. Popular Middle Kingdom spots were the "terrace of the great god" in Abydos and the shrine of Heka-ib, a deified man, at Elephantine. In later times popular cult centers to place memorials included those of Amen-Re in Thebes and Ptah in Memphis, or in the Late Period, animal cemeteries. Invitations and requests by the dead, of course, were not decipherable by the bulk of the population which was illiterate, and therefore must have been aimed at the educated scribal and priestly class.

90 Edward F. Wente, "Funerary Beliefs of the Ancient Egyptians: An Interpretation of the Burials and the Texts," *Expedition* Winter (1982) 17, says that at least in the New Kingdom during the imperial period even the lower classes practiced mummification.

91 Morenz, *Egyptian Religion*, 198–20.

92 Alan B. Lloyd, "Psychology and Society in the Ancient Egyptian Cult of the Dead," in William Kelly Simpson, ed., *Religion and Philosophy in Ancient Egypt* (New Haven: Yale University Press, 1989) 127.

93 Wente, "Funerary Beliefs of the Ancient Egyptians: An Interpretation of the Burials and the Texts," 19.

opening-of-the-mouth ritual, in which the priest restored the dead person's faculties to him, such as breathing and eating. It took place outside the door of the tomb and was an important step in the transformation of the dead person into his new state of existence.[94] This was a one-time ritual at the moment of burial, while the offering ritual was an ongoing endeavor.[95] Because the need for offerings was continual, interment of the mummy was not the end of the process. This required the endowment of a mortuary cult, in which priests were to make the requisite offerings and perform accompanying rituals. A portion of land and its produce would be set aside in perpetuity for two purposes, to provide the offerings themselves and pay the hired priests to offer them.[96] The main priest was called the ḥm-ka, the servant of the ka, but the function could be fulfilled by more than one person serving in rotation.[97] Of course the endowment did not really last in perpetuity, since the passage of generations led to a loss of interest and financial support, which is why the backup of inscribing requests to the living for a recitation of the offering formula if nothing else was at hand existed.[98] "Briefly summarized, Egyptian funerary practices consisted of a period of mourning and preparation of the corpse, the interment, and the conduct

---

[94] Lloyd, "Psychology and Society in the Ancient Egyptian Cult of the Dead," 126. A sm-priest performed the ritual with an adze. "I open for you your mouth. I open for you your mouth with the adze of Anubis with which the mouths of every god are opened."

[95] Roth, "The Social Aspects of Death," 57.

[96] Roth, "The Social Aspects of Death," 52.

[97] Roth, "The Social Aspects of Death," 53. This position was often filled by the tomb owner's son, which had the double advantage of providing for one's offspring while ensuring Osirian filial piety. Taking care of burying parents was a requirement of inheritance. Cf. also Morenz, *Egyptian Religion*, 195, who believes that this requirment dates to the earliest periods. Lloyd, "Psychology and Society in the Ancient Egyptian Cult of the Dead," 129, notes that even a paid professional priest, in his function of making the offerings, was considered to be the deceased's son.

[98] Wente, "Funerary Beliefs of the Ancient Egyptians: An Interpretation of the Burials and the Texts," 19. Derchain, "Death in Egyptian Religion," 112, also remarks that the gradual decline of one's mortuary endowment was a well-known fact to the Egyptians, and was compensated for by the funeral myth, which "integrates the individual into the universe rather than into the single small group of which he is a part, and thus guarantees him the possibility of an unlimited existence."

of a regular cult of the deceased which was intended to last indefinitely."[99]

By this point a seeming contradiction in attitudes with regard to the fate of the dead emerges. The mortuary literature describes a transference of the deceased to the sky or the underworld, where, by the time of the Book of the Dead if not earlier, he must pass a judgment of his moral worth in life, while the tomb, grave goods, and offerings suggest that the person stays within the sepulchre and retains life through physical means.[100] Which is it? The answer is that the Egyptians were able to hold all of these conceptions together in a single system. Although part of the reason for this is that they simply were untroubled by a multiplicity of approaches, it also helps to understand their ideas about the composition of an individual person, which comprised a number of components. Egyptian thoughts on the matter seem complex to the modern student, but it is an important element in understanding their views about what happened at and after death to any single individual.

During life, the physical frame was called the body, and the corpse or mummy after death.[101] The "shadow" most often appears in the context of the dead, although it also existed in life. It seems to be associated with

---

[99] Lloyd, "Psychology and Society in the Ancient Egyptian Cult of the Dead," 124.

[100] Morenz, *Egyptian Religion*, 204, states the question thus: "did Egyptians visualize life in the beyond as taking place solely in the tomb (through the conservation of the body or the presence of the ka as the life-force)?" His answer is "no." Cf. also Murnane, "Taking It With You: The Problem of Death and Afterlife in Ancient Egypt," 43. He writes "The range of options that Egyptian mortuary religion seems to offer hints at unresolved ambiguities in the conception of death and the afterlife. One strategy, to all appearances the oldest, centered on the continued sustenance that the dead required from the world of the living—in a real sense 'taking it with them.' Its alternative involved a journey from this world to another part of the universe, where the deceased joined the circuit of nature or took up residence in the realm of Osiris.... The otherworldly orbit of the dead was not seen as a bar to their inhabiting their tombs or participating in the feasts of the living. Most Egyptologists explain the inconsistency of these notions in terms of the conservatism of Egyptian society." Although the Egyptians often avoid simply rejecting one conception for another, their multiple views of the fate of the dead are not just a salad of mutually exclusive beliefs. This becomes clear when seen in light of their ideas about the human makeup, as the discussion will show.

[101] Lloyd, "Psychology and Society in the Ancient Egyptian Cult of the Dead," 119.

the mummy and in artistic representation is a black silhouette of the deceased.[102] The "name" and the "heart" were more significant to the Egyptians than their literal meanings might suggest. The name comprised a person's essence, so much so that if nothing else survived, memory of the name by the living could sustain the deceased's existence. The heart was the source of the intellect, as well as emotion.[103] In the moment of judgment after death the deceased might plead with the heart not to betray him, and many spells were concerned to prevent one's heart being taken away.

Every living person was the possessor of a "ka."[104] Iconographically the ka was depicted as the person's double, and is usually described by scholars as "a sustaining vital force,"[105] "the vital element within a human being,"[106] or a "life-force."[107] This force is not individual to a person, but suffuses all the living, including the gods.[108] It is born at the same moment as the individual and continues to exist after death. When offerings are made at a tomb, it is specifically to the ka that they are given.[109]

In addition to the ka there existed the "ba," often translated as "soul," though others reject this translation for the confusion it can cause when equated with the modern idea of the soul. It approximates the notion of "personality" or "character" and unlike the ka is individual to every person.[110] While it exists during life it really comes into its own at death. The ba is the aspect of the person that can detach from the body after death and move about through the earth, and for this reason is

---

[102] Lloyd, "Psychology and Society in the Ancient Egyptian Cult of the Dead," 119.

[103] Lloyd, "Psychology and Society in the Ancient Egyptian Cult of the Dead," 119.

[104] Originally only the king had a ka, but eventually everyone does.

[105] Wente, "Funerary Beliefs of the Ancient Egyptians: An Interpretation of the Burials and the Texts," 19.

[106] Lloyd, "Psychology and Society in the Ancient Egyptian Cult of the Dead," 119.

[107] Allen, "Funerary Texts and Their Meaning," 43.

[108] Allen, "Funerary Texts and Their Meaning," 44.

[109] Wente, "Funerary Beliefs of the Ancient Egyptians: An Interpretation of the Burials and the Texts," 19.

[110] Allen, "Funerary Texts and Their Meaning," 43.

usually drawn as a human-headed bird.[111] A well-known expression states "the corpse to the earth, the ba to heaven,"[112] which emphasizes the ba's mobility. "The ba was that aspect of the deceased's personality that functioned outside the natural limitations imposed upon a material body. The corpse remained permanently in the tomb, but the ba was free to move throughout the cosmos."[113]

The "akh" is something like a ghost,[114] and is unlike all the other components because instead of being one aspect out of many parts that make up the whole person, it was "the total person in a state of beatitude and power beyond the grave."[115] The akh functioned as a member of the social world of the beyond, and could affect matters in this world.[116] People in the world of the living acted on behalf of the dead in terms of their interaction with the ka, by making offerings to it; the dead acted on behalf of the living in their aspect as an akh.[117]

These elements functioned together as a unified whole, forming a complete human being in the physical, intellectual, and spiritual aspects. Although to today's reader this may seem a complex approach for understanding all those indefinable things that make a person a unique entity, it does help make the mortuary traditions more comprehensible. The preservation of the corpse, the tomb, and the ongoing offerings

---

111 Lloyd, "Psychology and Society in the Ancient Egyptian Cult of the Dead," 119.

112 Wente, "Funerary Beliefs of the Ancient Egyptians: An Interpretation of the Burials and the Texts," 20; see also Miriam Lichtheim, *Maat in Egyptian Autobiographies and Related Studies* (Göttingen: Vandenhoeck & Ruprecht, 1992) 51, who translates a text in which appears the following line, "[I] now rest in the beautiful west, my Ba in heaven, my corpse in the graveyard...."

113 Wente, "Funerary Beliefs of the Ancient Egyptians: An Interpretation of the Burials and the Texts," 20.

114 Wente, "Funerary Beliefs of the Ancient Egyptians: An Interpretation of the Burials and the Texts," 19.

115 Lloyd, "Psychology and Society in the Ancient Egyptian Cult of the Dead," 119–120. Allen, "Funerary Texts and Their Meaning," 45, describes the akh as the state that is achieved when the ba and the ka rejoin one another.

116 Wente, "Funerary Beliefs of the Ancient Egyptians: An Interpretation of the Burials and the Texts," 19–20. Derchain, "Death in Egyptian Religion," 112, describes the akh similarly, as the form in which the dead would interact with the living.

117 Wente, "Funerary Beliefs of the Ancient Egyptians: An Interpretation of the Burials and the Texts," 19–20.

assured the well-being of the body and the ka, while the ba could join Re in the sun bark or travel through the underworld. As an akh each person could play a role in the community of dead as well as the living, just as when alive on earth. So the cult and the literature were not contradictory; everything worked together in an overall system that made sense.

ANALYSIS: THE VIEW OF DEATH

Community

The preceding pages provide a description of the texts and cult of ancient Egyptian mortuary traditions, but it remains to synthesize the material in an attempt to discern what the overall shape of Egyptian attitudes towards death was. What trends emerge, and what can be said about the Egyptian response as a system? The first observation is that death, for all of its importance on an individual level, is essentially a community event, and much of the concern of the cult and literature is to overcome the inevitable separation that death brings about and to reintegrate the deceased back into the community as soon as possible. "Community" includes not just the world of the living, but that of the dead as well. This feature of the Egyptian response to death can be seen in a number of ways.

First of all, there is the mortuary cult with its provision for ongoing offerings to the dead, preferably by the heir or, if this was not to be, by a priest who takes on the role of the deceased's son. Family obligation does not cease with death, in other words. It simply takes on a new form. In addition, the dead and the living continued to join together in the celebration of important holidays.[118] A well-known example is the case of the Theban "Feast of the Valley," a popular New Kingdom festival day when the god Amun would leave his temple on the east bank of the Nile and cross over to visit the royal mortuary temples on the west bank. At the same time the families of the dead also crossed the river and held feasts in the chapels of their departed loved ones. "This feast, in which the dead were thought to join, helped the living to continue their relationships with their dead relatives, and enabled the dead to continue

---

[118] Lloyd, "Psychology and Society in the Ancient Egyptian Cult of the Dead," 129.

to participate in the festivals of the community."[119] The sense of continued community between the two worlds is also evident in tomb paintings in which several generations are depicted sharing a banquet together. There is no apparent distinction between those who are still living and those who have died, which suggests that death is not a factor in the determination of family membership.[120]

The continuation of family obligation was a two-way street. Just as the living continued to bear responsibilities toward the dead, so was the opposite true, as the practice of writing letters to the dead shows.[121] As noted earlier, letters were always addressed to the akh, and might request assistance in a crisis in the form of legal action in the beyond, or plead that unpleasant interference cease.[122] A famous example of the latter is a letter from a man to his wife where he demands to know what he has done that prompted her to make his life difficult after she died. He insists that he never did anything against her, and threatens to make a formal complaint against her before the Divine Ennead of the West.[123] Again,

---

[119] Roth, "The Social Aspects of Death," 59. She adds that even in modern times the Egyptians pay visits to their dead at important festivals, "a remnant of the ancient Egyptians' communal view of the afterlife and the important role given to the dead in ancient Egyptian society." Cf. also Murnane, "Taking It With You: The Problem of Death and Afterlife in Ancient Egypt," 39, for similar comments.

[120] Murnane, "Taking It With You: The Problem of Death and Afterlife in Ancient Egypt," 39.

[121] Such letters were left in the tomb chapel, sometimes written on a bowl which was then filled with food. When the deceased came for the food he would find the letter; cf. Derchain, "Death in Egyptian Religion," 112. These letters, says Lesko, "Death and the Afterlife in Ancient Egyptian Thought," 1765, shows that the dead were not thought to be much different from the living. "The continuity of life and the afterlife was assumed and reunification with family members was expected. The dead were approachable and reproachable; they could be cajoled, and they could meddle in the affairs of the living. People expected justice and were not afraid to insist on a quid pro quo...."

[122] Wente, "Funerary Beliefs of the Ancient Egyptians," 20. Gardiner, *The Attitude of the Ancient Egyptians to Death and the Dead*, 24, says the concept of writing letters to the dead shows that the Egyptians considered ties unaltered by death. "It is as though death had no more effect than to set a barrier analogous to that of physical distance."

[123] Lloyd, "Psychology and Society in the Ancient Egyptian Cult of the Dead," 124.

family interaction, although certainly not identical to what it was in life, does not stop with death.

Further, one concern that emerges in the Coffin Texts is that the deceased be rejoined with family members who were already in the netherworld; he goes "seeking his father and mother, seeking his children and brethren, seeking his loved ones, seeking his friends, seeking his associates and his servants who worked for N on earth and seeking his concubines whom he has known."[124] This spell is an attempt to reconstruct in full the immediate family circle of the deceased, as well as the wider social structure, including friends and servants.

The deceased makes a transition from the world of the living to the world of the dead, but the members of each maintain relations with the other, and the latter reflects the former in that it too functions as a community.[125] The rituals, funeral, guides, and spells all help the deceased become a functioning member of the netherworld's society.[126] "Personal identity is, for the Egyptian, a function of social integration and approval. A human being is a person only within the limits of the image which the (significant) others hold of him."[127] Therefore in order to exist as a person after death the individual must once again become part of a community, that of the other spirits and the gods, which makes it possible to continue to interact with one's original society on earth.[128] A person's

---

[124] For full citation of the passage, see page 132. Faulkner, *The Ancient Egyptian Coffin Texts*, spell 146 (I:123–24). See also spells 131–145 (I:113–124).

[125] Assmann, "Death and Initiation in the Funerary Religion of Ancient Egypt," 152, remarks that the community of the dead is modelled on earthly society.

[126] Assmann, "Death and Initiation in the Funerary Religion of Ancient Egypt," 144, writes, "The netherworld appears therein first and foremost as a social sphere, in which the deceased must move and, eventually, integrate himself by means of the spoken word: by appealing, conjuring, intimidating, beseeching, threatening, answering, etc...."

[127] Assmann, "Death and Initiation in the Funerary Religion of Ancient Egypt," 151.

[128] Baines, "Society, Morality, and Religious Practice," 147, says "People hoped that death would lead them to a desired state in the hereafter, but death did not necessarily end their role in this life. Here the Western view that society consists only of the living blocks comprehension. The Egyptian living and dead were part of the same community, and the dead could intervene positively or negatively among the living."

home base, as it were, shifts from one world to the other, but together the two worlds remain part of a whole.

In other words, the ancient Egyptians functioned on the basis of a sense of collective self, and this is reflected in their views of death. This is not to say that they had no notion of individual identity, because they did, and the notion of continuity in the face of death is oriented toward individual existence, but the community is writ large in much of their way of living and thus in their mortuary traditions. "[W]hen they defined what they were, essentially and fundamentally, when they related their existence to life and death, the social community was their preferred reference point."[129] By becoming Osiris, the deceased merges not only with this god but with all the other dead as well.[130] In both life and death, then, the ancient Egyptian was always part of the larger entity comprised of all Egyptians. Neither life nor death takes place on a purely individual level.[131]

Memory

A second consistent feature that emerges from the many texts and practices of ancient Egyptian mortuary religion is the importance of memory. One scholar approaches this topic from an interesting direction when he questions the usual interpretation of the cult of the dead. The tomb, grave goods, and ongoing offerings were not a literal attempt "to take it with you."[132] In fact, the texts that have survived make it clear that

---

[129] Ragnhild Bjerre Finnestad, "The Pharaoh and the 'Democratization' of Post-mortem Life," in Gertie Englund, ed., *The Religion of the Ancient Egyptians: Cognitive Structures and Popular Expressions* (Stockholm: Almqvist & Wiksell International, 1989) 91.

[130] Finnestad, "The Pharaoh and the 'Democratization' of Post-mortem Life," 91.

[131] Finnestad, "The Pharaoh and the 'Democratization' of Post-mortem Life," 92, remarks that in light of the Egyptian emphasis on community in life and death both, to call the opening of access to the afterlife beyond the royal sphere a 'democratization' is misleading in that this word's meaning is based on the rights of the individual. Yet the Egyptian afterlife was not so much a matter of individual attainment as it was of community integration.

[132] Herman te Velde, "Commemoration in Ancient Egypt," in H. G. Kippenberg et al, eds., *Visible Religion: Annual for Religious Iconography, Vol. I: Commemorative Figures* (Leiden: E. J. Brill, 1982) 138. He calls this a "completely stupid idea" which does the ancient Egyptians little credit, although he adds later

one's existence after death is not identical to life on earth. So what was the point of the tombs, offerings, and so on? They function to preserve the memory of the dead among the living.[133] Those who are not remembered, or commemorated, by another slip into non-being.[134] Mortuary art is one example of the effort for commemoration. "Art for the dead is really art for life. It is a protest against death and transience. The striving is to perpetuate, to hold fast, to keep in memory...."[135] Only by means of memory in the minds of others can a person be kept rooted in the community. The fact that merely reciting a person's name is enough to preserve that individual's existence further supports the point.

Not only is memory of the deceased in the minds of others important, but he must also retain his own memory after death. As noted in the discussion of the different compendia of spells that existed, one concern was that the dead person be able to remember his name. Memory of one's name signified retaining individual consciousness and identity. The ba, that element of the person which retains personality, gains its power from the fact that it *remembers* its life.[136] When the deceased seeks out the family and associates who have already reached the netherworld, this is an attempt to reintegrate into society and requires before anything else the preservation of personal identity, memory of the self, in other words.

An especially interesting text from a New Kingdom papyrus relates to the matter of memory.[137] It claims that the names of the scribes "have

---

that they "may sometimes have talked one another into it" (139).

[133] Te Velde, "Commemoration in Ancient Egypt," 142, states that grave goods are a material way of remembering the dead. Derchain, "Death in Egyptian Religion," 111, says that tomb has three functions, a home for the deceased, a place where the living and the dead can meet, and "a support for the memory of his existence."

[134] Te Velde, "Commemoration in Ancient Egypt," 140. Cf. also Derchain, "Death in Egyptian Religion," 112: "Survival is nothing but the remembrance of the dead, which rituals strive to prolong."

[135] Te Velde, "Commemoration in Ancient Egypt," 141. It should be noted that he does not claim the Egyptians had no idea of an objective life after death, but that it depended not on the physical apparatus of the tomb as much as on commemoration (140).

[136] Derchain, "Death in Egyptian Religion," 111.

[137] Te Velde, "Commemoration in Ancient Egypt," 143 also cites this in the conclusion of his argument.

become everlasting," while their relatives are forgotten.[138] The scribes had neither tombs nor heirs "to pronounce their names." Instead they made heirs out of books and instructions. The metaphor of the book as an heir is developed, and the writer states that all people become the children of the scribe through the guidance of the book he leaves.

> Their graves are forgotten.
> Their name is pronounced over their books,
> Which they made while they had being;
> *Good is the memory of their makers,*
> *It is forever and for all time!*

A second metaphor that treats the book as a tomb follows. "Surely useful in the graveyard/ Is a name in people's mouth!" The text then goes on to state that a book is actually better than a house, a chapel, or a stela. It lists a number of famous people of the past who left writings behind, and interestingly, most of them are known today.[139] The last words are "Death made their names forgotten/ But books made them remembered!"

The sentiments here did not become mainstream. People continued to practice the traditional means of burial, as did probably even the author of this text. But besides being interesting in its own right, it offers two points to the present discussion. One is the fact that memory was able to lend itself to such a powerful expression of human endurance in the face of oblivion, even to the denigration of the rest of the mortuary tradition with which it normally worked in tandem. The other is that even in this new formulation of immortality, the importance of the community has not lessened; heirs of the body may fail, but succeeding generations take on that role instead. The scribe attains his eternal life through his survival in the community mind. It turns out, then, that community and memory are

---

[138] The quotations come from Miriam Lichtheim, *Ancient Egyptian Literature*, II:176–78.

[139] There really could not be better proof of the author's point; the scribes *are* remembered! Edward F. Wente, "The Scribes of Ancient Egypt," in Jack M. Sasson, ed., *Civilizations of the Ancient Near East*, Vol. IV (New York: Charles Scribner's Sons, 1995) 2219, states that six of the eight people the text names have left writings, and four of them are portrayed in a tomb chapel of the Ramesside period at Saqqara as mummified beings. He further points out that the papyrus on which this text appears (Chester Beatty) was found in Deir el-Medina, a village whose sole purpose for existence was to build and paint royal tombs (2220).

inextricably linked to one another. The former is the means through which the latter is sustained.

Death as Threat

The student of the ancient Egyptian ways of confronting death cannot help but feel something bordering on awe at the sheer scope of the mortuary traditions. For a people typically regarded as bureaucratic and bourgeois in their way of life, they certainly took on death in grand fashion. The initial impression is that death is neutralized from every conceivable angle. On the physical level, pyramids, tombs, coffins, grave goods, food and drink offerings, mummification of the body, all represent a concerted effort to preserve existence in a concrete, tactile way.[140] On the level of myth, the deceased has different possible destinies, union with Osiris, joining the sun-god Re on his heavenly circuits, or association with the stars. On yet another level, the deceased continues to live through interaction with the earthly community, and is incorporated into the community of the dead. Memory maintains the individual's existence among the living. No avenue appears to be neglected, and the culture was amenable to letting new conceptions join the tradition without demanding that others be weeded out. Moral justification, knowledge, magic, were equally useful in the process of attaining a secure place as one of the blessed dead.[141] In sum, there was every reason for confidence that death was not annihilation, and the system should have been, and was, a source of some optimism.

However, there is more to be found in the ancient Egyptian psyche with respect to death than this somewhat cheery picture would suggest. Without question the system worked well for millennia and was successful in its ability to confront human fears about death, but it did not eliminate these fears. If death were as defanged as the above might suggest, then logically the Egyptian should have felt no reticence at

---

140 Probably this aspect of Egyptian tradition has made the deepest impression on the modern mind, since it is the most easily displayed in museums and noticed in Egypt itself; a pyramid or a mummy is more immediate than a myth or a text.

141 Morenz, *Egyptian Religion*, 210, observes that the idea of a moral judgment of the dead might seem contradictory to having burial rituals and tombs, but the Egyptians were completely comfortable with the combination. Wente, "Funerary Beliefs of the Ancient Egyptians," 26, states that a moral life and a ritual burial were both considered advisable.

hastening to the good life to be had in the beyond. But the Egyptian wanted to live just as much as anyone else, and the longer the better.[142] A standard form of address in invitations to tomb chapel visitors is "O you who love life and despise death."[143] An early instruction text remarks "death humbles us."[144] Even the standard mortuary literature reveals underlying fears about what happens to the dead, as has been mentioned already in the description of the main compendia.[145]

A number of nasty things might await the deceased on the other side. References to the "wrath of the dead,"[146] "your enemies," "those who would harm you in the realm of the dead,"[147] severed heads, souls whisked away to slaughter-houses, hearts cut out, starvation,[148] "the lords of butchery," whiplashes,[149] nets,[150] snakes, crocodiles,[151] and various other unpleasant beings and experiences reveal an extensive range of fears about what might happen.[152] The afterlife was a place that had much to offer in the way of happiness and peace, but many dangers, too. Even

---

[142] Much as people today. "My horror is dying before I have become old, before I have come to venerableness." Cf. Jan Zandee, *Death as an Enemy According to Ancient Egyptian Conceptions* (Leiden: E. J. Brill, 1960) 70 (a citation from the Coffin Texts, spell 40). .

[143] Wente, "Funerary Beliefs of the Ancient Egyptians: An Interpretation of the Burials and the Texts," 17. Cf. also Zandee, *Death as an Enemy*, 54, who adds a variation, "Oh you that hates dying."

[144] "The Instruction of Prince Hardjedef," Lichtheim, *Ancient Egyptian Literature*, I:58. Murnane, "Taking It With You: The Problem of Death and Afterlife in Ancient Egypt," 45, remarks, "All told, the Egyptians never lost their deep-seated sense of uncertainty about any of the strategies they had developed for overcoming death. Keenly fond of life's pleasures, they were nonetheless haunted by an awareness of their own mortality."

[145] Says one speaker, "death is my detestation." Cf. Faulkner, *The Ancient Egyptian Book of the Dead*, spell 85 (82–83).

[146] Faulkner, *The Ancient Egyptian Pyramid Texts*, 21, utterance 93.

[147] Faulkner, *The Ancient Egyptian Coffin Texts*, spell 225 (I:177).

[148] Faulkner, *The Ancient Egyptian Coffin Texts*, spell 229 (I:182–83).

[149] Faulkner, *The Ancient Egyptian Coffin Texts*, spell 273 (I:206).

[150] Faulkner, *The Ancient Egyptian Coffin Texts*, spell 343 (I:277).

[151] Faulkner, *The Ancient Egyptian Book of the Dead*, examples include spells 31–37, 39–50, 153A–154, 163–164 (56–58, 60–65, 149–153, 158–160).

[152] None of these are part of an Egyptian "hell" in the sense that the evil are singled out for eternal punishment; those who were not found worthy were destroyed. The slaughterers, demons and so on seem rather to be simply an integral part of the un-earthly realm who must be sidestepped.

some of the less immediately horrifying aspects of the deceased's experiences after death, such as the judgment, are a source of apprehension. The person who did not successfully achieve justification experienced the "second death," which was permanent annihilation.[153] While there is no record of anyone who was believed to have failed, it must have been regarded as a moment of stress. In the Papyrus of Ani, for example, Ani begs his heart not to make him fail his test of moral worthiness.[154]

Apart from the dangers and traps to be avoided or passed, the Egyptians clearly had a fear of not retaining their physical and mental capabilities. Numerous spells in the mortuary literature are proof of this. Hunger and thirst,[155] blindness,[156] and immobility[157] are all anathema, as is forgetfulness.[158] All of these must arise from the observation that the corpse does not eat, drink, breathe, move, or have consciousness. In spite of procedures such as the opening-of-the-mouth ritual, the worry persisted that somehow the deceased would be stuck without any of his earthly faculties. This is less a fear of demons and torture than it is of stasis.[159]

In addition, the Egyptians felt fully the grief and loneliness brought about by the death of a loved one. Even in the best of circumstances,

---

[153] Zandee, *Death as an Enemy*, 48, 186. To those so punished the Book of Gates makes the remark, "Your souls belong to non-being."

[154] See footnote #66. Assmann, "Death and Initiation in the Funerary Religion of Ancient Egypt," 147, says that "justification," is the core of Egyptian funerary traditions and functions in three ways. These are justification in the face of *the* enemy, i.e. death; *an* enemy, who might accuse him in the netherworld court; and finally, the divine judge. The afterlife in this respect seems highly litigious.

[155] Faulkner, *The Ancient Egyptian Pyramid Texts*, 109; Faulkner, *The Ancient Egyptian Coffin Texts*, spells 70, 164–67, 173–221 (I:66, 142–44, 147–75). See also spells 581, 661, 772 (II:184–85, 234, 302). Similarly cf. spells 1011 and 1012–14 (III:110–12, 112–15); Faulkner, *The Ancient Egyptian Book of the Dead*, examples include spells 54–59, 62 (65–68). See also 148–149, 178, 189 (137–145, 176, 185–188).

[156] Faulkner, *The Ancient Egyptian Coffin Texts*, spell 20, I:11.

[157] Zandee, *Death as an Enemy*, 11–12, says that the idea of not being able to move about is not due to the fact that the mummy is bound in bandages, but refers to rigor mortis.

[158] Faulkner, *The Ancient Egyptian Coffin Texts*, spells 410–412, 453–454 (I:63–64, 84–85).

[159] Zandee, *Death as an Enemy*, 66, expresses this as "a decline of life, a distressful existence."

when a proper burial and its accompanying rituals were carried out, the survivors were aware that no matter what the future might hold by way of relation to the newly dead, the deceased's way of living on earth had changed irrevocably. In one tomb scene a woman clings to her husband's mummy and cries "I am your sister [=wife], Merit-Re. You great one, do not leave Merit-Re. Your character was good. You good father, my being far from you, how is that? I go alone and behold, I walk behind you. You who liked to talk to me, you are silent, you do not talk."[160] The widow is keenly aware of her abandonment. In spite of the traditions which keep the dead a part of the family through offerings, festival celebrations, even correspondence, she feels separation and silence. In another example, a scene of a funeral procession carries a lament which reads "Woe to you, who were rich of people. He passes all his relations. He has hurried to the eternal land of darkness, where there is no light."[161] One official of the late Ramesside age named Butehamon enclosed a letter with his wife's coffin which contains the ensuing melancholy observation. "The sun-god has departed and his company of gods following him, the kings as well, and all humanity in one body following their fellow men. There is no one who shall stay alive, for we will all follow you."[162] Apparently his wife's mortality has led him to the reflection that her death is one small part of a greater, comprehensive state which will envelop all beings, human as well as divine. While the man's comment does not explicitly express fear or horror at the thought, it does evoke a sense of sadness and finality.

An especially interesting interchange takes place between Atum and Osiris in the Book of the Dead. Osiris asks "O Atum, how comes it that I travel to a desert which has no water and no air, and which is deep,

---

[160] Zandee, *Death as an Enemy*, 53–54.

[161] Zandee, *Death as an Enemy*, 90–91. He adds, "It is striking that the people who lament at the funeral procession sing of this negative side of death, as if the funerary ritual with which they are occupied, is of no use."

[162] Wente, "Funerary Beliefs of the Ancient Egyptians," 23; also see his article, "The Scribes of Ancient Egypt," 2220. In the Egyptian view of things, the gods were subject to death just like humanity. See Gardiner, *The Attitude of the Ancient Egyptians to Death and the Dead*, 14; also see Hornung, *Conceptions of God in Ancient Egypt: The One and the Many*, 160. He remarks that the Book of the Dead, chapter 154, says death awaits every god, goddess, animal, and insect, and similar claims appear in the Book of Gates; then he quotes Thomas Mann's comment that in Egypt "your dead are gods and your gods dead" (156–57).

dark, and unsearchable?" Atum replies, "Live in it in content!" O: "But there is no love-making there!" A: "I have given spirit-being instead of water, air and love-making, contentment in place of bread and beer—so says Atum. Do not be sorry for yourself, for I will not suffer you to lack."[163] Osiris himself, the prototypical example of how to emerge from death into new life, here shies away from the new existence with which he is confronted, because it is nothing like life as it is usually known but instead a dark and mysterious place without bodily pleasures. Atum assures him that it is not a bad place, but does not claim that it is like anything on earth. Instead, one has "spirit-being" there. Osiris does not seem particularly comforted.

Scholars often remark that the chief characteristic of the ancient Egyptian view of death is based on the notion of restoration. "The idea of a cycle of death and regeneration, of an incessant renewal of life through death, was the background of all mortuary rituals and beliefs...."[164] Again, "from a very early period the Egyptians saw rejuvenation and regeneration as the true meaning of death."[165] As a general model this analysis is persuasive, but it should be kept in mind that the system was not regarded as fail-safe, and that the mortuary religion itself was willing to express the persistent fears that somehow something might go wrong. In the letter of the scribe Butehamon to his deceased wife and in the interchange between Atum and Osiris there is even a conception of a final end-point at which the cycles of renewal stop. On a related matter, early in this chapter it was pointed out that the mainstream interpretation of the Egyptian focus on death insists that the ancients were not morbid, but had such a love of life they wanted it to continue forever.[166] "They did spend an extraordinary amount of time and energy in denying and circumventing death, but the spirit was not one of gloomy foreboding. On the contrary, it was a spirit of hopeful triumph, a vigorous relish of life, and an expectant assertion of continued future life as over against the

---

163 Faulkner, *The Book of the Dead*, spell 175 (175). In further conversation Atum reveals that that in time he will destroy creation and let it return to the abyss, and only he and Osiris will remain.

164 Jørgen Podemann Sørensen, "Major Issues in the Study of Ancient Egyptian Religion," *Temenos* 30(1994) 138–39.

165 Hornung, *Conceptions of God in Ancient Egypt: The One and the Many*, 160. Existence was not an unchanging state but one of ongoing renewal, and "to be dead is not the same as not to exist."

166 See footnote #2 for specific quotations.

finality or doom of death. Self-assurance, optimism, and a lust for life produced an energetic assertion of eternally continuing life rather than elaborate defenses against death."[167] However, the argument here, again, is that while the framework of the mortuary apparatus was based in many ways on assurance and optimism, this still left room for concern and doubt.

DEATH AND EGYPTIAN SCEPTICISM

As has just been discussed in the previous section, apprehension about death does crop up in the tradition, in the sense of anguish at being separated from one's loved ones when they die and also fear of falling into an unpleasant fate once death has come. On occasion, however, a voice will go beyond apprehension and express scepticism about the system as a whole. Although these voices are not the mainstream, they are part of the overall picture and for that reason should be explored so as to provide a fuller flavor of ancient Egyptian thinking about death.

The Dispute of a Man with His Ba

This text goes by a variety of names, including the Lebensmüde, the Man Who Was Tired of Life, and A Dispute Over Suicide. It comes from Papyrus Berlin 3024 and dates from the Middle Kingdom, c. 2000–1800 BCE[168] The beginning of the work is missing, small lacunae are scattered throughout along with scribal errors, and some of the vocabulary is otherwise unknown,[169] all of which leaves ample room for a variety of interpretations of the text. However, the general outline is as

---

167 Wilson, *The Burden of Egypt*, 78. It should be pointed out that Wilson later notes that by the Nineteenth and Twentieth Dynasties tomb iconography shifts from happy scenes of daily life to a focus on death, the funeral, and the netherworld, and thus the mood has shifted some from one of optimism.

168 William Kelly Simpson, ed., *The Literature of Ancient Egypt* (New Haven: Yale University Press, 1973) 201. This was not long after the traumatic political events of the First Intermediate Period when the central government of the Old Kingdom collapsed. See pages 129–30 for a quick review of the social and political situation in the First Intermediate Period, which is the same time that the Coffin Texts came into being.

169 R. J. Williams, "Reflections on the Lebensmüde," *Journal of Egyptian Archaelogy* 48(1962), 49. It has 155 columns in all. Cf. Lichtheim, *Ancient Egyptian Literature*, I:163.

follows. A man who has suffered personal disaster and who sees society all around him in turmoil decides that life is no longer worth living. As he is about ready to take the plunge, his ba begins arguing with him.[170] The ba challenges the man's decision to kill himself, and what follows in the rest of the text is a debate between the two.[171]

The man begins by expressing his consternation at the fact that his own ba refuses to support him. "Behold, my soul wrongs me," he says.[172] After some complaint and irritation he tries to cajole his ba's acquiescence by promising it extensive tomb comforts, afraid that it will abandon him if he cannot win it over, which would be the equivalent of annihilation. The ba is not impressed, and says that all these thoughts of burial are nothing but sadness and tears, considering that one can no longer see the sun or home again. As far as the enticement of a good tomb burial, the ba points out that even those who had fine pyramids made for themselves now receive nothing on their offering stones, and have fared no better than the dead on the riverbank.[173] So much for funerary arrangements. Instead, one should "pursue the happy day and forget care."[174]

The man answers in four poems, each of which repeats a constant refrain. In the first he says, "Behold, my name will reek through thee (i.e. the ba), more than...," where a pair of items is fitted into the slot eight times, usually having to do with bad smells. If the ba insists that the man live, it will be an unhappy business for the man. In the second poem he

---

[170] See pages 143–46 for a discussion of the "ba" and the other elements that make up an individual's being and consciousness.

[171] The setup is interesting, since the man is literally arguing with himself.

[172] James B. Pritchard, ed., *Ancient Near Eastern Texts Relating to the Old Testament* (Princeton: Princeton University Press, 1955) 405.

[173] The New Kingdom text which extols the making of books as a better means of immortality than leaving behind a tomb and mortuary endowment is an interesting echo of this sentiment. See pages 173–74.

[174] Pritchard, ed., *Ancient Near Eastern Texts Relating to the Old Testament*, 405. Two brief parables which are obscure in meaning follow this statement. In the first a man is trying to hurry home by boat with his family when a storm suddenly arises and kills all but him, whereupon he mourns for his unborn children. In the second a poor man asks his wife for a midday meal, but is told he must wait until dinner, which makes him grumble and sulk. The footnotes suggest that the point of the stories may be that unnatural death is a bad business, and one should not try to hurry an event before its appointed time (406, nn. 13–14).

repeatedly asks "To whom can I speak today?" followed by an observation bearing on social and moral chaos.

> To whom can I speak today?
> > Hearts are rapacious;
> > Every man seizes his fellow's goods.
> To whom can I speak today?
> > The gentle man has perished,
> > (But) the violent man has access to everybody.[175]

This poem is sixteen stanzas long. The third poem consists of six stanzas beginning "Death is in my sight today like...," where the comparison is an advantageous one.

> Death is in my sight today
> > (Like) the recovery of a sick man,
> > Like going out into the open after a confinement.[176]

The final poem is three stanzas in length, in which the refrain, "Why surely, he who is yonder" marks a reflection on the happy condition of the person who has died, namely, that he can punish sinners, acquire choice offerings, and obtain direct access to the sun-god Re. The conclusion is the ba's response, which is not entirely clear in its particulars. It does, however, seem to be reconciled with the man and agree to stand by him whenever he should die.

The purpose of the story has been the subject of a great deal of discussion.[177] Despite the variety of interpretations, a common thread

---

175 Pritchard, ed., *Ancient Near Eastern Texts Relating to the Old Testament*, 406. Lichtheim, *Ancient Egyptian Literature*, I:167, translates the second half of the quotation in terms of qualities, not types of people: "Kindness has perished/ Insolence assaults everyone." The idea is the same.

176 Pritchard, ed., *Ancient Near Eastern Texts Relating to the Old Testament*, 407.

177 Erman, Suys, and Williams consider it a reflection of growing scepticism regarding the effectiveness of elaborate funerary arrangements. Junker said it was a statement on the chaos of the world, which had reached such an extent that only the blessed dead could set things aright, this being the reason for suicide. De Buck felt that the text was about the opposition of the conservative religious tradition with newer heretical ideas acted out by the man and his hedonistic ba, while Weill said the ba insisted on "a total denial of immortality." Cf. Williams,

emerges. Clearly a debate is taking place between two different world-views, both of which are surprising. On the one hand, the man rejects the idea that there is any pattern or order to current events. In fact, the world seems to be a jumbled, lawless mess. Therefore, death is a desirable fate.[178] This line of thought undermines the traditional teachings that human activities are part of divinely regulated cosmic stability permeated by maat, truth/justice/order. On the other hand, the ba counsels present enjoyment, not such an odd piece of advice in itself, except that it comes on the heels of denying the validity of the funerary cult and, by implication, the afterlife, and is given as the only possible course of action in light of that denial. In other words, each disputant finds fault with the mainstream tradition, one regarding the present world, the other the hereafter. The man seeks solace in the hereafter while the ba wants to find it in the here and now. In the final analysis, the man's view of death appears to win out, since his ba gives up its opposition and promises to stand by him, but even if this is the case the questions about the validity of the mortuary tradition are pointed.[179]

"Reflections on the Lebensmüde," 49–51. In his book-length discussion of the subject, Goedicke identifies the story's theme as "the eternal problem of man's dichotomy between life-oriented hedonism and spiritually-minded idealism." Hans Goedicke, *The Report About the Dispute of a Man with His Ba* (Baltimore: The Johns Hopkins Press, 1970) 13. According to him, the crux of the debate is not the value of funerary preparations as so many others believe. The man is actually trying to attain the philosophical ideals much later fleshed out by the gnostic movements (66, n. 78). In short, "the quest for knowledge (l. 139) is the dominating purpose in life and is found to be thwarted by the encumbrance of the *physis*" (42). Goedicke's analysis of the text is flawed in many respects, one of the main ones being that he wants to paint the man as a gnostic philosopher, and greatly overdraws the "knowledge" language by forced translations in order to do so.

[178] Breasted, *Development of Religion and Thought in Ancient Egypt*, 191, found this conclusion, that death is better than life, to be the text's most remarkable feature.

[179] Breasted, *Development of Religion and Thought in Ancient Egypt*, 177–181, attributed the text's scepticism to a growing realization that, first of all, the already-ruined remains of the great pyramids and cemeteries of the Old Kingdom stood as testimony to the futility of human efforts at permanence, and secondly, to a frank appraisal of the "low moral level of society." Morenz, *Egyptian Religion*, 206, rejects this common interpretation of the text and says that it is really about the problem of how the body and the ba relate to one another after death. Donald B. Redford, "Ancient Egyptian Literature: An Overview," in Jack M. Sasson, ed., *Civilizations of the Ancient Near East*, Vol. IV (New York: Charles Scribner's

The Harper Song Tradition

Tombs as far back as the Old Kingdom contain scenes in which harpers are portrayed, but rarely were their songs recorded.[180] In the Middle Kingdom the scenes with harpers have shifted from the older agricultural and domestic contexts to largely funerary ones, such as offering-table scenes. These scenes appear in tombs as well as on stelae, and now the actual songs are recorded occasionally.[181] They consist of invocations of the dead and ceremonial hymns.[182] By the New Kingdom recording of the songs is common. Scenes usually show the deceased sitting before the offering table while he is served by the rest of his family and being entertained by a musician's song; the accompanying texts can come under the more general heading of an "entertainment song."[183] The content of the pieces may simply declare how content the tomb owner is in his new existence, or contain actual exhortations to the deceased to make merry in his afterlife.[184]

Sons, 1995) 2234, reasserts the view that the text concerns doubts about the mortuary cult.

180 Miriam Lichtheim, "The Songs of the Harpers," *Journal of Near Eastern Studies* 4(1945) 187. She knows of only one exception, a single Sixth Dynasty tomb.

181 Lichtheim, "The Songs of the Harpers,"187. With some frequency in the Middle Kingdom, and very often in the New Kingdom, harpers are depicted as blind, a tendency for which there is no really good explanation. "Whatever the origin of the practice, it is likely that in the course of time it became an artistic formula of characterization and, as such, independent of observed reality or of a specific meaning" (188).

182 Lichtheim, "The Songs of the Harpers," 191.

183 Michael V. Fox, "The Entertainment Song Genre in Egyptian Literature," in Sarah Israelit-Groll, ed. *Scripta Hierosolymitana, Vol. XXVII: Egyptological Studies* (Jerusalem: The Magnes Press, 1982) 269. These scenes are often labeled in the inscription by the phrase "diverting the heart," which supports the genre designation of entertainment song.

184 Edward F. Wente, "Egyptian 'Make Merry' Songs Reconsidered," *Journal of Near Eastern Studies* 21(1962) 119–21, disagrees with Lichtheim that the songs are purely funerary, and suggests that they were originally secular songs transferred to the tomb. Fox, "The Entertainment Song Genre in Egyptian Literature," 270–71, concludes that many of the ideas probably came from present-world banquets, but in the tomb context become funerary.

The harper is not merely entertaining his deceased master, however. Literally, his job is to "keep his name alive."[185] In one example of such a song the harper sings:

> How abiding you are in your... place
> of eternity, in your everlasting tomb!
> It is filled with offerings and provisions,
> for every good thing is contained within it,
> while your *ka* is with you....[186]

The point is that the dead is perpetually in a state of well-being and able to enjoy the comforts of his tomb. The song praises not the deceased, but his condition.[187] This is a feature common to the genre as a whole. The make-merry advice, similarly, does not just exhort the deceased to enjoy himself, but implies that he is in a condition whereby he is capable of doing so.[188] These songs also have a second function, and that is to teach the living, when they visit the dead, that those who fulfill the requirements of the mortuary religion can expect to reach the same kind of happy state in death themselves.[189]

All of this is a standard part of the mortuary tradition and fits right in with that tradition's promise of everlasting life. The scepticism emerges as a small but striking countercurrent in which the promise is not technically denied, but seriously questioned. The first and main example of this is a text known as the Antef Song, and it appears in two places. One is Papyrus Harris 500, the other is the New Kingdom tomb of Paatenemheb at Saqqara.[190] Its name comes from the introduction in the papyrus version which, though written in the New Kingdom (19th

---

[185] Fox, "The Entertainment Song Genre in Egyptian Literature," 289.

[186] Fox, "The Entertainment Song Genre in Egyptian Literature," 290.

[187] Fox, "The Entertainment Song Genre in Egyptian Literature," 290. He adds, "The singer is sustaining him by declaring that he *is* sustained." These songs, then, he designates "beatitudes" (292). In some cases the songs are hymns to the gods (296).

[188] Fox, "The Entertainment Song Genre in Egyptian Literature," 295–96.

[189] Fox, "The Entertainment Song Genre in Egyptian Literature," 300, says they teach "the basic doctrine of Egyptian mortuary religion: that the man who is morally and ritually fit and who has made the necessary mortuary arrangements may be sure of attaining a blessed afterlife, free from want and loneliness."

[190] Lichtheim, "The Songs of the Harpers," 192; Michael V. Fox, "A Study of Antef," *Orientalia* 46(1977) 400.

dynasty), attributes the song to the house of King Antef, one of a number of possible Middle Kingdom monarchs.

The date of composition is uncertain. Both surviving sources are from the New Kingdom, but most have dated it to the Middle Kingdom. The ascription to a King Antef, the Middle Egyptian style of language, and the tone of the song hark back to some time not long after the First Intermediate Period. On the other hand, no Middle Kingdom sources survive, and the song generated quite some interest only in the New Kingdom, prompting one cycle of songs similar in tone along with another string of opposing songs that counter Antef's message.[191] It also needs to be pointed out that scepticism is not just a Middle Kingdom phenomenon. In addition, the Middle Egyptian grammar often uses constructions rare before the 18th dynasty,[192] and the association with Antef could well be pseudepigraphal. The name itself, 'Intwf, literally means "he has been taken" and could just describe the deceased, who had been taken by death. No royal honorifics appear anywhere in the song itself, which is odd if the royal attribution is genuine.[193] The translations that follow are by Michael Fox,[194] from Papyrus Harris 500.

In the opening the song is ascribed to an "Antef" the justified, i.e. the deceased. It states that the deceased is flourishing and declares that his fate is good.[195] The generations pass while others come into their place,

[191] Lichtheim, "The Songs of the Harpers," 191–92, 207. She decides for a Middle Kingdom origin nonetheless, although she analyzes it along with other New Kingdom songs because of its affinities with them.

[192] Michael V. Fox, "A Study of Antef," 401, points to 1) the first-present construction (old perfective, or, noun plus the preposition ḥr plus an infinitive, in main clauses), which is rare before the Eighteenth Dynasty, but frequent in Antef; 2) Use of bn and bw for negation, not to be found before the Eighteenth Dynasty. Fox acknowledges that Lichtheim offers an explanation for this, namely, scribal modification, but suggests that the argument is circular without other evidence that the text is really Middle Egyptian.

[193] Fox, "A Study of Antef," 401–02. See also Hans Goedicke, "The Date of the 'Antef-Song,'" in *Fragen an die altägyptische Literatur: Studien zum Gedenken an Eberhard Otto* (Wiesbaden: Dr. Ludwig Reichert Verlag, 1977) 186–89 for similar arguments supporting a date of origin in the New Kingdom.

[194] Fox, "A Study of Antef," 403–07. See also Lichtheim, "The Songs of the Harpers," 192–93 and her later translation in *Ancient Egyptian Literature*, 196–97.

[195] This line is tricky; Fox and Lichtheim can be consulted for the philological analysis.

as has always happened. The dead are all resting in their tombs. Then comes the discordant comment that

> Those who built tombs—they have no (burial) places.
> Look what has become of them![196]

The speaker has heard the wisdom of sages like Imhotep and Djedef-Hor, but then points out that *their* burial places have crumbled and are as if they had never existed. As for the afterlife,

> There is no one who returns from there
> to tell their condition,
> to tell their needs,
> and thus to heal our hearts;
> before we hasten to the place they went to.

His advice, then, is to be cheerful and forget such things. The best solution is to follow one's heart, anoint oneself with myrrh, dress in fine linen, and get as much pleasure as possible

> until there comes to you that day of lamentation—
> And the Weary of Heart[197] cannot hear their wailing;
> weeping cannot save a man from the Netherworld.

In what may be a refrain, the harper advises the reader to have a good life, because the time for it is limited. The final words are,

> No one can make his property go with him.
> There is no one who goes who will return.

The message which emerges is startling. First, the tombs of the past, including those of famous men, have fallen into nothingness. In earlier harper songs one is assured "O tomb, you were built for

---

[196] Fox, "A Study of Antef," 408, comments on the parallel between this thought and the Dispute of a Man with His Ba, and suggests that Antef may have based the observation directly on the earlier text. See also Lichtheim, "The Songs of the Harpers," 191, for analogous remarks on the parallels.

[197] A reference to Osiris; see Lichtheim, *Ancient Egyptian Literature*, 197.

eternity,"[198] but now they are transitory. The following reference to Imhotep and Djedef-Hor may not be random examples of famous men. Both were well-known Old Kingdom sages associated in some way with the tomb. Imhotep left no known words of wisdom, but achieved fame as the tomb architect who designed the step pyramid of King Zoser in the 3rd dynasty. Djedef-Hor left to posterity a text, the preserved fragment of which says, "Make excellent thy dwelling place of the west... the house of death is for life."[199] The harper's comment is an acute irony considering their claims to fame.

Secondly, he reflects on the human inability to know anything about what really happens after death. No one returns to tell what it is like on the other side and to "heal our hearts." While he does not insist that there is no existence on the other side, the mortuary religion depended on the belief that one's experience after death was both well-understood and controllable, and to question this is a blow to confidence in the tradition.[200] The fact that no one can really know about what happens after death causes a condition of dissatisfaction that cannot be "healed."

Finally, although technically the singer takes an agnostic position on the question of an afterlife, by the end he insists that nobody can take along his property, and re-emphasizes that no one can come back. So not only can the deceased not return to the pleasures and relationships of this world, he cannot take any of this world with him into death. The two states, life and death, are completely disjunct and unbridgeable.

These are potent points which did not go unanswered in subsequent compositions. One strand of songs appears to be an explicit rejection of Antef's claims, all from the New Kingdom. The song known as Neferhotep I comes from a tomb in the reign of Haremhab. It too expresses themes found in Antef, but with an additional comment on the

---

198 Leiden V, 68. See Fox, "A Study of Antef," 414. He writes that in this matter the Antef song is "a direct attack on Egyptian mortuary beliefs."

199 See Fox, "A Study of Antef," 414 and Lichtheim, "The Songs of the Harpers," 193 for the observation.

200 Fox, "A Study of Antef," 15, remarks that the harper "sweeps aside centuries of amassed 'knowledge' of the after-life by the simple observation that no one returns from the realm of the dead." In his "The Entertainment Song Genre in Egyptian Literature," 313, he calls Antef a "reverse" beatitude, since it suggests the opposite of what the entertainment songs normally claim and instead of praising the state of the dead condemns it.

repeated rising and setting of the sun. This may be a way of tempering the melancholy since human birth and death now fit into the larger cosmic context of decline and renewal.[201] Merrymaking in the present is not a makeshift replacement for funeral preparations but exists in addition to them.[202] The song may express some gloom at death, but it becomes too fragmentary to follow very well. Neferhotep II appears in the same tomb, and here there can be no doubt about its polemic.

> I have heard those songs that are in the tombs of old
> And what they relate in extolling the earthly
> And in belittling the land of the dead.
> Wherefore is the like done to the land of eternity
> The just and fair that holds no terror?[203]

The poet is obviously disgusted at such impudence, and offers assurance that the deceased will reach the other side safely. Death is *not* a cause for terror. Neferhotep III is on the very same wall and though it begins by acknowledging the inevitability of death, it describes in detail how all the gods will personally aid the deceased in very traditional terms.[204] A different tomb, dating to the beginning of the Nineteenth Dynasty, contains a song that also appears to counter the scepticism of Antef,

---

201 Lichtheim, "The Songs of the Harpers," 196. "This perspective does not induce a negative attitude toward death. And, indeed, the outcry against oblivion which in the Antef song follows on the theme of transitoriness is suppressed altogether." Although on a later page (208) she says that this song still has a little of Antef's skepticism, her main argument suggests that while some reflection on the fleetingness of life may be found, the song is one of assurance, not doubt.

202 Fox, "A Study of Antef," 421.

203 Lichtheim, "The Songs of the Harpers," 197. See also László Kákosy and Zoltán Imre Fábián, "Harper's Song in the Tomb of Djehutimes," *Studien zur Altägyptischen Kultur* 22(1995) 211–225, for two harper songs which are closely based on those in Neferhotep's tomb. The two songs are joined into one.

204 Lichtheim, "The Songs of the Harpers," 199. Khai-Inheret is from a later tomb in the reign of Ramses III and uses language quite similar to Antef's, but to assert that tombs do remain. Thus, one is both to make merry now and prepare a tomb for the afterlife. Paser, from a tomb dating to the reigns of Seti I and Ramses II, reflects on death and urges enjoyment of the present, but without the doubts that Antef contains. See Lichtheim, "The Songs of the Harpers," 201–04. She further discusses (202–07) other harpers songs which continue to offer assurance that death is not the end, minus even the make-merry advice. These are the songs of Piay, of Neferrenpet, of Penniut, and of Tjanefer.

though not as bluntly as the Neferhotep songs. It too advises one to
follow one's heart, and remarks that the dead are forgotten; then it goes
on to express "une croyance orthodoxe inébranlée dans l'au-delà et dans
le service du culte."[205]

Apparently, then, Antef provoked a counter-tradition which went
to some trouble to refute its doubts. On the other hand, a series of songs
continues in his spirit throughout tombs of Ramses III's reign in the 20th
dynasty.[206] "Do not cease to act according to your desire until the day of
mooring comes and until the one who sees but who is not seen and who
has no fixed date arrives [on the day that grieves hearts], the one who
causes the house to tumble [to the groun]d when he arrives, so that all
work is come to naught, which one has done as his (own). No one who
has gone has ever returned."[207] The tone of these songs has the same
melancholy quality as in Antef.[208] Once again death becomes the deadline
before which all enjoyment must be had. It annihilates one's efforts and
is fundamentally unknowable.

---

[205] Jürgen Osing, "Les chants du harpiste au Nouvel Empire," in Jürgen
Osing, *Aspects de la Culture Pharaonique: Quatre leçons au Collège de France
(Février-mars 1989)* (Paris: Diffusion de Boccard) 21. He adds that this song takes
a middle position between the "orthodox" and "heretical" harper songs.

[206] Wente, "Egyptian 'Make Merry' Songs Reconsidered," 122.

[207] This comes from the tomb of Tjoy; cf. Wente, "Egyptian 'Make Merry'
Songs Reconsidered," 124–26. He provides translations of four different songs in
all. What makes all of these songs remarkable is that they appear in the tombs, the
very embodiments of the religion that they doubt. One reason for this could be that
the harper song would be only one small element of a tomb apparatus mostly
consisting of numerous prayers and spells from the cult. Since it was not one of the
required texts that the deceased needed for a safe journey into the hereafter, it did
not suffer the restrictions placed on the traditional forms, and this might make it
more flexible for expressing non-standard ideas (cf. Lichtheim, "The Songs of the
Harpers," 210).

[208] Jan Assmann, *Stein und Zeit: Mensch und Gesellschaft im alten Ägypten*
(Munich: Wilhelm Fink, 1991) 223–226, has some interesting comments to make
on the message of these harpers songs compared to traditional Egyptian mores. He
suggests that the command to follow one's heart is not meant as a universally
applicable life principle, but applies within the specific context of the festival or
holiday banquet. The "memento mori" element functions to bring one's attention
away from mundane matters and allow a momentary setting aside of daily cares
(225). The everyday world and world of the banquet embody two different sets of
values (226).

The fact that the first attested appearance of the Antef song is in a tomb dating to the time of Akhenaten is not without interest.[209] This is the Amarna period, when the king forced a radical shift in religious theory and practice by purging the other gods in favor of the Aten, or sun-disc, alone.[210] The daily mortuary offerings ceased, the gods of the underworld were ignored, and generally the operations of the mortuary cult as it had previously existed no longer functioned. Death had no role in the Amarna religious system, at least not in the traditional sense.[211] What the people got instead was a king who was the sole mediator between them and the only divine principle in the universe, the Aten. In one of the sun hymns from Amarna[212] the address to the Aten reads

> When you set in the western horizon
> the earth is in darkness
> in the condition of death....

Later in the same hymn is the statement that the creatures of the world live when the sun dawns, and die when it sets. Death is reinterpreted as the absence of the Aten. This is interesting from the historian of religion's point of view, but was less interesting to the people at large. Akhenaten's theology did not pass the survival test in Egyptian culture once he died.

---

209 Lichtheim, "The Songs of the Harpers," 192.

210 B. G. Trigger, et al, *Ancient Egypt: A Social History*, 220.

211 David P. Silverman, "Divinity and Deities in Ancient Egypt," in Byron E. Shafer, ed., *Religion in Ancient Egypt: Gods, Myths, and Personal Practice* (Ithaca, NY: Cornell University Press, 1991) 87, writes "death was a reality that played no part in the new theology." Also see John Baines, "Society, Morality, and Religious Practice," 190, who comments "Another important omission from the monuments at Akhetaten was the mention of the world of the dead. Akhenaten and his courtiers built large tombs at the site, and in doing so they superficially continued earlier practices and aspirations. But the nonroyal tombs lack scenes relating to the hereafter, and the royal tomb, which contains mourning scenes commemorating the death of one of Akhenaten's daughters, includes nothing that points to a specific destiny in the next world.... There is no evidence for an ethical judgment after death, and the realm of the dead is only vaguely alluded to. Because so much of moral discourse and social competition had traditionally been conducted in terms of the next life, a whole area of meaning, which was crucial for this life as well as the next, must have seemed to be lost."

212 See Assmann, *Egyptian Solar Religion in the New Kingdom*, 99, for the translation; another translation can be found in Lichtheim, *Ancient Egyptian Literature*, II:96–100.

It is not implausible that the Antef song could be reflecting, in part, a general sense of lost confidence after the upheavals of the period.[213]

CONCLUSION

That the Egyptians did not take a facile approach to death, then, is plain. It was something to which they responded full-heartedly and on a variety of levels, in ways that changed over time in answer to changing needs. The goal was to achieve personal survival within the community of the dead and the living alike. Although the mortuary religion assured its practitioners, which is to say Egyptian society, that this goal could and would be achieved, even the official tombs and texts can reveal an underlying apprehension of death from time to time. Also, on occasion, sceptical voices emerge which questioned whether the living really knew as much about death and its realm as they claimed. The point is not that the system was therefore ineffective, only that it acknowledged the reality of human fears and emotions. In fact, as a system, the mortuary religion was successful and remained at the heart of the Egyptian culture for at least three millennia.

---

213 Fox, "A Study of Antef," 403, remarks that it is believable these events might "undermine faith in the permanency and validity of the mortuary cult in general." While it would be impossible to pin definitively Antef's origin to this era, the other factors pointing to the time, such as the late grammar, become stronger when the same time also offers such fertile ground for the doubts it expresses. Some in fact have seen the entire Ramesside period as an era where people had lost confidence in the stability of the cosmos as a whole. See Assmann, *Egyptian Solar Religion in the New Kingdom*, 195. A possible source of evidence for this might be found in letters from the period in which ordinary people repeatedly make remarks on the unknowability of what the next day has in store. "I am alive today, but I don't know my condition tomorrow" is a phrase that appears regularly. See Edward F. Wente, *Letters From Ancient Egypt* (Atlanta: Scholars Press, 1990) 32–34, 116–17 for examples, all from the reign of Ramesses II. A variation from the Twentieth Dynasty is "Indeed I'm alive today; tomorrow is in God's hands" (178–79,185).

Chapter 5
THE ANCIENT EGYPTIAN BIOGRAPHIES

GENRE

One of the oldest and most enduring elements of the ancient Egyptian mortuary tradition was the self-presentation by the deceased to any outside reader who might pass by. Unfortunately, scholars are not agreed on just how to designate these self-presentations. Are they biographies, autobiographies, "biographical" or "autobiographical" narratives, any known literary genre, or what exactly? Browsing through what little has been written on the phenomenon in the context of the ancient world is an interesting study in dissension. Says one writer, "The genre of biography was not known in pharaonic Egypt. Autobiographies, however, are well attested."[1] Another states "there is no autobiography as such in the ancient world, if we describe 'autobiography' as the retrospective interpretation of the author's own life—a contemplative self-scrutiny of the past."[2] He goes on to say that some writings do seem autobiographical, however, so that one can talk of ancient "autobiographical" texts. Often in discussions of the rise of autobiography, Augustine's *Confessions* (fifth century CE)

---

[1] Olivier Perdu, "Ancient Egyptian Autobiographies," in Jack M. Sasson, ed., *Civilizations of the Ancient Near East*, Vol. IV (New York: Charles Scribner's Sons, 1995) 2243.

[2] Edward L. Greenstein, "Autobiographies in Ancient Western Asia," in Jack M. Sasson, ed., *Civilizations of the Ancient Near East*, Vol. IV (New York: Charles Scribner's Sons, 1995) 2421. The fact that both of these statements come from the same volume of essays is an interesting detail.

is cited as the beginning of the tradition.[3] One such author offers an interesting summary of what was necessary for the rise of the autobiographical genre: "the breakup of the traditional community, increasing sensitivity to change, new forms of self-consciousness and religious awareness, a shift from deductive to inductive modes of thought, the alteration of the class structure, and increased literacy." In short, the appearance of the type of person "whose true self could not be captured by any universal model."[4]

On biography, the *Encyclopedia of Religion's* introductory essay immediately defines the discussion in terms of *sacred* biography, accounts of people considered to be holy. The essay largely concentrates on narratives about the founders of religions, and thus deals with material which does not even come into existence until near the end or after the end of ancient Egyptian culture.[5] Similarly in the *Anchor Bible Dictionary*, the entry for "ancient biography" centers on the gospels and designates as the starting point for the investigation the Greek "lives."[6] Just after the turn of the century a large work on the genre of autobiography actually does devote its first chapter to ancient civilizations, and it offers a number of thoughts on the Egyptian case in particular.[7] At first the genre under discussion is called biography, despite the book's title.[8] The author then remarks that part of the tomb preparation required "a biography of the departed, which often was an

---

[3] Janet Varner Gunn, "Autobiography," in Mircea Eliade, ed., *The Encyclopedia of Religion*, Vol. 2 (New York: Macmillan Publishing Company, 1987) 7. She acknowledges that her essay is based on Western examples. Greenstein, "Autobiographies in Ancient Western Asia," IV:2421, also remarks on the fact that many regard the *Confessions* to be the the first autobiography. "The introspective nature of Augustine's work is often taken as the sine qua non of genuine autobiography. If that criterion were strictly applied, few ancient near eastern autobiographical texts would meet it."

[4] Gunn, "Autobiography," 2:7.

[5] William R. LaFleur, "Biography," in Mircea Eliade, ed., *The Encyclopedia of Religion*, Vol. 2 (New York: Macmillan Publishing Company, 1987) 220.

[6] Charles Talbert, "Biography, Ancient" in D. N. Freedman, ed., *The Anchor Bible Dictionary*, Vol. 1 (New York: Doubleday, 1992) 745.

[7] Georg Misch, *A History of Autobiography in Antiquity* (Leipzig and Berlin: B. G. Teubner, 1907; trans. E. W. Dickes, 2 Vols., London: Routledge & Kegan Paul Ltd., 1950).

[8] Misch, *A History of Autobiography in Antiquity*, I:21.

autobiography."[9] This intriguing statement is not unpacked, and the discussion continues to speak of "biographies" until a later paragraph where the question is raised as to what extent the subject of the narrative also would have composed it. Sometimes the ancient text states that a descendant of the tomb-owner is responsible for the inscription (or burial) or that family documents had been consulted. The author comments that "this does not matter very much,"[10] but then seems to shift to the label "autobiography" in the ensuing discussion. In the *Lexikon der Ägyptologie* the entry under "Autobiographie," refers the reader to "Biographie," although the article uses both terms throughout.[11]

The use of the terms "biography" and "autobiography" as interchangeable labels with reference to the ancient Egyptian material is fairly common among scholars, in fact, though most seem to settle for "biography" as the overarching genre. One of the most active scholars in the field however insists that ancient Egypt never had the genre "biography."[12] She makes a special note of this because of the fact that Egyptologists are, as she puts it, apologetic about using the term autobiography and instead lean on the phrase "biographical inscriptions."[13] This is partly explained by the general assumption that autobiography is, by definition, a recent Western genre, and nothing before Augustine counts.[14] But if the literary type under question is one of "the narration of bits of one's life from a position of self-awareness and reflection, then the ancient Egyptian autobiographical inscriptions were true autobiographies."[15] Nevertheless, the heading for the essay on

---

[9] Misch, *A History of Autobiography in Antiquity*, I:23.

[10] Misch, *A History of Autobiography in Antiquity*, I:27.

[11] Baudouin van der Walle, "Biographie," in Wolfgang Helck et al, eds., *Lexikon der Ägyptologie*, Vol. I (Wiesbaden: Otto Harrassowitz,1975) 816, early in the essay states "la biographie égyptienne prend logiquement la forme de l'autobiographie...." At one point (817) he writes "(auto)biographie."

[12] Miriam Lichtheim, *Ancient Egyptian Autobiographies Chiefly of the Middle Kingdom* (Göttingen: Vandenhoeck & Ruprecht, 1988) 2. See also Perdu in footnote #1 for a similar view.

[13] Lichtheim, *Ancient Egyptian Autobiographies*, 2.

[14] Lichtheim, *Ancient Egyptian Autobiographies*, 2. She further says, regarding Augustine's *Confessions*, that it is "a mountain of an autobiography, to be sure, and one which appears to be blocking the view into the two millennia that preceded it."

[15] Lichtheim, *Ancient Egyptian Autobiographies*, 2.

the subject in the recent *Anchor Bible Dictionary* is to be found under "Egyptian Literature: Biographies." Here the author says "biography is the first literary genre known from ancient Egypt and the best attested."[16] This essay later remarks that most of the time one cannot know whether the inscriptions were written by their subjects; most are in the first person and "appear to be autobiographical."[17]

In short, there seems to be no consensus on the question. Some say Egypt had only biography, some say it had only autobiography, while the rest do not discuss the genre issue at all, and tend to switch back and forth between terms.[18] Clearly all parties agree that one is dealing with some form of presentation of an individual, the key features and development of which will be discussed below, and Lichtheim has the right of it in her suggestion that many people do not regard the Egyptian texts as autobiographies, or even as biographies depending on the focus of the discussion, simply because they are non-Western and very old, and thus do not come within the purview of most authors, many of whom probably are not even aware of them. However, having acknowledged this, for the sake of consistency in what follows it would be helpful to choose a name for these texts and stick with it, and in spite of Lichtheim's insightful comments, the present project will regard the Egyptian materials as "biographies."

---

[16] Elizabeth J. Sherman, "Egyptian Biographies," in David Noel Freedman, ed., *The Anchor Bible Dictionary*, Vol. II (New York: Doubleday, 1992) 390. See also van der Walle, "Biographie," 815, "De tous les genres littéraires, la genre biographique est le plus anciennement attesté en Egypt."

[17] Sherman, "Egyptian Biographies," 391. See also Elizabeth J. Sherman, "Ancient Egyptian Biographies of the Late Period (380 BCE Through 246 BCE)," in *The American Research Center in Egypt Newsletter* 119(1982) 38: "Although most of these inscriptions employ the first person, it is unclear whether they were authored by the subjects themselves or by pious family members who lived after them, and it is safer to consider them biographies rather than autobiographies."

[18] As noted earlier, Misch, *A History of Autobiography in Antiquity*, moves between both terms. So does Heike Guksch, *Königsdienst: Zur Selbstdarstellung der Beamten in der 18. Dynastie* (Heidelberg: Heidelberger Orientverlag, 1994), see pages 1–2. A careful reading of other works would probably reveal the same thing. This is not necessarily a flaw, it just goes to show that the question, in reference to the Egyptian materials, is complex. Karl Jansen-Winkeln, *Ägyptische Biographien der 22. und 23. Dynastie*, 2 Vols. (Wiesbaden: Otto Harrassowitz, 1985) appears to favor the term "biography" over "autobiography."

The reason rests on nothing more than the fact that some of the texts are known not to have been written by the subject.[19] Generally an individual commissioned a tomb inscription, stela, or statue, and thus did not personally execute the text, though he probably influenced its preparation.[20] Leaving aside all questions of how self-reflective or individualistic the modern "autobiography" is expected to be, one thing the word certainly means is that the person of focus is the author. Trying to talk about an "autobiography" which is composed by someone else is too big a semantic strain on the word for personal comfort. One must acknowledge that no doubt some of the relevant texts were self-composed, in which case "biography" would not be as exact a term as one might like. Yet biography is a more general category that might reasonably include autobiography, whereas the reverse is not true. So choosing "biography" is something of an imperfect compromise. The problem is one for moderns, not the Egyptians, who would have understood their own genre quite well. In our terms, a life narration is either by the individual, or by an outside person. It appears that today we

---

[19] In addition to the comments already cited by Misch, *A History of Autobiography in Antiquity*, I:27, and Sherman, "Egyptian Biographies," 391, see Greenstein, "Autobiographies in Ancient Western Asia," IV:2421, who categorically states that the Egyptian inscriptions, which might be viewed as "autobiographical," were still "nearly all the direct product of scribes, not of the autobiographical subjects themselves." While it is difficult to know with such certainty that the scribes were usually responsible, Miriam Lichtheim herself acknowledges on occasion that a given text may be composed by someone else. See Lichtheim, *Ancient Egyptian Autobiographies*, 38, where one example is the case of women's texts, which were composed for them by a father, husband, or son. "Women did not produce their own autobiographical inscriptions." Later (143), in reference to the inscription of one Intef, she says in regard to a stylistic point that it is "fortunate that Intef *or his scribe* had stopped...." These remarks suggest that the term "*auto*biography" is not the best.

[20] See Guksch, *Königsdienst*, 1. Eberhard Otto, *Die biographischen Inschriften der ägyptischen Spätzeit* (Leiden: E. J. Brill, 1954) 123, raises the question of who the real authors of the texts are and makes the plausible suggestion that temples had workshops in which the priests, over the course of time, assembled handbooks of a variety of material that might be used in a biographical text. These would include old tomb inscriptions, wisdom sayings, quotations from mortuary writings and so on, from which an individual could draw, as well as add personal touches.

do not have an appropriate word which describes "narrative self-presentation, whether by the subject, family member, or hired scribe."

HISTORY AND CONTENT

Now that the label "biography" has been chosen, the time has come to investigate the substance and history of the ancient Egyptian genre. The Egyptian biographies are mortuary writings and are always the presentation of the deceased to posterity within the funerary context. They appear in inscriptions, either in the tomb chapel or on a separate stela which itself may appear in the tomb or be erected somewhere else, such as a temple.[21] Typically they are in the first-person singular.[22] Their intended audience is those who will visit or pass by the tomb or monument in future generations, more particularly, those who can read.[23] Commonly the biography will specifically address every priest and every scribe who can read the writing.[24] The purpose of these texts has been described in different ways. They are a means for the owners to "invoke their own personalities."[25] They function to "construct and project a certain self-image."[26] They are "das Mittel der Selbstvorstellung des Toten gegenüber einem erwarteten und erhofften Publikum."[27] Through

---

[21] Perdu, "Ancient Egyptian Autobiographies," IV:2244. In the temples, stelae (and statues) were deposited in the courtyards. Rarely, starting in the Twenty-Sixth Dynasty and later, the biographical inscription might appear on the sarcophagus (2246).

[22] Perdu, "Ancient Egyptian Autobiographies," IV:2243; Sherman, "Egyptian Biographies," 391. Sherman notes that occasionally a text will appear in the third person, and quite rarely in the second person.

[23] Perdu, "Ancient Egyptian Autobiographies," IV:2243. J. Gwyn Griffiths, *The Divine Verdict: A Study of Divine Judgement in the Ancient Religions* (Leiden: E. J. Brill, 1991) 195, says that they appeal to passers-by "so that survival in their remembrance is the aim."

[24] John Baines, "Society, Morality, and Religious Practice," in Byron E. Shafer, ed. *Religion in Ancient Egypt: Gods, Myths, and Personal Practice* (Ithaca, NY: Cornell University Press, 1991) 140, makes the comment that only those in the upper classes could read, so that the content of the biography is really aimed at the elite; he adds that the morality of the texts, however, likely reflected that of the broader scope of society.

[25] Perdu, "Ancient Egyptian Autobiographies," IV:2243.

[26] Greenstein, "Autobiographies in Ancient Western Asia," IV:2422.

[27] Guksch, *Königsdienst*, 24.

them the subject "recorded the essential aspects of his life and person which he wished to perpetuate."[28]

All of these statements are true, and it should be noted that the genre is quite selective in preserving the *desired* image of the individual, that is, an ancient Egyptian biography does not attempt to portray failures in the best light or explain away shortcomings, because it does not acknowledge such things. Nor does the genre attempt to describe an individual's life in its entirety. Its focus is the successful course of the person's career, with a strong emphasis on his moral worthiness.[29] Moreover, the biography is confined to the "private sector," meaning that it was not a form used by royalty. It is true that many of the subjects of the texts were closely involved with the king and the court, so that "private" does not exactly mean the same thing in ancient Egypt as it does in the modern West, but the fact remains that the genre was restricted to the non-royal realm.[30]

Ancient Egyptian biographies serve a purpose that goes beyond merely preserving the noteworthy events of one's life for posterity's admiration. They attempt to impress the reader with the subject's moral worth as well as with his attainments, and thereby elicit offerings, if not literal ones at least the spoken offering formula, for the maintenance of

---

[28] Lichtheim, *Ancient Egyptian Autobiographies*, 5.

[29] Lichtheim, *Ancient Egyptian Autobiographies*, 5. Jørgen Podemann Sørensen, "Divine Access: The So-called Democratization of Egyptian Funerary Literature as a Socio-cultural Process," in Gertie Englund, ed., *The Religion of the Ancient Egyptians: Cognitive Structures and Popular Expressions* (Stockholm: Almqvist & Wiksell International, 1989) 116, describes the genre's aims in terms of *status*. "The career, the events, the deeds, and the lifestyle that it recounts purport to the social, moral, and religious status of the deceased."

[30] Lichtheim, *Ancient Egyptian Autobiographies*, 5. She explains that the kingship was too sacred and ceremonially regulated to lend itself to private narrative expression. The "Instructions to Merikare" and "Instructions of Amenemhet," she adds, have some points of contact with the genre but were in essence political tracts. Jan Assmann, "Schrift, Tod und Identität: Das Grab als Vorschule der Literatur im alten Ägypten," in Aleida Assmann, et al, eds., *Schrift und Gedächtnis: Beiträge zur Archäologie der literarischen Kommunikation* (Munich: Wilhelm Fink, 1983) 79, examines the concept of "personality" which the biographies make possible, and concludes that although the king lent "personality" to his subjects and thereby made it viable for them to achieve endurance for posterity, personality is not itself a royal category. This is because according to the dogma the king is exempt from death, and thus does not need personality.

the deceased's well-being in the beyond.[31] A successful biographical text is one which arouses admiration in its readers and leads to some manner of offering on behalf of the deceased. Obviously this aim dictates the actual content of the biographies. The subject must show himself to be deserving, and thus it is that the texts consistently portray their owners as effective in their jobs, compassionate towards their colleagues and underlings, devoted to and admired by the king, and so on.[32] Here emerges one of the features of the Egyptian tradition of self-presentation which runs against the grain of typical modern custom. Earlier in this chapter a scholar was quoted as remarking that the idea of presenting a personal narrative of a life to posterity requires a sense that the individual's "true self could not be captured by any universal model."[33] In the Egyptian context, although one may get a feel for individual personalities, the goal is just the opposite, that is, to show just how perfectly the subject *did* exemplify the universal model of the Egyptian ideal man.

In spite of a general consistency in purpose and substance throughout Egypt's history, the biographical texts do exhibit signs of change and development. The earliest examples date to the Old Kingdom

---

[31] Perdu, "Ancient Egyptian Autobiographies," IV:2243, says of the genre that "its goal is less to inform [passersby] than to serve the autobiographer's goals for the afterlife." Guksch, *Königsdienst*, 1, adds that it illustrates "das ägyptische Bewußtsein von der inneren Beziehung zwischen den beiden Phasen menschlicher Existenz, der diesseitigen und der jenseitigen...." Van der Walle, "Biographie," 815, similarly explains "[the deceased] voulait laisser aux visiteurs de sa tombe une impression avantageuse de sa personne et les inciter par là à réciter la formule d'offrandes...." Assmann, "Schrift, Tod und Identität," 67, puts a slightly different turn on this point. He says that one of the main purposes of the tomb was to keep the deceased's name alive. "*Denn in Gedächtnis, nicht im Grabe leben die Toten weiter*; das Grab ist nur die 'Außenstabilisierung' dieser sozialen Fortdauer und als solche ein soziales Phänomen" (italics his). The biography serves this maintenance of social memory. His point is well taken, though the importance of the belief in the afterlife itself should not be overly attenuated.

[32] Guksch, *Königsdienst*, 1–2, remarks that because of the underlying consciousness the biographies have of the connection between this world and the next, the texts are not simply a description of what really happened in the course of a life. "Je besser [an official] im geltenden System funktioniert hat, desto preisungswürdiger ist ein Beamter und um so größer siene Chance, durch die gleichen Normen anerkennende Nachwelt versorgt zu werden mit dem, was er als Toter benötigt: ehrendes Andenken und Totenopfer" (2).

[33] Gunn, "Autobiography," 2:7.

in the tombs next to Memphis, where the royal court was located. They appear in a very basic form in the Fourth Dynasty and then fuller versions in the Fifth and Sixth Dynasties.[34] At first there were separate elements that stood independently of one another, such as the prayers for offerings, and warnings against violation of the tomb, which in the Sixth Dynasty, along with the self-presentation, were tied into one text.[35] As the offering formula expanded it led to a separate appeal to the living which is where the specific request for assistance from visitors came in.[36] In this period it was the officials tied to the administration of the court who had the means to build tombs for themselves, that is, they had a warrant from the king, and therefore the subject's proficiency at fulfilling the king's wishes and the ensuing royal praise and appreciation are central to the genre.[37] Examples of such officials include viziers, courtiers, governors of the provinces, and high priests.[38] The king is the unchallenged focus of attention, and even the other gods receive short notice.[39]

In the First Intermediate Period the political scene changed considerably as the central monarchy lost its hold on authority and power shifted to provincial centers. The individual nomes, or districts, and towns became self-governing. Now even common people could acquire

---

[34] Lichtheim, *Ancient Egyptian Autobiographies*, 5. Perdu, "Ancient Egyptian Autobiographies," IV:2247, says of the Fourth Dynasty examples that the narrator describes how the tomb was built and says a few words about himself.

[35] Lichtheim, *Ancient Egyptian Autobiographies*, 5–6. Perdu, "Ancient Egyptian Autobiographies," IV:2247, regards the Sixth Dynasty as the time when the genre really begins to develop. Places outside of Memphis where a few biographies also appear are Elephantine, Edfu, Abydos, and Dayr al-Gabrawi.

[36] Lichtheim, *Ancient Egyptian Autobiographies*, 6. She sums up (144) that the main elements of the genre were established by the end of the Old Kingdom and include "the career narration; the moral profile; and the prayerful speeches—the offering formula, the appeal to the living, and the warning to visitors."

[37] Lichtheim, *Ancient Egyptian Autobiographies*, 6; Van der Walle, "Biographie," 817–818. Assmann, "Schrift, Tod und Identität," 73, says of this time that "der König verleiht seinen Beamtem ihre Biographie und ihre 'Persönlichkeit'.... Der König personifiziert die Kategorie der sozialen Anerkennung."

[38] Perdu, "Ancient Egyptian Autobiographies," IV:2247.

[39] Sherman, "Egyptian Biographies," 391.

property and some local power and thus construct at least simple tombs.[40]
A royal warrant was no longer necessary. Biographical texts of the ruling
authorities in this period focus on how the individual provides order,
food, or protection in an age of chaos.[41] Lesser officials describe their
political and economic successes as the result of their own labor, or at
times the result of some assistance from the town gods, but not as the
benefaction of pharaoh.[42] Self-worth is measured in terms of one's
relations to fellow-citizens and native town.[43] The new themes are
expressed in new formulae, not the old phrases of the preceding period.[44]
The king is no longer the center of all value.

In the Middle Kingdom the central monarchy was reestablished,
and the biographies also reflect the changes in social temperament
brought on by the event. Even more people than before, of more classes,
began to express themselves in this genre and the content became fuller.[45]
Interestingly, by now the majority of biographical texts are to be found
in the provinces, rather than the capital.[46] Although the king once again
held a central role in the self-narration, the tone was still different than in
the Old Kingdom. The servant emphasizes his loyalty to the king, as

---

[40] Lichtheim, *Ancient Egyptian Autobiographies*, 21, 142. On the latter page
she states that rich, poor, and the rising middle class alike composed
self-presentations.

[41] Perdu, "Ancient Egyptian Autobiographies," IV:2249.

[42] Lichtheim, *Ancient Egyptian Autobiographies*, 21, 142. She sums up the
characteristic feature of this period as the person's discovery of "his 'self.'" See
also Miriam Lichtheim, *Maat in Egyptian Autobiographies and Related Studies*
(Göttingen: Vandenhoeck & Ruprecht, 1992) 23. Griffiths, *The Divine Verdict*,
196, says that this is a period when the nome rulers show some measure of
independence, or as he phrases it, a "sturdier standing" in relation to the king.

[43] Sherman, "Egyptian Biographies," 391. Lichtheim, *Ancient Egyptian
Autobiographies*, 37, comments that women in the First Intermediate Period, like
the rest of the population, experienced "an advance in the display of selfhood."
Women possess stelae in which they are shown alone, not with a husband or any
other male. However, because women did not have careers, they did not have
biographies, and their inscriptions consist only of names, titles, and references to
their good character, along with the typical funerary prayers and offerings (37–38).

[44] Lichtheim, *Ancient Egyptian Autobiographies*, 22; Sherman, "Egyptian
Biographies," 391.

[45] Perdu, "Ancient Egyptian Autobiographies," IV:2249. He adds that texts
in later periods of Egyptian history borrowed extensively from the Middle
Kingdom biographies.

[46] Perdu, "Ancient Egyptian Autobiographies," IV:2249.

before, but now this is attached to the motif of pharaoh's loyalty to his subject.[47] The development of independence in the First Intermediate Period had a lasting effect. In addition, the stelae at Abydos form a group in their own right which emphasize successfully achieving an Osirian afterlife. These texts stress the moral aspect of the subject at the expense of specific details of the career.[48]

Subsequently, the Theban warlords successfully drove the Hyksos of the Second Intermediate Period out of Egypt and the period now called the New Kingdom began. It was at this time that the greatest number of [preserved] biographies were produced. Most of the known tomb texts are to be found in the tombs at Thebes, while temple monuments with biographical inscriptions appear throughout the country.[49] Again, the king is at the center of attention,[50] though one of the chief characteristics of biographies from the Eighteenth Dynasty is the expansive description of events in the individual's life and the pride in personal initiative.[51] The texts of this era also continue two trends that began as the Middle

---

[47] Lichtheim, *Ancient Egyptian Autobiographies*, 45, 142–43. She describes this as "reciprocal loyalty," which "implies a large gain in selfhood and personal pride, a gain which the kingless First Intermediate time had fostered, and which the return of kingship did not weaken" (45). Jan Assmann, "State and Religion in the New Kingdom," in William Kelly Simpson, ed., *Religion and Philosophy in Ancient Egypt* (New Haven: Yale University Press, 1989) 72, remarks that in the Old Kingdom the biographies portray people as acting only on the order of pharaoh, who "seems to monopolize initiative, planning, and motivation," while in the Middle Kingdom the individual is directed by his own heart.

[48] Lichtheim, *Ancient Egyptian Autobiographies*, 55–134, 143.

[49] Perdu, "Ancient Egyptian Autobiographies," IV:2251. He states that the rising prosperity of the city led to the construction of numerous tombs, where many of the texts appear, but that private temple monuments, especially statues at this stage, account for the largest numbers of new texts. The temple monuments appear in Karnak (at Thebes) as well as in the provinces, particularly provincial capitals.

[50] Guksch, *Königsdienst*, 3. "Im Zentrum der Selbstdarstellung steht in der 18. Dynastie das Verhältnis zum König. Für den König zu handeln, sich vor ihm zu bewähren, von ihm belohnt zu werden, erfüllt in dieser Zeit so sehr den Mittelpunkt des offiziellen Daseins, daß daneben alle weiteren Bezugspunkte des Lebens eines Beamten sekundär werden." Griffiths, *The Divine Verdict*, agrees that the king is important in the biographical texts, especially during the reign of Akhenaten, but with more attention to the details of the subject's career.

[51] Perdu, "Ancient Egyptian Autobiographies," IV:2251; Sherman, "Egyptian Biographies," 391; Guksch, *Königsdienst*, 102; Van der Walle, "Biographie," 818.

Kingdom drew to a close, detailed descriptions of the afterlife and the intimate relationship between the individual and the gods.[52] An example of an Eighteenth Dynasty biography which provides a sketch of what the deceased will experience in the netherworld is the text of Paheri from el-Kab.[53]

> Thou goest in, thou comest out, while thy heart is glad in the favor of the Lord of Gods. A fine burial after a venerable old age, when old age has come. Thou takest thy place in the Lord of Life, thou unitest thyself to the earth in the Necropolis of the West in order to become a Living Soul. Indeed, she [the soul] has bread, water, and wind, and may take the form of a phoenix, a swallow, a hawk, a heron, as thou wishest. Thou crossest over in a ferryboat without being hindered, thou sailest on the water of the flood. It so happens that thou livest again. Thy soul will not be kept away from thy body. Thy soul is divine with the spirits, the accomplished souls speak to thee. Thy image is among them and thou receivest what is upon earth. Thou hast water, thou breathest the air, thou drinkest to thy heart's content. Thy two eyes are given to thee to see, thy two ears to hear what is being said, thy mouth to speak, thy feet to walk. Thy arms and shoulders have movement, thy flesh is flourishing, thy vessels are pleasant—thou art satisfied with all thy members....

In the Ramesside period (the Nineteenth and Twentieth Dynasties) further change can be seen as the trend towards piety, a closer sense of connection with the gods, becomes pronounced.[54] At the same time the experiences and deeds of an individual career slip into the background, while hymns to the gods, prayers for a safe arrival in the netherworld, and insistent claims that the individual is righteous come to the fore.[55]

---

[52] Lichtheim, *Maat in Egyptian Autobiographies*, 109. She states (112) that references to a judgment after death are uncommon in the first half of the Eighteenth Dynasty, then become increasingly frequent, as do denials of any wrongdoing, and further remarks (121) on the fact that the development of afterlife wishes in the biographies occurs at the same time the Book of the Dead texts were being compiled.

[53] The translation is from Alexandre Piankoff and N. Rambova, *The Mythological Papyri* (New York: Pantheon Books, 1957) 3–4.

[54] Lichtheim, *Maat in Egyptian Autobiographies*, 75. One example she cites is the prayer of Userhat in which "observance of right-doing and personal devotion to the gods are linked with the utmost precision."

[55] Lichtheim, *Maat in Egyptian Autobiographies*, 134–35.

One interesting example of a Ramesside text is a hymn that comes from the stela of Bak-aa.[56] He addresses Osiris and at one point says:

> Those to come in their millions,
> in the end they land with you;
> in the womb they face toward you,
> there's no tarrying in Egypt.
> They are with you, all come to you,
> great and small alike;
> yours are they who live on earth,
> one and all will reach you.

Lichtheim regards this text as an important example of the notion of Osiris as "lord of death" in the Ramesside period;[57] the speaker has a keen consciousness of the fact that all creatures are heading towards death, even from the womb. However, somber though this thought be, the hymn as a whole expects a happy existence in the netherworld for the righteous Bak-aa. The work does show a deeper reflection on the fact of mortality and a concomitant insistence on moral perfection than is apparent in earlier periods, though.

With the end of the New Kingdom the last thousand years of Egyptian history before the turn of the millennium saw government authority once again devolve to regional lords, with a succession of foreign dynasties divided by periods of native control, the particular details of which are described in the following chapter. A reasonable description of the age is that it was one of upheaval and political disorder. Scholars call this time the Late Period, which extends from the Twenty-Second Dynasty to the Roman takeover, about a thousand years.[58] The extant biographies continue to develop and change in this era, although until a resurgence in the Ptolemaic period not as many appear in the tomb funerary chapels, perhaps because it had become too costly to have them built. Temple monuments however continued in frequency so that the biographical genre did not experience a decline in

---

[56] Lichtheim, *Maat in Egyptian Autobiographies*, 136–38. The same hymn appears on the stelae of Minmose and Amenmose, also Ramesside, as well as in part in Ani's copy of the Book of the Dead. The translation is Lichtheim's.

[57] Lichtheim, *Maat in Egyptian Autobiographies*, 139.

[58] Otto, *Die biographischen Inschriften*, 5.

usage.[59] The three texts which will be discussed in detail further in the chapter all date to the Late Period, but before the translations commence a few words should be said on the general characteristics of the biographies as a whole in this stage of Egyptian history.

The form of the biography has undergone a rearrangement. The appeal to the reader comes forward in the text so that the entire work is now a direct address. At the same time, the request at the end for an offering is often lacking; instead the subject of the text wants the reader to take his life as an example and utter his name.[60] The bulk of the biographies stem from priests, civil servants, and military officers.[61] The language used is mostly still Middle Egyptian, just as in the older texts, although by now it had long passed out of common usage and was utilized only for formal inscriptions and religious materials. Narrative portions are all in Middle Egyptian, with an occasional example of Late Egyptian in cases where the composer wants to imitate the current speech, and this only during the Twenty-Second and -Third Dynasties. All later texts are in Middle Egyptian.[62]

---

[59] Perdu, "Ancient Egyptian Autobiographies," IV:2252. He names Karnak, Memphis, Sais, and the Serapeum (Saqqara) among others as places that supply a large number of Late Period biographies. Most were inscribed on statues in this time, except at the Serapeum, where stelae continued to be the favored form. Sherman, "Egyptian Biographies," 392, also states that biographical texts were now set up in temple courtyards more than anywhere else, though she offers a somewhat different explanation for this, which is that the temples had defensive walls which offered protection from the destructive forces of war and that people "could no longer trust in isolated necropolis priests and the occasional passerby to remember their souls."

[60] Otto, *Die biographischen Inschriften*, 16. He gives an interesting example of how the request for uttering an offering formula has (at least in some cases) changed in the Late Period. In the biography of the priest Hor, Hor begins by addressing all those who will come to the tomb and says "hört den Ausspruch! Nicht wird ja euer Mund müde vom Sprechen; nichts Übles ist es ja für den Sprechenden (sondern) etwas Gutes!" (17). The old plea for uttering the offering formula because it is not something that requires effort and will be of benefit to the speaker is quite recognizable here, but makes poor sense because the actual request is not for the formula, but for hearing (=paying attention).

[61] Otto, *Die biographischen Inschriften*, 9.

[62] Otto, *Die biographischen Inschriften*, 19. Otto adds that one can find single elements of Late Egyptian and even Coptic interspersed in the materials. An exception to his general point is that in the case of one family of Memphite priests in the Ptolemaic period, the Middle Egyptian text of one stela would be copied on a

One new feature of the texts is that the individual will speak directly to the gods, not merely to the reader or the local priests.[63] As time progressed the biographies came to be centered around what deeds the subject had performed for the sake of the gods.[64] In earlier periods the deities tended to be a less central consideration in the biographies, but after the New Kingdom ended they came to the fore.[65] The deeper feeling of connection with the gods is mirrored by a strong sense of relationship to the family and immediate milieu.[66] At the same time the idea of dependence on the king, which had existed in various degrees of interpretation throughout Egyptian history, slips into the background.[67] Some view these tendencies as a sign that the Egyptians were turning away from the political disturbances and uncertainties of life in order to concentrate on the more attractive promise of an agreeable existence in the afterlife.[68] It should of course be kept in mind that pious trends had already emerged some time before, during the New Kingdom, but the increasing focus on the individual's piety towards the gods at the expense of much actual biographical detail does seem to reflect a new attitude towards the world and one's sense of self. For some, even reliance on the afterlife will come into question.

Otto makes an interesting observation about the view of act and consequence that appears in these texts. He explains that in the older period a good deed automatically led to an appropriate outcome, whereas now God is the personal arbiter of each result and acts according to the divine will, i.e. in a way that cannot be predicted with certainty. The regularity of the system where everyone is to receive their "just deserts" no longer holds, and it is now up to God to see to it that the good receives

---

second stela, but in Demotic. See footnote #91.

[63] Perdu, "Ancient Egyptian Autobiographies," IV:2252.

[64] Perdu, "Ancient Egyptian Autobiographies," IV:2252.

[65] Guksch, *Königsdienst*, 3. Otto, *Die biographischen Inschriften*, 20, writes that the characteristic of the late biographies is that "die persönliche Verbundenheit mit der Gottheit deutlich in den Vordergrund tritt."

[66] Otto, *Die biographischen Inschriften*, 17.

[67] Baines, "Society, Morality, and Religious Practice," 196.

[68] Sherman, "Egyptian Biographies," 392.

its proper reward.[69] Moreover, as the coming examples in particular will show, there appears to be a loss of confidence for some in the age-old expectation of immortality in an afterlife.[70]

In the Late Period biographies in general, the focus of the notion of immortality turns from the netherworld to the present life and seeks fulfillment in the fame of one's good name, good deeds, and more importantly, one's descendants.[71] Even if the other known late biographical writings do not offer the extreme arguments of the examples about to be discussed, this trend provides an understandable context into which they fit. The desire that one's children take over one's position in life, common to the biographical genre from days of old, achieves a particular urgency and frequency at this time.[72] Once death becomes the end of life, immortality is possible through this-worldly means alone, children and fame.[73] As the preceding chapter showed, descendants and reputation were always part of the wide repertoire the Egyptians had at

---

[69] Otto, *Die biographischen Inschriften*, 23–24. Baines, "Society, Morality, and Religious Practice," 187–89, questions Otto's analysis here. He says that he draws his supporting quotations for the idea of the mechanical operation of act and consequence from earlier wisdom literature texts, which tend to be more impersonal and abstract by definition. These are writings that describe the general principles of the universe. The biographies however are a personal account of an individual's life, so that a more intimate relation to the divine is described. In other words, genre differences, not time period, account for the emphasis on divine involvement. This is a perceptive point to bring up, and it also true that even the wisdom literature acknowledges divine intervention. Nevertheless, Otto is right in that the gods have a new prominence in the biographies than they had had in the past (as also says Guksch, *Königsdienst*, 3), and that there is a general loss of confidence in the order of the world of which this is only one example. So Baines brings in an important nuance but this does not break Otto's point.

[70] Otto, *Die biographischen Inschriften*, 31.

[71] Otto, *Die biographischen Inschriften*, 51. See page 53 where he says that the idea of the judgment of the dead generally recedes, as the belief in the afterlife became uncertain. See also page 59 where he reiterates the point: "das Vertrauen zu den theologischen Dogmen, besonders wenn sie sich mit Tod und Jenseits befassten, schwach geworden war. So auf doppelte Weise auf sich selbst und sein Geschlecht angewiesen, sieht der Mensch den noch überzeugenderen Teil seiner Unsterblichkeit im Nachleben seines Geschlechtes und seines guten Namens liegen. Und diesen zweiten Punkt behandeln unsere Inschriften ebenfalls mit besonderer Vorliebe."

[72] Otto, *Die biographischen Inschriften*, 59.

[73] Otto, *Die biographischen Inschriften*, 64–65.

hand for achieving some form of eternal endurance of the self,[74] but these were part and parcel of a deep-seated belief in individual immortality in an afterlife. This is the heart of the ancient Egyptian symbolic system. The outright denial of it is not just a shift in emphasis, but a shift in essence. Most late biographies do not actually deny it, instead adjusting their focus. But three are known to have done so, even though they themselves retain the old, but now thoroughly undermined, offering requests.

As a whole, late biographies can be said to reveal a new disquiet about the patterns of the world, about whether an upright life brings its reward as hoped, and there is an increased sense that well-being is purely at the choice of a mysterious divine will.[75] Late Period trends in the age-old biographical tradition show a deepening anxiety towards life and in particular reserve toward the notion of life after death which is characteristic of the time in a way that it was not of the earlier periods.[76] One has to remember that many of the texts continue in the tradition of the past, but some of these different trends do seem to merge with one another: the not uncommon lack of a request that the reader utter an offering-formula to supply the needs of the dead, the intense focus on the gods instead of the king, the turning towards family and the inner circle rather than one's participation in the world at large, a sense that there is no reliable pattern of deed and consequence in life which further heightens the dependence on the gods, and the outright declaration that the afterlife is empty, which in itself would seem to run counter to a reliance on the deities. The loss of confidence in the afterlife is the focus of this chapter and is best seen through the relevant texts.

---

[74] Herman te Velde, "Commemoration in Ancient Egypt," in H. G. Kippenberg et al, eds., *Visible Religion: Annual for Religious Iconography, Vol. I: Commemorative Figures* (Leiden: E. J. Brill, 1982) 142–143, questions Otto's conclusions about the state of Egyptian belief in the Late Period since the need for remembering the dead had been important for a long time. He also notes that leaving memory of oneself on earth is not something that necessarily excludes a belief in the afterlife (143). He is right in his basic point, but Otto is not trying to suggest that memory is a new idea, or that this in itself excludes the afterlife. Rather he is talking about the evidence as a whole and new emphases, in which his argument is persuasive.

[75] Lichtheim, *Ancient Egyptian Literature*, III:5.

[76] Morenz, *Egyptian Religion*, 213, also comments on this late scepticism towards the afterlife.

THE TEXTS

Isenkhebe

The first composition for consideration is the stela of Isenkhebe,[77] the date of which has been set in the early Saite period, 650-630 BCE.[78] The stela is round-topped, made of limestone, and is 0.52 meters high.[79] At the top Isenkhebe worships Isis and Osiris, with two columns of text on the right, behind her, and two on the left, behind Isis and Osiris. The left columns are the beginning of the biography proper and continue below the picture in six horizontal lines.[80] The translation:

> I worship your Ka, Lord of the Gods, although[81] I am still a child. This is an injury against me,[82] while I was a child, without fault. [I?] tell what has

---

[77] Miriam Lichtheim, *Ancient Egyptian Literature: A Book of Readings*, 3 Vols. (Berkeley: University of California Press, 1973, 1976, 1980) III:59, explains that the name was a common one in the Late Period and means "Isis in Chemmis."

[78] Peter Munro, *Die spätägyptischen Totenstelen* (Glückstadt: J. J. Augustin, 1973) 284–85. Adolf Erman, "Zwei Grabsteine griechischer Zeit," in Gotthold Weil, ed., *Festschrift Eduard Sachau* (Berlin: Georg Reimer, 1915) 111, on the other hand, considered the stela to be Ptolemaic. Otto, *Die biographischen Inschriften*, 187, tentatively suggests a Ptolemaic date, though he adds a question mark. Lichtheim, *Ancient Egyptian Literature*, III:58, does not explicitly say she agrees with Munro's dating but she does remark that he uses archeological criteria, and may therefore agree with him. Ursula Rößler-Köhler, *Individuelle Haltungen zum Ägyptischen Königtum der Spätzeit: Private Quellen und ihre Königswertung im Spannungsfeld zwischen Erwartung und Erfahrung* (Wiesbaden: Otto Harrassowitz, 1991) 214, dates it as Munro does.

[79] Lichtheim, *Ancient Egyptian Literature*, III:58.

[80] Lichtheim, *Ancient Egyptian Literature*, III:58.

[81] Erman, "Zwei Grabsteine griechischer Zeit," 104, translates "*während* ich (noch) ein Kind bin," and comments that "ḥr ḫpr.i" has some sort of nuance, which in the context of the entire work is likely the idea that the speaker has reached Osiris too quickly. Lichtheim, *Ancient Egyptian Literature*, III: 58, has "*though* I am but a child." Otto, *Die biographischen Inschriften*, 187, offers "*da* ich noch ein Kind bin."

[82] The meaning of this phrase is obscure. The Egyptian is "ḥḏ nn ḥr.i." Erman, "Zwei Grabsteine griechischer Zeit," 104, reads "(Dich) der dieses an (?) mir schädigte...." He admits that the grammar is odd, but the gist is clear, so the phrase in his view is a euphemism for "die." "Dieses" refers to the years that have been destroyed for the girl. Otto, *Die biographischen Inschriften*, 187, translates "Das (d.h. das Leben) wurde mir vermindert (?)...." He notes that his translation is uncertain, and refers the reader to Erman. Lichtheim, *Ancient Egyptian Literature*, III:58, perhaps stays closest to the Egyptian with "Harm is what befell me!"

happened [?].[83] I sleep in the valley, a girl, thirsting though water is beside me. I was driven away from my childhood before it was time. I turned away from my house as a youth,[84] without my having been satisfied in it. The dark, the abomination of a child, rose up over me while the breast was still in my mouth. The watchers [?][85] of this gate/hall of judgement turn away all people from me, who am not in the (proper) time of solitude.[86] My heart was happy at seeing many people. I was one who loved gaiety.

Everyone seems to agree however that the phrase is a reference to death, and as Lichtheim points out (59) the word "ḥd" is used in the same way in the Antef Song (cf. the preceding chapter for a brief discussion of this text).

[83] This is another difficult phrase, in Egyptian "ḏd ḫpr.f." Erman, "Zwei Grabsteine griechischer Zeit," 104, has "Der sagte und es (?) geschah...." He explains that the idea is that Osiris gave his command regarding the girl, and thus it happened, a notion which is not unusual for the Egyptians. Siegfried Schott, *Altägyptische Liebeslieder, mit Märchen und Liebesgeschichten* (Zürich: Artemis, 1950) 145, translates similarly. Otto, *Die biographischen Inschriften*, 187, suggests "Ich sage, was mir geschah (?)." In his view Erman's translation makes poor sense. Lichtheim, *Ancient Egyptian Literature*, III:59, breaks the line up differently than the others by ending the preceding sentence with "When I was but a child!" Her next sentence is "A faultless one reports it." The present translation does what most have done by attaching "without fault" or some such to the "but a child" line of thought, and beginning a new idea with "ḏd ḫpr.f."

[84] Erman, "Zwei Grabsteine griechischer Zeit," 104, translates this as "und so wandte ich mich fort von meinem Hause in meiner Kindheit...." Otto, *Die biographischen Inschriften*, 187, says "Ich kehrte meinem Hause den Rücken als ein Kleines...." Lichtheim, *Ancient Egyptian Literature*, III:59, gives "Turned away from my house as a youngster...."

[85] The Egyptian word here is "ḥtpw." R. O. Faulkner, *A Concise Dictionary of Middle Egyptian* (Oxford: The Griffith Institute, 1988) 180, renders the word "the peaceful ones = the blessed dead." Adolf Erman and and Hermann Grapow, *Wörterbuch der Aegyptischen Sprache*, 7 Vols. (Leipzig: J. C. Hinrichs'sche Buchhandlung, 1926–63) III:195, translate it "seligen Toten." Erman, "Zwei Grabsteine griechischer Zeit," 106, says "Die Wächter (?)," and explains that these refer to gods of the netherworld, as proven by the Book of the Dead. Schott, *Altägyptische Liebeslieder*, 146, translates as Erman does. Otto, *Die biographischen Inschriften*, 188, says "Die Totengeister." Lichtheim, *Ancient Egyptian Literature*, III:59, has "the demons." Obviously Isenkhebe is confronting some kind of otherworldly beings who are not acting in a friendly way towards her.

[86] Erman, "Zwei Grabsteine griechischer Zeit," 106, points out that the Egyptian is literally "Der nicht in der Zeit des Alleinseins ist." Otto, *Die biographischen Inschriften*, 188, and Lichtheim, *Ancient Egyptian Literature*, III:59, render this as a first person construction.

O King of the Gods, Ruler of Eternity, to whom come all people, give me
bread, milk, incense, water which come from your offering-table. I am a child
without fault.

Although the composition is not very long, it manages to convey
powerful ideas and images in the space that it has available. As in the
Antef Song, discussed in the previous chapter, Isenkhebe calls death an
"injury," which in her case appears to be related to the fact that she has
died before the full span of her life had a chance to run. She says she was
driven from her youth, forced to leave her home unfulfilled. Death is, on
the one hand, a state of sleep, which implies unconsciousness, while on
the other it appears to cause feelings of deprivation. The girl is thirsty,
even though water is beside her. The dark, which she especially abhors,
has consumed her. Some type of supernatural beings will not let anyone
near her in the netherworld, which brings on untimely solitude. The
reader does not learn why they bar her from companionship; she says
repeatedly that she is innocent of any fault, which rules out punishment.
The phrasing however suggests that this may be a normal state of affairs
for the dead, since she did not reach "the time for solitude." This implies
that death is a form of isolation for everyone, but perhaps those who lived
their lives out do not chafe against it as she does. The piquancy of the
point is drawn out when she describes how particularly she loved being
around people and enjoying gaiety. The text concludes with the common
request that Osiris, "to whom come all people," give her some of the
sustenance from his offering-table, but in light of the preceding the plea
is hollow. She already has water beside her, which means the proper cult
is being maintained, but it does no good. The problem appears not to be
one of having no access to what she needs, but being unable to make use
of it. These same ideas are developed in more detail in the following text.

Taimhotep

The next biography under consideration is that of Taimhotep, who
was born in 73 BCE[87] and died at thirty years of age. Her stela is
round-topped and of limestone with a picture on the upper portion
showing Taimhotep adoring six gods, first among them Osiris. The text

---

[87] Lichtheim, *Ancient Egyptian Literature*, III:64; Munro, *Die
spätägyptischen Totenstelen*, 165.

runs in twenty-one horizontal lines below the relief.[88] She was the wife of the high priest of Ptah in Memphis, Pshereneptah, whom she married at age fourteen. Unlike Isenkhebe, Taimhotep is of high status.[89] The biography begins with a detailed offering formula, then takes up the narrative of Taimhotep's life. The story is an interesting one. It happened that she gave birth to three daughters, until she and her husband finally prayed together to the god Imhotep, a popular divinity in this period who was a deified sage from the Old Kingdom, for a son. Pshereneptah had a revelatory dream in which the god said he would give them their son if the high priest would perform a deed for him in his sanctuary. This he did, employing sculptors for whatever it was exactly and performing a sacrifice.[90] Taimhotep then became pregnant, and sure enough, when she gave birth, the child was a boy.[91] Four years later, in 42 BCE, Taimhotep

---

[88] Lichtheim, *Ancient Egyptian Literature*, III:69; Robert Bianchi, et al, *Cleopatra's Egypt: Age of The Ptolemies* (New York: The Brooklyn Museum, 1988), 230–31, has a photograph, as does H. R. Hall, *A General Introductory Guide to the Egyptian Collections in the British Museum* (London: Harrison and Sons, 1930) 216; E. A. E. Reymond, *From the Records of a Priestly Family from Memphis* (Wiesbaden: Otto Harrassowitz, 1981) plate 12; and Dietrich Wildung, *Imhotep und Amenhotep: Gottwerdung im alten Ägypten* (Munich: Deutscher Kunstverlag, 1977) plate 13. The stela has two large cracks but is still quite readable.

[89] Reymond, *From the Records of a Priestly Family from Memphis*, 51, notes that in the late second century BCE her husband's grandfather married a daughter of Ptolemy IX, Berenice.

[90] For a partial translation of this segment cf. Wildung, *Imhotep und Amenhotep*, 68–70; Hall, *A General Introductory Guide*, 407, also has a brief discussion of this first part of the work. An English translation of Pshereneptah's stela, as well as part of Taimhotep's, can be found in Edwyn Bevan, *A History of Egypt under the Ptolemaic Dynasty* (London: Methuen & Co., Ltd., 1927) 347–48. The actual translation is done by S. R. K. Glanville. Pshereneptah refers to the birth of his son, the gift of Imhotep, but does not offer the detail of his wife's stela on the matter.

[91] Munro, *Die spätägyptischen Totenstelen*, 165, lists stelae for various members of this family. Besides Taimhotep he cites stelae for her husband, her son, and her younger sister. He shows the family relationships in a chart on page 166, and describes the individual stelae one by one on pages 338–39, 341. Also Jan Quaegebeur, "The Genealogy of the Memphite High Priest Family in the Hellenistic Period," in Dorothy Crawford, et al, eds., *Studies on Ptolemaic Memphis* (Leuven: 1980) 69–71, lists all known stelae and the family relationships they reveal. Jan Quaegebeur, "Contribution à la Prosopographie des Prêtres

died.[92] What follows is a long address by the dead woman to her husband.

> O (my) brother, husband, friend, high priest:[93] do not weary of drink, food,
> deep drinking, and loving. Make a holiday! Follow your heart day and night!
> Do not set sorrow[94] in your heart. What are the years which are not on earth?[95]
> As for the West, it is a land in sleep, heavy darkness, the dwelling-place of
> those who are there.[96] Sleep is in their (mummy) forms.[97] They do not awake

Memphites à l'Époque Ptolémaïque," *Ancient Society* 3(1972) 77–109, discusses
several of the family's stelae in more detail, Taimhotep in particular on pages 93–
96 (his purpose does not include a discussion of the part of her biography under
study here). See Wildung, *Imhotep und Amenhotep*, 65–67 and 70–73 for
discussion of the husband's and sons stelae, respectively. Reymond, *From the
Records of a Priestly Family from Memphis*, discusses the entire family at length
(see pages 165–94 on Taimhotep). Bianchi, et al, *Cleopatra's Egypt*, 231, remarks
that in this group of stelae the hieroglyphic text is frequently translated into
Demotic on a separate stela. Jan Quaegebeur, "Taimhotep," in Wolfgang Helck et
al, eds., *Lexikon der Ägyptologie*, Vol. VI (Wiesbaden: Otto Harrassowitz, 1986)
184, says that Taimhotep's Demotic stela, also in the British Museum, adds nothing
new. See Rößler-Köhler, *Individuelle Haltungen zum Ägyptischen Königtum der
Spätzeit*, 327–329, for short discussions of Taimhotep's two stelae with respect to
what they reveal about attitudes towards the king (remarks on other family stelae
follow).

[92] Lichtheim, *Ancient Egyptian Literature*, III:64.

[93] Faulkner, *A Concise Dictionary of Middle Egyptian*, 170, notes that the
phrase "wr-ḥrp-ḥm(w)" specifically refers to the high priest of Ptah at Memphis.

[94] The word here is listed in Erman and Grapow, *Wörterbuch der
Aegyptischen Sprache*, II:120, under a slightly different spelling.

[95] This is a difficult sentence, and the translation above assumes the
interpretation of Erman, "Zwei Grabsteine griechischer Zeit," 108, in which "iṯw"
is read as "iwty." Otto, *Die biographischen Inschriften*, 193, and Schott,
Altägyptische Liebeslieder, 144, follow Erman. Lichtheim, *Ancient Egyptian
Literature*, III:64, disagrees. She feels the sentence should continue the preceding
idea that one ought to enjoy life, and remarks that time in the netherworld was not
measured in "years," so that the notion of years which are not spent on earth is
unlikely. Instead, she takes the first word, "iḥy," not as the interrogative particle
"iḥ" but the verb "3ḥ." Secondly, "iṯw" she reads as the verb "iṯi," "to pass time."
Thus she translates the whole as "Value the years spent on earth!" No rendering is
very certain.

[96] Lichtheim, *Ancient Egyptian Literature*, III:64, takes "n nty imw" as "n3
nty imw" and uses it for the beginning of the following sentence: "Darkness weighs
on the dwelling-place, Those who are there sleep...." This translates "dns" as a
transitive verb, which she notes must have been possible or else a preposition is
missing. Erman, "Zwei Grabsteine griechischer Zeit," 108, also states that one
might translate "dns" transitively, except he knows of no other examples and so
discounts this reading. Otto, *Die biographischen Inschriften*, 193, follows Erman.

to see their brothers, they do not see their fathers or their mothers, their hearts lack[98] their wives and their children. The water of life which is food for all, it is thirst for me. It comes (only) to the one who is on earth; I am thirsty, (though) water is beside me. I do not know the place in which it is (?),[99] since (I) reached this valley. Give me running water, say to me[100] "You are not far from water,"[101] turn my face to the northwind on the shore of the water.

---

[97] Erman, "Zwei Grabsteine griechischer Zeit," 108 and Lichtheim, *Ancient Egyptian Literature*, III:64, read "sm" as "form," while Otto, *Die biographischen Inschriften*, 193, takes the word in its other meaning, "occupation"; "Schlafen ist ihre Beschäftigung."

[98] Erman, "Zwei Grabsteine griechischer Zeit," 108, suggests that their hearts "vermißt (?)" their wives and children, noting that the word "wh" would normally have the preposition "m." Otto, *Die biographischen Inschriften*, 193, says their hearts "entbehren" them. Schott, *Altägyptische Liebeslieder*, 144, says "vergessen," and Lichtheim, *Ancient Egyptian Literature*, III:63, translates "Their hearts forgot...."

[99] This is another puzzling construction. The Egyptian runs "n rḫ.i bw nty is im.i." Any intelligible translation requires emendation. Erman, "Zwei Grabsteine griechischer Zeit," 109, Schott, *Altägyptische Liebeslieder*, 144, and Lichtheim, *Ancient Egyptian Literature*, III:63, all choose the translation offered above. Otto, *Die biographischen Inschriften*, 193, suggests "Ich kenne nicht den Ort, wo ich bin (?)...." To get the former translation one must read "is" as "iw.s," Erman notes, which is a normal spelling in Late Period names. Then, "im.i" would be read as "im." This still leaves the problem of the third-person feminine "s" in the emended "iw.s." Is it an incorrect reference to the water? Since the Egyptian appears to be garbled, various emendations are plausible, though Erman may have a point when he says that the text continues to speak of water and thus water should be taken as the subject of the present sentence, too (i.e. not the speaker).

[100] The hieroglyphs literally read "iw.i ḏd n.i....", but this makes poor sense. Erman, "Zwei Grabsteine griechischer Zeit," 109, believes that what looks like "iw.i" may be taken as a writing of the imperative prefix "i" (in other words, the reed leaf and the sitting man, minus the quail chick) to the verb, which renders a better translation. Lichtheim, *Ancient Egyptian Literature*, III:63, Schott, *Altägyptische Liebeslieder*, 144, and Otto, *Die biographischen Inschriften*, 193, do the same.

[101] The translation "you" is based on the word "ḥm" which usually means "majesty (of the king)." Erman, "Zwei Grabsteine griechischer Zeit," 109, translates it as "majesty," with the explanation that the phrase could just be from a traditional formula used for the king which, although here addressing a private individual, still retains its original form. Lichtheim, *Ancient Egyptian Literature*, III:57, states that "ḥm" often just means "person, self," and so she reads it as a simple address to Taimhotep, where "your person" equals "you," as above. Otto, *Die biographischen Inschriften*, 193, uses the more literal translation "deine Gestalt."

Surely[102] then my heart will be cooled in its suffering.

As for Death, "Come" is his name.[103] All whom he has summoned come to him immediately, their hearts terrified with fear of him.[104] There is none who sees him among gods or humanity. The great ones are in his hand just like the small. None opposes him from all whom he loves. He steals the son from his mother rather than the aged one who is (already) walking about in his vicinity.[105] All the frightened plead before him, (but) he does not give them his ear. He[106] does not come to the one who calls upon him,[107] he does not[108] listen to the one who pays him honor. He is not seen, that gifts of any sort can be given to him.

O all who come to this necropolis, give to me incense on the flame, water in every festival of the West.

The scribe, sculptor, and scholar, the initiate of the goldhouse in Tenent, the

---

[102] Erman, "Zwei Grabsteine griechischer Zeit," 110, does not think the meaning "surely" for "smwn" fits the context, and Otto, *Die biographischen Inschriften*, 193, puts a question mark after his translation "sicherlich." Lichtheim, *Ancient Egyptian Literature*, III:63, says "perhaps." Yet the sentence with "surely" can fit in the sense that she is saying: if only this could be done for me, then surely I would feel better—but, she has already explained that such assistance can no longer have any effect on her, which lends added poignancy here.

[103] Erman, "Zwei Grabsteine griechischer Zeit," 111, remarks that the sounds for "death" (mou) and "come" (amou) in the Egyptian are quite close, which makes a pun. Schott, *Altägyptische Liebeslieder*, 145, brings out the connection a bit in his translation, "Was den Tod betrifft, so ist sein Name: Komm!"

[104] Otto, *Die biographischen Inschriften*, 193, breaks the sentence up differently. "Der Tod, 'Komm' ist sein Name, er ruft jeden zu sich. Sie kommen zu ihn sogleich...."

[105] That is, the old person is already practically at death's door.

[106] The verb does not have an explicit subject, which causes Erman, "Zwei Grabsteine griechischer Zeit," 110, to put a question mark after the "he," but clearly Death is still the subject, as Otto, *Die biographischen Inschriften*, 193, and Lichtheim, *Ancient Egyptian Literature*, III:63, also translate it.

[107] Erman, "Zwei Grabsteine griechischer Zeit," 111, discusses the odd spelling of the verb "sm3'," which is written "sm3'ḥw." According to Grapow the "ḥw" is an incorrect representation of the elephant tusk determinative, which is sometimes used in words with "ḥw" as the phonetic value. For the latter confer Alan H. Gardiner, *Egyptian Grammar* (3rd edition; Oxford: Griffith Institute, 1957) 463. The word "sm3'" is listed in Erman and Grapow, *Wörterbuch der Aegyptischen Sprache*, IV:125.

[108] The Egyptian mistakenly has "not" twice.

prophet of Horus, Imhotep son of the prophet Khahapi,[109] justified, has made it.

The very end of this text is an interesting little glimpse into how such materials were composed, since the scribe Imhotep essentially signs his work. Unfortunately, it is not entirely certain just what Imhotep is responsible for, since the phrasing is ambiguous. Some believe that he both composed the text and designed the stela.[110] Others credit Taimhotep's husband for commissioning and composing it.[111] The reader notices that the dead woman says at one point that the deceased do not recognize their wives, which suggests that the author, whether husband, brother, or someone else, was male and not the subject herself.

Taimhotep's discourse takes the ideas in Isenkhebe and deepens their ramifications. The opening exhortation to her still-living husband to live life to the fullest attains real urgency in light of her personal account of what it is like to be dead. The West is a place of sleep and darkness, which is what Isenkhebe also said. Taimhotep dwells on the insensibility of death in more detail, however. Everyone lies still in their mummified state, and nobody awakens to see their family, whether parents, spouses, or children. Their hearts, the seat of thinking and consciousness, are empty or forgetful of their loved ones.

Then she takes up Isenkhebe's theme of thirst and develops the idea extensively. She too is thirsty, although water is present at her side. The problem is that water is only effective for the living. It nourishes them, but is thirst for her. She does not even know where it is to be found,

---

[109] Bianchi, et al, *Cleopatra's Egypt*, 231, says that this Imhotep is the brother-in-law of Taimhotep. According to Quaegebeur, "The Genealogy of the Memphite High Priest Family in the Hellenistic Period," 70, he is her brother. He adds that while the identification of his parents with hers is not provable, it "seems obvious that the man who drafted the original inscriptions was a close relative of those commemorated in the original texts." Quaegebeur's outline suggests that the names do match up when all the different family stelae are cross-referenced. An additional note is that both Bianchi and Quaegebeur read this man's name as "Harimouthes," meaning that they take the "Horus" in "prophet of Horus" instead as part of the proper name.

[110] Lichtheim, *Ancient Egyptian Literature*, III:65; also Quaegebeur, "The Genealogy of the Memphite High Priest Family in the Hellenistic Period," 70.

[111] Dorothy Crawford, "Ptolemy, Ptah and Apis in Hellenistic Memphis," in Dorothy Crawford, et al, eds., *Studies on Ptolemaic Memphis* (Leuven: 1980) 21.

anymore.[112] Her plea for water immediately follows, and as in the case of Isenkhebe there is little hope that it can be granted. "Water" is a drumbeat throughout this whole section. Water is thirst for me.... water is beside me.... give me water.... say "you are not far from water...." the shore of the water.... She begs for offerings, for reassurance, for help, so that her anguish can be assuaged, or literally, "cooled," which also requires water. Yet Taimhotep herself seems to regard the situation as irremediable.

The following commentary on Death personified is unforgettable. Death's very name is "Come," its essence is that all creatures must come to it, which is something Isenkhebe had said, too. Death is all-powerful, treats everyone exactly alike, and cannot be delayed or opposed. Although terrified, people cannot resist his summons. Death takes whom he pleases in spite of age or wish of the victim; perversely, he ignores those who want him and takes those who abhor him. Neither pleas nor bribes affect him, and though omnipotent, Death is unseen (this is stated two different times), even by the gods. Again, Taimhotep concludes with a request for offerings, incense and water, just like Isenkhebe had, but there is faint hope that they can do much for her. The implication of this last point is astonishing, in that the mortuary cult simply ceases to function.[113]

The stela is especially interesting in that it gives a detailed account of Taimhotep's life before the soliloquy under discussion begins, and clearly it was a successful one. She married well and had four children, including the desired son as she and her husband had wanted. Although she has not died of old age by any means, she has lived an adult life and fulfilled the role expected by her society. The birth of the son appears to be something of a coup. Unlike Isenkhebe, then, her problem is not one of childhood death, nor does she claim that she did not get her fair share

---

[112] One cannot make too much of this particular point, since the Egyptian text here is garbled; the problems are spelled out in the footnotes to the translation above. If the meaning of the text is rather that Taimhotep does not know where *she* is since having died, the point is still arresting, as then she is saying that death removes any sense of space or location.

[113] Siegfried Morenz, *Egyptian Religion*, trans. Ann E. Keep (New York: Cornell University Press, 1973) 191; see also Otto, *Die biographischen Inschriften*, 47, who says the idea means that the offering-formula is no longer trusted.

of life. This is not an issue and is a difference between the two texts.[114] Yet Taimhotep takes little comfort in the life she lived, so melancholy is her current state of existence. By the end of the narration, Death itself has almost become the main character. The one who is dead is beyond succor, the one who is alive faces a losing battle with a force that stands outside all bounds, human or divine, and there is no answer or comfort to be offered. Death truly comes as the end.

Petosiris

Unlike the preceding two texts which both come from mortuary stelae, the material relating to the family of Petosiris is located in a tomb. The excavation of the tomb, which was discovered in 1919, followed by the description, photography, transcription and translation of texts, were carried out and produced by Gustave Lefebvre in the early 1920's. As he remarks, this is not really the "tomb of Petosiris," since a large part of the structure was dedicated by Petosiris to his father and older brother and the subterranean chamber on discovery still contained the sarcophagi of his wife and one of his sons.[115] In other words this is a family tomb, but Petosiris built it and is the main personality that comes through. Five generations of the family, beginning with his grandparents and ending

---

[114] Quaegebeur, "Taimhotep," 184, says otherwise, that she "se plaint de sa mort prématuré," and that the text's scepticism "paraît surprenant pour une personne ayant fait preuve d'une grande piété personnelle." So also Lichtheim, *Ancient Egyptian Literature*, III:13. However, unlike Isenkhebe, and unlike the text next to be translated, that of Thothrekh the son of Petosiris, Taimhotep nowhere claims that she died too young, nor is it obvious that having reached her fourth decade and raised several children, anyone of the time would regard her death as unusually early. Pieter W. van der Horst, *Ancient Jewish Epitaphs: An Introductory Survey of a Millennium of Jewish Funerary Epigraphy (300 BCE–700 CE)* (Kampen: Kok Pharos, 1991) 73–84, discusses the average age of death for people in the ancient Near East around the turn of the millennium. Although a number of factors makes it difficult to establish a figure with certainty, what evidence there is suggests a common average age of death in the upper twenties to lower thirties, depending on location. Greek, Roman, and Jewish epitaphs frequently mourn early deaths of children (45–46) as well as death that occurred before marriage (46–48). However, although Taimhotep's age of death is young by today's standards, it is not certain that the death of a thirty-year-old mother of four would have been considered a remarkable event. She herself does not comment on it.

[115] Gustave Lefebvre, *Le tombeau de Petosiris*, 3 Vols. (Cairo: Institut francais d'archéologie orientale, 1923–24) I:1.

with a son of his oldest son, appear in the inscriptions.[116] Petosiris and other male members of his family in turn held the office of high priest for the god Thoth in Hermopolis.

Although no cartouches or dates are to be found on the tomb walls, Lefebvre persuasively dates the tomb to the fourth century BCE. Vocabulary, proper names, and comparison with other late inscriptions reinforce one another in his conclusion. Specifically, the older generations of the family lived during the final native dynasties, then the second Persian domination (342–332 BCE), while the younger lived under Greek rule.[117] More than one inscription refers to a chaotic period when "foreigners" were in control of Egypt,[118] which would refer to the second Persian period when the country was in an uproar. In one of the biographical inscriptions for Petosiris he describes holding one of his offices "while the Ruler-of-foreign-lands" was Protector in Egypt, and nothing was in its former place, "since fighting had started inside Egypt, the South being in turmoil, the North in revolt.... The priests fled, not knowing what was happening."[119]

In response to the mayhem Petosiris takes it upon himself to restore order to the priestly rites and rebuild various temples, structures, and park grounds. "I made splendid what was found ruined anywhere."[120] In light of recent historical events he is no doubt speaking the literal truth, but it is interesting that his claims were traditionally made only by pharaohs, who might describe their accessions in terms of an age-old restoration of order out of chaos. Petosiris is also portrayed in some of the tomb reliefs as performing offering rites to various gods, which was usually the prerogative of the king.[121] He "stretched the cord, released the

---

[116] Lefebvre, *Le tombeau de Petosiris*, I:3–6, discusses the generations one by one and provides a family tree.

[117] Lefebvre, *Le tombeau de Petosiris*, I:10. See also Rößler-Köhler, *Individuelle Haltungen zum Ägyptischen Königtum der Spätzeit*, 287–292, for discussion of the tomb and the dates during which various family members probably lived.

[118] See Lefebvre, *Le tombeau de Petosiris*, I:10–11, for discussion, and 80, 82, and 137 for the actual texts in which the comments occur.

[119] Lichtheim, *Ancient Egyptian Literature*, III:46. She agrees (49) that this refers to the end of the Persian domination.

[120] Lichtheim, *Ancient Egyptian Literature*, III:47.

[121] Lefebvre, *Le tombeau de Petosiris*, I:9.

line, to found the temple of Re....," another royal function.[122] He even
uses the royal epithet "ankh, wd3, seneb," "living, prosperous, hale," after
his name.[123] The final touch to this multifarious approach to royalty is
that the tomb became something of a pilgrimage site after the death of
Petosiris and Greek graffiti left at the site by later visitors describes it as
a "temple," while someone refers to Petosiris himself as a "sage."[124]
Petosiris reached a semi-divine status not unlike that of the Old Kingdom
sage Imhotep or the New Kingdom Amenhotep son of Hapu.

One of the interesting things about the inscription translated below
is that it should come from this context, that of a successful and important
family whose claim to fame is bringing the local area and temples back
to their proper condition, and in a tomb most of whose inscriptions are
properly oriented toward the funeral cult and if anything, whose owner
assimilates himself to the highest traditional authority figure in Egyptian
society, the king. Yet the following text, that of a son of Petosiris named
Thothrekh, is anything but traditional. Apparently he died in his youth but
the exact age is unknown. The inscription consists of eleven vertical lines
with a lacuna of 12 centimeters at line 2. The translation:

> Speech by the Osiris, the Great One of the Five, the Master of the Seats,[125]
> Thothrekh,[126] justified, son of the Great One of the Five, the Master of the
> Seats, the Prophet Petosiris,[127] possesser of honor, born to the mistress of the
> house Renpetnefret. O you who are alive on earth, who will come to this desert,

---

[122] Translation by Lichtheim, *Ancient Egyptian Literature*, III:47; comment
on page 49. See Lefebvre, *Le tombeau de Petosiris*, I:9 for comments; for the
French translation of the biographical inscriptions for Petosiris see I:79–84, 136–
145; for a German translation see Otto, *Die biographischen Inschriften*, 180–83.

[123] Lefebvre, *Le tombeau de Petosiris*, I:9, see pp. 45, 46, and 85 for actual
textual examples. Lefebvre counts eleven examples. Rößler-Köhler, *Individuelle
Haltungen zum Ägyptischen Königtum der Spätzeit*, 292, also comments on the use
of this royal formula.

[124] Lefebvre, *Le tombeau de Petosiris*, I:9, 21–25.

[125] Lefebvre, *Le tombeau de Petosiris*, I:1–2, discusses these titles which
are common epithets for the male members of the family. They designate the bearer
as the high priest of Thoth in Hermopolis. In the case of Thothrekh, however,
Lefebvre notes that he was too young to have really functioned in this position, and
suggests that they appear here as a custom of protocol.

[126] The name in the hieroglyphs is "dhwty-rh," "known by Thoth." See
Lefebvre, *Le tombeau de Petosiris*, II:27, for the hieroglyphic text.

[127] The name in the hieroglyphs is "p3-di-Wsir," "gift of Osiris."

all who will come to make offerings in this necropolis, pronounce my name with water-offerings.[128] Thoth will favor you because of [it].[129] It is rewarding to act for one who cannot act; it is Thoth who will repay the deed for him who acts for me. [He who does me a good deed, such will be done for him; whoever praises my Ka], his Ka will be praised.[130] He who does a bad thing against me, [a bad thing][131] will be done against him. I am a man who is worthy to have his name pronounced. He who hears my story,[132] his heart will be distressed because of it, because I was a little child, seized through robbery,[133] shortened[134] in years[135] among the unknowing children, seized quickly as a little one, like a man snatched by sleep.[136] I was a youth of [?] years,[137] when

---

[128] Erman and Grapow, *Wörterbuch der Aegyptischen Sprache*, IV:118, note that "sfsf 3w" is a common combination. "Sfsf" means "wasser spenden," or more generally, "spenden," as does "sfsf 3w."

[129] In the Egyptian the "it" is missing but is safely assumed, thus read "ḥr[.s]."

[130] A lacuna in the text, but translators agree on the same kind of reconstruction based on the context and parallels. The above follows Lefebvre, *Le tombeau de Petosiris*, I:113. Lichtheim, *Ancient Egyptian Literature*, III:53, offers a shorter reading with just the second part of the phrase, "[He who praises my ka], his ka will be praised." Otto, *Die biographischen Inschriften*, 174, has "[Wer mir opfert o.ä.], dem wird sein Ka gnädig sein."

[131] Another easily filled lacuna.

[132] Literally, who hears "my word."

[133] Lefebvre, *Le tombeau de Petosiris*, I:115, thinks that "ḥ'd3" may be a mistake for "'d3" and that "m 'd3" would provide a better meaning in the context. Thothrekh would then be saying that he was seized "injustement." Faulkner, *A Concise Dictionary of Middle Egyptian*, 51, translates "m 'd3" as "falsely," and Erman and Grapow, *Wörterbuch der Aegyptischen Sprache*, I:241, say "m 'd3w" means "verbrecherisch, lügnerisch." These meanings do not seem to make as much sense for the present context, however. The *Wörterbuch*, III:43, translates "m ḥ'd3" on the other hand as "räuberisch," which fits better. All these meanings are related, and the *Wörterbuch* even refers the reader to "'d3" in the entry for "ḥ'd3." The image of death as a thief seems better, though.

[134] The word is spelled "sḥ'w," but properly it should be "sḥw'." See the entry in Faulkner, *A Concise Dictionary of Middle Egyptian*, 238, and Erman and Grapow, *Wörterbuch der Aegyptischen Sprache*, IV:213.

[135] The above follows Lichtheim, *Ancient Egyptian Literature*, III:53, and Otto, *Die biographischen Inschriften*, 175. Lefebvre, *Le tombeau de Petosiris*, I:114, translates "qui fus enlevé par violence: mes années furent abrégeés...."

[136] There seems to be an "s" floating in the construction, "mi s iṯ.n s kd." Lefebvre, *Le tombeau de Petosiris*, I:115, takes "s" to be "sw," thus, as the direct object, "like a man whom sleep has seized." Otto, *Die biographischen Inschriften*, 175, has "wie ein Mann, der *aus* dem Schlaf gerissen wurde."

[137] Faulkner, *A Concise Dictionary of Middle Egyptian*, 166, defines the word "ḥwn" as "child" or "young man." Erman and Grapow, *Wörterbuch der*

I was taken to the city of eternity, to the place of perfect ba-souls.[138] Because of it[139] I arrived before the Lord of Gods without having had my share.[140] I was rich in friends among all the men of (my) town. Not one among them could save me![141] Every one of the town, men and women, mourned very greatly because they saw what had happened to (me), because (I) was excellent in their hearts. All (my) friends were in lamentation.[142] (My) father and mother beseeched death,[143] my brothers were head-on-knee.[144] Since (I) arrived at this land of deprivation, where people were judged in the presence of the Lord of the Gods, no fault (in me) was found. Bread was given to me in the hall of the Two Truths, water from the sycamore like the perfect ba-souls.[145] You will

---

Aegyptischen Sprache, III:52–53, have "Knabe, Jüngling, junger Mann." No number specifying the quantity of years survives, and though there is a small lacuna next to "years," it might simply have contained part of the writing of this word. In any event, no one knows just how old Thothrekh was when he died, and the term used for him, ḥwn, could mean anything from little kid to very young adult. Otto, *Die biographischen Inschriften*, 175, does not treat this passage as if his years were ever given. He says "[Ich] war noch jung an Jahren...."

[138] Twice in this sentence "nty" appears for "n."

[139] That is, because of having died.

[140] Lefebvre, *Le tombeau de Petosiris*, I:115, notes that another possible translation for "wḏ" is "judge," which is how Otto, *Die biographischen Inschriften*, 175, translates "werde ich nicht gerichtet werden."

[141] Lichtheim, *Ancient Egyptian Literature*, III:53, breaks the phrases up thus: "I was rich in friends, all the men of my town, not one of them could protect me!"Lefebvre, *Le tombeau de Petosiris*, I:114, translates "J'étais riche en amis, à savoir (m) tous les gens de ma ville, (mais) pas un d'eux qui pût me défendre (contra la mort)!" Otto, *Die biographischen Inschriften*, 175, has "Ich war reich an Freunden unter jedermann meiner Stadt. Aber keiner ist darunter, der mir (jetzt) helfen kann."

[142] An extra sitting man determinative appears at the end of this statement. Lefebvre and Otto ignore it, while Lichtheim may emend it to "ḥr.i" since she translates "All my friends mourned *for me*...."

[143] This phrase is tricky. The Egyptian is "it mwt ḥr nht[.i] mt." The [i] does not fit, unless it stands for the similar sitting man but with the hand to mouth, which would then be the expected determinative for this word; see Faulkner, *A Concise Dictionary of Middle Egyptian*, 136. Lichtheim, *Ancient Egyptian Literature*, III:53, has "Father and Mother implored death," while Lefebvre, *Le tombeau de Petosiris*, I:114, says "mon père, ma mère suppliaient la mort." However, Otto, *Die biographischen Inschriften*, 175, translates "mein Vater und meine Mutter wünschen zu sterben," which is grammatically possible.

[144] A sign of mourning. An odd "iṯw" appears after "brothers," which Lefebvre, *Le tombeau de Petosiris*, I:116, explains should be "irw."

[145] Lichtheim, *Ancient Egyptian Literature*, III:54, is persuasive when she insists that the verbs here ought to be translated as past tenses, since the deceased is

endure in life, you will follow Sokar, you will see the face of Re in the morning on the feast of the New Year when he rises in the great house of the temple of Khmun, you will follow Thoth on this beautiful day of the beginning of the 3ht-season, you will hear the sound of jubilation in the temple of Khmun when the Golden One arises[146] to make her love (visible),[147] according as you say on each occasion of (your) approaching this necropolis, "All good things for your Ka, little child whose time passed so quickly without following his desires on earth."

The father of Petosiris, Sishu, utters reflections on life which do not equal Thothrekh's speech for scepticism, but are not without interest. On more than one occasion Sishu exhorts the visitor of the tomb to heed his words and take the description of his own life as an example of how one should live. "Come, I will lead you on the way of life...."[148] In another inscription he says again "I will lead you on the way of life, I will tell you your (proper) conduct."[149] In this latter text he goes on to advise the reader to enjoy himself and follow his heart, because "when a man departs, his goods depart.... there is no sun for the rich, there is no messenger of death who accepts a bribe in order to forget that for which [he] was sent...."[150] The next line is lost. Then, "He goes quickly, like a dream. There is no one who knows the day when he will come; it is the skill of God that hearts are forgetful over it.[151] [Presumably the "he" refers to death or death's messenger]. But a pulled-up plant is the one

---

describing what happened to him when he died and entered the netherworld.

[146] I.e. Hathor; cf. Lichtheim, *Ancient Egyptian Literature*, III:54.

[147] This approximates Lichtheim, *Ancient Egyptian Literature*, III:54, "to show her love." Lefebvre, *Le tombeau de Petosiris*, I:114, translates "pour agir à son gré"; Otto, *Die biographischen Inschriften*, 175, has "um ihre Liebenswürdigkeit zu zeigen."

[148] Lefebvre, *Le tombeau de Petosiris*, I:158 and II:83, for the hieroglyphic text; Lichtheim, *Ancient Egyptian Literature*, III:50; Otto, *Die biographischen Inschriften*, 183.

[149] Lefebvre, *Le tombeau de Petosiris*, I:161 and II:90; Lichtheim, *Ancient Egyptian Literature*, III:51; Otto, *Die biographischen Inschriften*, 183.

[150] Lefebvre, *Le tombeau de Petosiris*, I:161, does not attempt to translate most of this line because of a lacuna, but in II:90 he transcribes almost a full hieroglyphic line. Lichtheim, *Ancient Egyptian Literature*, III:51; Otto, *Die biographischen Inschriften*, 184, both translate much like the above.

[151] The last part is a little tricky. Lefebvre, *Le tombeau de Petosiris*, I:161, suggests that "smḫ ibw" means to make hearts forget, and subsequent translators agree.

seized as a child...."[152] These lines are in the tradition of something like the Antef song, in that they advise enjoyment of life now because death is unpredictable and final.[153] Even the rich cannot enjoy the sun once they are dead, and death itself cannot be bribed like some local official. Sishu makes the interesting comment that the reason people are not obsessed by this thought is because the deity makes them forget mortality. The reference to the death of a young person is intriguing in view of the long oration by the young Thothrekh.

Thothrekh's inscription has a number of parallels with those of Isenkhebe and Taimhotep. Like Isenkhebe, he died without having had his fill of life. This is a key point, in fact. He explains that he had many friends, but they were powerless to protect him from death. His parents pleaded on his behalf, but as Taimhotep also says, this is to no avail. He too insists that he is without fault, and he too calls the netherworld a land of deprivation. He then proceeds, as do the other two, to request assistance from the living in making offerings to him; the final line is that the visitor should address him as one who did not get the chance to fulfill his desires on earth. Again, the feeling is that the offerings are not going to do much good because he now exists in a land of deprivation. In all three cases the thought that the traditional funerary cult is ineffective appears in a traditional funerary genre and is attached to the usual

---

[152] This image of a pulled-up plant appears also in the biography of Padisobek, translated by Lichtheim, *Maat in Egyptian Autobiographies*, 191–201. Here the speaker bemoans the fact that he died without ever having had a child and says of such a person (198), "For behold, a man to whom no child was born is one who does not exist! He has really not been born! His deeds will not be remembered; his name will not be pronounced, like one who has not existed! [I am] a tree that was torn out with its roots, because of what happened to me!" One is interested to see how the motif of the ripped-up plant is applied in this case not to a person who dies too young, but to an individual who reached a full age but still could leave no decendants.

[153] Lefebvre, *Le tombeau de Petosiris*, I:162, rejects the conclusion that Sishu is advising "carpe diem," because he says this contrasts too much with the moral teachings of the tomb in general and this speech in particular. Therefore he suggests that a refutation existed in the lacuna of line 4. But this seems unnecessary. Not only does the speech of Thothrekh reveal that a wide variety of ideas could appear in the same tomb, but Sishu's speech as whole is still coherent even with the carpe diem advice. The injunction to life enjoyment and moral responsibility are not mutually exclusive ideas in the ancient Egyptian context.

formulae, which leads to an even greater sense of dissonance. The ramifications of these texts is that one does not continue to enjoy a fulfilling existence in the netherworld, which is especially chilling for those who die young, because then they have lost their only chance for "their share."

DISCUSSION

In the case of the tomb of Petosiris the question of Greek influence comes into consideration. In Lefebvre's view, the tomb itself reveals Greek influence, particularly in some of its reliefs. In these one finds art which steps outside the traditional canons of ancient Egyptian presentation. One scene in particular is that of the deceased's family gathering at his tomb to offer a sacrifice "au mort héroïsé."[154] In addition some of the figures are wearing a distinctively Greek form of clothing, the "manteau macédonien."[155] He does make the point that the Hermopolitan traditions of art had always been somewhat independent of the norm, and therefore does not believe that the Greek style is fully responsible for the peculiarities of the tomb; but he does feel that some Hellenic influence has accentuated the Hermopolitan tradition.[156] Most subsequent scholars are in agreement with Lefebvre on this matter,[157] which usually leads to the assumption that the texts have been influenced

---

[154] Lefebvre, *Le tombeau de Petosiris*, I:25.

[155] Lefebvre, *Le tombeau de Petosiris*, I:24–25.

[156] Lefebvre, *Le tombeau de Petosiris*, I:31, 34, 94.

[157] Susanne Nakaten, "Petosiris," in Wolfgang Helck et al, eds., *Lexikon der Ägyptologie*, Vol. IV (Wiesbaden: Otto Harrassowitz, 1982) 995–96; Philippe Derchain, "Death in Egyptian Religion," in Yves Bonnefoy, ed., *Mythologies*, Vol. 1 (Chicago: The University of Chicago Press, 1991) 115; Sherman, "Egyptian Biographies," 392; Lichtheim, *Ancient Egyptian Literature*, III:45; Rößler-Köhler, *Individuelle Haltungen zum Ägyptischen Königtum der Spätzeit*, 287. See also M. Picard, "Les Influences Étrangères au Tombeau de Petosiris: Grèce ou Perse?" *Bulletin de L'Institut Français d'Archéologie Orientale* 30(1931) 201–227, for his argument against the suggestion of M.P. Montet, "Note sur le Tombeau de Petosiris, por servir à l'histoire des Perses en Égypte," *Revue archéologique* 1(1926) 161–81, that the tomb reveals Persian influence. Van der Walle, "Biographie," 819, on the other hand, does not specifically refer to the Greeks, and comments only that tomb seems to reflect the spirit of the priestly and intellectual milieu of the area.

by Greek thought as well, though this latter idea is generally stated in passing.

However, nothing in the tomb's inscriptions needs the "Greek influence" theory for explanation, either with respect to general content or specific phrasing, and the theory itself seems to be not so much a heartfelt scholarly conviction as a supposition that sceptical thought is probably attributable to hellenic influence. Taimhotep's biography likewise consists of themes which are consistent with the native Egyptian context.[158] Erman remarks that both Isenkhebe and Taimhotep may seem at first sight to be indebted to Greek ideas, but that nothing in them is foreign to Egyptian intellectual traditions.[159] The previous chapter has shown that scepticism with respect to death was known in preceding periods of Egyptian history, but not in the biographical tradition.[160] The

---

[158] See Bianchi, et al, *Cleopatra's Egypt*, 231, for this view as well.

[159] Erman, "Zwei Grabsteine griechischer Zeit," 111.

[160] Mention should be made here of the biography of a priest of Amon in the Twenty-Second Dynasty named Nebneteru, written sometime in the mid-800's BCE. It is inscribed on a statue and comes from Karnak, and was translated by Hermann Kees, "Die Lebensgrundsätze eines Amonspriesters der 22. Dynastie," *Zeitschrift für Ägyptische Sprache und Altertumskunde* 74 (1938) 73. Nebneteru proudly announces that he spent his life pleasurably, without sorrow or sickness, and lived to be 96 years old. Nevertheless, the whole land mourns him, and Kees translated the following passage as an arresting description of death. "Verhüte, daß etwas ihm Gleiches geschieht! Der Ausgang des Lebens (ist) Trauer, bedeutet Dürftigkeit an dem, was früher bei dir war, und Leerheit an deinem Besitz; bedeutet Sitzen in der Halle der Bewußtlosigkeit beim Verkünden ein Morgen, das doch nicht kommt, bedeutet als Ersatz ein Auge, das trieft—verhüte, dass es kommt!— bedeutet Nichtwissen, bedeutet Schlafen, wenn die Sonne zur Linken (im Osten) steht, bedeutet Dürsten zur Seite des Bieres!" (79). Nebneteru then goes on to say that the West demands that one follow one's heart, because "the heart is a god, whose chapel is the stomach," and finally he concludes with a request for the standard offerings to his ka. However, Kees himself retranslated the passage in "Zu den Lebensregeln des Amonspriesters Nebneteru (Kairo Cat. 42225)," *Zeitschrift für Ägyptische Sprache und Altertumskunde* 88(1963) 24–26. See also Jansen-Winkeln, *Ägyptische Biographien der 22. und 23. Dynastie*, I:22 and II:426–27, and Lichtheim, *Ancient Egyptian Literature*, III:22, who follow the new translation. Otto, *Die biographischen Inschriften*, 46, 139, and Morenz, *Egyptian Religion*, 188, follow the original Kees translation. The newer interpretation does not read this passage as a description of the netherworld but as an exhortation to the living not to live in mourning, want, denial, thirst, and so on. The text is still interesting, because Nebneteru refers to the West as a place of "darkness" before his exhortation begins,

thought that the netherworld presents the danger not only of suffering but of unconsciousness, loss of self, and immobility is attested in the long line of mortuary texts, the purpose of which was to prevent these very things from happening. Lamentations for the dead express the fear that the deceased is permanently isolated from his loved ones and cut off from the pleasures of life.[161] The even graver suggestion that one may not really know whether the promises of the mortuary cult are reliable and therefore that people need to make the most of the present life is also attested in the harper song tradition. The point is not that such ideas were unthinkable to the ancient Egyptian mind.

What is interesting about the texts discussed above, however, is that these ideas had not appeared in the biographical tradition before the Late Period. Their presence in *this* genre lends a new pointedness to the ideas themselves for two reasons. First of all, the expressions of doubt and concern about death which existed up to this time were small parts of a larger and secure mortuary apparatus. Worries about discomfort in the beyond in the mortuary texts are ameliorated by remedies and spells in those same texts. The laments of family members for the deceased as presented in tomb illustrations represent natural human emotions which are easily incorporated into the main framework of the mortuary religion. The same is the case with the harper songs. None of the preceding categorically declare that the entire structure of the cult is pointless. Laments and songs were not essential elements of the tradition and thus could exercise a certain amount of freedom in straying from the dogma.[162] This was not the case with the biographies, which were integral to the mortuary traditions and, in spite of flexibility in details, were on no account expected to be the bearers of bad tidings. This means that the appearance of such intense scepticism here of all places is new and remarkable.[163]

---

a reading on which all still agree, and this is what leads to the advice to avoid self-denial and poverty.

[161] Morenz, *Egyptian Religion*, 187.

[162] Jan Assmann, "Fest des Augenblicks—Verheissung der Dauer: Die Kontroverse der ägyptischen Harfnerlieder," in Jan Assmann et al, eds., *Fragen as die altägyptische Literatur: Studien zum Gedenken an Eberhard Otto* (Wiesbaden: Dr. Ludwig Reichert, 1977) 84, remarks that the tomb could incorporate such expressions of doubt because the system as a whole was strong.

[163] Lichtheim, *Ancient Egyptian Autobiographies*, 201, observes that the expression of the fear of death in terms of "blank despair" in the biographical

Secondly, the ancient Egyptian biographical genre is inherently designed as a self-presentation, which means that for the first time there exist first-person accounts of death as, essentially, nothingness. Isenkhebe, Taimhotep, and Thothrekh tell us personally that death is a rapacious and terrifying being, that darkness, isolation, sleep, forgetfulness, and thirst characterize the state of the dead. This kind of claim is especially shocking in view of the assumption expressed in something like the afore-mentioned Eighteenth Dynasty biography of Paheri, "thou livest again.... thou hast water, thou breathest the air, thou drinkest to thy heart's content...." They can say these things because they themselves are dead.[164] Death is the universal leveller, and though no one specifically says so, the reader can only conclude that one's moral state is irrelevant not only with respect to when death makes its claim but also to what the individual will experience after death. Isenkhebe and Thothrekh both insist that they have no fault, and in other parts of Taimhotep's biography she too is morally pure. Certainly factors of age, wealth, and personal wishes make no difference, the reader is told. In the past the Antef Song had rhetorically asked the listener/reader, who ever returned from the dead to tell us of their condition? Now cases have appeared where this is exactly what happens. If the harper of the Antef Song had no testimony as to whether the dead live again, Isenkhebe, Taimhotep, and Thothrekh give certain testimony: they do not.

The messages of the biographies here are quite specifically aimed at preceding Egyptian tradition. In chapter four the analysis of the long-established view of death uncovered a series of basic points: 1) that death was treated not just as a matter of the individual, but also as a community event, where the deceased hoped to rejoin the family in the netherworld, 2) that continuation of memory was crucial, 3) and that underlying fears that one will experience bodily distress or want, possibly even suffering, were a constant concern for which many preventative spells were designed. In the biographies at hand, the first two points are

---

tradition is highly unusual, a comment she makes in reference to the Late Period biography of Padisobek (see footnote 152).

[164] Technically, testimony by the dead that death is non-existence is a contradiction in terms, since they should not be able to communicate any longer. It is the nature of the genre that gives them voice, even though the content of their message strictly speaking cancels out the genre itself.

negated, and the culture's worst fears are suddenly confirmed. As Otto remarks about these texts, the counsel to make merry does not counter the feelings of grief and helplessness, the offering formula is unconvincing, the idea of a judgment after death loses its power, and in short, "Tod triumphiert über die Hilfsmittel der Religion! Auch die Götter sind machtlos gegen ihn...."[165]

If it is true, and it is, that the genre in its very purpose of existence had always counted on the belief that "the person was indestructible,"[166] and that it could serve as a "bulwark against oblivion,"[167] one is left to consider the possibility that some Egyptians at least were beginning to have doubts about personal indestructibility and security from oblivion. One scholar remarks that the biographies, if perhaps they do not really serve as portraits of individuals, do serve as "a portrait of Egyptian society,"[168] and this being the case, one wonders just what in Egyptian society at the time was happening to lead to the changes in outlook intimated by this genre in the Late Period. Interestingly, circumstances in Egypt bear some similarity to the situation in Palestine in this era, which will be the subject of the following chapter.

---

[165] Otto, *Die biographischen Inschriften*, 50–51.
[166] Lichtheim, *Ancient Egyptian Autobiographies*, 2.
[167] Lichtheim, *Ancient Egyptian Autobiographies*, 146.
[168] Perdu, "Ancient Egyptian Autobiographies," IV:2252.

Chapter 6
LATE PERIOD EGYPT:
HISTORICAL AND INTELLECTUAL CONTEXT

HISTORICAL CONTEXT

The late biographies, not too surprisingly, are not a cultural aberration but reflect developments in Egyptian history and thought that can be seen in other areas, too. Unfortunately, Late Period Egypt is a time that has often been disdained by scholars as unworthy of much interest and therefore it is sometimes difficult to get a perspective on it untainted by distaste. Breasted's analysis is a good example of what has become a common pattern of treatment. He writes that

> the world was growing old, and men were dwelling fondly and wistfully on her far-away youth. In this process of conserving the old, the religion of Egypt sank deeper and deeper in decay, to become, what Herodotus found it, a religion of innumerable external observances and mechanical usages, carried out with such elaborate and insistent punctiliousness that the Egyptians gained the reputation of being the most religious of all peoples. But such observances were no longer the expression of a growing and developing inner life, as in the days before the creative vitality of the race was extinct.[1]

---

[1] James Henry Breasted, *Development of Religion and Thought in Ancient Egypt* (New York: Charles Scribner's Sons, 1912; reprinted New York: Harper & Row, 1959) 367. Somewhat earlier (363) he comments on the end of the Egyptian empire: "With the decline of the Empire from the thirteenth century onward, the forces of life both within and without were exhausted and had lost their power to stimulate the religion of Egypt to any further vital development. Stagnation and a deadly and indifferent inertia fell like a stupor upon the once vigorous life of the nation." Further down the page he refers to "this Amonite papacy" and its deleterious effect on the Egyptian spirit.

This kind of reflection on the era is not uncommon.[2] In the case of Alan Gardiner's history, the Late Period receives a cursory outline only and the outline does not even reach as far as the Ptolemies.[3] One recent comparative study of Egyptian and Israelite history continues to reveal these attitudes towards the Late Period. This book's epilogue, which sums up in two pages the events of both nations in the end of the first millennium BCE after the fall of Judah in 587, talks about the "stultifying trends" that emerged in both. Examples of these stultifying trends include Egyptian cryptography and the Mishna. "One might almost say that 'God was dead'"[4]

However, late Egyptian history has more to offer than these scholarly renditions would suggest, not as a sad footnote to the bygone glory days of the past but as an interesting, vital, and creative period in its own right. There certainly were changes in the culture, but whether these changes are a sign of *decay* is not a matter of fact, but of interpretation.[5] As one text on Egypt says about this time, the culture

---

[2] John A. Wilson, *The Burden of Egypt: An Interpretation of Ancient Egyptian Culture* (Chicago: University of Chicago Press, 1951) 307, writes that Herodotus describes the Egyptians as the most "god-fearing" of peoples and adds "Here we have a description of brightly polished automatons unceasingly performing solemn gestures but utterly empty of mind or heart. It is a true picture of the spiritual vacuum of late Egypt, which left the land exposed to invasion by otherworldliness, monasticism, or apocalyptic expectation."

[3] Alan H. Gardiner, *Egypt of the Pharaohs: An Introduction* (Oxford: Oxford University Press, 1961). He hurries through this period in fact so as to get to the final section more quickly, a treatment of what is known about the earliest stages of Egyptian history.

[4] Donald B. Redford, *Egypt, Canaan, and Israel in Ancient Times* (Princeton: Princeton University Press, 1992) 470–71. Frustrated resistance in both societies could come up with little better than apocalyptic hope, a sign of "disenfranchised cultures that have been outstripped by a new and imaginative way of life from across the seas." More will be said about this attitude in chapter 7.

[5] Robert K. Ritner, "Implicit Models of Cross-Cultural Interaction: A Question of Noses, Soap, and Prejudice," in Janet H. Johnson, ed., *Life in a Multi-Cultural Society: Egypt from Cambyses to Constantine and Beyond* (Chicago: The Oriental Institute, 1992) 283–90, provides a perceptive analysis of scholarly biases in the study of late Egyptian history. He describes the typical view as reflective of the "Biological Model" of cultural development, in which a culture is like a plant that "sprouts, grows, flowers, and decays." The Old Kingdom is the sprout, the Middle Kingdom the growth, the New Kingdom the flower, the Late Period the decay. "Loss of political independence is interpreted as a loss of cultural independence and vitality. Any evidence of subsequent change is viewed in terms

exhibits "complex and subtle responses by a flexible political and ideological system to greatly changed circumstances, but not a fundamental reordering or disintegration. Egypt did not need to, and apparently did not, perceive itself as in decline."[6] The biographies which were discussed above become more explicable when set into the context of their contemporary historical situation.

Among the more important events of the post-Ramessid age are the fact that Egypt once again experienced a weakening of royal political power during what scholars call the Third Intermediate Period (around 1070–656 BCE),[7] as well as several foreign invasions. The throne increasingly lost military strength and Egypt's borders began to contract from their earlier imperial location, while the succession experienced irregularities such as usurpation and assassination plots.[8] The Twentieth Dynasty had a string of short reigns, occasioned by the fact that Ramesses III lived a very long time and then was followed by several aged heirs.[9] The High Priest of Amun in Thebes began to take on more power at the expense of royal authority, and Ramesses XI made the unheard-of request of the Viceroy of Kush that he use his own forces and take command of Upper Egypt.[10] Subsequently two men named Herihor and Smendes acquired power in Thebes and divided Egypt, allowing Ramesses XI to

---

of degeneration or foreign influence" (284). His comments apply to the study of Jewish history as well. The concluding chapter will have more to say about these points.

[6] B. G. Trigger et al, *Ancient Egypt: A Social History* (Cambridge: Cambridge University Press, 1983) 195.

[7] Cf. Miriam Lichtheim, *Ancient Egyptian Literature: A Book of Readings*, 3 Vols. (Berkeley: University of California Press, 1973) III:ix for the dating. The period includes the Twenty-First through the Twenty-Fifth dynasties.

[8] Trigger, et al, *Ancient Egypt: A Social History*, 222–23.

[9] Trigger, et al, *Ancient Egypt: A Social History*, 224. This created a problem regarding confidence in the stability of the succession apparatus. "The concept of *ma'at* accommodated the limitations of humanity within royal quasi-divinity but in the context of a natural progression in the ruler's life from early maturity to a substantially later death. The comparatively rapid succession of elderly or dramatically mortal rulers stressed the ambiguous character of the kings' relationship to the supernatural."

[10] Trigger, et al, *Ancient Egypt: A Social History*, 231. This was close enough to an invasion that finally inhabitants of the area joined forces against him and he returned to Kush after a few years.

remain king of the whole country in name, but taking over the divisions themselves when he died.[11]

The country's political organization remained diffuse and complex until the Nubian kings from the south invaded and formed the Twenty-Fifth dynasty. When the Assyrians invaded, the Nubian dynasty fell, and in 663 BCE Thebes was sacked. From 664–525 a native dynasty, the Twenty-Sixth, gained control. The line came from Sais, a city of the Delta, and the Saite period was one of new political and cultural strength.[12] Egypt was unified and strong again in this "last great age of pharaonic civilization."[13] From 525–404 the Persians, led by Cambyses, made Egypt a Persian satrapy and functioned as the Twenty-Seventh Dynasty. Three dynasties of native kings followed, the Twenty-Eighth, Twenty-Ninth, and Thirtieth, until Persia retook Egypt in 343.[14] In 332 Alexander came and the country was subsequently in control of the Ptolemies.

Because invasion and kingship by non-natives were an on-again, off-again, state of affairs, one of the central questions regarding this time period is whether and to what extent the culture experienced psychological distress at the political irregularities. The problem was that in the Egyptian scheme of the world, pharaoh was the protector of order, Maat,[15] while foreigners represented disorder. A foreign pharaoh in this

[11] Trigger, et al, *Ancient Egypt: A Social History*, 231–32. Smendes was technically ruler of all Egypt, but really ruled Lower Egypt while Herihor's line had control of Middle and Upper Egypt.

[12] Lichtheim, *Ancient Egyptian Literature*, III:3. Trigger, et al, *Ancient Egypt: A Social History*, 232, remark that under this dynasty Egypt achieved "rapid and effective recentralization."

[13] Trigger, et al, *Ancient Egypt: A Social History*, 282. Later (284), they comment that the kings of the Saite dynasty showed renewed interest in traditional pharaonic activities, such as monumental construction and successful military actions internationally. An interesting note for biblicists is that one of the Saite kings is Necho II (610–595), who in II Kings 23:29 kills king Josiah at Megiddo. See II Chronicles 35:20–24 for a longer account of the same event.

[14] Trigger, et al, *Ancient Egypt: A Social History*, 286–87.

[15] Siegfried Morenz, *Egyptian Religion*, trans. Ann E. Keep (New York: Cornell University Press, 1973) 113, says "Maat is right order in nature and society, as established by the act of creation, and hence means, according to the context, what is right, what is correct, law, order, justice and truth." Trigger, et al, *Ancient Egypt: A Social History*, 74, notes that it was the king's responsibility to see to it that Maat functioned properly on earth. Erik Hornung, "Ancient Egyptian Religious Iconography," in Jack M. Sasson, ed., *Civilizations of the Ancient Near East* Vol.

system is potentially a contradiction in terms. In the Egyptian view of kingship, however, the situation is a little more complicated. If an individual fulfilled the role of pharaoh, was properly crowned, carried out his functions, and in fact acted as Egypt's protector, then that person *was* pharaoh.[16] The point here is not that the Egyptians paid no heed to whether their country had shifted hands to outside monarchs, but that the fact of a non-native king was not in itself necessarily a blow to the royal ideology. If the king did his job properly, then order was preserved.

An interesting window into this phenomenon is the inscription that appears on the statue of Udjahorresnet which was set in the temple of Neith around 519 BCE.[17] The text provides an account of Udjahorresnet's interactions with Cambyses, the first Persian king. The former had been an admiral of the Egyptian fleet before the Persians arrived, and continued to hold high office at court under Cambyses. He states that it was he who gave the Persian the proper royal titulary of an Egyptian king; in other words, who helped him assimilate to the traditional role of pharaoh. He goes on to relate how Cambyses restored the decrepit temple of Neith in Sais at Udjahorresnet's urging, and then personally made offerings to the goddess.[18] Cambyses seems to have made a real effort to

---

III (New York: Charles Scribner's Sons, 1995) 1723, adds that a common scene displayed on temple walls is that of the king offering Maat, in the form of a squatting goddess wearing a feather on her head, to the gods.

[16] Trigger, et al, *Ancient Egypt: A Social History*, 297. They point out that some of the foreign kings better fulfilled the pharaonic ideal than others. The Persians Cambyses and Darius for example showed respect and support for various Egyptian cults, and similarly Alexander. (In classical sources Cambyses has a bad reputation because he curbed temple privileges, but in reality he was lenient toward the Egyptians [286]). Xerxes and Artaxerxes III, on the other hand, come in for condemnation.

[17] Alan B. Lloyd, "The Inscription of Udjahorresnet: A Collaborator's Testament," in *Journal of Egyptian Archaeology* 68(1982) 166.

[18] Lloyd, "The Inscription of Udjahorresnet: A Collaborator's Testament," 170, writes "It will be observed that Udjahorresnet dwells with particular insistence on the way in which Cambyses had accepted the traditional model of Egyptian kingship, and regulated his behaviour by it." In view of this narrative and other texts of the time, Lloyd doubts the idea presented in classical sources that Cambyses was an impious king, which he attributes to the disgruntlement of priests at the temples Cambyses restricted financially (173). He cut their revenues to pay for his conquest, though three temples were exempt; see Ray, "Egypt, 525–404 BC," in John Boardman et al, eds., *The Cambridge Ancient History*, Vol. IV

act as an Egyptian pharaoh should act, as a protector of Egypt and its religious traditions, and the testimony of Udjahorresnet shows that in the minds of some at least, he was successful.[19] The inscription continues with reflections on the next Persian king, Darius, in a similar vein.[20] In a later stela, on the other hand, that of Smatawytefnakht, the second Persian conquest led by Artaxerxes III is described as a catastrophe, which fits with the fact that neither this king nor his successors showed any respect for Egyptian traditions. It would have been impossible, then, for such men to be assimilated to the ideal of kingship.[21]

The Demotic Chronicle supports the argument that a good king was judged by his actions, not his ethnic background. It comprises a series of oracular statements that cover historical events in Egypt during the fourth and possibly the early third centuries BCE,[22] and along the way offers interpretations of whether recent Egyptian kings were satisfactory or not. Although this writing is anti-Persian, it is not anti-foreigner. The Greeks, contrary to the common interpretation, are not reviled, while

---

(Cambridge: Cambridge University Press, 1988) 260.

[19] Ray, "Egypt, 525–404 BC," 258, says of Udjahorresnet that he "was obviously an arch-collaborator," though this scholar regards the inscription as reliable. Similarly, Lloyd takes it as a given that he was a "collaborator," as his article's title shows. He remarks that, like others, the man was willing "to collaborate and even champion the Persian cause." Cf. Lloyd, "The Inscription of Udjahorresnet: " Collaborator's Testament," 170. Yet in light of Lloyd's own persuasive analysis of the worldview behind Udjahorresnet's inscription, the accepted use of this term seems misplaced. The *American Heritage Dictionary*, 3rd edition, defines the verb as follows: "to cooperate treasonably, as with an enemy occupation force in one's country." Yet if Udjahorresnet's interest was in maintaining the proper balance of order in the country and seeing to it that the person sitting on the throne did his job properly, then treason is not the appropriate way to define his actions, and "collaborator" is a misnomer that carries inapplicable modern connotations. Lloyd himself remarks that simple pragmatism does not explain Udjahorresnet's warm feelings toward his new pharaoh (170).

[20] Lloyd, "The Inscription of Udjahorresnet: A Collaborator's Testament," 174–75, also points to a crude stela in which a man is shown praying to Darius in the form of a hawk (Horus) as evidence that the Egyptians, even those who were not officially ensconced in a court setting, could accept a Persian king as a true pharaoh.

[21] Lloyd, "The Inscription of Udjahorresnet: A Collaborator's Testament," 178–79.

[22] Janet Johnson, "The Demotic Chronicle as a Statement of a Theory of Kingship," *Journal of the Society for the Study of Egyptian Antiquities* 13(1983) 61.

some of the kings of the native 28th–30th dynasties are criticized.[23] The Chronicle's purpose, besides predicting the arrival of a new ruler from Herakleopolis, is actually to provide a statement of legitimate kingship,[24] which requires a correct coronation and proper behavior.[25] Such behavior includes beneficence to the temples and their deities, ritual activity, preservation of the law, and protection of Egypt from its enemies. In Egypt's past native kings were also not entirely free of reproach. In the Middle Kingdom text called the Admonitions of Ipuwer the speaker declares to the king that in spite of his power, he has allowed society to fall into chaos. "Authority, Knowledge, and Truth are with you—turmoil is what you let happen in the land, and the noise of strife."[26] It had long

---

[23] Johnson, "The Demotic Chronicle as a Statement of a Theory of Kingship," 65. Her interpretation is not that of all scholars. See J. Gwyn Griffiths, "Apocalyptic in the Hellenistic Era," in David Hellholm, ed., *Apocalypticism in the Mediterranean World and the Near East: Proceedings of the International Colloquium on Apocalypticism, Uppsala, August 12–17, 1979* (Tübingen: J. C. B. Mohr, 1983) 283; also cf. Alan B. Lloyd, "Nationalist Propaganda in Ptolemaic Egypt," *Historia* 31(1982) 42, who writes "the text insists on 'pinpointing' foreign enemies and activating xenophobia." His article is useful but on this question Johnson is more persuasive. It cannot be denied that there are examples of unmistakable hostility to foreign rule in late Egyptian writings, such as the Potter's Oracle, which portrays the Ptolemaic line as the enemy (Lloyd, 50–54); but see Janet Johnson, "Is the Demotic Chronicle an Anti-Greek Text?" in H. J. Thissen and K. T. Zauzich, eds., *Grammata Demotika, Festschrift für Erich Lüddeckens zum 15. Juni 1983.* (Würzburg: Gisela Zauzich Verlag, 1984) 116–17, who notes that the Potter's Oracle is unquestionably anti-Greek, but also points out that the Roman period papyri in which it appears, and which may reflect a late second century BCE original, have been repeatedly revised and "updated." In other words, the composition is not evidence of hostility towards the Greek rulers in the early Ptolemaic era, only in the Roman period.

[24] Johnson, "The Demotic Chronicle as a Statement of a Theory of Kingship," 66. In her article "Is the Demotic Chronicle an Anti-Greek Text?" 124, she states that the Herakleopolitan king will replace the Ptolemies not because they are "foreign," but because they have not acted according to Maat.

[25] Johnson, "The Demotic Chronicle as a Statement of a Theory of Kingship," 68. She adds that "law" (hp) equals "maat."

[26] Cf. Lichtheim, *Ancient Egyptian Literature*, I:160. She adds in a footnote that "Authority, Knowledge, and Truth" in the Egyptian are Hu, Sia, and Maat. Other Middle Kingdom works which contain criticisms of the state of Egyptian society in general are the Prophecies of Neferti and the Complaints of Khakheperre-sonb. Miriam Lichtheim regards all of them as part of genre that dwells on "national distress," with little or no historical reality behind it. A simple

been possible to conceive of a native king allowing disorder to run riot, even if this was more of a literary topos than fact. In the case of Akhenaten, his reign was later viewed as a time of chaos and abandonment by the gods, and a common epithet for this pharaoh was "the Enemy."[27]

On the matter of the principle involved in being able to accept a non-native as a proper Egyptian, the culture's attitudes toward more humble foreigners is in line with that toward an outside king. Those who considered Egypt to be their home and adopted its culture were Egyptians.[28] There were various revolts under the Persians as well as the Ptolemies, but they are not obviously the result of nativist sentiment. Economic factors and struggles between power groups appear to be primary motivations.[29] Right through the Ptolemaic period in fact there

---

change of dynasty could be the occasion for elaborating the theme "order versus disorder" (I:134).

[27] Trigger, et al, *Ancient Egypt: A Social History*, 201.

[28] Trigger, et al, *Ancient Egypt: A Social History*, 317. Ray, "Egypt, 525–404 BC," 275 sums it up succinctly: "anyone who spoke Egyptian, and who behaved in a recognizably Egyptian way, was Egyptian, no matter what his origin."

[29] Trigger, et al, *Ancient Egypt: A Social History*, 317. Johnson, "Is the Demotic Chronicle an Anti-Greek Text?" 120–21, points out that the Egyptians had always tended to rebel "against weak central government and against corrupt officials, when both the officials and the kings were 'native' Egyptians." Motives for rebellions in both the Persian and Ptolemaic periods no doubt varied, but chafing against a harsh economic system and official corruption was key. There has also been something of a debate as to whether more subtle resistance to the Ptolemies in particular took place among the priestly classes. Werner Huss, "Some Thoughts on the Subject "'State' and 'Church' in Ptolemaic Egypt," in Janet H. Johnson, ed., *Life in a Multi-Cultural Society: Egypt from Cambyses to Constantine and Beyond* (Chicago: The Oriental Institute, 1992) 163, states that officially the priests cooperated with the monarch, but that they resisted the Ptolemies in lesser ways. On the other hand, J. Gwyn Griffiths, "Egyptian Nationalism in the Edfu Temple Texts," in John Ruffle, et al, eds., *Glimpses of Ancient Egypt* (Warminster: Aris & Phillips, 1979) 178, questions the suggestion that temple inscriptions reveal any polemic against the Ptolemaic line, and notes that the Ptolemies fully embraced the tradition that the pharaoh was Horus and the son of Re. Johnson, "Is the Demotic Chronicle an Anti-Greek Text?" 116–17, concurs with the view that the priests were mostly supportive of Ptolemaic kingship. Priestly synods made decrees honoring them as proper kings who did their duty by the gods and the temples, and though there are instances where priests led rebellions, Egyptian temples were often attacked in local revolts, which suggests that they were not regarded as friends of the revolutionaries.

is little data which suggests ethnic hostility between differing groups.[30]

However, the cultural view of the kingship as an *office* does seem to have undergone some changes by the Late Period. While the requirements for proper fulfillment of it remained largely unaltered, it was regarded as less all-powerful. There exists a statue of Nectanebo II, the last native king, in which he is under the protection of a huge falcon representing the god Horus. In design it harks back to a statue of the Old Kingdom Khafra. But in the latter statue Horus is much smaller than the king and hovers at his head. In the Nectanebo version, the falcon dwarfs the king, suggesting a shift from kingly confidence to a pointed feeling of the king's dependence on the god's power.[31] This probably reflects a new awareness of the throne's precarious and changeable nature, no matter who is sitting on it. It has been remarked that in this period the idea emerges that the king depends on the gods and even, as the Demotic Chronicle shows, might act against divine will.[32] In earlier tradition the king was usually assumed to be, by definition, in accord with Maat, whereas in the Chronicle this is not necessarily the case. "From the end of the New Kingdom until the Macedonian conquest Egyptian history had been punctuated by long periods of fragmentation of authority which could not but diminish the aura of omnipotent and ineffable godhead surrounding the Pharaonic office." The principle that success or failure was a sign of a person's balance with Maat was an old one; now it was applied to the king as well.[33]

---

[30] See Ritner, "Implicit Models of Cross-Cultural Interaction: A Question of Noses, Soap, and Prejudice," 289. He adds that in the Roman period this is no longer the case, but that this was due to specific Roman actions in the governance of Egypt which went counter to the earlier status quo (290).

[31] Trigger, et al, *Ancient Egypt: A Social History*, 291; J. Gwyn Griffiths, *The Divine Verdict: A Study of Divine Judgement in the Ancient Religions* (Leiden: E. J. Brill, 1991) 175.

[32] Alan B. Lloyd, "Egypt, 404–332 BC," in D. M. Lewis et al, eds., *The Cambridge Ancient History*, Vol. VI (Cambridge: Cambridge University Press, 1994) 350. See also Eberhard Otto, *Die biographischen Inschriften der ägyptischen Spätzeit* (Leiden: E. J. Brill, 1954) 118, who comments on the fact that in the Demotic Chronicle, by holding the king to the same moral standard as mere mortals, for the first time the old identification of the kingship with ethics has split asunder.

[33] See Lloyd, "Nationalist Propaganda in Ptolemaic Egypt," 43, for quotation and comment.

It appears, then, that the mere fact of having a non-native Egyptian on the throne was not necessarily a cause for national demoralization in itself. Individual foreign kings who looked after Egypt's interests could be assimilated to the Pharaonic ideal. However, the general reality that the kingship as a principle had no stable anchor but continued to swing from one power base to another, sometimes native and sometimes not, throughout the last centuries of the final millennium BCE did have an effect on the culture. The king had been for Egyptian society, since the time of written records, the foundation of the country's identity.[34] Breaks in royal authority had occurred, but were temporary. The chaotic state of the kingship in the Late Period, however, was a new experience.

The biographies of the time are just one place where the weakening status of the kingship can be seen. As early as the Twenty-Second Dynasty individuals show markedly less dependence on the king, while the gods get the credit for one's earthly blessings. The by now familiar Petosiris does not mention a king at all;[35] when he refers to the current ruler of the land he calls him "hq3 n Kmt," not "king." In one inscription, in fact, he comments that he did such and such just as one did in earlier days "when there was a king in the palace...."[36] To imply that there is no king now, for an ancient Egyptian, is a significant statement. The husband of Taimhotep, Pshereneptah, is a member a priestly family that got on

---

[34] Otto, *Die biographischen Inschriften*, 102, says that the kingship formed "für das ganze Land wie für jeden Einzelnen die notwendige Voraussetzung seiner Existenz." Later he talks about the tension the Late Period Egyptians must have felt between their ideal for society, especially the kingship, and present reality (104). One sign of this is in late texts where individuals begin to blur the old topos of the King as the giver of orders and doer of deeds, with a current idea that only the gods have control over events (112). Otto refers to cases, as in the tomb of Petosiris, where the king acts on Thoth's orders (117), or where personal rewards are attributed to the gods. See also Rößler-Köhler, *Individuelle Haltungen zum Ägyptischen Königtum der Spätzeit*, 288, for comments on the fact that Petosiris credits his own promotion in life to Thoth.

[35] Griffiths, *The Divine Verdict*, 196–97. Rößler-Köhler, *Individuelle Haltungen zum Ägyptischen Königtum der Spätzeit*, 381, sets the first examples of withdrawal from the king in the biographical texts to the Twenty-First Dynasty.

[36] Rößler-Köhler, *Individuelle Haltungen zum Ägyptischen Königtum der Spätzeit*, 288. See also Otto, *Die biographischen Inschriften*, 114, for his remarks on this statement. Petosiris acknowledges that there is someone in charge, but not that the person is his king, apparently. His description of the turmoil of the land seems to be restricted to the last Persian domination, however; he makes no critical remarks about the present Greek overlords.

well with the Ptolemies, and he describes his friendly relations with the current ruler, whom he himself crowned as a very young priest. Yet it is interesting that even he refers to Alexandria as the "residence of the *Greek kings*,"[37] which suggests that he feels a distinction is necessary between them and an Egyptian king. This is not to be taken as a sign of hostility on the part of Pshereneptah, but his wording is noticeable. The political realities of the Late Period, then, were not without impact on the worldviews of the Egyptians.

RELIGIOUS AND INTELLECTUAL TRENDS

Egyptian religious interests did not remain static during the course of these events. They underwent shifts in focus and emphasis, just as they had always done, in fact. Animal cults became much more popular in the Late Period than previously.[38] Deified men, though a phenomenon of earlier times, gained more attention than ever before. An example is Amenhotep, son of Hapu, who was an architect and advisor to Amenhotep III in the Eighteenth Dynasty. Although the king himself first initiated this cult, it was in the Saite period that it really became popular, and the son of Hapu became a healer god.[39] Healing gods in general were another new feature of late Egyptian religiosity. Two common ones were Shed and Horus, both depicted as youths. Stelae of these gods, at the bottom of which were basins, were set up in temples or the necropolis; a person could pour water over the stela, which then took on the power

---

[37] Rößler-Köhler, *Individuelle Haltungen zum Ägyptischen Königtum der Spätzeit*, 330. The phrase is "hnw nyswwt h3w-nbw."

[38] Sadek Ashraf, *Popular Religion in Egypt During the New Kingdom* (Hildesheim: Gerstenberg, 1987) 270, writes "There is no doubt that a remarkable feature of Egyptian religion in the Late Period is the prominence of zoomorphic gods." Trigger, et al, *Ancient Egypt: A Social History*, 294–95, mention the ibis (Thoth), the sacred ram, and the Apis bull as examples. Cf. also J. D. Ray, "Egypt, 525–404 BC," 279; John Baines, "Society, Morality, and Religious Practice," in Byron E. Shafer, ed. *Religion in Ancient Egypt: Gods, Myths, and Personal Practice* (Ithaca, NY: Cornell University Press, 1991) 197.

[39] Ashraf, *Popular Religion in Egypt During the New Kingdom*, 276–79. Another example Ashraf gives is Imhotep, the vizier and architect of Zoser in the Third Dynasty. By the Thirtieth Dynasty he was an important god known for his wisdom and the power to cure, a patron for doctors and scribes, in short, another healer god (281–83).

inherent in the text and picture, scoop it out of the basin, and either drink the water or apply it to a wound.[40] The cult association became common. This was a religious society tied to a particular god in which members paid dues, followed rules, held offices, offered legal and financial help to colleagues, and so on.[41] Incubation is well attested in the Late Period. This is the practice of trying to receive a message from a deity through a dream, usually by spending the night in that god's temple. A common message people sought was one of healing.[42] Moreover, some gods gained greater prominence than in earlier times. A prime example is Isis, whose cult was particularly supported by the kingship.[43] Another is Osiris, who although well established already became so popular that he largely edged out the cult of the sun god, Re.[44] Finally, an increase in what are typically called "magical practices" is evident in this period.[45]

The wisdom tradition is a profitable place to turn to in order to discover new accents in Egyptian intellectual movements. Wisdom literature was an age-old genre in Egypt by this time, which makes it an

---

[40] Ashraf, *Popular Religion in Egypt During the New Kingdom*, 284–85.

[41] Ashraf, *Popular Religion in Egypt During the New Kingdom*, 286–88. Ashraf says that membership numbers ranged from 24–50 members in the surviving documents, and he is unsure as to whether these societies were only for the local, low-level clergy of a god, or also open to laymen (287).

[42] Ashraf, *Popular Religion in Egypt During the New Kingdom*, 288–89.

[43] Trigger, et al, *Ancient Egypt: A Social History*, 294, note that the first temple of Isis known to be built was ordered by Amasis. It stood in Memphis, another at Philae. Nectanebo II had one constructed at Behbet el-Hagar. They suggest three reasons for the state support of the goddess. Isis was associated with the kingship, and since kingship was experiencing ups and downs it made sense for the throne to tie itself as closely as possible to her. All of the Late Period native dynasties came from Lower Egypt, which was the origin of the Isis cult. Finally, the goddess was gaining popularity among the people, which would create sympathy toward a supportive royal dynasty. See also Alan B. Lloyd, "Egypt, 404–332 BC," 353–54.

[44] Jaroslav Cerny, *Ancient Egyptian Religion* (London: William Brendon and Son, 1952) 137–38. "In the Ptolemaic period Re hardly occurs, his role having been taken over by Osiris."

[45] Robert K. Ritner, "Horus on the Crocodiles: A Juncture of Religion and Magic in Late Dynastic Egypt," in William Kelly Simpson, ed., *Religion and Philosophy in Ancient Egypt* (New Haven: Yale University Press, 1989) 103. He notes that scholars often contrast this "magic" to "true religion" and falsely conclude that this is further evidence for the decline of Egyptian culture from an earlier "golden age."

especially useful source to look at for tracking changes in worldview throughout Egyptian history. The best texts for this purpose are Ankhsheshonqy and Papyrus Insinger. Each in their own way reveals attitudes which fit with the picture provided by the late biographies and the trends in Egyptian religion in this period. While they certainly do not reveal the despair of the texts in the preceding chapter, they do suggest a muted, cautious approach to an inscrutable world which is new to the tradition.

The first person to publish Ankhsheshonqy was S. R. K. Glanville in 1955.[46] Its arrangement is simple. In the tradition of the Egyptian instruction, it begins with a brief narrative that sets the scene for the upcoming admonitions. The hero is a priest of Re in Heliopolis, who goes to Memphis to visit his friend from childhood, Harsiese, the chief physician to Pharaoh. During the visit, Harsiese tells his friend that he is participating in a plot to assassinate the king. Ankhsheshonqy tries to persuade him not to do it, pointing out how many good things Pharoah did for him by making him chief physician, but Harsiese will not listen. Meanwhile, a servant overhears the whole conversation and reports same to the king, who proceeds to execute the would-be assassins and throw Anksheshonqy into prison for not informing on the plotters himself. Once in prison, he decides to write instructions for his son, which he does on the only available writing material, fragments of his broken meal crockery.

What follows is a series of sentences, sometimes but not necessarily loosely arranged by topic, that cover a wide variety of subjects. The moral tone is pragmatic and down to earth, with a healthy interest in self-preservation.[47] Some of the observations are so pointed as

---

[46] S. R. K. Glanville, *Catalogue of Demotic Papyri in the British Museum, Volume II: The Instructions of 'Onchsheshonqy* (London: Trustees of the British Museum, 1955). The text survives as Papyrus no. 10508 in the British Museum, which gained possession of it in 1896. The papyrus is complete, consisting of 27 ½ columns of Demotic that appears to be of late Ptolemaic date, with the actual composition possibly as old as the fifth century (xi–xiii).

[47] Glanville, *Catalogue of Demotic Papyri*, II:xiv, felt that these instructions are not, as in the past, aimed for the upper classes at court or the scribal profession, but specifically designed for the peasant farmer. Biblical scholars subsequently concurred, one saying that a "rural background" predominates; see B. Gemser, "The Instructions of 'Onchsheshonqy and Biblical Wisdom Literature," in

to strike the modern reader as humorous, and perhaps they were designed to be so. The original editor said the text transmits a low moral standard,[48] and the work has been described as opportunistic and downright cynical.[49] This is an overly pejorative description. Granted that its focus is on personal well-being, it still exhibits a sense of fair play and generosity unrelated to any possible gain for the exhortee.

The other text which is relevant is Papyrus Insinger.[50] Unlike Ankhsheshonqy, which is so loosely organized as to be free-form, P. Insinger's maxims are grouped into chapters of generally unified themes, each of which has a heading and is numbered. One of its distinctive features is that at the end of each chapter the author laid out a pattern of reversals brought about by fate and fortune, the purpose of which is to suggest that the preceding teaching does not always operate according to human ken. Sometimes the paradoxical conclusions have become disordered or garbled, but the pattern is well-enough preserved to be evident. A persistent theme throughout is the dichotomy between the wise man and the fool, the actions of each and the consequences that result.

Both Ankhsheshonqy and P. Insinger are well-rooted in Egyptian wisdom traditions, but at the same time they have their own individual flavor which allows a small window into the interests and concerns of the day. Ankhsheshonqy is down-to-earth and not overly inclined to brood, so one should not overdraw hints of melancholy in the text. As for death in particular, references are occasional. "Do well by your body in your

---

Supplements to Vetus Testamentum: Congress Volume VII (Leiden: E. J. Brill, 1960) 115. As Lichtheim points out, however, less than a tenth of its sayings relate to farming and the country, and at least some imagery from that realm in any ancient society would be expected; see Miriam Lichtheim, *Late Egyptian Wisdom Literature in the International Context: A Study of Demotic Instructions* (Freibourg, Schweiz: Universitätsverlag, 1983) 4.

[48] Glanville, *Catalogue of Demotic Papyri*, II:xiv.

[49] Gemser, "The Instructions of 'Onchsheshonqy and Biblical Wisdom Literature," 123.

[50] Lichtheim, *Ancient Egyptian Literature*, III:184. It was named after J. H. Insinger, the man who acquired it for the Rijksmuseum in 1895. The first five and a half of its twenty-five chapters are missing, though there are fragmentary papyri in the Carlsberg Collection in Copenhagen and elsewhere that reveal variant readings. The handwriting suggests the first century CE, while the actual text could have been composed in the late Ptolemaic period. See also Francois Lexa, *Papyrus Insinger*, 2 Vols. (Paris: Librairie Orientaliste Paul Geunther, 1926).

days of well-being. There is no one who does not die" (8:7–8).[51] This is in line with the advice of the harper songs, in that it views death with a sceptical eye and advises enjoying the present, yet it does not carry the same weight of despair as the afore-discussed biographies. Later in the text Ankhsheshonqy exclaims "May existence always follow death!" (10:25), which is a traditional sentiment.[52] This hope is the basis for the advice that one should be sure to have a tomb ready (12:5). Interestingly, the text further on states "There is none wretched except him who has died (or, is dying)" (19:17). Then, "death does not say 'I am coming'" (20:12). Death is not by any stretch a main theme for Ankhsheshonqy, but his scattered reflections reveal a certain ambivalence towards it, a hope for life after death coupled with an awareness that death is unpredictable and undesirable. Ankhsheshonqy also seems to feel that events in general are beyond human control. He says that fortune is from the hand of the god (20:6), and that nothing happens except what the god wishes (22:25). The impression is that everything is decided apart from the human realm. Near the end of the text, although the section is partly missing, appears an entire passage which acknowledges that act and consequence are often disjunct, because "All are in the hand of the fate and the god" (26:8).

This feeling for the paradoxes in life is heightened in P. Insinger with its repeated chapter conclusions which reveal how events can undo expectations. For example, the end of one chapter reads (7:13–19).

> There is one who lives on little so as to save, yet he becomes poor.
> There is one who does not know, yet the fate gives (him) wealth.
> It is not the wise man who saves who finds a surplus.
> Nor is it the one who spends who becomes poor.
> The god gives a wealth of supplies without an income.
> He also gives poverty in the purse without spending.
> The fate and the fortune that come, it is the god who sends them.

Like Ankhsheshonqy, the text emphasizes the all-controlling power of fate, which is itself controlled by the god. "Do not say 'the chance is good' and forget the fate in it" (4:12). "It is the god who gives the heart,

---

[51] Quotations for these two wisdom texts come from Lichtheim, *Ancient Egyptian Literature*, Vol. 3.

[52] The translation of this line is not entirely certain, as noted by Janet Johnson in a personal communication.

gives the son, and gives the good character" (9:19). "Before the god the strong and the weak are a joke" (11:20). "All these are in the power of the fate and the god" (30:15). Comments on death in particular are not prevalent, though the text does say "Death and the life of tomorrow, we do not know their <nature>" (17:6). The implications of such a statement are potentially far-reaching, but there is no further development of the idea. An added layer in the text is a thread that relates to personal misfortune and how to persist in spite of it. "It is the god who gives patience to the wise man in misfortune" (19:9). "The fate together with the god bring happiness after anxiety" (19:15). "What comes (or, has come) of hardship, leave yourself in the hand of god in it" (20: 13). The repeated counsel on prevailing in times of trouble lends a certain sombre quality to the work's mood. The reader's overall feeling is that the world is not a very happy or ordered place, and that all a person can do is try to ride out the vagaries of fortune and the unpredictability of the gods as patiently as possible. Together, the two wisdom texts offer a view of the world which certainly is intelligible in the Egyptian context, but which also shows a deeper feeling of human powerlessness and resignation towards life than that previously attested in the genre.

One of the key questions with respect to Ankhsheshonqy and P. Insinger is whether their themes and interests are explained as the result of foreign influence, especially Greek influence. This is an important question because, as in the case of the late biographies, and the book of Qoheleth too, it has to do with how one approaches and explains the nature of late ancient Near Eastern history. The scholar who has probably done the most with these two wisdom texts, Miriam Lichtheim, believes that they do reflect foreign influences. She makes a careful and detailed argument for her hypothesis, so it is worth some reflection to see how she goes about it.

Both Ankhsheshonqy and P. Insinger share a compositional characteristic which Lichtheim cites as the incentive that caused her to investigate possible Hellenistic influences on the texts. This characteristic is the use of the monostich, an individual sentence that by grammar and content is self-contained.[53] Earlier instructions did not have this feature, and she dubs it "newly invented" for the very reason that she could find

---

[53] Lichtheim, *Late Egyptian Wisdom Literature in the International Context*, 1.

no known precedent.[54] More will be said on this later. Concluding that this structural feature must not have been an intra-Egyptian one, she turns her frame of reference to the larger Hellenistic world. Her investigations lead her to suggest a number of possible parallels between the Egyptian texts and various Aramaic and Greek compositions.

She begins with Ankhsheshonqy and the Aramaic Wisdom of Ahiqar. Lichtheim believes that echoes of the latter can be seen in Ankhsheshonqy in various places, such as on the subject of quarrels,[55] wealth,[56] and speech.[57] She further investigates a series of proverbs which

---

[54] Lichtheim, *Late Egyptian Wisdom Literature in the International Context*, 11.

[55] Lichtheim, *Late Egyptian Wisdom Literature in the International Context*, 14–16. The passage in Ankhsheshonqy is "Do not insult the common man. When insult occurs beating occurs. When beating occurs killing occurs. Killing does not occur without the god knowing. Nothing occurs except what the god commands" (22:21–25). One Syriac version of Ahikar reads "Among those who quarrel do not stand, for from laughter there comes quarrel, and from quarrel there comes fighting, and from fighting there comes killing" (Berlin 165, no. 55); another runs "In the house of those who quarrel do not stand, for from a word there comes a quarrel, and from a quarrel is stirred up vexation, and from vexation comes killing" (BM Add 7200, no. 8). Because all of these examples are similar in content and share the chain syllogism, she suggests an Aramaic version of Ahiqar which has not survived is the source for Ankhsheshonqy and the Syriac translations. The argument for a common text between the Syriac translations is sound, but the similarities with Ankhsheshonqy are more generic. Its topic is insulting people, not quarrels; all pertain to violent acts, but violence is a broad category. The chaining style is similar, but chaining is one of the features of Ankhsheshonqy at large which helps make the separate monostichs cohere, as Lichtheim herself points out (4). If this form is a repeated trait, its appearance in any one passage is less compelling as an argument for specific outside influence on that passage.

[56] Lichtheim, *Late Egyptian Wisdom Literature in the International Context*, 18. The two proverbs she compares share the "better-than" form and impart similar messages. However, while the wording is similar, the "better-than" formulation is a standard proverbial characteristic both in other Egyptian as well as foreign wisdom writings (cf. Amenemope 8:19, 9:5, 9:7, 16:11, 16:13, 22:15; Proverbs passim), so that this shared feature by itself is not enough to warrant notice. In addition, wealth and poverty are among the staple topics in wisdom traditions.

[57] Lichtheim, *Late Egyptian Wisdom Literature in the International Context*, 19. Ankhsheshonqy has "You may trip over your foot in the house of a great man, you should not trip over your tongue" (10:7). Ahiqar says (Syr Berlin 165, no. 54) "Release not your word from your mouth until it is examined in your

Ankhsheshonqy shares in common with other Semitic and Greek writings. She makes no particular claims in these latter cases as to who influenced whom, but instead intends to show that the evidence is strong for Ankhsheshonqy's inclinations toward international borrowing.[58] One example concerns the act of spitting. Says Ankhsheshonqy, "He who sends spittle to the sky, upon his face it falls" (11:10). In Midrash Qoheleth Rabba 7:21 one finds "He who spits upwards, upon his face it falls." A Greek version reads, "He who spits toward heaven bespits his beard." Another example is the notion that he who digs a pit will fall into it, and he who shakes a stone will see it roll onto his own foot. These sayings appear in one form or another in Ankhsheshonqy 26:21, 22:5; Proverbs 26:27; Qoheleth 10:9; Ben Sira 27:25; and also in the Petubastis story as well as in Hesiod.[59] So also with the admonition not to muddy a

---

heart; for it is better for a man to trip with his foot than to trip with his tongue." These are so similar in expression and content that it does seem possible they are both making use of the same proverb. This saying also appears in Ben Sira, however, as "A slip on the pavement is better than a slip of the tongue" (20:18), and Diogenes Laertius cites it from Zeno as "It is better to slip with the feet than with the tongue (Lichtheim 1983, 19; Jack T. Sanders, *Ben Sira and Demotic Wisdom* [Chico, CA: Scholars Press, 1983] 103). Lichtheim herself acknowledges it as "a truly international proverb."

[58] Lichtheim, *Late Egyptian Wisdom Literature in the International Context*, 29–30.

[59] Cf. Sanders, *Ben Sira and Demotic Wisdom*, 43. The arguments offered by P. Walcot, "Hesiod and the Instructions of 'Onchsheshonqy," *Journal of Near Eastern Studies* 21(1962) 215–19, for Ankhsheshonqy's dependence on Hesiod's "Works and Days" are also slender. He sets up the problem by stating that the Egyptian text is so unlike the other wisdom writings of the culture, before and after, that by implication one is motivated to look for some sort of outside influence (216). He considers its standard of morality well below the typical level, though partially redeemed by sayings of higher sentiment. Hesiod's work exhibits the same combination of self-aggrandizing cynicism and lofty ideals. He further notes, just as Glanville had, that Ankhsheshonqy is aimed at the peasant farmer and is thus "in a class by itself among our Egyptian texts" (216). So too is Hesiod's poem. However, as mentioned earlier, Lichtheim points out that this emphasis on the farming imagery in Ankhsheshonqy is out of proportion to the relatively small percentage of relevant sayings. Even if one considers the countryside details significant, the text would still not be "in a class by itself." In a recently published hieratic wisdom text from the Late Period, Brooklyn Papyrus 47.218.135, the editor remarks that his text exhibits such agricultural topics as well, and he further cites Ptahhotep (maxim 9) and Amenemope (chapter 6) as evidence for older attestation of rural interests. He goes on to acknowledge the three-way parallels between the hieratic composition,

well for others after one has had a drink, and the observation that he who fights along with his town rejoices with it. Such statements are fundamental observations, ethics, and warnings that have to do with the mechanics of daily life among all cultures. The very extent of attestation for such ideas suggests less that Ankhsheshonqy is absorbing outside elements than that the text is, in these cases, one more witness to the commonality of human experience.

Regarding P. Insinger, one of the central themes that Lichtheim draws out is the role of "character" in the text. Although character as a concept makes an appearance in Ankhsheshonqy, it is only in P. Insinger that it takes the center stage.[60] The particular spin that character receives here is primarily in the juxtaposition between the sage and the fool. The sage, or "rmṯ rḫ," has self-control, shame, patience, and a healthy respect for the deity, while the fool, or "lḫ," "ḥne," "rmṯ swg," exhibits the opposite qualities. This kind of dichotomy is one that begs for comparison with counterparts in biblical and Greek texts, she feels. "As far as one can judge from the presently known Egyptian sapiential texts, the prominence of the sage/fool dichotomy is, in Egypt, a feature of *late* wisdom."[61] Thus she turns to non-Egyptian works to see where the idea might have come from.[62] Where P. Insinger finds its closest company is

---

Ankhsheshonqy, and the Works and Days with respect to admonishing unceasing field labor, but concludes that direct connections "should not be assumed." See Richard Jasnow, *A Late Period Hieratic Wisdom Text (Papyrus Brooklyn 47.218.135)* (Chicago: The Oriental Institute, 1992) 37–38. As for the bluntly pragmatic morality of the Egyptian piece and Hesiod's, it should be noted that the didactic strain of wisdom literature by nature tends toward the pragmatic, with differing degrees of self-interest between texts and even within texts. Considering the lack of specifically noteworthy parallels between the two works and the evidence that Ankhsheshonqy is not the cultural oddity that some have taken it to be, one again concludes that direct influence is not a necessary or even particularly likely assumption.

[60] Lichtheim, *Late Egyptian Wisdom Literature in the International Context*, 118–20.

[61] Lichtheim, *Late Egyptian Wisdom Literature in the International Context*, 48.

[62] Lichtheim, *Late Egyptian Wisdom Literature in the International Context*, 122. She correctly notes the same pairings of sage and fool, righteous and wicked, throughout Proverbs and Qoheleth, although in the latter book everyone suffers the same in life despite social, intellectual, or moral categories. She also feels, with some justification, that P. Insinger struggles more with problems of

with the Hellenistic moral philosophies. Epicureanism and Stoicism both use the sage/fool pair for their reflections, but she feels the Stoic mentality to be much more relevant to the Egyptian material.[63] "This view of man and the universe was in essential harmony with the world view of Ancient Egypt." When the Egyptian sages ran across Stoic philosophy, they felt an affinity with it, and P. Insinger developed the wise man into a moral exemplum in a manner much like the philosophers.

However, what does it mean to say that the Stoic view of the world was in harmony with Egypt's? Lichtheim does not go so far as to suggest that the more particular features of Stoic philosophy have counterparts in the late Egyptian wisdom. Her claim seems to be a much more general one, that the belief in an ordered world populated by some intelligent people, some stupid ones, and a number of average types who would benefit from a little teaching, bears a similarity to Egyptian thought. But this can be said about many peoples' views of life. On this level the comparison is very generic—interesting, but not persuasive as an argument for Stoic influence. The toehold for making the comparison in the first place is the perceived change in the Late Period wisdom from the preceding tradition regarding the division between the wise man and the fool. A brief glimpse at earlier Egyptian wisdom texts suggest that the novelty of this division is overdrawn, however.

The distinction first appears in the Instruction of Ptahhotep, who discusses it in some detail in the epilogue.

> The wise is known by his wisdom,
> The great by his good actions.
> His heart matches his tongue,
> His lips are straight when he speaks:
> He has eyes that see,

---

human versus divine responsibility in the use of its juxtapositions than does the book of Proverbs. Ben Sira is the Hebrew work that best approaches P. Insinger's interests in this regard.

[63] See Lichtheim, *Late Egyptian Wisdom Literature in the International Context*, 124, for her description of the Stoic worldview: the universe has been ordered by the deity, who is the source and cause of its goodness. Evil exists, but suffering does not shake the wise man. He is free of the passions and ruled by reason, which means that he is the possessor of an unassailable freedom that consists of doing what is right. The fool is the opposite in every way. Most people, however, can improve themselves through education as they strive for virtue.

His ears are made to hear what will profit his son,
Acting with truth he is free of falsehood.

The fool who does not hear,
He can do nothing at all;
He sees knowledge in ignorance,
Usefulness in harmfulness.
He does all that one detests
And is blamed for it each day;
He lives on that by which one dies.
His food is distortion of speech.[64]

Amenemope revolves around the distinction between the silent man and the heated man, which Lichtheim herself acknowledges as a precursor to the Demotic wisdom.[65] The pairing of fools (ḥmw) and sages (rḫw) also appears in the stele of Mentuhotep; Papyrus Chester Beatty IV pl. 20, verso 6,6; the Instruction by a Man for His Son IV 5; and the Eloquent Peasant B1 287.[66] This evidence has led at least one scholar to question Lichtheim's belief that the wise/fool focus of P. Insinger is so new and unusual as to require explanation.[67] Egyptian tradition, in short, had a long-standing familiarity with the juxtaposition of human types, while P. Insinger does not insist on the typology to the point of dogmatism. It may be the case that P. Insinger develops the idea in more detail, but not in a way that goes beyond the conceivable limits of the native framework. The incentive to find Stoic influence is unnecessary.

Another aspect which Lichtheim discusses is the repeated appearance of Fate and Fortune in the paradoxical chapter endings. The main body of each chapter generally assumes that the individual has the ability to make decisions based on a reliable pattern of cause and effect.

---

[64] Lichtheim, *Ancient Egyptian Literature*, I:73–75.

[65] Lichtheim, *Late Egyptian Wisdom Literature in the International Context*, 45.

[66] Nili Shupak, *Where Can Wisdom Be Found? The Sage's Language in the Bible and in Ancient Egyptian Literature* (Fribourg, Switzerland: University Press, 1993) 184.

[67] Shupak, *Where Can Wisdom Be Found? The Sage's Language in the Bible and in Ancient Egyptian Literature*, 259. Shupak further points to the recognition in P. Insinger that the demarcation between wise man and fool can get fuzzy (222). Some "wise men" do not know (P. Ins. 4:19) while sometimes those who have a hard life are not fools (P. Ins. 5:6).

The conclusions of the chapters, however, show that this order does not unwaveringly follow a set of mechanical rules. Sometimes events are inscrutable, and in these cases, all one can do is chalk it up to the mysterious workings of fate and fortune (š3y and šḥne). Lichtheim acknowledges that the idea of reversal of fortune (šḥne) is not new to the Egyptian material.[68] The Instruction of Any says "It is the god who judges the righteous, his fate comes and takes him away."[69] Several lines later one finds this passage:

> As to him who was rich last year,
> He is a vagabond this year;
> Don't be greedy to fill your belly,
> You don't know your end at all....
> Man does not have a single way,
> The lord of life confounds him.[70]

The use of "fate" (š3y), on the other hand, meaning that life is unpredictable and ever-changing, she feels to be new, since earlier it had referred only to the individual's predetermined lifespan.[71] However, Morenz in his discussion of the term "fate" says "by 'fate' we also understand particular events in a man's life, ordained from above, which guide him directly."[72] While lifespan is the central meaning of the term,

---

[68] Lichtheim, *Late Egyptian Wisdom Literature in the International Context*, 140.

[69] Lichtheim, *Ancient Egyptian Literature*, 141.

[70] Lichtheim, *Ancient Egyptian Literature*, 142. Similarly the seventh chapter of Amenemope opens with "Do not set your heart on wealth, There is no ignoring Fate and Destiny." In chapter twenty, Any admonishes "Don't use for yourself the might of god, As if there were no fate and destiny." Chapter twenty-five reflects that
> Man is clay and straw,
> The god is his builder.
> He tears down, he builds up daily,
> He makes a thousand poor by his will,
> He makes a thousand men into chiefs.

[71] Lichtheim, *Late Egyptian Wisdom Literature in the International Context*, 140. See also her "Observations on Papyrus Insinger," in Erik Hornung and Othmar Keel, eds., *Studien zu altägyptischen Lebenslehren* (Freiburg, Schweiz: Universitätsverlag; Göttingen: Vandenhoeck & Ruprecht, 1979) 303.

[72] Morenz, *Egyptian Religion*, 68.

the content of a person's life is also a present idea.[73] In his monograph on š3y, Quaegebeur says it represents "the human condition," both outside factors imposed on a person or predestined for him at birth, and the vital energy within each individual. He goes on to say that in his opinion, š3y does not primarily mean lifespan, though this is one of its implications.[74] Since š3y is obviously a dynamic word that could mean a variety of things, one wonders whether its function in P. Insinger is so new to Egyptian thought. The notion that the unexpected can always happen is the same idea one finds all the way back to Ptahhotep, so the presence of such a belief in the present text does not strike the reader as all that alien.

Lichtheim however suggests Greek influence. She points out that in Ptolemaic decrees "sḥne" was translated by "tyche," "and there can be little doubt that P. Insinger employed it in this sense." Likewise for "š3y," whose Greek translations were "ananke" and "heimarmene," that is, "necessity."[75] The reason for stating that the Egyptian composition used an old Egyptian word in the exact sense meant by its Greek equivalent is unclear. In content, the fate and fortune of which the text speaks seem to express the native belief that there is a power which sometimes undoes human plans and inverts expectations. The observation that the best-laid plans can go awry is common to many cultures and based on human experience.[76] Lichtheim has not shown that there is anything distinctively Greek to the Egyptian formulation. When she draws this part of the discussion to a close by asking whether the author must have learned to use the paradox from Greek and particularly Stoic models,[77] the evidence from earlier Egyptian texts suggests that the answer is no.[78]

---

[73] Morenz, *Egyptian Religion*, 72.

[74] Jan Quaegebeur, *Le Dieu Égyptien Shaï dans la Religion et l'Onomastique* (Leuven: Leuven University Press, 1975) 125.

[75] Lichtheim, *Late Egyptian Wisdom Literature in the International Context*, 140.

[76] Cf. Proverbs 21:30, 16:1, 16:19.

[77] Lichtheim, *Late Egyptian Wisdom Literature in the International Context*, 149. She is probably right, though, when she disagrees with others that comments about fate and divine determinism are in conflict with the assumption that each person has the responsibility to make the right choices, as some scholars have suggested. The Egyptians were most likely not losing sleep over this logical inconsistency. In daily experience, both views would have been verified (133–34).

[78] Lichtheim, *Late Egyptian Wisdom Literature in the International Context*, 176. Yet another area in which she feels P. Insinger reflects its Hellenistic

After reviewing some of the main arguments for foreign influence and finding that they are not especially persuasive, one is inclined to go back to the starting point, which was the fact that both Ankhsheshonqy and P. Insinger use the monostich. Interestingly enough, in the recently published hieratic wisdom text mentioned earlier, the editor notes that while the Brooklyn Papyrus has a lot of couplets, there are also passages composed of monostichs. This leads him to question Lichtheim's statement that the monostich must be a foreign element.[79] The date of the Brooklyn Papyrus is uncertain. The editor feels that it dates to the fifth or fourth century BCE, although the composition could be Saite. This fact, plus his overall investigation, leads him to say that "the Demotic wisdom texts are firmly rooted in native tradition and that foreign influence need not be invoked to explain their apparent differences from their predecessors."[80] Outside influence from individual texts and philosophical schools is not a necessary factor to explain the kinds of development visible in Egypt's Late Period wisdom literature.[81]

---

influence is in the sixteenth chapter. In a passage on death the author notes that no matter how much wealth one manages to hoard during his lifetime, it all gets left behind when the person dies. Most attestations of this thought are from the Hellenistic age throughout Egyptian, Hebrew, Aramaic, and Greek works. On the other hand, the same idea that you can't take it with you also appears, as discussed in a previous chapter, in a variety of New Kingdom harper songs, where it is drawn out in great detail. The concept is nothing new in the Egyptian context.

[79] Jasnow, *A Late Period Hieratic Wisdom Text (Papyrus Brooklyn 47.218.135)*, 41.

[80] Jasnow, *A Late Period Hieratic Wisdom Text (Papyrus Brooklyn 47.218.135)*, 42. See Lexa, *Papyrus Insinger*, II:104, who says that with rare exception, "je n'ai trouvé dans le papyrus d'Insinger rien que l'on pourrait prendre pour un produit de la penseé grecque." Also see Mark Smith, "Weisheit, demotische," in Wolfgang Helck and Wolfhart Westendorf, eds., *Lexicon der Ägyptologie* (Wiesbaden: Otto Harrassowitz, 1986) VI:1195, who comments "There are differences, innovations, and shifts of emphases, but these are only to be expected.... it is clear that [the late wisdom] texts are products of the same cultural tradition." So also Didier Devauchelle, "De l'originalité des sagesses égyptiennes tardives du IVe siècle avant au Ier siècle après J.-C.," in Jacques Trublet, ed., *La sagesse biblique: De l'Ancien au Nouveau Testament* (Paris: Cerf, 1995) 228, who feels the evidence is not sufficient to suggest foreign influence on late Egyptian wisdom literature.

[81] Sanders, *Ben Sira and Demotic Wisdom*, 27–28, offers some useful points regarding the whole comparative investigation. First, one needs to be clear about when a text is actually appropriating another work or just using a phrase that had gained popularity in its own right. A modern example is the use of Shakespeare. If

CONCLUSION

In fact, the kinds of changes the wisdom literature reveals fit into the social and political conditions of the times. It exhibits a subdued quality, a keen recognition that the best of human plans go awry and that everything is in the hands of an enigmatic deity. At the same time, religious practices increasingly focus on deified men, healing gods, dream interpretation, and religious associations. These shifts suggest a growing sense of a need for solace or salvation, a cure for ills, disclosure of information or revelation, or redefinition of one's religious community. Meanwhile, the biographies become distant towards the idea of the king, and now tend to regard all things as utterly dependent on the gods. Scholars who traditionally regard the Late Period as a time of stagnation and creative turpitude have it backwards. This is a period of distress, and of inquiry, and even of scepticism, but for this very reason the artifacts that have survived, textual as well as physical, reveal a high level of thought and creativity, of an attempt by individuals to address changing circumstances in a variety of ways and to reorient themselves in a shifting world. The Egyptians continued to confront life vigorously, but in new ways.

And because life was presenting itself as unfamiliar and chaotic, there were people who drew new conclusions about death. A handful of the biographies personally testify to the view that death has become omnipotent, and announce that the traditional mortuary religion is empty,

---

someone is writing a piece in which he says "all that glitters is not gold" (note the misquotation), is the reader to assume that he consciously incorporates Shakespeare, or is simply making use of an everyday expression without even thinking about the source? Has he even read Shakespeare? Quite possibly he has not, and this hypothetical example applies to a person and textual source within the same culture, much less to potential international borrowing. Secondly, when it is claimed, for example, that Ben Sira contains Greek "expressions and allusions," one should not accept this claim merely because similar Greek examples can be found for some of Ben Sira's ideas. When a point appears that finds parallels both to Hebrew and Greek traditions, without anything in particular to demonstrate Greek ties, the biblical traditions are the more likely source (29). Sanders himself is not sympathetic to the idea of much Greek influence for Ben Sira, and instead tries to demonstrate ties to none other than P. Insinger. In fact, the Hebrew text may exhibit a few Greek points of contact, but the methodology Sanders exhorts is sound.

because death is deprivation and ultimately, insensibility. Death was not the continuation of life as it had always been; death was final. That such a view might appear in this period should not, in light of the historical context, related shifts in the biographical genre in particular, and developments in the religion in general, be surprising. The move away from the traditional answers to death is one move among many that were taking place in the intellectual and religious spheres, and reflects on perceptions of life. The fact is that life was changing. Most especially, the foundation of the ancient Egyptian world, the office of pharaoh, was not regarded as the all-powerful cornerstone of cosmic order that it once had been. The gradual, fitful, and eventual collapse of the cornerstone created pressures which released themselves in different ways. "Foreign influence" is not a persuasive, nor a necessary, explanation for what was happening. The old ways were passing, and with them passed the entire symbolic framework that lent order to chaos. And so the individual might find that, without this framework, something such as death became an unattenuated force, without the moderating support on which one's ancestors had been able to rely. Death became the end.

Chapter 7
CONCLUSIONS

Both the book of Qoheleth and the late Egyptian biographies that have been studied here are usually regarded by readers as singular and strange, and understandably so. The aim of this project has been to discover how the texts could come to be. In both sets of material, death is a problem such that each culture's established ways for confronting death's disruptions are, for these authors, no longer effective. Qoheleth regards death as an event which stands for the disjunction of every previously conceivable form of human continuity. The immortalities of descendants, community, memory, or the preservative qualities of wisdom and righteousness, are naught. In the same time period, Egypt also shows signs of regarding death as an insoluble problem, in ways which specifically negate Egyptian traditions of endurance, in this case based on an individual immortality where one's physical needs will continue to be fulfilled in a reunited existence with one's family and the community of the dead at large.

Whenever an attempt is made to understand what has motivated these authors, and since the Late Egyptian materials are not studied much the attempt is usually made in the case of Qoheleth, the answer typically rests on the idea of foreign influence. However, by setting these respective writings in the context of contemporary or later materials, one could see that although they depart in significant ways from earlier traditions they do end up fitting into religious and intellectual trends that were getting under way in each society. The project has taken a two-pronged attack to the question, in that it looked at the history of an idea, the attitude toward death, within two cultures in order to trace changes in that idea, as well as compared this development between the cultures, using the Jewish book of Qoheleth and the Egyptian biographies as the points of comparison. What arises from this developmental comparison is the fact that in both civilizations, in the same time period, some people began to lose confidence in their society's ways of confronting death. Both Qoheleth and the Egyptian biographies have a double context, first within their own traditions, and then cross-culturally. Within the traditions, each is part of a broader pattern of change where a wide spectrum of religious beliefs, expectations, and emphases are coming in for new reflection. Moreover, this pattern of change appears in two very different societies at approximately the same time.

Various explanations are conceivable for such a situation, not excluding the hypothesis that the authors have been influenced by material foreign to the culture, as is most commonly suggested, by Greek writings or ideas. For the reasons stated in earlier chapters, this answer, while a reasonable theory that should be tested, turns out to have little explanatory force for the particular cases at hand. The search for foreign influence is understandable when the specific texts are studied in isolation from the fuller religious environment, because the content of the ideas then appears to come out of nowhere, unless an outside cause is supposed. What seems inexplicable in the materials individually, however, is understandable as part of growing shifts in religious thinking as a whole throughout the Near East in the last half millennium BCE or so.

J. Z. SMITH
AND THE SHIFT IN RELIGIOUS PATTERNS

Productive work in understanding the shape of religious life across the ancient Near East in this time has been done by the historian of religions J. Z. Smith. In a series of essays he has analyzed a variety of religious texts, practices, and trends in this environment and found that the evidence reveals a fundamental change in the nature of religious expression in the period. The traditional pattern of religiosity was giving way to a new type, which he describes as a shift from a "locative" to a "utopian" worldview.

In the traditional, locative model of religion, people believe that a cosmic order, consisting of the realm of the gods, pervades reality and that human society should imitate the divine, which task is seen to by the kings and priests. A common feature of this view of life is the creation myth that occurs throughout the Mediterranean and Near East, where the divine forces struggle with chaos and successfully achieve order, which enables creation. The duty of the individual is to learn what his place in the grand framework of creation is. The sage is "the one who can discern the pattern of things and aid the king and the people in fulfilling their appointed role. Man is charged with the task of harmonizing himself with the great rhythms of cosmic destiny and order."[1] A typical figure in this kind of worldview is the "hero-that-failed," who in a myth or story attempts to escape death or the limits of human nature and eventually comes to accept that this is impossible. A famous example is Gilgamesh. The key feature of the cosmos, then, is that it has limits, boundaries.[2] Everyone, god and man alike, must constantly work together to maintain the delicate framework of order within the cosmic boundaries in the face of the eternal threat of chaos.[3]

However, in the Hellenistic period (more on this time frame below), a "radical revaluation" came about.[4] What had been a reassuring, reliable structure in which a person's place and responsibilities in the cosmos were well and fully understood became an inscrutable, threatening prison. The powers with whom human society had earlier worked to maintain the system were now dangerous. The accepted limits on humanity which helped preserve order and stability were felt to be oppressive. The goal of the individual is no longer to fit into the cosmic organization, but to escape it, and the "hero-that-failed" is replaced by the "hero-that-succeeded." Instead of the threat of a return to chaos, the threat is other men, demons, evil, or *death*.[5] The sage is supplanted by the savior, the one who knows not how to fit in, but how to escape.[6]

> ....each locative culture was to discover that its cherished structures of limits, the gods that ordained and maintained these limits, and the myths which described the creation of the world as an imposition of limits were perverse. Each culture rebelled against its locative traditions, developing a complex series of techniques for escaping limitation, for achieving individual and cosmic freedom now.[7]

---

[1] Jonathan Z. Smith, *Map Is Not Territory: Studies in the History of Religions* (Leiden: E.J. Brill, 1978) 133, 160–61.

[2] Smith, *Map Is Not Territory*, 134.

[3] Smith, *Map Is Not Territory*, 136–37.

[4] Smith, *Map Is Not Territory*, 138, 161. Smith attributes this phrase to Hans Jonas.

[5] Smith, *Map Is Not Territory*, 187, italics mine.

[6] Smith, *Map Is Not Territory*, 138–39, 161–62.

[7] Smith, *Map Is Not Territory*, 140. See also Jonathan Z. Smith, "European Religions: Ancient: Hellenistic," in *The Encyclopedia Brittanica*, Vol. 18 (15th edition: 1985) 925–27, as well as Jonathan Z. Smith, *Drudgery Divine: On the Comparison of Early Christianities and the Religions of Late Antiquity* (Chicago: University of Chicago Press, 1990) 121–124, for a similar discussion.

The "locative" view of the world stresses the value of location or place, the "utopian," taking the word in its technical sense, stresses "the value of being in no place."[8]

And why, exactly, does this basic change in religious worldview come about? Smith first cites the hypothesis that with the conquests of Alexander the old style of civic organization, based on the polis, disintegrated and people were now, literally, "cosmopolitan," or cosmic citizens. This was overwhelming and led to feelings of rootlessness, which underlay the general feelings of anomie.[9] Smith himself, at this point, avoids the search for a cause or causes and concentrates on the situation as it presents itself once the changes start coming about. However, in a different chapter, he does offer his personal view of the source of the Hellenistic religious shift, which was "the almost total cessation of native kingship and sovereignty in the domains of Alexander's successors."[10]

This suggestion is persuasive to a certain extent. Shifts in power throughout the Near East and Mediterranean led to successive dominations of local cultures, in which Greece also took part. The loss of native kingship was a key factor in the locative cultures in which a king was a central part of the delicate framework that kept chaos at bay. These societies did not employ modern distinctions between politics and religion; king, god(s), priests, army, bureaucrats, people, all alike were mutually joined in the ongoing effort to protect the age-old order. The loss of one of the main components in the system created a fundamental crisis for the entire locative approach to life. The explanation is convincing in the case of the Jewish tradition. In the case of Egypt, the matter is a little more complicated, since the Egyptian tradition of kingship was not abruptly cut off in the same fashion as it was for the Jews. It did suffer serious battering, and was taken over by foreign overlords. Yet, if these new kings fulfilled traditional pharaonic functions, as both Persian and Greeks sometimes did, the system was sustainable. The question for the Egyptians had to do with whether the actions of the king were proper or not. However, if the kingship in particular did not cease to exist, it is true that the office of the king seems to have lost its aura of irreproachability, and as a whole Egypt was experiencing some of the same systemic changes in its traditions that other cultures were.

---

[8] Smith, *Map Is Not Territory*, 101.

[9] Smith, *Map Is Not Territory*, 163.

[10] Smith, *Map Is Not Territory*, 186.

Another point at which one would rephrase Smith's formulation is the part where he speaks of Alexander's successors as the ones under whom nations began losing their kings. Alexander did not conquer native kings in either Judah or Egypt; this was the job of the Babylonians and Persians. In fact, native kingship had been succumbing to the imperial aspirations of various empires since the Assyrians went on the march. Judah and Egypt had lost (and Egypt regained and lost again) native kings before Alexander appeared on the scene, although Greek domination certainly contributed to the pattern. For Judah the key date was 587 BCE; for Egypt, the process was more sporadic, but the Persian conquest in 525 BCE may have been the watershed for Egyptian culture.[11] In short, the different societies of the entire region were bound in a series of mutually affecting events which began in the centuries preceding the Hellenistic period, and continued to gain momentum through it. Much of the evidence for the kind of religious shift that Smith describes comes from the period after Alexander, which is understandable since it would take a while for people to consider their new situation and attempt to deal with it. But the situation itself does not begin in 332.

Smith's model for understanding the permutations in religious goals that resulted from these events is suggestive, with the change that the events which led to the religious shifts were underway even before Alexander officially inaugurated the Hellenistic period, and that the question of kingship, in particular, has somewhat different ramifications for Israel and Egypt. However, the traditional mode of religiosity, the bounded, hierarchical, locative worldview, began to crumble, and when that happened, people were forced to rethink their cosmic position, their relationship to gods and society alike. Old ways of dealing with the enduring questions and problems of life seemed invalid. New answers were needed, sought, and found, a wide variety of them, in fact. As Smith explains, "social change is preeminently symbol or symbolic change," and the questions that lie at the core of such change are: where does one stand in the universe, what are one's limits?[12] He goes on to say that in

---

[11] The Greeks had been experiencing their own socio-political stresses during the series of wars they suffered before Alexander even began his string of conquests. More will be said about this below.

[12] Smith, *Map Is Not Territory*, 143. Gilbert Murray, *Stoic, Christian, and Humanist* (London: C. A. Watts, 1940) 64, in a more pejorative description of the cultural changes of time, refers to the peoples in the period immediately before Jesus as experiencing a sort of mental "failure of nerve," in which "superstition and emotionalism" held sway.

his view there are two basic answers to the questions, the locative and utopian, that each describes what is to be taken as the center of value, either conforming to the order or escaping the order, and that all other symbolization arises from the respective position taken by a society (or, one might add, from the position taken by an individual within a society).[13]

Smith's model helps one understand the struggle with death that appears in Qoheleth and the relevant Egyptian biographies as something which is comprehensible in their changing religious environments. The foregoing chapters showed that contemporary and subsequent trends within each tradition bear out the notion that there is a new religious and intellectual ferment within both cultures and that some people were beginning to experience doubt or anxiety about old answers and seek out new ones. Death is one of many matters that came in for discussion, which makes sense considering that it is an elemental fact of human life which cries out for interpretation. The writers of these texts of course did not say to themselves "due to the pressures of historical change, we need to refashion our conceptual universe...." Their circumstances would have been much more personal and immediate than that.[14] They were experiencing the cultural stresses of the times as their traditional organization of society and associated way of viewing the cosmos were breaking down.

What is interesting to note, however, is that the particular texts in question do not appear to exemplify either the locative *or* the utopian worldviews. In fact, the authors seem to be stuck between the two, meaning that their locative traditions no longer supply compelling answers to death, and yet they have not made that step into the utopian framework in order to find new ones. This may be what makes them so poignant and disturbing, because they really have no answers to offer that would serve as the basis for cultural reconstruction. The closest any of them comes to an answer is the advice to enjoy life in the here and now while there is still time, but this is not much of a solution, nor do they

---

[13] He adds that he assumes no evolutionary schema between locative and utopian worldviews, where the former is old and the latter new. Emphases shift from one to the other throughout history; in this particular time, the shift is away from the locative (Smith, *Map Is Not Territory*, 143; also see 101 where he says that both views "have been and remain coeval existential possibilities which may be appropriated whenever and wherever they correspond to man's experience of his world").

[14] Nor is it to be expected that they would analyze their socio-cultural circumstances in the manner of present-day historians of religion.

really claim that it is. The call to make the most of the present, in the context of the claim that there no possible long-term solution to the problem of death, is in itself an ephemeral remedy. This does not mean that the locative/utopian model is therefore negated, but perhaps it can be expanded. Smith says that he feels there are two answers to the question regarding the place in which one stands in the cosmos and the limits one must face in life, but perhaps there are more.

It may be that, in the course of a move from one way of looking at the world to another, that is, from one way of symbolizing reality to oneself, and society's self, to another way of doing so, there is a third position which is neither locative nor utopian; this would be the case of a person who no longer has confidence in one type of answer to fundamental human questions and is left then without his locative framework for interpreting his experiences, but also does not make the qualitative leap to the utopian approach, and this seems to be the case for Qoheleth and the Egyptian texts. This is not really all that surprising, that in these centuries a wide spectrum of reactions to events should come into being. Some people are going to stick with what they know, some will reinterpret their traditions, some will seek entirely new answers to the new circumstances of their lives, and some will no longer find comfort in tradition nor find themselves willing or able to enter a new symbolic framework. One notices that Qoheleth even appears to be aware of a belief that the fate of humans and animals after death might be different (3:21), but he dismisses the notion.[15]

What the locative/utopian model does for the scholar is provide a structure for understanding religion in the late ancient Near Eastern world, which Smith assigns particularly to the period after Alexander but finds its roots beforehand. One change in society that affected cultures throughout the region was when native kingship began to fail. In Egypt, the kingship did not cease until the Roman period, but it did not remain unaffected by successive invasions, and the realities of Persian and Ptolemaic rule had their own political and economic ramifications for the country. Though the details of this change varied from one culture to

---

[15] It is interesting that the Hebrew and Egyptian texts start from quite different premises, one from a background where personal immortality is not a cultural tradition, the others from a background where it is, yet reach the same conclusion, that there is no known way to overcome the human finitude that is the result of death. The traditional Egyptian view, that the individual might achieve immortality, could be an answer to Qoheleth, one that he seems to have heard of, but which he rejects.

another, the fact that change was occurring is a constant between societies; the old systems of social and religious organization were shifting, or even breaking. The move from the traditional place-centered understanding of the cosmos, society, and the individual to one where the individual seeks to escape the cosmic system is widespread. The texts at hand are a small part of this shift, although they themselves do not seem to fall within either worldview, but rather slip through the crack between them. Naturally the process was not a neat, linear development, but one where people were jumping both directions by fits and starts. But in the long run, the model is descriptive of the religious environment. Qoheleth and the Egyptian biographies appear to represent an intermediate step in the overall transformation, to mark a transitional moment. The really useful aspect of the model is that it gets away from the typical effort to understand changes in religious temperament at this time as a matter of influence of one culture on another. No doubt there was influence, too, but the influences are secondary to the main issue, which is that universal shifts in the political horizons and societies across the area were creating a need for responses within the societies themselves, which then also may have been disposed to incorporating ideas from others who were dealing with their own internal shifts.

In a discussion of the scholarly act of comparison, Smith points out that a comparison between one feature or detail in a given tradition with another, if it stops there, is a thin endeavor that in itself typically leads to the same old question of borrowing, whereas the comparison of whatever detail or idea under study in both traditions "with respect to a more generic pattern" refrains from conclusions of influence,[16] and this is often a much more useful way of understanding the traditions as a whole. Moreover, he emphasizes that a key feature of a proper method of comparison is *"the recognition and role of historical development and change."*[17] The scholar of late antiquity confronts cultures that were in the process of energetically reinterpreting their traditions, and any given interpretation that a people chose represented a "particular way of relating themselves to their historical past and social present."[18]

This means that, in the case of Qoheleth and the late Egyptian biographies, it would be a matter of less interest to note that both sets of material regard death as an insurmountable problem, than it is to set each within their respective histories and understand how distinctive they are

---

[16] Smith, *Drudgery Divine*, 99.

[17] Smith, *Drudgery Divine*, 106, italics his.

[18] Smith, *Drudgery Divine*, 107.

with regard to their traditions, how they specifically target the ways their traditions had confronted death, and how they fit into new movements of questioning and rethinking old answers that are taking place contemporaneously. When this fuller context is considered, the question no longer appears to be a matter of influence, but of an historical pattern which finds its roots in events within the cultures, events of a type that were occurring across the region more or less simultaneously. The intent of this project is not to argue that one needs to cut Greece out of the comparative enterprise, but to bring other cultures in and look at the course of developing religious changes throughout the period. In fact, Greek thought shows similar trends in views of death and rethinking of tradition which are comparable with those in Israel and Egypt.

GREEK ATTITUDES TOWARDS DEATH

The Greek view of death was originally not unlike the general attitudes presented in the Hebrew Bible. The Greeks had a place where the dead go after death, Hades, just as the Israelites had Sheol. Like Sheol, it was not a place of judgment or reward and punishment. Everyone experiences the same, bland, listless existence.[19] The first surviving evidence for a belief in post-mortem reward and punishment is in the *Hymn to Demeter* (7th century BCE), and the key here is not good conduct, but knowledge of the ritual and witnessing the mysteries. The Orphics also believed in a dualistic afterlife.[20] In general, however, even though Hades could be a place of punishment for selected spectacular crimes as far back as Homer, the dead were not considered to be differentiated.[21] Beginning in the mid-fifth century a new idea seems to have arisen where the psychai of the dead went upwards instead of into Hades, but this did not entail a belief in personal immortality. Rather it was a description of the separation of the person's different component parts,[22] much like the biblical notion of the body returning to dust, the life-breath to God.

Lattimore agrees that notions of immortality for the Greeks were not widespread, and were usually related either to the mysteries or to

---

[19] Robert Garland, *The Greek Way of Death* (Ithaca, NY: Cornell University Press, 1985) 60, says "There is no hint of a reckoning on the other side of the grave. Good and evil alike lead an equally cheerless existence."

[20] Garland, *The Greek Way of Death*, 61.

[21] Garland, *The Greek Way of Death*, 67.

[22] Garland, *The Greek Way of Death*, 75.

Orphism, neither of which appear very often in the surviving epitaphs.[23] The fourth century BCE is when Greek epitaphs which do disclose a belief in immortality first appear, with the majority dating to the Roman period.[24] The development in Greece was somewhat similar to that among the Jews. A notion that death is the end of individual existence appears to have been the norm, with an emergence of some idea of immortality in epitaphs starting to appear in the 300's BCE. There was a gradual shift from a low level of concern with death to an increasing interest in an individual survival.[25] Other evidence includes accounts of descents into the netherworld and ideas of reincarnation, along with a more upscale view, materially speaking, of existence in Hades, where the dead live a rich existence filled with plenty.[26]

Interestingly, the Greek world itself was undergoing a number of changes which are related to one another. The fourth century was a time of political disintegration and economic upheaval. Constant wars had a deleterious effect on the land, crops, travel, and therefore trade, not to mention the defeated cities. Political instability, poverty, and destruction

---

[23] Richmond Lattimore, *Themes in Greek and Latin Epitaphs* (Urbana: University of Illinois Press, 1962) 342. An example of an epitaph that represents the earlier Greek view of death reads as follows:

> Wayfarer, do not pass by my epitaph, but stand and listen, and then, when you have learned the truth, proceed. There is no boat in Hades, no ferryman Charon, no Aeacus keeper of the keys, nor any dog called Cerberus. All of us who have died and gone below are bones and ashes: there is nothing else. What I have told you is true. Now withdraw, wayfarer, so that you will not think that, even though dead, I talk too much (Lattimore, *Themes in Greek and Latin Epitaphs*, 75).

[24] Lattimore, *Themes in Greek and Latin Epitaphs*, 53–54. The bulk of them are not from Greece but Asia Minor, with a fair number from Egypt and Italy.

[25] Jan N. Bremmer, "The Soul, Death and the Afterlife in Early and Classical Greece," in J.M. Bremer et al, eds., *Hidden Futures: Death and Immortality in Ancient Egypt, Anatolia, the Classical, Biblical and Arabic-Islamic World* (Amsterdam: Amsterdam University Press, 1994) 96.

[26] Bremmer, "The Soul, Death and the Afterlife in Early and Classical Greece," 102–04. He notes that descent stories go back as far as the *Odyssey*, and include the tales of Heracles, Theseus, and Orpheus (102). Pythagoras in the late sixth century was one among a number of others at the time who taught reincarnation (102–03). As for Hades, this god came to be called Pluto, or "rich one," and in the late fourth century people began to offer him sacrifices (103). The dead, who in Homer were called "the powerless heads of the dead," are later named "eudaimones" or "makarioi" (104).

went hand in hand.[27] A depression set in.[28] Competition for scarce resources led to increasing specialization. The constant revolutions created professionals whose specialty was fighting. Advanced banking meant specialized careers in finance, and so on in many areas of life.[29] The city-state lost its position as the main Greek form of political organization.[30]

Late Greece and classical Greece were not the same society. Smith sketches out a number of contrasts between the two:

1) The main form of land holding in the classical world was small plots owned by the average citizen, while in the hellenistic world it tended toward larger estates owned by a king, temple, or high official.

2) The classical world was organized by city states, "of small extent and homogenous population, with some form of conciliar government." In the hellenistic world, the new political unit was the monarchy, which included many peoples and lands.

3) In the classical world, society was based mostly on local custom. In the hellenistic world, written law codes with authority over large territories came to the fore.

4) In the classical world, the city gods were the focus of religious interest and civic feeling. In the hellenistic world, the ruler cult became the center of patriotic expression, while religious assistance was commonly sought from gods lacking any important political tie.

5) In the classical world, "because the economic and political units were so small, private individuals were of relatively great importance...." In the hellenistic world, as the forms of organization expanded in size, the private individual became less important "and the average man was less interested in politics, more in his private affairs."

6) In the classical world the bureaucracy and army were mostly composed of citizens who normally held other jobs. In the hellenistic world both were run by professionals. "Most of these contrasts resulted from developments which had already begun in the earlier years of the fourth century, when classical culture was disintegrating."[31]

---

[27] Morton Smith, *The Ancient Greeks* (Ithaca, NY: Cornell University Press, 1960) 90.

[28] Smith, *The Ancient Greeks*, 91.

[29] Smith, *The Ancient Greeks*, 93–94.

[30] F. W. Walbank, *The Hellenistic World* (Cambridge, MA: Harvard University Press, 1993) 338. The city-state could not deal with monarchs backed by professional armies. Monarchical resources were also greater than city resources.

[31] Smith, *The Ancient Greeks*, 120–22 for all six points listed and quotations.

The stresses and changes in the status quo to which Greeks were forced to react are matched by alterations in religious and philosophical attitudes. A growing interest in individual survival after death was only one example of this. A small but indicative case appears in the arts. Whereas before, sculpture had been tied to its architectural setting, the statues of Praxiteles reveal an emphasis on the individual statue. No longer is the sculpted deity portrayed as interested in the observer's worship. The gods under his chisel tended to come out as totally heedless and unobservant of the worshiper. Moreover, his subjects were deities like Eros, god of love, and Dionysius, god of drunkenness, ecstasy, and individual immortality.[32] As the world became larger, people became increasingly alone.[33] The emerging sense of isolation and individualism of the age is reflected in the growing number of various organizations one could join, in particular religious groups, which may have been a move to overcome isolation through membership in a larger entity.[34] The philosophies of Epicurus and the Stoics also reveal the new concerns of the time.

> Both were individual adjustments to the insecurity and indifference of the hellenistic world. What could be done? One could withdraw from the world, practice frugality, live content in the enjoyment of one's wisdom, *and face death without fear*. Or one could by practice achieve indifference to misfortune, follow unhesitatingly the moral teaching of the sect, live content in the enjoyment of one's virtue, *and face death with assurance*.[35]

---

[32] Smith, *The Ancient Greeks*, 95–96. He adds "these had become the gods of private life and of the individual. As loyalty to the city-state declined, so did the representation of the civic deities and so did their worship (except as prescribed by law....)." In particular, Smith comments, Asclepius, the god of healing, had many devoted adherents.

[33] Smith, *The Ancient Greeks*, 125. "The city-state had been home; the Seleucid or Ptolemaic kingdom was merely where you lived."

[34] Smith, *The Ancient Greeks*, 126. Walbank, *The Hellenistic World*, 218, remarks that as the power of the city-states declined and the people lost faith in their cults, the mystery religions became increasingly popular. These latter may have functioned as a replacement for the lost city-state cults.

[35] Smith, *The Ancient Greeks*, 129 (italics mine). See also Jacques Choron, *Death and Western Thought* (New York: Collier Books, 1963) 64, who says that "the individual, deprived of the emotional security and self-evident meaningfulness of existence in and for the sake of the city-state and confronted with a wide and strange world, was not only in need of support and guidance on how to live in it; he also became conscious of being an isolated individual, and this new awareness of his individuality of necessity brought into a sharper focus the old problem of death."

A rising scepticism was fueled by the sophistic movement, and traditional worship started to turn to abstractions such as Peace or Democracy.[36] The abstracting, or depersonalizing, of the gods can be seen for the first time in the fourth century BCE. One popular abstract figure was *Tyche*, or Fortune.[37] Part of Fortune's popularity may have been related to the fact that in an age of mobility, the assistance of one's city gods was made difficult by distance.[38] Greek and Latin epitaphs of the period reveal "an uncomfortable feeling that one is at the mercy of certain gods, vague but powerful, quick-tempered and vindictive, whom one would be careful not to irritate if one only knew how to keep from doing it.... It means that death comes by chance; and chance then as now was a mystery with no clear name."[39] So the gods were either uninterested and remote from humanity, or cantankerous and to be given a wide berth, if possible. Yet another trend was a turn to oriental cults which provided personal interaction with particular gods or hope for personal immortality.[40]

In any event there appears to have been a sense that the old mechanisms for confronting the vagaries of life were no longer reliable,

---

[36] Walbank, *The Hellenistic World*, 209–210. "Old certainties had gone and though ancient rites were still zealously performed in the conviction that what was traditional should be preserved, many people were at bottom agnostics or even atheists.... The expansion into new lands could only accentuate these often contradictory trends. For many reasons the new world of monarchic states with their new city foundations and, equally, the old cities of Greece proper and the Aegean basin now felt the impact of fresh religious attitudes and came to adopt new forms of religious experience. Contact with non-Greek populations who worshipped different gods, the deliberate encouragement of certain cults for reason of state policy, the adoption either spontaneously or in reply to official hints or pressure of ruler-cult, the consciousness in individuals of new, personal emotional needs amid social isolation, the response to the uncertainties of a world in which swift changes brought frequent striking reversals of fortune (so that Fortune herself was often invoked as a powerful deity)—all these combine to create a confused and kaleidoscopic picture of change hard to get into focus."

[37] Walbank, *The Hellenistic World*, 220. Hengel, "The Interpenetration of Judaism and Hellenism in the Pre-Maccabean Period," 181, remarks "The early Hellenistic period, especially the third century, was predominantly a time of decline of traditional religion and of enlightenment. Tyche, the goddess of chance, was the dominant deity...."

[38] Elias Bickerman, *Four Strange Books of the Bible* (New York: Schocken Books, 1967) 146.

[39] Lattimore, *Themes in Greek and Latin Epitaphs*, 158.

[40] Walbank, *The Hellenistic World*, 220–21.

and new ones were needed. The political, social, and economic changes that were taking place in Greece, with the associated cultural stresses, is by now a familiar pattern in light of similar happenings in Israel and Egypt. In Greece, the problem is tied to the decline of the polis as the center of social organization and breakdown of classical culture which was taking place by the early fourth century. In Israel, the disruption of the kingship by expanding empires was the root of the cultural pressure, and while the matter of the kingship is a little more complex in Egypt, that culture was experiencing the same kinds of political onslaught as the rest of the region. In all cases the socio-political shifts are related to ongoing and often interconnected processes of power struggle in the region, which eventually dovetailed when the Persians were finally pushed back and replaced by Alexander and his successors across the Mediterranean and Near East. Alexander's arrival was not, however, the first sign of the new age, but came after the processes of change not only in the Near Eastern cultures but the Greek as well were underway. Certainly he was a significant part of that process, but not the initiator of it.

People in many places were experiencing a growing feeling of spiritual dislocation and isolation; the gods became more depersonalized, chance seemed to be the ruling principle of the world, and the individual was left on his own to negotiate the complexities of life. One manifestation of this is a new concern with death, which led to a variety of ways for dealing with it. Amongst the Greeks, one approach aimed for preservation of the individual in a new notion of Hades, where the soul lived in plenty. Some turned to reincarnation. Others, such as the Epicureans and the Stoics, attempted instead to ameliorate the fear of death. Yet others turned to mystery religions. Gods like Asclepius, the healer, became increasingly popular. In other words, Greek society exhibits political upsets of its own, and concomitant religious and intellectual responses, not unlike Judah and Egypt. The exact details are not the same, but the trends are analogous. The changes begin in the latter cultures somewhat before those in Greece, as foreign invasions were already well underway in Judah and Egypt, but by the time of Alexander the upheavals had spread throughout the entire region.

"THE HELLENISTIC WORLD"

In view of the fact that this study has been devoted to investigating texts of the of the second half of the last millennium BCE, some of which come from the Hellenistic era, it would be useful to look at the word "Hellenistic" and see what exactly it means, because it has defined scholarly inquiry in ways that affect not only the answers, but also the questions scholars ask of the period. In the case of Qoheleth, for example, when some describe the book as Hellenistic, the statement appears to be equivalent to saying not simply that it was written after Alexander, which it may have been, but that it contains ideas, expressions, or worldviews that derive from Greek culture. In other words, sometimes there is a lack of clarity about whether "Hellenistic" refers to a time period or a culture. This is a confusion akin to that between "parallel" and "influence," but is at least somewhat understandable considering the implications of the word.

Hengel has an interesting discussion of the terminology and concepts attached to "Hellenism" and "Hellenistic."[41] He notes that the idea of Hellenism in the sense of a world culture was first propounded by Gustav Droysen, whose views were based on a Hegelian notion of history. Greece was the antithesis of the Orient, and Hellenism the synthesis. A similar idea found a home among some Roman authors. Hengel specifically points to *De fortuna aut virtute Alexandri Magni*, by Plutarch. Here Alexander conquers the world, but also is a tutor and civilizer of the barbarians who spreads law and peace among the savages.[42] However, the idea of a "world-empire" was not indigenous to the Greek mindset, which had been based rather on the polis as a political entity. The first Hellenistic rulers (from the Diadochi on) had little interest in spreading the benefits of Greek culture to their peoples, and rather more interest in solidifying their political power. It was Rome that

---

[41] Martin Hengel, "The Interpenetration of Judaism and Hellenism in the Pre-Maccabean Period," in W. D. Davies and Louis Finkelstein, eds., *The Cambridge History of Judaism*, Vol. I (Cambridge: Cambridge University Press, 1984) 167–228.

[42] Hengel, "The Interpenetration of Judaism and Hellenism in the Pre-Maccabean Period," 168. This idea, Hengel adds, is founded on the Stoic notion of the "world-citizen."

made "Hellenism" a real, worldwide phenomenon.[43] The meaning of the verb "hellenizein" was "to speak Greek," not to pick up prescribed elements of Greek culture.[44]

One scholar, in reference to the particular question of the usage of the Greek language among the Jews, emphasizes the continuing preference for Hebrew among non-Diasporic Jewish writers.

> ....the sacred writers of Palestine continued to write in Hebrew, or even in Aramaic, throughout the third century B.C.E. So lively was the ancestral tongue that even at this period of intensive Hellenization it could still produce a poetic masterpiece in the Song of Songs; serious historical works such as Chronicles and Ezra-Nehemiah; and a work of religious edification like the book of Esther [he adds also Deutero-Zechariah, the second half of Daniel, Ecclesiastes, Ben Sira, and the bulk of the Dead Sea Scrolls to the list].[45]

Likewise, in the case of Late Period Egypt, where scholars previously thought that the Ptolemies had brought in a dominating Greek culture that embedded itself in and merged with the native traditions in an unavoidable process of syncretism, this now appears not to be the case. The fact that Egyptian legal custom and Greek law officially existed side by side, with neither overriding the other, has been known for some time.[46] More recently it has become apparent that Egyptian religion and literature also continued to flourish, with little real interest in

---

[43] Hengel, "The Interpenetration of Judaism and Hellenism in the Pre-Maccabean Period," 169. He adds (174) that when discussing "Hellenization" a number of different aspects should be kept in mind. "These are: firstly, purely occupational and business contacts; secondly, the physical mixture of peoples through mixed marriages; thirdly, the adoption by orientals of Greek language and culture; fourthly, the full assimilation of orientalized Greeks and Hellenized Orientals. Lack of women was one reason why mixed marriages could not always be avoided in the new military settlements and newly-founded cities. However, full assimilation was a rare exception, at least in the early part of the third century. We most frequently encounter assimilation of orientals, but, viewing the population as a whole, it does not usually affect broad classes of people. A real interpenetration first occurs in the Roman period."

[44] Hengel, "The Interpenetration of Judaism and Hellenism in the Pre-Maccabean Period," 183.

[45] Mathias Delcor, "Jewish Literature in Hebrew and Aramaic in the Greek era," in W. D. Davies and Louis Finkelstein, eds., *The Cambridge History of Judaism*, Vol. I (Cambridge: Cambridge University Press, 1984) 355–56.

[46] Alan E. Samuel, *From Athens to Alexandria: Hellenism and Social Goals in Ptolemaic Egypt* (Louvain: Imprimerie Orientaliste, 1983) 114. The individual could choose which system of law and associated courts to utilize.

intermingling on either side.[47] The Egyptians went about their religious, literary, artistic, and legal activities mainly unaffected by Greek customs in these matters;[48] the Greeks largely did the same.[49] These conclusions are in contrast to a typical kind of argument exemplified by Momigliano, who felt that "Egyptian culture declined during the Hellenistic period because it was under the direct control of the Greeks and came to represent an inferior stratum of the population."[50] As one Egyptologist has pointed out, this view of the period carries the assumption that, once Alexander and his successors moved in, native culture lost its independence and any changes that occurred in it from that point on are to be explained as "degeneration or foreign influence."[51]

Hengel in his own investigation of the notion of "Hellenism" or "Hellenistic" culture has suggested these very labels, in their academic origin, imply notions of a world culture and unified civilization which do not accurately reflect the desires or the realities of the time. The Hegelian concept of a synthesis of East and West does not in fact describe the

---

[47] Alan E. Samuel, *The Shifting Sands of History: Interpretations of Ptolemaic Egypt* (Lanham, MD: University Press of America, 1989) 9.

[48] Samuel, *The Shifting Sands of History*, 46. See also Samuel, *From Athens to Alexandria*, 107–117. The corpus of Demotic texts, much still untranslated, is extensive (109). The bureaucracy continued to make use of native officials (111), even at the higher levels, as did the army and police forces. For similar views cf. Janet Johnson, "Is the Demotic Chronicle an Anti-Greek Text?" in H. J. Thissen and K. T. Zauzich, eds., *Grammata Demotika, Festschrift für Erich Lüddeckens zum 15. Juni 1983* (Würzburg: Gisela Zauzich Verlag, 1984) 119–120.

[49] Samuel, *The Shifting Sands of History*, 45–46. "While the notion of 'syncretism' of Greek and Oriental themes in religion is hard a-dying, the evidence goes very much against it...." (46). The Greeks, as always, were willing to accept new gods, but their religious practice and treatment of them was still Hellenic.

[50] Arnaldo Momigliano, *Alien Wisdom: The Limits of Hellenization* (Cambridge: Cambridge University Press, 1975) 3–4. For an argument against this kind of approach and a pointed analysis of assumptions in scholarship regarding this era, see Robert K. Ritner, "Implicit Models of Cross-Cultural Interaction: A Question of Noses, Soap, and Prejudice," in Janet H. Johnson, ed., *Life in a Multi-Cultural Society: Egypt from Cambyses to Constantine and Beyond* (Chicago: The Oriental Institute, 1992) 283–90 (he also quotes Momigliano on page 284).

[51] Ritner, "Implicit Models of Cross-Cultural Interaction: A Question of Noses, Soap, and Prejudice," 284. He also denies that Egyptian culture was somehow in a "pure" and untouched state as far as interaction with foreign cultures before the Greeks, and holds up the Semitic influences in the military, religious, and literary spheres in the New Kingdom as an example. He remarks that scholars regularly confuse cultural "vitality" with cultural "purity" (285).

nature of the contacts between the different Near Eastern cultures of the late first millennium BCE. The idea is instead a template that became, and continues to be, popular among modern scholars who study this period of history. The closest ancient worldview that can be found to fit the template is that of the Romans, which is to say a good two centuries after the conquests of Alexander the Great at the least. Hengel notes that the word "hellenizein" referred not to cultural assimilation, but to use of the Greek language, no more and no less. While use of a culture's language may open doors into other aspects of its traditions, it does not allow one to make assumptions regarding the extent of cultural influence. As Delcor points out, the language of choice in Judea continued to be Hebrew, which suggests further caution about making assumptions with regard to the amount of interest a Judean Jew would have in Greek attitudes, philosophies, and literatures. Similarly in Egypt, Demotic continued to be an active and vital language. No doubt there was exposure to Greek views in both cultures, but the extent and nature of it is not a given and the fact that a Jewish or Egyptian text is written after Alexander does not in itself say much about whether it is going to reflect Greek influence.

Part of the difficulty is related to the very term "Hellenistic." Scholars have agreed for purposes of mutual understanding to label the period from Alexander the Great through Roman hegemony as "the Hellenistic Era." This is fair enough. Historians are well aware of the fact that these labels are not precise and that movements and conditions of the period in question did not turn on and then turn off on the given dates. However, this particular label may be a problem. The confusion lies in the fact that the word consists of a root, *hellen*, that designates that which is "Greek." Moreover, although it properly refers only to Greek language, the label naturally lends itself to taking in Greek traditions, mores, and civilization as a whole. But this chapter's argument, based on the preceding chapters of the book, is that the time period in question is not properly described as essentially "Hellenistic" if this is taken to mean "Greek," in the sense of Greek civilization arriving on the scene and proceeding to sow its cultural seed far and wide. That Greek culture affected and was affected by those of the rest of the Mediterranean and Near East is unquestionable, but it is not clear that it dominated them, nor that it was the fundamental and primary source of the political, social, and religious changes that appeared across the area.

In short, the period under discussion may not be, literally, *Hellen*istic. By using such terminology, one is subtly and understandably led to regard the period as a time to be characterized as Greek in nature, and this affects one's assumptions in the course of study. In an admittedly simplistic formulation of the problem, it becomes easy to move along the following equation: here is a text written in the Hellenistic Era, thus the text is Hellenistic (*hellen*-like), thus the text can be read in light of assumed likely Greek influence of greater or lesser degree. This is not to say that distinct and often parallel changes were not taking place in the political systems, cultures, economies, and religions of the Mediterranean and Near East, but that it is not the case that the scholar should turn to Greece as the primary cause. Yet the very terminology used in the study of the time already colors expectations. It would be less prejudicial to use a label that does not inherently suggest that Greece was the heart of the changes experienced in the Near East in this time, though tradition no doubt will preserve the usage. Just as a parallel is not necessarily an influence (although it *may* reflect influence), writings from the last centuries of the the final millennium BCE, in spite of the nomenclature "Hellenistic," are not necessarily Greek in nature (though some *may*, and do, reveal Greek ideas).

An investigation of the word "Hellenistic" actually yields interesting insights into modern critical study. When Droysen's expression *Hellenismus* entered the academic scene a century and a half ago, and subsequently the new term "Hellenistic," "the concepts attached to this term and the new period were similar to those which had emerged as part of the ideology of colonialism and imperialism: the carrying of the rationalism of advanced civilization to the more primitive; the spread of more progressive governmental forms; the gift of technology to those unfamiliar with it; the quickening of economic activity in areas long sluggish or dormant; the enjoyment and adaptation of the exotic art forms of the easterners by the west."[52] The events and attitudes of the mid-nineteenth century world in which the scholars of this new field of study lived also appear in the approach they took to the time period known as Hellenistic. Just as the modern West was exploring and spreading through Eastern cultures of the day, presumably bringing them an advanced way of life and uniting the worlds into a greater one, so did it happen when Alexander swept through the Near East many centuries earlier and inaugurated a new age where Greek culture penetrated the old civilizations and bound all into a new, Hellenistic world. This original understanding of the Hellenistic period no longer holds the full allegiance of the academy. "No longer can we assert confidently that the world which Alexander opened to the Greeks provided an opportunity for

---

[52] Samuel, *The Shifting Sands of History*, 1.

Hellenism to blend with many local cultures to create a new and universal culture for the Mediterranean."[53] Nevertheless, the reigning view has had many decades to become ingrained, and it retains a subtle but tenacious hold.

This discussion of the Hellenistic period has two consequences for the study of the material at hand, and more generally, for the study of all pre-turn of the era Jewish and Egyptian materials. The first is that, if Alexander did not inaugurate a syncretistic world culture in which Hellas and the Orient merged with one another, then it is not safe to assume that a text written after 332 BCE, whether Jewish, Egyptian, or something else, can be explained in terms of Greek ideas, worldview, writings, etc. This is true for Qoheleth and the late Egyptian biographies in particular, and the study of the time period in general. Secondly, traditional academic interest in Alexander and his heirs as the watershed stage in late Near Eastern religion may be overshadowing an equally significant time beforehand, when one by one the cultures of the region were losing their native kings, or suffering other forms of societal pressure as the nature of kingship was affected by outside assumption, and thus having to address new circumstances and needs. Qoheleth may plausibly have been written in the Persian period. His problem is equally understandable if the text originated in the fifth, fourth, or third centuries. Of the three Egyptian biographies used for comparison, one is probably from the seventh century, one from the time when Persian hegemony in Egypt shifted to Greek, and one from the end of Greek rule.

In sum, a person's understanding of, first, the nature of the Hellenistic age itself, and second, its role in the wider time frame of the last several hundred years BCE in the Near East, are going to affect one's basic premises for approaching materials from this stretch of time. The argument here is not an attempt to denigrate the importance of the Hellenistic period, but to expand the horizon under consideration. The era after Alexander's conquests plays an important part in a time frame of power shifts in which Near Eastern civilizations were losing and/or reinterpreting their traditional cultural systems, and when classical Greece began to disintegrate; however, it is a part of the watershed, not the whole. In the case of one particular manifestation of the resulting

---

[53] Samuel, *The Shifting Sands of History*, 10. The evidence rather leads to a picture of a diversity of non-homogenized cultures, he adds. Ritner, "Implicit Models of Cross-Cultural Interaction: A Question of Noses, Soap, and Prejudice," 286, adds his voice to the argument.

religious ferment, the problem of death, it seems that it started to arise for Jews and Egyptians alike before Alexander.

THE ZEITGEIST

Sometimes scholars speak of a "Hellenistic Zeitgeist," and if the adjective is dropped, "Zeitgeist" is a useful way of describing the situation where the cultures of the period were sharing in mutual shifts in political, social, and religious structures which resulted in attitudes and writings that share a great deal of similarity. It should be applied to a broader swath of history so as to take in the preceding two or three centuries. With respect to the Egyptian situation, Miriam Lichtheim talks about the new outlook of the *Hellenistic* world, which she sums up as "the quest for salvation," and adds "it was an age of spiritual distress and of groping for new answers."[54] Again, the only quibble is that the description need not be restricted to the time after Alexander, but applies to the foregoing centuries when societies were already experiencing the impact of foreign domination. She goes on to describe the Late Period biographies as a whole, and it should be noted that these include those before the Hellenistic era. She says that they are "subtly different from the attitudes of the past," because they are less optimistic about life. They do not assume, as in the past, that a righteous way of life will bring success. Success and contentment depend now on the will of the gods alone, and moreover, those same gods are inscrutable.[55] In a few

---

[54] Miriam Lichtheim, *Ancient Egyptian Literature: A Book of Readings*, 3 Vols. (Berkeley: University of California Press, 1973, 1976, 1980) III:4. This comment comes in the introduction to her final volume of translations which date to the Late Period.

[55] Lichtheim, *Ancient Egyptian Literature*, III:5. She makes similar comments about the later Egyptian world view in general in "Observations on Papyrus Insinger," in Erik Hornung and Othmar Keel, eds., *Studien zu altägyptischen Lebenslehren* (Freiburg, Schweiz: Universitätsverlag: Göttingen: Vandenhoeck & Ruprecht, 1979) 293–94: "[The Egyptian's] experience of the rightness and benevolence of this all-embracing order had been conceptualized in the term Maat; and he had deeply felt that living in accordance with the divinely established order was doing right and disturbing it was evil. But when there had been sufficient experience with disorder and suffering the Egyptian developed the notion, though not the term, of the reversal of fortune. Both Any and Amenemope dwelled on it, and Amenemope attributed it explicitly to the inscrutable designs of the god, who 'tears down and builds up' (Amenemope 24/15). In the Late Period the concept of Maat had been narrowed to meaning 'truth' and 'justice,' and the universal order was now viewed as depending directly on the actions of the gods."

biographies, the differences from past attitudes are quite unsubtle, and the muted tone to be found in general in the Late Period gives way to an anguished claim that death is an omnipotent force that abolishes the traditional Egyptian ways of establishing the coherence of existence.

Lichtheim later makes a very interesting comment right at the end of her discussion of the Late Period. She is speaking about Papyrus Insinger, which was discussed in chapter six, and the fact that it emphasizes endurance, acceptance of whatever happens, and the feeling that the unfathomable will of the gods is expressed through the vicissitudes of fortune. She concludes:

> Greeks and Egyptians alike were participating in, and being transformed by, the currents of Hellenistic universalism, syncretism, and pessimism which were undermining all the polytheistic cultures of the Mediterranean world and paving the way for the new gospel of the kingdom of heaven.[56]

This is a recognition that something of a broader nature was taking place in this era than simple influence, something that affected Greeks and Egyptians alike and, in an even wider realm, the traditional modes of religiosity in many cultures. The insight is not unlike Smith's. The phrasing is still tied to the notion of the post-Alexandrine period as the locus of the changes, and again, one should point out here that while such changes may be most evident in the age of Alexander's successors, their roots go back to before this time.[57] Another scholar, commenting more

---

[56] Lichtheim, *Ancient Egyptian Literature*, III:10. One could add that these currents were also paving the way for gnostic religions, Rabbinic Judaism, new philosophies, etc.

[57] That a key problem for Egypt and Judah both was based on the state of the kingship was suggested by Samuel K. Eddy, *The King is Dead: Studies in Near Eastern Resistance to Hellenism 334–31 B.C.* (Lincoln: University of Nebraska Press, 1961), whose thesis was that the end of native kingship in the Near East was the prime cause of the resistance to Hellenic overlords. Eddy has a valid insight in that the loss of the kingship was central to the upheavals of the era, though again the focus on the Hellenistic period does not go back far enough. The upheavals of 334–31 were not *caused* by the arrival of Alexander; they go back to when the native kings actually fell, and then they continued in the Hellenistic period. Some of his specific analyses need to be regarded with caution, such as the belief that a deep racial hatred existed between Egyptians and Greeks (257), or that Greek law ousted the Egyptian (311). See also Jørgen Podemann Sørensen, "Native Reactions to Foreign Rule and Culture in Religious Literature," in Per Bilde et al, eds., *Ethnicity in Hellenistic Egypt* (Aarhus: Aarhus University Press, 1992) 164–81, for a study of how Egyptians responded to foreign rule.

generally on the nature and conditions of any historical breakthrough, not just the emergence of Christianity to which Lichtheim refers, says that a new message must provide meaning in a set of circumstances "that has rendered the old ways impracticable."[58]

Similarly, the Second Temple period in Judah could also be described as a time of "groping for new answers." Without temple and king, the Jews were in a precarious position to say the least, and though they rebuilt the temple, their situation would never be like it was before the Exile. God was viewed as removed from events, as more transcendent,[59] and the feeling of a gap between humanity and God grew intense; this led to "a real change in attitudes to the structure of the cosmos.... [which] is the dual transformation of the perceptions of time and of space...."[60] The sensation of God's distance created a feeling of cosmic aporia, and this required cosmic redemption.[61] This at least was one response to the new existential situation. For some, however, the turn to cosmic redemption was not temperamentally possible. Thus, like some of the Egyptian biographies, Qoheleth is left with the conclusion that death abolishes his tradition's understanding of continuity. One scholar makes a perceptive comment when he says of Qoheleth that he "is reflecting on problems which are being raised in different parts of the world during the fifth, fourth, and third centuries B.C."[62]

---

[58] Eric Weil, "What is a Breakthrough in History?" *Daedalus* 104(1975) 28. He later adds (30) that in these situations the goal is to find "a new meaning for human life and the world after the failure of an older meaning. The divinities of the City have been defeated, the rites have shown themselves ineffective, the moral ideals and ideas have become inapplicable in a radically changed situation...."

[59] Michael E. Stone, "Eschatology, Remythologization, and Cosmic Aporia," in S. N. Eisenstadt, ed., *The Origins and Diversity of Axial Age Civilizations* (Albany: State University of New York Press, 1986) 246.

[60] Stone, "Eschatology, Remythologization, and Cosmic Aporia," 248. At the same time, the torah became a written tradition, and the center of power for religious learning shifted from the priests to a variety of groups who competed for exegetical authority (241–44). The shift to a new kind of elite was "inextricably entwined with the profound changes in the intellectual and religious world-view" (251).

[61] Stone, "Eschatology, Remythologization, and Cosmic Aporia," 249.

[62] Ernest Horton Jr., "Koheleth's Concept of Opposites," *Numen* 19(1972) 21. See also Christoph Uehlinger, "Qohelet im Horizont mesopotamischer, levantinischer und ägyptischer Weisheitsliteratur der persischen und hellenistischen Zeit," in Ludger Schwienhorst-Schoenberger, ed., *Das Buch Kohelet: Studien zur Struktur, Geschichte, Rezeption und Theologie* (Berlin: Walter de Gruyter, 1997) 1–2, 57–58, who from a somewhat different angle, not that of time period but of

The problem of death, along with many related questions, such as the individual's place in the world, relation to humanity or nation or ethnic group, position with respect to the divine, moral responsibilities, and purpose in life, would become a point of debate amongst a number of peoples, and many answers to it were offered. Later in Egyptian tradition, Egyptian gnostics would compose a dualistic Hermetic work, "Asclepius," in which one learns that there will be a time:

> ....when Egyptians will seem to have served the divinity in vain, and all their activity in religion will be despised. For all divinity will leave Egypt and will flee upward to heaven. And Egypt will be widowed; it will be abandoned by the Gods. For foreigners will come into Egypt, and they will rule it. Egypt! And in that day the country that was more pious than all countries will become impious. No longer will it be full of temples, but it will be full of tombs. Neither will it be full of gods, but it will be full of corpses. O Egypt! [63]

Death here is the image which portrays the complete destruction of Egyptian religion. Tomb replaces temple, corpse replaces god.[64] On the

---

cultural analogies, argues that scholars should stop trying to understand Qoheleth merely within either the Israelite wisdom tradition or the sphere of Greek philosophy, but should consider the "third horizon," that of other Near Eastern literatures.

[63] Daniel McBride, "The Egyptian-Gnostic View of Death," in Sara E. Orel, ed., *Death and Taxes in the Ancient Near East* (Lewiston, NY: The Edwin Mellen Press, 1992) 132. His text citation is VI, 8.70.2, from James M. Robinson ed., *The Nag Hammadi Library in English*, trans. James Brashler, Peter A. Dirkse, and Douglas M. Parrot (Leiden: E. J. Brill, 1988) 330. McBride remarks "It is clear that over seven hundred years of foreign occupation in the Nile valley prior to the rise of the Gnostic movement can be expected to have had a rather profound watershed effect upon the Egyptian psyche, in large part perhaps explaining the the rise of dualist cosmologies that were still essentially 'Egyptian' in their outlook."

[64] Hans Dieter Betz, ed., *The Greek Magical Papyri in Translation, Including the Demotic Spells* (Chicago: University of Chicago Press, 1986) xlvi–xlvii, makes the interesting point that the magical papyri, which come from Greco-Roman Egypt and include Greek and Demotic spells alike, focus extensively on the underworld and its deities. He says "human life seems to consist of nothing but negotiations in the antechamber of death and the world of the dead.... In other words, there is a consensus that the best way to success and worldly pleasures is by using the underworld, death, and the forces of death" (xlvii). This stance towards death and the dead regards it as a powerful cosmic principle which one must bargain with and manipulate in order to achieve one's aims. Unlike Qoheleth or the late biographies, and Taimhotep's poem on death as something that is utterly uncontrollable comes especially to mind, this mindset attempts to take hold of the forces of death and use them to one's own ends. A little further down the page Betz

brighter side, a different text[65] proclaims that someday:

> "The Enemy, on the contrary, Death, shall go to the chains, into the place of confinement of the souls of the liars and thieves, those who loved the Darkness."

The last quotation is similar to Paul's promise in I Corinthians 15:24–26

> Then comes the end, when he [Christ] hands over the kingdom to God the Father, after he has destroyed every ruler and every authority and power. For he must reign until he has put all his enemies under his feet. The last enemy to be destroyed is death.[66]

The idea that death is an enemy that will someday be destroyed for all time is a view of the world that is quite different from what one finds in either traditional Egyptian religion or the Hebrew Bible. A fundamental change in thinking has come about. Qoheleth and the Egyptian biographies do not come anywhere near this kind of worldview; what they show is the early signs that the traditional responses to death are beginning to break down for some. They do not claim to be abandoned by their gods, nor do they treat death as a cosmic principle of evil, but they stand at a crossroads which led to many paths, some to gnostic movements, some to Pauline Christianity, some to Rabbinic Judaism, and many other possibilities as well. Death had escaped from its lair and had to be re-tamed, and in time, it was. But then, as now, its bonds never seem very secure.

---

remarks that the magician at this time, in his religious function, was able to reassure people that "he could make things work in a world where nothing seemed to work the way it used to..... While other people could no longer make sense of the old religions, he was able to."

[65] McBride, "The Egyptian-Gnostic View of Death," 135. The text is from the *Kephalia*, chapter 66, "Concerning the Envoy," 165.

[66] From the NRSV.

Bibliography

Albertz, Rainer. *A History of Israelite Religion in the Old Testament Period*, Vols. I-II. Louisville, KY: Westminster/John Knox Press, 1994.

Allen, James P. "Funerary Texts and Their Meaning." In *Mummies and Magic: The Funerary Arts of Ancient Egypt*, ed. Sue D'Auria et al., 38-49. Boston: Museum of Fine Arts, 1988).

Anderson, William H. U. *Qoheleth and Its Pessimistic Theology: Hermeneutical Struggles in Wisdom Literature*. Lewiston: Mellen Press, 1997.

Andrews, Carol. "Introduction." In R. O. Faulkner, *The Ancient Egyptian Book of the Dead*, 11-16. Austin: The University of Texas Press, 1993.

Assmann, Jan. "Death and Initiation in the Funerary Religion of Ancient Egypt." In *Religion and Philosophy in Ancient Egypt*, ed. William Kelly Simpson, 135-159. New Haven: Yale University Press, 1989.

_____. *Egyptian Solar Religion in the New Kingdom: Re, Amun and the Crisis of Polytheism*. Translated by Anthony Alcock. London and New York: Kegan Paul International, 1995.

_____. "Fest des Augenblicks—Verheissung der Dauer: Die Kontroverse der ägyptischen Harfnerlieder." In *Fragen an die altägyptische Literatur: Studien zum Gedenken an Eberhard Otto*, ed. Jan Assmann et al., 55-84. Wiesbaden: Dr. Ludwig Reichert, 1977.

_____. "Schrift, Tod und Identität: Das Grab als Vorschule der Literatur im alten Ägypten." In *Schrift und Gedächtnis: Beiträge zur Archäologie der literarischen Kommunikation*, ed. Aleida Assmann, 64-93. Munich: Wilhelm Fink, 1983.

_____. "State and Religion in the New Kingdom." In *Religion and Philosophy in Ancient Egypt*, ed. William Kelly Simpson, 55-88. New Haven, Yale University Press, 1989.

_____. *Stein und Zeit: Mensch und Gesellschaft im alten Ägypten*. Munich: Wilhelm Fink, 1991.

Bagnall, Roger S. "Greeks and Egyptians: Ethnicity, Status, and Culture." In *Cleopatra's Egypt: Age of the Ptolemies*, ed. Robert S. Bianchi, 21-27. Brooklyn: Brooklyn Museum, 1988.

Bailey, Lloyd R. *Biblical Perspectives on Death*. Philadelphia: Fortress Press, 1979.

_____. "Death as a Theological Problem in the Old Testment." *Pastoral Psychology* 22 (1971): 20-32.

Baines, John. "Society, Morality, and Religious Practice." In *Religion in Ancient Egypt: Gods, Myths, and Personal Practice*, ed. Byron E. Shafer, 123-200. Ithaca, NY: Cornell University Press, 1991.

Barr, James. *The Semantics of Biblical Language*. Oxford: Oxford University Press, 1961.

Barton, George A. *The Book of Ecclesiastes*. New York: Charles Scribner's Sons, 1908.

Becker, Ernst. *The Denial of Death*. New York: The Free Press, 1973.

Bergman, Jan. "Introductory Remarks on Apocalypticism in Egypt." In *Apocalypticism in the Mediterranean World and the Near East: Proceedings of the International Colloquium on Apocalypticism, Uppsala, August 12-17, 1979*, ed. David Hellholm, 51-60. Tübingen: J. C. B. Mohr, 1983)

Bernand, E. *Inscriptions métriques de l'Égypte greco-romaine*. Paris: Belles Lettres, 1969.

Betz, Hans Dieter, ed. *The Greek Magical Papyri in Translation, Including the Demotic Spells*. Chicago: University of Chicago Press, 1986.

Bevan, Edwyn. *A History of Egypt under the Ptolemaic Dynasty*. London: Methuen & Co., Ltd., 1927.

Bianchi, Robert. "The Cultural Transformations of Egypt as Suggested by a Group of Enthroned Male Figures from the Faiyum." In *Life in a Multi-Cultural Society: Egypt from Cambyses to Constantine and Beyond*, ed. Janet H. Johnson, 15-39. Chicago: The Oriental Institute, 1992.

_____ et al. *Cleopatra's Egypt: Age of The Ptolemies*. New York: The Brooklyn Museum, 1988.

Bickerman, Elias. *Four Strange Books of the Bible*. New York: Schocken Books, 1967.

Blank, S. H. "Prolegomenon." In Christian D. Ginsburg, *The Song of Songs and Coheleth (Commonly Called the Book of Ecclesiastes)*. Reprint, New York: Ktav Publishing House, Inc., 1970.

Blenkinsopp, Joseph. "Ecclesiastes 3.1-15: Another Interpretation." *Journal for the Study of the Old Testament* 66 (1995): 55-64.

Bloch-Smith, Elizabeth. "The Cult of the Dead in Judah: Interpreting the Material Remains." *Journal of Biblical Literature* 111 (1992): 213-224.

_____. *Judahite Burial Practices and Beliefs about the Dead*. Sheffield: Journal for the Study of the Old Testament Press, 1992.

Bowker, John. *The Meanings of Death*. Cambridge: Cambridge University Press, 1991.

Bowman, Alan K. *Egypt after the Pharaohs: 332 BC–AD 642, from Alexander to the Arab Conquest*. California: The University of California Press, 1986.

Braun, Rainer. *Kohelet und die frühhellenistische Popularphilosophie*. Berlin: Walter de Gruyter, 1973.

Bream, Howard N. "Life Without Resurrection: Two Perspectives From Qoheleth." In *A Light Unto My Path (Jacob M. Myers Festschrift)*, ed. H. N. Bream et al., 49-65. Philadelphia: Temple University Press, 1974.

Breasted, James Henry. *The Dawn of Conscience*. New York: Charles Scribner's Sons, 1933.

_____. *Development of Religion and Thought in Ancient Egypt*. New York: Charles Scribner's Sons, 1912. Reprint, New York: Harper & Row, 1959.

Bremer, Jan N. "The Soul, Death and the Afterlife in Early and Classical Greece." In *Hidden Futures: Death and Immortality in Ancient Egypt, Anatolia, the Classical, Biblical and Arabic-Islamic World*, ed. J. M. Bremer et al., 91-106. Amsterdam: Amsterdam University Press, 1994.

Brenton, Sir Lancelot C. L. *The Septuagint with Apocrypha: Greek and English*. London: Samuel Bagster & Sons, 1851. Reprint, Grand Rapids, MI: Zondervan, 1983.

Brichto, Herbert C. "Kin, Cult, Land and Afterlife—A Biblical Complex." *Hebrew Union College Annual* 44 (1973): 1-54.

Brown, Francis, S. R. Driver, and Charles A. Briggs. *The New Brown-Driver-Briggs-Gesenius Hebrew and English Lexicon*. Peabody, MA: Hendrickson Publishers, 1979.

Brugsch, H. K. *Thesaurus Inscriptionum Aegyptiacarum*, 6 parts. Leipzig: J. C. Hinrichs, 1883-1891. Reprint, 1965.

Burkitt, F. C. "Is Ecclesiastes a Translation?" *Journal of Theological Studies* 23 (1921-22).

Camp, Claudia. *Wisdom and the Feminine in the Book of Proverbs*. Sheffield: Journal for the Study of the Old Testament Press, 1985.

Campbell, Ernest Q. "Death as a Social Practice." In *Perspectives on Death*, ed. L. O. Mills, 209-230. Nashville: Abingdon, 1969.

Carse, James P. *Death and Existence: A Conceptual History of Human Mortality*. New York: John Wiley & Sons, 1980.

Cerny, Jaroslav. *Ancient Egyptian Religion*. London: William Brendon and Son, 1952.

Charles, R. H. *A Critical History of the Doctrine of a Future Life*. London: Black, 1913.

Charlesworth, James H., ed. *The Old Testament Pseudepigrapha*, Vols. I & II. New York: Doubleday, 1983.

Chilton, Bruce D. "'Not to Taste Death': A Jewish, Christian and Gnostic Usage." In *Studia Biblica 1978: II. Papers on the Gospels*, ed. E. A. Livingstone, 29-36. Sheffield: Journal for the Study of the Old Testament Press Press, 1980.

Choron, Jacques. *Death and Western Thought*. New York: Collier Books, 1963.

Cohen, A., trans. *Midrash Rabbah: Ecclesiastes*. London: Soncino Press, 1939.

Collins, John J. "Apocalyptic Eschatology as the Transcendence of Death." *Catholic Biblical Quarterly* 36 (1974): 21-43.

_____. *The Apocalyptic Imagination: An Introduction to the Jewish Matrix of Christianity*. New York: Crossroad, 1989.

_____. *Between Athens and Jerusalem: Jewish Identity in the Hellenistic Diaspora*. New York: Crossroad, 1983.

_____. "Cosmos and Salvation: Jewish Wisdom and Apocalyptic in the Hellenistic Age." *History of Religions* 17 (1977): 121-142.

_____. *Daniel*. Minnneapolis: Fortress Press, 1993.

_____. *Jewish Wisdom in the Hellenistic Age*. Louisville: Westminster John Knox Press, 1997.

_____. "Proverbial Wisdom and the Yahwist Vision." *Semeia* 17 (1980): 1-17.

_____. *Proverbs-Ecclesiastes*. Atlanta: John Knox Press, 1980.

_____. "The Root of Immortality: Death in the Context of Jewish Wisdom." *Harvard Theological Review* 71 (1978): 177-192.

_____. "Sibylline Oracles." In Vol. 1, *The Old Testament Pseudepigrapha*, ed. James H. Charlesworth, 317-473. New York: Doubleday, 1983.

_____. "Wisdom, Apocalypticism, and Generic Compatibility." In *In Search of Wisdom: Essays in Memory of John G. Gammie*, ed. Leo G. Perdue et al., 165-85. Louisville, KY: Westminster/John Knox Press, 1993.

Cosser, William. "The Meaning of 'Life' in Prov., Job and Ecc." *Glasgow University Oriental Society Transactions* (15): 48-53.

Crawford, Dorothy. "Ptolemy, Ptah and Apis in Hellenistic Memphis." In *Studies on Ptolemaic Memphis*, ed. Dorothy Crawford, et al., 1-42. Leuven: [s.n.], 1980.

Crenshaw, James L. *Ecclesiastes: A Commentary*. Philadelphia: The Westminster Press, 1987.

_____. *Old Testament Wisdom: An Introduction*. Atlanta: John Knox Press, 1981.

_____. "Popular Questioning of the the Justice of God in Ancient Israel." In *Studies in Ancient Israelite Wisdom*, ed. James L. Crenshaw, 289-304. New York: Ktav Publishing House, 1976.

_____. "Qoheleth in Current Research." In *Hebrew Annual Review*. Vol. 7, *Biblical and Other Studies in Honor of Robert Gordis*, ed. Reuben Ahroni, 41-56. Ohio: Ohio State University, 1983.

_____."Qoheleth's Understanding of Intellectual Inquiry." In *Qohelet in the Context of Wisdom*, ed. Antoon Schoors, 205-24. Leuven: Leuven University Press, 1998.

_____. "The Shadow of Death in Qoheleth." In *Israelite Wisdom: Theological and Literary Essays in Honor of Samuel Terrien*, ed. John G. Gammie, 205-216. New York: Scholars Press, 1978.

_____, ed. *Studies in Ancient Israelite Wisdom*. New York: Ktav Publishing House, 1976.

_____, ed. *Theodicy in the Old Testament*. Philadelphia: Fortress Press, 1983.

_____. *A Whirlpool of Torment*. Philadelphia: Fortress Press, 1984.

Crüsemann, Frank. "The Unchangeable World: The 'Crisis of Wisdom' in Koheleth." In *God of the Lowly: Socio-Historical Interpretations of the Bible*, ed. Willy Schottroff and Wolfgang Stegemann, 57-77. Maryknoll, NY: Orbis Books, 1984.

Dahood, Mitchell. *Psalms*, 3 Vols. Garden City, NY: Doubleday, 1966-1970.

Davis, Barry C. "Ecclesiastes 12:1-8—Death, and Impetus for Life." *Bibliotheca Sacra* 148 (1991): 298-318.

de Jong, Stephan. "God in the Book of Qohelet: A Reappraisal of Qohelet's Place in Old Testament Theology." *Vetus Testamentum* 47 (1997): 154-67.

Delcor, Mathias. "Jewish Literature in Hebrew and Aramaic in the Greek Era." In Vol. 1, *The Cambridge History of Judaism*, ed. W. D. Davies and Louis Finkelstein, 352-384. Cambridge: Cambridge University Press, 1984.

Delitzsch, F. *Biblischer Commentar IV, Hoheslied und Koheleth*. Leipzig: 1875. Reprint, *Commentary on the Song of Songs and Ecclesiastes*. Grand Rapids: Eerdmans, 1982.

Derchain, Philippe. "Death in Egyptian Religion." In Vol. 1, *Mythologies*, ed. Yves Bonnefoy, 111-115. Chicago: The University of Chicago Press, 1991.

Devauchelle, Didier. "De l'originalité des sagesses égyptiennes tardives du IVe siècle avant au Ier siècle après J.-C." In *La sagesse biblique: De l'Ancien au Nouveau Testament*, ed. Jacques Trublet, 217-228. Paris: Cerf, 1995.

Di Lella, Alexander. "Conservative and Progressive Theology: Sirach and Wisdom." *Catholic Biblical Quarterly* 28 (1966): 139-54.

Dodds, E. R. *Pagan and Christian in an Age of Anxiety: Some Aspects of Religious Experience from Marcus Aurelius to Constantine*. Cambridge: Cambridge University Press, 1965.

Eddy, Samuel K. *The King is Dead: Studies in Near Eastern Resistance to Hellenism 334-31 BC*. Lincoln: University of Nebraska Press, 1961.

Eichhorn, David. *Musings of the Old Professor: The Meaning of Koheles*. New York: Jonathan David, 1963.

Eisenstadt, S. N. "Introduction: The Axial Age Breakthroughs—Their Characteristics and Origins." In *The Origins and Diversity of Axial Age Civilizations*, ed. S. N. Eisenstadt, 1-25. Albany: State University of New York Press, 1986.

Elliger, K., and W. Rudolph, ed. *Biblia Hebraica Stuttgartensia*. Stuttgart: Deutsche Bibelgesellschaft, 1967.

Ellul, Jacques. *Reason for Being: A Meditation on Ecclesiastes*. Grand Rapids, MI: Eerdmans, 1990.

Englund, Gertie. "Gods as a Frame of Reference: On Thinking and Concepts of Thought in Ancient Egypt." In *The Religion of the Ancient Egyptians: Cognitive Structures and Popular Expressions*, ed. Gertie Englund, 7-28. Stockholm: Almqvist & Wiksell International, 1989.

Erman, Adolf. *The Ancient Egyptians: A Sourcebook of Their Writings*. New York: Harper and Row, 1966.

_____. "Zwei Grabsteine griechischer Zeit." In *Festschrift Eduard Sachau*, ed. Gotthold Weil, 103-112. Berlin: Georg Reimer, 1915.

_____ and Hermann Grapow. *Wörterbuch der Aegyptischen Sprache*, 7 Vols. Leipzig: J. C. Hinrichs'sche Buchhandlung, 1926-63.

Faulkner, R. O. *The Ancient Egyptian Book of the Dead*. Austin: The University of Texas Press, 1993.

_____. *The Ancient Egyptian Coffin Texts*, 3 Vols. Warminster: Aris & Phillips, Ltd., 1973, 1977, 1978.

_____. *The Ancient Egyptian Pyramid Texts*. Oxford: Oxford University Press, 1969.

_____. *A Concise Dictionary of Middle Egyptian*. Oxford: The Griffith Institute, 1988).

Finnestad, Ragnhild Bjerre. "The Pharaoh and the 'Democratization' of Post-mortem Life." In *The Religion of the Ancient Egyptians: Cognitive Structures and Popular Expressions*, ed. Gertie Englund, 89-93. Stockholm: Almqvist & Wiksell International, 1989.

Fishbane, Michael. *Biblical Interpretation in Ancient Israel*. New York: Oxford University Press, 1985.

Forman, Charles G. "The Pessimism of Ecclesiastes." *Journal of Semitic Studies* 3 (1958): 336-343.

Foster, John L. "The Hymn to Aten: Akhenaten Worships the Sole God." In Vol. III, *Civilizations of the Ancient Near East*, ed. Jack M. Sasson, 1751-1761. New York: Charles Scribner's Sons, 1995.

Fox, Michael V. "The Entertainment Song Genre in Egyptian Literature." In *Scripta Hierosolymitana*. Vol. XXVII, *Egyptological Studies*, ed. Sarah Israelit-Groll. Jerusalem: The Magnes Press, 1982.

_____. "Frame-Narrative and Composition in the Book of Qohelet." *Hebrew Union College Annual* 48 (1977): 83-106.

_____. "The Inner-Structure of Qohelet's Thought." In *Qohelet in the Context of Wisdom*, ed. Antoon Schoors, 225-38. Leuven: Leuven University Press, 1998.

_____. "Qoheleth 1.4." *Journal for the Study of the Old Testament* 40 (1988): 109.

_____. *Qohelet and His Contradictions*. Sheffield: The Almond Press, 1989.

_____. "A Study of Antef." *Orientalia* 46 (1977): 393-423.

_____. "Two Decades of Research in Egyptian Wisdom Literature." *Zeitschrift für Ägyptische Sprache und Altertumskunde* 107 (1980): 120-135.

_____. "Wisdom in Qoheleth." In *In Search of Wisdom*, ed. Leo G. Perdue, B. B. Scott, and W. J. Wiseman, 115-131. Louisville, KY: Westminster/John Knox Press, 1993.

Frankfort, H. *Ancient Egyptian Religion*. New York: Harper and Row, 1948.

Fredericks, Daniel C. *Coping with Transience: Ecclesiastes on Brevity in Life*. Sheffield: Journal for the Study of the Old Testament Press, 1993.

Fredericks, Daniel C. *Qoheleth's Language: Re-Evaluating Its Nature and Date*. Lewiston, NY: The Edwin Mellen Press, 1988.

Frymer-Kensky, Tikva. "The Planting of Man: A Study in Biblical Imagery." In *Love & Death in the Ancient Near East: Essays in Honor of Marvin H. Pope*, ed. John H. Marks and Robert M. Good, 129-136. Guilford, CT: Four Quarters Publishing Company, 1987.

Galling, Kurt. "Der Prediger." In *Die Fünf Megilloth*, ed. Ernst Würthwein, 73-125. Tübingen: J. C. B. Mohr [Siebeck], 1969.

Gammie, John G. "Spatial and Ethical Dualism in Jewish Wisdom and Apocalyptic Literature." *Journal of Biblical Literature* 93 (1974): 356-385.

_____. "Stoicism and Anti-Stoicism in Qoheleth." In *Hebrew Annual Review,* Vol. 9, *Biblical and Other Studies in Memory of S. D. Goitein,* ed. Reuben Ahroni, 169-187. Columbus: Ohio State University, 1986.

_____ and Leo G. Perdue, ed. *The Sage in Israel and the Ancient Near East.* Winona Lake: Eisenbrauns, 1990.

_____ et al., ed. *Israelite Wisdom: Theological and Literary Essays in Honor of Samuel Terrien* (New York: Scholars Press, 1978).

Gardiner, Alan H. *The Attitude of the Ancient Egyptians to Death and the Dead.* Cambridge: Cambridge University Press, 1935.

_____. *Egypt of the Pharoahs: An Introduction.* Oxford: Oxford University Press, 1961.

_____. *Egyptian Grammar,* 3rd edition. Oxford: Griffith Institute, 1957.

_____. and Kurt Sethe. *Egyptian Letters to the Dead, Mainly From the Old and Middle Kingdoms.* Oxford: Oxford University Press, 1928.

Garland, Robert. *The Greek Way of Death.* Ithaca, NY: Cornell University Press, 1985.

Gatch, Milton McC. *Death: Meaning and Mortality in Christian Thought and Contemporary Culture.* New York: Seabury Press, 1969.

Gemser, B. "The Instructions of 'Onchsheshonqy and Biblical Wisdom Literature." In *Supplements to Vetus Testamentum: Congress Volume VII.* Leiden: E. J. Brill, 1960.

Gese, Hartmut. "The Crisis of Wisdom in Koheleth." In *Theodicy in the Old Testament,* ed. James L. Crenshaw, 141-153. Philadelphia: Fortress Press, 1983.

Gilbert, M. "Wisdom Literature." In *Jewish Writings of the Second Temple Period* ed. M. E. Stone, 283-324. Philadelphia: Fortress Press, 1984.

Ginsberg, H. Lewis. "The Quintessence of Koheleth." In *Biblical and Other Studies,* ed. A. Altmann, 47-59. Cambridge: Harvard University Press, 1963.

_____. *Studies in Koheleth.* New York: Jewish Theological Seminary of America, 1950.

Ginsburg, Christian D. *The Song of Songs and Coheleth (Commonly Called the Book of Ecclesiastes).* Reprint, New York: Ktav Publishing House, Inc., 1970.

Glanville, S. R. K. *Catalogue of Demotic Papyri in the British Museum.* Volume II, *The Instructions of 'Onchsheshonqy.* London: Trustees of the British Museum, 1955.

Goedicke, Hans. "The Date of the 'Antef-Song.'" In *Fragen an die altägyptische Literatur: Studien zum Gedenken an Eberhard Otto,* 185-196. Wiesbaden: Dr. Ludwig Reichert Verlag, 1977.

_____. "A Neglected Wisdom Text." *Journal of Egyptian Archeology* 48 (1962): 25-35.

_____. *The Report About the Dispute of a Man with His Ba.* Baltimore: The Johns Hopkins Press, 1970.

Goff, Beatrice L. *Symbols of Ancient Egypt in the Late Period: The Twenty-First Dynasty*. The Hague: Mouton Publishers, 1979.

Gordis, Robert. "Koheleth—Hebrew or Aramaic." *Journal of Biblical Literature* 71 (1952): 93-109.

_____. *Koheleth—The Man and His World*. New York: Bloch Publishing Company, 1955.

_____. Gordis, Robert. "The Original Language of Qohelet." *Jewish Quarterly Review* 37 (1946-47): 67-84.

_____. "The Translation Theory of Qohelet Re-examined." *Jewish Quarterly Review* 40 (1949-50): 103-16.

Greenspoon, Leonard J. "The Origin of the Idea of Resurrection." In *Traditions in Transformation: Turning Points in Biblical Faith*, ed. Baruch Halpern and Jon D. Levenson. Winona Lake, IN: Eisenbrauns, 1981.

Greenstein, Edward L. "Autobiographies in Ancient Western Asia." In Vol. IV, *Civilizations of the Ancient Near East*, ed. Jack M. Sasson, 2421-2432. New York: Charles Scribner's Sons, 1995.

Griffiths, J. Gwyn. "Apocalypticism in the Hellenistic Era." In *Apocalypticism in the Mediterranean World and the Near East: Proceedings of the International Colloquium on Apocalypticism, Uppsala, August 12-17, 1979*, ed. David Hellholm, 273-293. Tübingen: J. C. B. Mohr, 1983.

_____. *The Divine Verdict: A Study of Divine Judgement in the Ancient Religions*. Leiden: E. J. Brill, 1991.

_____. "Egyptian Nationalism in the Edfu Temple Texts." In *Glimpses of Ancient Egypt*, ed. John Ruffle, 174-179. Warminster: Aris & Phillips, 1979.

_____. "Hellenistic Religions." In Vol. 6, *The Encyclopedia of Religion*, ed. Mircea Eliade, 252-266. New York: Macmillan Publishing Company, 1987.

_____. *Plutarch's De Iside et Osiride*. Cambridge: University of Wales Press, 1970.

Gualtieri, Antonio R. *The Vulture and the Bull: Religious Responses to Death* Lanham, MD: University Press of America, 1984.

Guksch, Heike. *Königsdienst: Zur Selbstdarstellung der Beamten in der 18. Dynastie*. Heidelberg: Heidelberger Orientverlag, 1994.

Gunn, Janet Varner. "Autobiography." In Vol. 2, *The Encyclopedia of Religion*, ed. Mircea Eliade, 7-11. New York: Macmillan Publishing Company, 1987.

Hall, H. R. *A General Introductory Guide to the Egyptian Collections in the British Museum*. London: Harrison and Sons, 1930.

Hayman, A.P. "Qohelet, the Rabbis, and the Wisdom Text from the Cairo Geniza." In *Understanding Poets and Prophets: Essays in Honour of George Wishart Anderson*, ed. A. Graeme Auld, 149-165. Sheffield: Journal for the Study of the Old Testament Press, 1993.

Hengel, Martin. "The Interpenetration of Judaism and Hellenism in the Pre-Maccabean Period." In Vol. 1, *The Cambridge History of Judaism*, ed. W. D. Davies and Louis Finkelstein, 167-228. Cambridge: Cambridge University Press, 1984.

_____. *Judaism and Hellenism: Studies in their Encounter in Palestine during the Early Hellenistic Period*, 2 Vols. Philadelphia: Fortress, 1974.

_____. "The Political and Social History of Palestine from Alexander to Antiochus III (333-187 BCE)." In Vol. 1, *The Cambridge History of Judaism*, ed. W. D. Davies and Louis Finkelstein, 35-78. Cambridge: Cambridge University Press, 1984.

Herrmann, Wolfram. "Human Mortality as a Problem in Ancient Israel." In *Religious Encounters with Death: Insights from the History and Anthropology of Religions*, ed. Frank E. Reynolds and Earle H. Waugh, 161-169. University Park, PA: The Pennsylvania State University Press, 1977.

Hertzberg, H. W. *Der Prediger*. Leipzig: A. Deichertsche Verlagsbuchhandlung D. Werner Scholl, 1932. Reprint, Gütersloh: G. Mohn, 1963.

Hirshman, Marc. "The Greek Fathers and the Aggada on Ecclesiastes: Formats of Exegesis in Late Antiquity." *Hebrew Union College Annual* 59 (1988): 137-165.

Holm-Nielsen, Svend. "On the Interpretation of Qoheleth in Early Christianity." *Vetus Testamentum* 24 (1974): 168-77.

Hooke, S. H. "Israel and the Afterlife." *Expository Times* 76 (1965): 236-39.

Hopkins, Thomas J. "Hindu Views of Death and Afterlife." In *Death and Afterlife: Perspectives of World Religions*, ed. Hiroshi Obayashi, 143-155. New York: Greenwood Press, 1992.

Hornung, Erik. "Ancient Egyptian Religious Iconography." In Vol. III, *Civilizations of the Ancient Near East*, ed. Jack M. Sasson, 1711-1730. New York: Charles Scribner's Sons, 1995.

_____. *Conceptions of God in Ancient Egypt: The One and the Many*. Translated by John Baines. Ithaca, NY: Cornell University Press, 1982.

Horton, Ernest Jr. "Koheleth's Concept of Opposites. *Numen* 19 (1972): 1-21.

Humbert, Paul. *Recherches sur les sources égyptiennes de la littérature sapientale d'Israël*. Neuchatel: Delachaux & Niestlé, 1929.

Humphreys, S. C. *The Family, Women, and Death: Comparative Studies*. London: Routledge & Kegan Paul, 1983.

_____ and Helen King, eds. *Mortality and Immortality: The Anthropology and Archaeology of Death*. London: Academic Press, 1981.

Humphreys, W. Lee. *The Tragic Vision and the Hebrew Tradition*. Philadelphia: Fortress Press, 1985.

Huss, Werner. "Some Thoughts on the Subject 'State' and 'Church' in Ptolemaic Egypt." In *Life in a Multi-Cultural Society: Egypt from Cambyses to Constantine and Beyond*, ed. Janet H. Johnson, 159-163. Chicago: The Oriental Institute, 1992.

Illman, Karl-Johan. *Old Testment Formulas About Death*. Abo: Abo Akademi, 1979.

Isaksson, Bo. *Studies in the Language of Qoheleth: With Special Emphasis on the Verbal System*. Stockholm: Almqvist & Wiksell International, 1987.

Jansen-Winkeln, Karl. *Ägyptische Biographien der 22. und 23. Dynastie*, 2 Vols. Wiesbaden: Otto Harrassowitz, 1985.

Japhet, Sara and Robert B. Salters. *The Commentary of R. Samuel Ben Meir Rashbam on Qoheleth*. Leiden: E. J. Brill, 1985.

Jasnow, Richard. *A Late Period Hieratic Wisdom Text (Papyrus Brooklyn 47.218.135)*. Chicago: The Oriental Institute, 1992.

Jastrow, Morris. *A Gentle Cynic*. Philadelphia: J. B. Lippincott Company, 1919.

Johnson, Aubrey R. *The One and the Many in the Israelite Conception of God*. Cardiff: University of Wales Press Board, 1942.

Johnson, Janet. "The Demotic Chronicle as a Statement of a Theory of Kingship." *Journal of the Society for the Study of Egyptian Antiquities* 13 (1983): 61-72.

_____. "The Demotic Chronicle as an Historical Source." *Enchoria* 4 (1974): 1-17.

_____. "Is the Demotic Chronicle an Anti-Greek Text?" In *Grammata Demotika, Festschrift für Erich Lüddeckens zum 15. Juni 1983*, ed. H. J. Thissen and K. T. Zauzich, 107-124. Würzburg: Gisela Zauzich Verlag, 1984.

_____. "The Role of the Egyptian Priesthood in Ptolemaic Egypt." In *Egyptological Studies in Honor of Richard A. Parker*, ed. Leonard H. Lesko, 70-84. Hanover, NH: University Press of New England.

_____ and Robert K. Ritner. "Multiple Meaning and Ambiguity in the 'Demotic Chronicle.'" In Vol. 1, *Studies in Egyptology: Presented to Miriam Lichtheim*, ed. Sarah Israelit-Groll, 494-506. Jerusalem: The Magnes Press, 1990.

Jones, Bruce William. "From Gilgamesh to Qoheleth." In *The Bible in the Light of Cuneiform Literature: Scripture in Context III*, ed. William W. Hallo et al., 349-379. Lewiston, NY: The Edwin Mellen Press, 1990.

Kaiser, Otto and Eduard Lohse, eds. *Death and Life*. Nashville: Abingdon, 1981.

Kákosy, László and Zoltán Imre Fábián. "Harper's Song in the Tomb of Djehutimes." *Studien zur Altägyptischen Kultur* 22 (1995): 211-225.

Kaminsky, Joel S. *Punishment Displacement in the Hebrew Bible*, 2 Vols. Ph.D. Diss., University of Chicago, 1993. Published as *Corporate Responsibility in the Hebrew Bible*. Sheffield: Sheffield Academic Press, 1995.

Kees, Hermann. "Die Lebensgrundsätze eines Amonspriesters der 22. Dynastie." *Zeitschrift für Ägyptische Sprache und Altertumskunde* 74 (1938): 73-87.

_____. "Zu den Lebensregeln des Amonspriesters Nebneteru (Kairo Cat. 42225)." *Zeitschrift für Ägyptische Sprache und Altertumskunde* 88 (1963): 24-26.

Kemp, Barry J. *Ancient Egypt: Anatomy of a Civilization*. New York: Routledge, 1989.

Kitchen, Kenneth A. "The Basic Literary Forms and Formulations of Ancient Instructional Writings in Egypt and Western Asia." In *Studien zu altägyptischen Lebenslehren*, ed. Erik Hornung and Othmar Keel., 235-282. Freiburg Schweiz: Universitätsverlag; Göttingen: Vandenhoeck & Ruprecht, 1979.

_____. *The Third Intermediate Period In Egypt*. Warminster: Aris & Phillips, 1973.

Knobel, Peter S. "The Targum of Qohelet." In *The Aramaic Bible: The Targums*, ed. Kevin Cathcart, Michael Maher, and Martin McNamara. Collegeville, MN: The Liturgical Press, 1991.

Kolarcik, Michael. *The Ambiguity of Death in the Book of Wisdom 1-6*. (Rome: Pontifical Biblical Institute, 1991.

Kristensen, W. Brede. *Life Out of Death: Studies in the Religions of Egypt and Ancient Greece*. Louvain: Peeters Press, 1992.

Kugel, James L. "Qohelet and Money." *Catholic Biblical Quarterly* 51 (1989): 32-49.

Kurtz, Donna C. and John Boardman. *Greek Burial Customs*. Ithaca, NY: Cornell University Press, 1971.

LaFleur, William R. "Biography." In Vol. 2, *The Encyclopedia of Religion*, Mircea Eliade, 220-224. New York: Macmillan Publishing Company, 1987.

Lattimore, Richmond. *Themes in Greek and Latin Epitaphs*. Urbana: University of Illinois Press, 1962.

Lauha, Aarre. *Kohelet*. Neukirchen-Vluyn: Neukirchener Verlag, 1978.

Lavoie, Jean-Jacques. "Bonheur et Finitude Humaine: Étude de Qo 9,7-10." *Science et Esprit* 45 (1993): 313-24.

_____. *La penseé du Qohélet: Étude exégétique et intertextuelle*. Quebec: Fides, 1992.

_____. "Temps et finitude humaine: Étude de Qohélet ix 11-12." *Vetus Testamentum* 46 (1996): 439-47.

Lefebvre, Gustave. *Le tombeau de Petosiris*, 3 Vols. Cairo: Institut francais d'archéologie orientale, 1923-24.

Lesko, Leonard H. "Ancient Egyptian Cosmogonies and Cosmology." In *Religion in Ancient Egypt: Gods, Myths, and Personal Practice*, ed. Byron E. Shafer, 88-122. Ithaca, NY: Cornell University Press, 1991.

_____. Lesko, Leonard H. *The Composition of the Book of Two Ways*, Ph.D. Diss., The University of Chicago, 1969.

_____. "Death and the Afterlife in Ancient Egyptian Thought." In Vol. III, *Civilizations of the Ancient Near East*, ed. Jack M. Sasson, 1763-1774. New York: Charles Scribner's Sons, 1995.

Lewis, Theodore J. *Cults of the Dead in Ancient Israel and Ugarit*. Atlanta: Scholars Press, 1989.

Lexa, Francois. *Papyrus Insinger*, Vol. II. Paris: Librairie Orientaliste Paul Geunther, 1926.

Lichtheim, Miriam. *Ancient Egyptian Autobiographies Chiefly of the Middle Kingdom*. Göttingen: Vandenhoeck & Ruprecht, 1988.

_____. *Ancient Egyptian Literature: A Book of Readings*, 3 Vols. Berkeley: University of California Press, 1973, 1976, 1980.

_____. "Autobiography as Self-Exploration." In Vol. I, *Sesto Congresso Internazionale di Egittologia*, ed. G. Zaccone, 409-14. Torino, Italy: International Association of Egyptologists, 1992.

_____. Lichtheim, Miriam. "Demotic Proverbs." In *Grammata Demotika, Festschrift für Erich Lüddeckens zum 15. Juni 1983*, ed. H. J. Thissen and K. T. Zauzich, 125-140. Würzburg: Gisela Zauzich Verlag,1984.

_____. *Late Egyptian Wisdom Literature in the International Context: A Study of Demotic Instructions*. Freibourg Schweiz: Universitätsverlag, 1983.

_____. *Maat in Egyptian Autobiographies and Related Studies*. Göttingen: Vandenhoeck & Ruprecht, 1992.

_____. "Observations on Papyrus Insinger," In *Studien zu altägyptischen Lebenslehren*, ed. Erik Hornung and Othmar Keel, 283-305. Freiburg Schweiz: Universitätsverlag; Göttingen: Vandenhoeck & Ruprecht, 1979.

_____. *The Songs of the Harpers*. Ph.D. Diss.,The University of Chicago, 1944.

_____. "The Songs of the Harpers." *Journal of Near Eastern Studies* 4 (1945): 178-212.

Lloyd, Alan B. "Egypt, 404-332 BC." In Vol. VI, *The Cambridge Ancient History*, ed. D. M. Lewis et al., 337-360. Cambridge: Cambridge University Press, 1994.

_____. "The Inscription of Udjahorresnet: A Collaborator's Testament." *Journal of Egyptian Archaeology* 68 (1982): 166-80.

_____. "Nationalist Propaganda in Ptolemaic Egypt." *Historia* 31 (1982): 33-55.

_____. "Psychology and Society in the Ancient Egyptian Cult of the Dead." In *Religion and Philosophy in Ancient Egypt*, ed. William Kelly Simpson, 117-133. New Haven: Yale University Press, 1989.

Loader, J. A. *Ecclesiastes*. Translated by John Vriend. Grand Rapids: Eerdmans, 1986.

_____. *Polar Structures in the Book of Qoheleth*. Berlin and New York: Walter de Gruyter, 1979.

Loewenstamm, Samuel E. *From Babylon to Canaan: Studies in the Bible and Its Oriental Background*. Jerusalem: The Magnes Press, 1992.

Lohfink, Norbert. *The Christian Meaning of the Old Testament*. Translated by R. A. Wilson. Milwaukee: Bruce, 1968.

_____. *Kohelet*. Wurzburg: Echter Verlag, 1980.

_____. "Qoheleth 5:17-19—Revelation by Joy." *Catholic Biblical Quarterly* 52 (1990): 625-635.

_____. "Technik und Tod nach Kohelet." In *Strukturen Christlicher Existenz: Beiträge zur Erneuerung des Geistlichen Lebens*, ed. H. Schlier et al., 27-35. Würzburg: Echter Verlag, 1968.

Longman, Tremper. *The Book of Ecclesiastes*. Grand Rapids: Eerdmans, 1998.

Loretz, Oswald. *Qohelet und der alte Orient: Untersuchungen zu Stil und theologischer Thematik des Buches Qohelet*. Freiburg: Herder, 1964.

Machinist, Peter. "Fate, *miqreh*, and Reason: Some Reflections on Qohelet and Biblical Thought." In *Solving Riddles and Untying Knots: Biblical, Epigraphic, and Semitic Studies in Honor of Jonas C. Greenfield*, ed. Ziony Zevit, Seymour Gitin, Michael Sokoloff. Winona Lake, IN: Eisenbrauns, 1995.

Martin-Achard, Robert. *From Death to Life*. Edinburgh and London: Oliver and Boyd, 1960.

Matties, Gordon H. *Ezekiel 18 and the Rhetoric of Moral Discourse*. Atlanta: Scholars Press, 1990.

McBride, Daniel. "The Egyptian-Gnostic View of Death." In *Death and Taxes in the Ancient Near East*, ed. Sara E. Orel, 129-143. Lewiston, NY: The Edwin Mellen Press, 1992.

McKenna, John E. "The Concept of *Hebel* in the Book of Ecclesiastes." *Scottish Journal of Theology* 45 (1992): 19-28.

McNeile, A. H. *An Introduction to Ecclesiastes*. Cambridge: Cambridge University Press, 1904.

Meulenaere, H. de. "De Vrouw in de Laat-Egyptische Autobiografie." *Phoenix* 7 (1961): 134-8.

Mendenhall, George E. "From Witchcraft to Justice: Death and Afterlife in the Old Testament." In *Death and Afterlife: Perspectives of World Religions*, ed. Hiroshi Obayashi, 67-81. New York: Greenwood Press, 1992.

Mertens, Jan. "Bibliography and Description of Demotic Literary Texts: A Progress Report." In *Life in a Multi-Cultural Society: Egypt from Cambyses to Constantine and Beyond*, ed. Janet H. Johnson, 233-35. Chicago: The Oriental Institute, 1992.

Mertz, Richard Rolland. *Some Aspects of Egyptian Autobiography Before the New Kingdom*. Ph.D. Diss., University of Chicago, 1953.

Metzger, Bruce M. and Roland E. Murphy, ed. *The New Oxford Annotated Bible: New Revised Standard Version*. New York: Oxford University Press, 1991.

Michel, Diethelm. *Qohelet*. Darmstadt: Wissenschaftliche Buchgesellschaft, 1988.

Milde, Henk. "'Going Out Into the Day.' Ancient Egyptian Beliefs and Practices Concerning Death and Immortality." In *Hidden Futures: Death and Immortality in Ancient Egypt, Anatolia, the Classical, Biblical and Arabic-Islamic World*, ed. J. M. Bremer et al, 15-35. Amsterdam: Amsterdam University Press, 1994.

Misch, Georg. *A History of Autobiography in Antiquity*. Leipzig and Berlin: B. G. Teubner, 1907. Translated by E. W. Dickes, 2 Vols. London: Routledge & Kegan Paul Ltd., 1950.

Momigliano, Arnaldo. *Alien Wisdom: The Limits of Hellenization*. Cambridge: Cambridge University Press, 1975.

Moore, Michael S. "Resurrection and Immortality: Two Motifs Navigating Confluent Theological Streams in the Old Testament (Dan 12:1-4)." *Theologische Zeitschrift* 39 (1983): 17-34.

Morenz, Siegfried. *Egyptian Religion*. Translated by Ann E. Keep. New York: Cornell University Press, 1973.

Muilenberg, James. "A Qoheleth Scroll from Qumran." *Bulletin of the American Schools of Oriental Research* 135 (1954): 20-28.

Munro, Peter. *Die spätägyptischen Totenstelen*. Glückstadt: J. J. Augustin, 1973.

Murnane, William J. "Taking It With You: The Problem of Death and Afterlife in Ancient Egypt." In *Death and Afterlife: Perspectives of World Religions*, ed. Hiroshi Obayashi, 35-48. New York: Greenwood Press, 1992.

Murphy, Roland E. "Dance and Death in the Song of Songs." In *Love & Death in the Ancient Near East: Essays in Honor of Marvin H. Pope*, ed. John H. Marks and Robert M. Good, 117-119. Guilford, CT: Four Quarters Publishing Company, 1987.

_____. *Ecclesiastes*. Dallas: Word Books, 1992.

_____. "On Translating Ecclesiastes." *Catholic Biblical Quarterly* 53 (1991): 571-579.

_____. "The Sage in Ecclesiastes and Qoheleth the Sage." In *The Sage in Israel and the Ancient Near East*, ed. J. G. Gammie and Leo G. Perdue, 263-271. Winona Lake: Eisenbrauns, 1990.

_____. "Wisdom in the Old Testament." In Vol. 6, *The Anchor Bible Dictionary*, ed. D. N. Freedman, 920-931. New York: Doubleday, 1992.

_____. *The Wisdom Literature*. Grand Rapids: Eerdmans, 1981.

Murray, Gilbert. *Stoic, Christian, and Humanist*. London: C. A. Watts, 1940.

Nakaten, Susanne. "Petosiris." In Vol. IV, *Lexikon der Ägyptologie*, ed. Wolfgang Helck et al., 995-98. Wiesbaden: Otto Harrassowitz, 1982.

Nickelsburg, George W. E., Jr. *Resurrection, Immortality, and Eternal Life in Intertestamental Judaism*. Cambridge: Harvard University Press, 1972.

Obayashi, Hiroshi. "Introduction." In *Death and Afterlife: Perspectives of World Religions*, ed. Hiroshi Obayashi, ix-xxii. New York: Greenwood Press, 1992.

Ogden, Graham S. "The Interpretation of רוּחַ in Ecclesiastes 1.4." *Journal for the Study of the Old Testament* 34 (1986): 91-92.

_____. Graham S. *Qoheleth*. Sheffield: Journal for the Study of the Old Testament Press, 1987.

_____. "Qoheleth IX 1-16." *Vetus Testamentum* 32 (1982): 158-69.

Orel, Sara E., ed. *Death and Taxes in the Ancient Near East*. Lewiston, NY: The Edwin Mellen Press, 1992.

Osing, Jürgen. "Les chants du harpiste au Nouvel Empire." In *Aspects de la Culture Pharaonique: Quatre leçons au Collège de France (Février-mars 1989)*, ed. Jürgen Osing, 11-24. Paris: Diffusion de Boccard.

Otto, Eberhard. *Die biographischen Inschriften der ägyptischen Spätzeit*. Leiden: E. J. Brill, 1954.

Palgi, Phyllis and Henry Abramovitch. "Death: A Cross-Cultural Perspective." *Annual Review of Anthropology* 13 (1984): 385-417.

Perdu, Olivier. "Ancient Egyptian Autobiographies." In Vol. IV, *Civilizations of the Ancient Near East*, ed. Jack M. Sasson, 2243-2254. New York: Charles Scribner's Sons, 1995.

Perdue, Leo. *Wisdom and Creation: The Theology of Wisdom Literature*. Nashville: Abingdon, 1994.

Pfeiffer, Robert H. "The Peculiar Skepticism of Ecclesiastes." *Journal of Biblical Literature* 53 (1934): 100-109.

Piankoff, Alexandre and N. Rambova. *The Mythological Papyri*. New York: Pantheon Books, 1957.

Picard, M. "Les Influences Étrangères au Tombeau de Petosiris: Grèce ou Perse?" *Bulletin de L'Institut Français d'Archéologie Orientale* 30 (1931): 201-227.

Plumptre, E. H., *Ecclesiastes*. Cambridge: The University Press, 1892.

Polzin, Robert. *Late Biblical Hebrew: Toward an Historical Typology of Biblical Hebrew Prose*. Missoula, MT: Scholars Press, 1976.

Poortman, Bartel. "Death and Immortality in Greek Philosophy: From the Presocratics to the Hellenistic Era." In *Hidden Futures: Death and Immortality in Ancient Egypt, Anatolia, the Classical, Biblical and Arabic-Islamic World*, ed. J. M. Bremer et al., 197-220. Amsterdam: Amsterdam University Press, 1994.

Posener, Georges, and Jean Sainte Fare Garnot. "Sur une Sagesse égyptienne de basse époque (Papyrus Brooklyn no. 47.218.135)." In *Les Sagesses du Proche-Orient Ancien, Colloque de Strasbourg 17-19 mai 1962*, 153-57. Paris: Presses Universitaires de France, 1963.

Porter, J. R. "The Legal Aspects of the Concept of 'Corporate Personality' in the Old Testament." *Vetus Testamentum* 15 (1965): 361-80.

Priest, J. "Humanism, Scepticism, and Pessimism in Israel." *Journal of the American Academy of Religion* 36 (1968): 311-326.

Pritchard, James B, ed. *Ancient Near Eastern Texts Relating to the Old Testament* Princeton: Princeton University Press, 1955.

Puech, Émile. *La croyance des Esséniens en la vie future: Immortalité, résurrection, vie éternelle? Histoire d'une croyance dans le judaïsme ancien*. Vol I, *La résurrection des morts et le contexte scripturaire*. Paris: Librairie Lecoffre/J. Gabalda, 1993.

Quaegebeur, Jan. "Contribution à la Prosopographie des Prêtres Memphites à l'Époque Ptolémaïque." *Ancient Society* 3 (1972):77-109.

_____. *Le Dieu Égyptien Shaï dans la Religion et l'Onomastique*. Leuven: Leuven University Press, 1975.

_____. "The Genealogy of the Memphite High Priest Family in the Hellenistic Period." In *Studies on Ptolemaic Memphis*, ed. Dorothy Crawford, et al., 43-81. Leuven: [s.n.], 1980.

_____. "Taimhotep." In Vol. VI, *Lexikon der Ägyptologie*, ed. Wolfgang Helck et al., 184-85. Wiesbaden: Otto Harrassowitz, 1986.

Rahlfs, Alfred. *Septuaginta*. Stuttgart: Deutsche Bibelgesellschaft, 1979.

Rainey, Anson F. "Study of Ecclesiastes." *Concordia Theological Monthly* 35 (1964): 148-57.

Rankin, Oliver S. *Israel's Wisdom Literature*. Edinburgh: T&T Clark, 1936.

Ranston, Harry. *Ecclesiastes and the Early Greek Wisdom Literature*. London: Epworth Press, 1925.

_____. "Koheleth and the Early Greeks." *The Journal of Theological Studies* 24 (1923): 160-69.

Ray, J. D. "Egypt, 525-404 BC" In Vol. IV, *The Cambridge Ancient History*, ed. John Boardman et al., 254-286. Cambridge: Cambridge University Press, 1988.

Redford, Donald B. "Ancient Egyptian Literature: An Overview." In Vol. IV, *Civilizations of the Ancient Near East*, ed. Jack M. Sasson, 2223-2241. New York: Charles Scribner's Sons, 1995.

_____. *Egypt, Canaan, and Israel in Ancient Times*. Princeton: Princeton University Press, 1992.

Reese, James M. *Hellenistic Influence on the Book of Wisdom and Its Consequences*. Rome: Biblical Institute Press, 1970.

Reymond, E. A. E. *From the Records of a Priestly Family from Memphis*. Wiesbaden: Otto Harrassowitz, 1981.

Ritner, Robert K. "Horus on the Crocodiles: A Juncture of Religion and Magic in Late Dynastic Egypt." In *Religion and Philosophy in Ancient Egypt*, ed. William Kelly Simpson, 103-116. New Haven: Yale University Press, 1989.

_____. "Implicit Models of Cross-Cultural Interaction: A Question of Noses, Soap, and Prejudice." In *Life in a Multi-Cultural Society: Egypt from Cambyses to Constantine and Beyond*, ed. Janet H. Johnson, 283-290. Chicago: The Oriental Institute, 1992.

Robins, Gay. "Wisdom from Egypt and Greece." In *Discussions in Egyptology* 1 (1985): 35-41.

Robinson, H. Wheeler. *Corporate Personality in Ancient Israel*. Philadelphia: Fortress Press, 1964.

Rogerson, J. W. "The Hebrew Concept of Corporate Personality: A Re-Examination." *Journal of Theological Studies* 21 (1970): 1-16.

Rosenberg, A. J, trans. *The Five Megilloth*. Vol. 2, *Lamentations, Ecclesiastes*. New York: Judaica Press, 1992.

Rößler-Köhler, Ursula. *Individuelle Haltungen zum Ägyptischen Königtum der Spätzeit: Private Quellen und ihre Königswertung im Spannungsfeld zwischen Erwartung und Erfahrung*. Wiesbaden: Otto Harrassowitz, 1991.

Roth, Ann Macy. "The Social Aspects of Death." In *Mummies and Magic: The Funerary Arts of Ancient Egypt*, ed. Sue D'Auria et al, 52-59. Boston: Museum of Fine Arts, 1988.

Sadek, Ashraf Iskander. *Popular Religion in Egypt During the New Kingdom*. Hildesheim: Gerstenberg, 1987.

Salters, R. B. "Qoheleth and the Canon." *Expository Times* 86 (1975): 339-42.

Samuel, Alan E. *From Athens to Alexandria: Hellenism and Social Goals in Ptolemaic Egypt*. Louvain: Imprimerie Orientaliste, 1983.

_____. *The Shifting Sands of History: Interpretations of Ptolemaic Egypt* Lanham, MD: University Press of America, 1989.

Sanders, E. P. "Testament of Abraham." In *The Old Testament Pseudepigrapha*, 2 Vols., ed. James H. Charlesworth, 871-902. New York: Doubleday, 1983.

Sanders, Jack T. *Ben Sira and Demotic Wisdom*. Chico, CA: Scholars Press, 1983.

Schmidt, Brian B. *Israel's Beneficent Dead: Ancestor Cult and Necromancy in Ancient Israelite Religion and Tradition*. Tübingen: J. C. B. Mohr [Siebeck], 1994.

Schoors, Antoon. "Ketibh-Qere in Ecclesiastes." In *Studia Paulo Naster Oblata II. Orientalia Antiqua*, ed. J. Quaegebeur, 215-222. Leuven: Department Oriëntalistiek, 1982.

_____. "Koheleth: A Perspective of Life After Death?" *Ephemerides Theologicae Lovanienses* 61 (1985): 295-303.

_____. *The Preacher Sought to Find Pleasing Words: A Study of the Language of Qoheleth*. Leuven: Departement Oriëntalistiek, 1992.

_____. "The Verb ראה in the Book of Qoheleth." In *"Jedes Ding hat seine Zeit...": Studien zur israelitischen und altorientalischen Weisheit*, ed. Anja A. Diesel, Reinhard G. Lehmann, Eckart Otto, and Andreas Wagner, 227-241. Berlin: Walter de Gruyter, 1996.

Schott, Siegfried. *Altägyptische Liebeslieder, mit Märchen und Liebesgeschichten*. Zürich: Artemis, 1950.

Schwienhorst-Schönberger, Ludger. *Nicht im Menschen Gründet das Glück" (Koh 2,24): Kohelet im Spannungsfeld jüdischer Weisheit und hellenistischer Philosophie*. Freiburg: Herder, 1994.

Scott, R. B. Y. *Proverbs-Ecclesiastes*. New York: Doubleday, 1965.

Segal, Alan. "Some Observations about Mysticism and the Spread of Notions of Life after Death in Hebrew Thought." In *Society of Biblical Literature 1996 Seminar Papers*, ed. Eugene H. Lovering, 385-99. Atlanta: Scholars Press, 1996.

Seow, C. L. "'Beyond Them, My Son, Be Warned': The Epilogue of Qoheleth Revisited." In *Wisdom, You Are My Sister*, ed. Michael L. Barre, 125-41. Washington, D.C.: Catholic Biblical Association of America, 1997.

_____. *Ecclesiastes*. New York: Doubleday, 1997.

_____. "Linguistic Evidence and the Dating of Qohelet." *Journal of Biblical Literature* 115 (1996): 643-666.

_____. "Qohelet's Autobiography." In *Fortunate the Eyes that See: Essays in Honor of David Noel Freedman in Celebration of His Seventieth Birthday*, ed. Astrid B. Beck et al., 275-287. Grand Rapids, MI: Eerdmans, 1995.

_____. "The Socioeconomic Context of 'The Preacher's' Hermeneutic," *Princeton Seminary Bulletin* 17 (1996): 168-195.

Shead, Andrew G. "Reading Ecclesiastes 'Epilogically.'" *Tyndale Bulletin* 48 (1997): 67-91.

Sheppard, Gerald T. "The Epilogue to Qoheleth as Theological Commentary." *Catholic Biblical Quarterly* 39 (1977): 182-89.

Sherman, Elizabeth J. "Ancient Egyptian Biographies of the Late Period (380 BCE Through 246 BCE)." *The American Research Center in Egypt Newsletter* 119 (1982): 38-41.

_____. "Egyptian Biographies." In Vol. 2, *The Anchor Bible Dictionary*, ed. David Noel Freedman, 390-93. New York: Doubleday, 1992.

Shupak, Nili. *Where Can Wisdom Be Found? The Sage's Language in the Bible and in Ancient Egyptian Literature*. Fribourg, Switzerland: University Press, 1993.

Silberman, L. H. "Death in the Hebrew Bible and Apocalyptic Literature,"
    Perspectives on Death, ed. L. O. Mills, 13-32. Nashville: Abingdon, 1969.

Silverman, David P. "Divinity and Deities in Ancient Egypt." In *Religion in
    Ancient Egypt: Gods, Myths, and Personal Practice*, ed. Byron E. Shafer, 7-
    87. Ithaca, NY: Cornell University Press, 1991.

_____. *For His Ka: Essays Offered in Memory of Klaus Baer*. Chicago:
    University of Chicago Press, 1994.

_____. "Textual Criticism in the Coffin Texts." In *Religion and Philosophy in
    Ancient Egypt*, ed.William Kelly Simpson, 29-53. New Haven: Yale
    University Press, 1989.

Simpson, William Kelly, ed. *The Literature of Ancient Egypt*. New Haven: Yale
    University Press, 1973.

Skehan, Patrick W. *The Literary Relationship Between the Book of Wisdom and the
    Protocanonical Wisdom Books of the Old Testament*. Washington, D.C.:
    The Catholic University of America, 1938.

Smalley, Beryl. *Medieval Exegesis of Wisdom Literature: Essays by Beryl Smalley*,
    ed. Roland Murphy. Atlanta: Scholars Press, 1986.

Smith, David L. "The Concept of Death in Job and Ecclesiastes." *Didaskalia* 4
    (1992): 2-14.

Smith, Jonathan Z. *Drudgery Divine: On the Comparison of Early Christianities
    and the Religions of Late Antiquity*. Chicago: University of Chicago Press,
    1990.

_____. *Map is Not Territory: Studies in the History of Religion*. Chicago:
    University of Chicago Press, 1978.

Smith, Mark. *The Demotic Mortuary Papyrus Louvre E. 3452*. Ph.D. Diss.,The
    University of Chicago, 1979.

_____. "Weisheit, demotische," In Vol. 6, *Lexicon der Ägyptologie*, ed. in
    Wolfgang Helck and Wolfhart Westendorf, 1192-1204. Wiesbaden: Otto
    Harrassowitz, 1986.

_____. and Elizabeth Bloch-Smith. "Death and Afterlife in Ugarit and Israel,"
    Journal of the American Oriental Society 108 (1988): 277-84.

Smith, Morton. *The Ancient Greeks*. Ithaca, NY: Cornell University Press, 1960.

Smith, Robert C. and John Lounibos. *Pagan and Christian Anxiety: A Response to
    E. R. Dodds*. Lanham, MD: University Press of America, 1984.

Sørensen, Jørgen Podemann. "Divine Access: The So-called Democratization of
    Egyptian Funerary Literature as a Socio-cultural Process." In *The Religion
    of the Ancient Egyptians: Cognitive Structures and Popular Expressions*,
    ed. Gertie Englund, 109-125. Stockholm: Almqvist & Wiksell International,
    1989.

_____. "Major Issues in the Study of Ancient Egyptian Religion," *Temenos* 30
    (1994): 125-52.

_____. "Native Reactions to Foreign Rule and Culture in Religious Literature."
    In *Ethnicity in Hellenistic Egypt*, ed. Per Bilde et al. Aarhus: Aarhus
    University Press, 1992.

Spangenberg, Isak J. J. "Irony in the Book of Qohelet." *Journal for the Study of the
    Old Testament* 72 (1996): 57-69.

Spencer, A. J. *Death in Ancient Egypt*. New York: Penguin Books, 1982.

Spronk, Klaas. *Beatific Afterlife in Ancient Israel and in the Ancient Near East*. Kevelaer: Butzon und Bercker; Neukirchen-Vluyn: Neukirchner Verlag, 1986.

Stone, Michael E. "Eschatology, Remythologization, and Cosmic Aporia." In *The Origins and Diversity of Axial Age Civilizations*, ed. S. N. Eisenstadt, 241-251. Albany: State University of New York Press, 1986.

Talbert, Charles. "Biography, Ancient." In Vol. 1, *The Anchor Bible Dictionary*, ed. D. N. Freedman, 745-749. New York: Doubleday, 1992.

Te Velde, Herman. "Commemoration in Ancient Egypt." In *Visible Religion: Annual for Religious Iconography*. Vol. I, *Commemorative Figures*, ed. H. G. Kippenberg et al., 135-153. Leiden: E. J. Brill, 1982.

_____. "Funerary Mythology." In *Mummies and Magic: The Funerary Arts of Ancient Egypt*, ed. Sue D'Auria et al., 27-37. Boston: Museum of Fine Arts, 1988.

_____. "Theology, Priests, and Worship in Ancient Egypt." In Vol. III, *Civilizations of the Ancient Near East*, ed. Jack M. Sasson, 1731-1749. New York: Charles Scribner's Sons, 1995.

Thériault, Carolyn A. "The Literary Ghosts of Pharaonic Egypt." In *Death and Taxes in the Ancient Near East*, ed. Sara E. Orel, 193-211. Lewiston, NY: The Edwin Mellen Press, 1992.

Tigay, Jeffrey H. "What is Man that You Have Been Mindful of Him? (On Psalm 8:4-5)." In *Love & Death in the Ancient Near East: Essays in Honor of Marvin H. Pope*, ed. John H. Marks and Robert M. Good, 169-171. Guilford, CT: Four Quarters Publishing Company, 1987.

Torrey, C. C. "The Question of the Original Language of Qohelet." *Jewish Quarterly Review* 39 (1948-49): 151-60.

Trigger, B. G. et al. *Ancient Egypt: A Social History*. Cambridge: Cambridge University Press, 1983.

Tromp, Nicholas J. *Primitive Conceptions of Death and the Nether World in the Old Testament*. Rome: Pontifical Biblical Institute, 1969.

Tsevat, M. "The Meaning of the Book of Job." In *Studies in Ancient Israelite Wisdom*, ed. James L. Crenshaw, 341-374. New York: Ktav Publishing House, 1976.

Uehlinger, Christoph. "Qohelet im Horizont mesopotamischer, levantinischer und ägyptischer Weisheitsliteratur der persischen und hellenistischen Zeit." In *Das Buch Kohelet. Studien zur Struktur, Geschichte, Rezeption und Theologie*, ed. Ludger Schwienhorst-Schoenberger, 1-70. Berlin: Walter de Gruyter, 1997.

Van der Horst, Pieter W. *Ancient Jewish Epitaphs: An Introductory Survey of a Millennium of Jewish Funerary Epigraphy (300 BCE - 700 CE)*. Kampen: Kok Pharos, 1991.

Van der Walle, Baudouin. "Biographie." In Vol. 1, *Lexikon der Ägyptologie*, ed. Wolfgang Helck et al., 815-821. Wiesbaden: Otto Harrassowitz, 1975.

Van Uchelen, Nico. "Death and the After-Life in the Hebrew Bible of Ancient Israel." In *Hidden Futures: Death and Immortality in Ancient Egypt, Anatolia, the Classical, Biblical and Arabic-Islamic World*, ed. In J. M. Bremer et al., 77-90. Amsterdam: Amsterdam University Press, 1994.

Van Walsem, René. "The Usurpation of Royal and Divine Actions and/or Attributes in the Iconography of Late 21st–Early 22nd Dyn. Coffins." In Vol. 1: *Sesto Congresso Internazionale di Egittologia*, ed. G. Zaccone, 643-49. Torino, Italy: International Association of Egyptologists, 1992.

Vawter, Bruce. "Intimations of Immortality and the Old Testament." *Journal of Biblical Literature* 91 (1972): 158-71.

Vergote, Joseph. "La notion de Dieu dans les Livres de sagesse égyptiens." In *Les Sagesses du Proche-Orient Ancien, Colloque de Strasbourg 17-19 mai 1962*, 159-190. Paris: Presses Universitaires de France, 1963.

Von Rad, Gerhard. *Wisdom in Israel*. Nashville: Abingdon Press, 1972.

Walbank, F. W. *The Hellenistic World*. Cambridge: Harvard University Press, 1993.

Walcot, P. "Hesiod and the Instructions of 'Onchsheshonqy." *Journal of Near Eastern Studies* 21 (1962): 215-219.

Wanke, Gunther. "Prophecy and Psalms in the Persian Period." In Vol. 1, *The Cambridge History of Judaism*, ed. W. D. Davies and Louis Finkelstein, 162-188. Cambridge: Cambridge University Press, 1984.

Weil, Eric. "What is a Breakthrough in History?" *Daedalus* 104 (1975): 21-36.

Weil, Gotthold, ed. *Festschrift Eduard Sachau*. Berlin: G. Reimar, 1915.

Weisengoff, John. "Death and Immortality in the Book of Wisdom." *Catholic Biblical Quarterly* 3 (1941):104-133.

Wente, Edward F. "Egyptian 'Make Merry' Songs Reconsidered." *Journal of Near Eastern Studies* 21 (1962): 118-128.

_____. "Egyptian Religion." In Vol. 2, *The Anchor Bible Dictionary*, ed. David Noel Freedman, 408-412. New York: Doubleday, 1992.

_____. "Funerary Beliefs of the Ancient Egyptians: An Interpretation of the Burials and the Texts." *Expedition* Winter (1982): 17-26.

_____. *Letters From Ancient Egypt*. Atlanta: Scholars Press, 1990.

_____. "The Scribes of Ancient Egypt." In Vol. IV, *Civilizations of the Ancient Near East*, ed. Jack M. Sasson, 2211-2221. New York: Charles Scribner's Sons, 1995.

Whitley, Charles F. *Koheleth: His Language and Thought*. Berlin, New York: Walter de Gruyter, 1979.

Whybray, R. N. *Ecclesiastes*. Grand Rapids: Eerdmans, 1989.

_____. "Qoheleth, Preacher of Joy." *Journal for the Study of the Old Testament* 23 (1982): 87-98.

_____. "A Time to Be Born and a Time to Die: Some Observations on Ecclesiastes 3:2-8." In *Near Eastern Studies: Dedicated to H. I. H. Prince Takahito Mikasa on the Occasion of His Twenty Fifth Birthday*, ed. Masao Mori et al., 469-83. Wiesbaden: Otto Harrassowitz, 1991.

Wildung, Dietrich. *Imhotep und Amenhotep: Gottwerdung im alten Ägypten*. Munich: Deutscher Kunstverlag, 1977.

Williams, James G. "Proverbs and Ecclesiastes." In *The Literary Guide to the Bible*, ed. Robert Alter and Frank Kermode, 263-282. Cambridge: Harvard University Press, 1987.

Williams, R. J. "Egyptian Wisdom Literature." In Vol. II, *The Anchor Bible Dictionary*, ed. David Noel Freedman, 395-99. New York: Doubleday, 1992.

_____. "Reflections on the Lebensmüde." *Journal of Egyptian Archaelogy* 48 (1962): 49-56.

_____. "Some Fragmentary Demotic Wisdom Texts." In *Studies in Honor of George R. Hughes*, ed. Janet Johnson and Edward Wente, 263-71. Chicago: The Oriental Institute, 1976.

_____. "What Does it Profit a Man?: The Wisdom of Koheleth." In *Studies in Ancient Israelite Wisdom*, ed. James L. Crenshaw, 375-389. New York: Ktav Publishing House, 1976.

Wilson, John A. *The Burden of Egypt: An Interpretation of Ancient Egyptian Culture*. Chicago: University of Chicago Press, 1951.

Winston, David. *The Wisdom of Solomon*. New York: Doubleday, 1979.

Wintermute, O. S. "Jubilees." In Vol. 1, *The Old Testament Pseudepigrapha*, ed. James H. Charlesworth, 35-142. New York: Doubleday, 1983.

Wise, Michael. "A Calque from Aramaic in Qoheleth 6:12; 7:12; and 8:13." *Journal of Biblical Literature* 109 (1990): 249-257.

Wright, Addison D. G. "Additional Numerical Patterns in Qoheleth." *Catholic Biblical Quarterly* 45 (1983): 32-43.

_____. "The Riddle of the Sphinx Revisited: Numerical Patterns in the Book of Qoheleth." *Catholic Biblical Quarterly* 42 (1980): 35-51.

_____. "The Riddle of the Sphinx: The Structure of the Book of Qoheleth." *Catholic Biblical Quarterly* 30 (1968): 313-334.

Würthwein, Ernst. "Egyptian Wisdom and the Old Testament." Translated by Brian W. Kovacs. In *Studies in Ancient Israelite Wisdom*, ed. James L. Crenshaw, 175-207. New York: Ktav Publishing House, 1976.

Zaleski, Carol. "Death, and Near-Death Today." In *Death, Ecstasy, and Other Worldy Journeys*, ed. John J. Collins and Michael Fishbane, 383-407. Albany: State University Press of New York, 1995.

Zandee, J. *Death as an Enemy According to Ancient Egyptian Conceptions*. Leiden: E. J. Brill, 1960.

Zimmerli, Walther. "Concerning the Structure of Old Testament Wisdom." Translated by Brian W. Kovacs. In *Studies in Ancient Israelite Wisdom*, ed. James L. Crenshaw, 113-133. New York: Ktav Publishing House, 1976.

Zimmermann, Frank. "The Aramaic Provenance of Qohelet." *Jewish Quarterly Review* 36 (1945-46): 17-45.

_____. "The Question of Hebrew in Qohelet." *Jewish Quarterly Review* 40 (1949-50): 79-102.

Zuck, Roy B. "God and Man in Ecclesiastes." *Bibliotheca Sacra* 148 (1991): 46-56.

Indexes

Author Index

Passage Index

Hebrew Bible

Subject Index